The Norton Sampler

XXXXXXXXXXXXXXXXXXXXXXXXXXXXXXXXXXXXXXXXXXXXXXXXXXXXXXXXXXXXXXXXXX

SIXTH EDITION

THE NORTON SAMPLER

SHORT ESSAYS FOR COMPOSITION

Sixth Edition

XXXXXXXXXXXXXXXXXXXXXXXXXXXXXXXXXXXXXXXXXXXXXXXXXXXXXXXXXX

THOMAS COOLEY

THE OHIO STATE UNIVERSITY

W·W·NORTON & COMPANY

NEW YORK·LONDON

Manufacturing by Courier Companies.
Book design by Martin Lubin.
Production manager: Diane O'Connor.

Library of Congress Cataloging-in-Publication Data
The Norton sampler : short essays for composition / [edited by]
Thomas Cooley.—6th ed.
p. cm.
Includes index.

ISBN 0-393-97882-6 (pbk.)
ISBN 0-393-97943-1 (Instructor's Edition)

1. College readers. 2. English language—Rhetoric. 3. Essays.
I. Cooley, Thomas, 1942– II. Title.
PE1417 .N6 2003
808'.0427—dc21   2002032979

W. W. Norton & Company, Inc., 500 Fifth Avenue, New York, NY 10110
www.wwnorton.com
W. W. Norton & Company Ltd., Castle House, 75/76 Wells Street, London W1T 3QT

6 7 8 9 0

Contents

Miss Dennis always wore a variation of one outfit—a dark-colored, flared woolen skirt, a tailored white blouse and a cardigan sweater, usually black, thrown over her shoulders and held together by a little pearl chain.

Can you see her? I can. And the image of her makes me smile. Still.

"He's mostly silver, but the silver is somehow made up of *all* the colors, if you know what I mean." I stopped. "Do you know what I mean by colors?"

At the door to 309, I pause, adjusting my eyes to the darkness. The only light in the room is coming from an infusion pump, which is flashing its red beacon as if in warning, and the dim hall light that barely confirms the room's furnishings and the shapeless form on the bed.

As alarming as the Gaines-burgers were, their soy meal began to seem like an old friend when the time came to try some *canned* dog foods.

CHAPTER TWO: **NARRATIVE** 54

XXXXXXXXXXXXXXXXXXXXXXXXXXXXXXXXXXXXXXXXXXXXXXXXXXXXXXX

Thomas Beller ❦ THE ASHEN GUY: LOWER BROADWAY, SEPTEMBER 11, 2001 60

At first glance he looked like a snowman, except instead of snow he was covered in gray, asbestos-colored ash. . . . A small plume of dust drifted off the top of his head as he walked, echoing the larger plume of smoke drifting off of One World Trade behind him.

Sebastian Junger ❦ THE LION IN WINTER 65

Dogs were barking in the distance, and a soldier shouted into his radio that the wounded were coming in and they needed more medicine, *now.*

Mary Mebane ❦ THE BACK OF THE BUS 72

Most Americans have never had to live with terror. I had had to live with it all my life—the psychological terror of segregation, in which there was a special set of laws governing your movements. You violated them at your peril. . . .

Richard Rodriguez ❦ NONE OF THIS IS FAIR 81

Affirmative Action programs had made it all possible. The disadvantages of others permitted my promotion; the absence of many Mexican-Americans from academic life allowed my designation as a "minority student."

Kelly Simon ❦ FRANK SINATRA'S GUM 88

He leaned his elbows on the table. His face was inches from mine. His baby blues twinkled at me. I could smell the Juicy Fruit on his breath.

CHAPTER THREE: **EXAMPLE** 93

XXXXXXXXXXXXXXXXXXXXXXXXXXXXXXXXXXXXXXXXXXXXXXXXXXXXXXXXXXXXXXX

In total, 347 individual acts of sin were committed at the bake sale, with nearly every attendee committing at least one of the seven deadly sins as outlined by Gregory the Great in the Fifth Century.

The reasoning techniques of thought experiments are not necessarily difficult. To test the statement that the world is infested by invisible flying cats which invariably avoid human beings, we would consider the consequences of such a situation.

Sometimes you have to believe that all English speakers should be committed to an asylum for the verbally insane. In what other language do people drive in a parkway and park in a driveway? . . . In what other language can your nose run and your feet smell?

I was eleven when I first heard jazz. Walking down a street in Boston, I was stopped by the sound coming out of a public address system attached to a record store. I was so exhilarated that I yelled in delight—something I had never done before on the proper streets of Boston. The music was Artie Shaw's "Nightmare."

My grandmother has bound feet. Cruelly tethered since her birth, they are like bonsai trees, miniature versions of what should have been.

CHAPTER FOUR: **CLASSIFICATION AND DIVISION** 127

Amy Tan ♠ MOTHER TONGUE 132

I spend a great deal of my time thinking about the power of language—the way it can evoke an emotion, a visual image, a complex idea, or a simple truth. Language is the tool of my trade. And I use them all—all the Englishes I grew up with.

Eric A. Watts ♠ THE COLOR OF SUCCESS 140

"Hitting the books," expressing oneself articulately, and, at times, displaying more than a modest amount of intelligence—these traits were derided as "acting white."

Isaac Asimov ♠ WHAT DO YOU CALL A PLATYPUS? 146

All the mammals are divided into two subclasses. In one of these subclasses ("Protheria" or "first-beasts") are the duckbill and five species of the spiny anteater. In the other ("Theria" or just "beasts") are all the other 4,231 known living species of mammals.

Freeman J. Dyson ♠ SCIENCE, GUIDED BY ETHICS, CAN LIFT UP THE POOR 154

We all know that green technology has a dark side, just as gray technology has a dark side. Gray technology brought us hydrogen bombs as well as telephones. Green technology brought us anthrax bombs as well as antibiotics.

Jeff Jacoby ♠ THE RISE OF THE BLENDED AMERICAN 159

The population of blended citizens is soaring, and with it the realization that racial divisions are only skin deep. Tens of millions of Americans have learned to think outside the racial box. It's time the government followed suit.

CHAPTER FIVE: **PROCESS ANALYSIS** 163

XXXXXXXXXXXXXXXXXXXXXXXXXXXXXXXXXXXXXXXXXXXXXXXXXXXX

Contrary to popular opinion, the shark's nose is not the area to attack, unless you cannot reach the eyes or gills.

No. A chicken would probably have had the sense to get out of the way. This boy was already well on the road to becoming a *man*, having learned one of the central ethics of his gender: Experience pain rather than show fear.

Meanwhile, the wasp, having satisfied itself that the victim is of the right species, moves off a few inches to dig the spider's grave. . . . Now and again the wasp pops out of the hole to make sure that the spider is still there.

Don't worry about form. It's not a term paper. When you come to the end of one episode, just start a new paragraph. You can go from a few lines about the sad state of pro football to the fight with your mother to your fond memories of Mexico to your cat's urinary-tract infection to a few thoughts on a personal indebtedness and on to the kitchen sink and what's in it.

Every culture comes up with tests of a person's ability to get out of a sticky situation. . . . When they slam the [car] trunk, though, you're helpless unless someone finds you. You would think that such a common worry should have a ready fix, and that the secret of getting out of a locked trunk is something we should all know about.

CHAPTER SIX: COMPARISON AND CONTRAST 200

XXXXXXXXXXXXXXXXXXXXXXXXXXXXXXXXXXXXXXXXXXXXXXXXXXXXXXXXX

Our daughter, Jill, has two grandmothers who are as different as chalk and cheese. One grandmother taught her how to count cards and make her face as blank as a huge, white Kleenex when she bluffed at blackjack. . . . The other grandmother taught her where to place the salad forks.

Children, in contrast, found my appearance clearly fascinating. One small girl came up to me and stared with unabashed curiosity at my empty pantlegs.

No part of either man's life became him more than the part he played in this brief meeting in the McLean house at Appomattox. Their behavior there put all succeeding generations of Americans in their debt. Two great Americans, Grant and Lee—very different, yet under everything very much alike.

But the woman I married was not Mexican but Japanese. It was a surprise to me. For years, I went about wide-eyed in my search for the brown girl in a white dress at a dance.

Male students are more likely to be comfortable attacking the readings and might find the inclusion of personal anecdotes irrelevant and "soft." Women are more likely to resist discussion they perceive as hostile, and, indeed, it is women in my classes who are most likely to offer personal anecdotes.

Certain events are parallel, but compared with Hugh's, my childhood was unspeakably dull. When I was seven years old, my family moved to North Carolina. When he was seven years old, Hugh's family moved to the Congo. We had a collie and a house cat. They had a monkey and two horses named Charlie Brown and Satan.

CHAPTER EIGHT: **CAUSE AND EFFECT** 276

XXXXXXXXXXXXXXXXXXXXXXXXXXXXXXXXXXXXXXXXXXXXXXXXXXXXXXXXX

REALTIME WRITING / *OUTSIDE* MAGAZINE Q&A 282

Marissa Nuñez ♠ CLIMBING THE GOLDEN ARCHES 284

Working at McDonald's has taught me a lot. . . . I'd like to have my own business someday, and working at McDonald's is what showed me I could do that.

John Edwards ♠ PRISON MAN CONSIDERS TURKEY 290

I got up, leaving my decent federal Thanksgiving dinner to the vultures. Up in the visiting room, families were arriving. Some inmates would let their families wait while they ate, but for most of us, family came first, even if that meant missing a special meal.

Jared Diamond ♠ WHO KILLED EASTER ISLAND? 295

They . . . turned to the largest remaining meat source available: humans, whose bones become common in late Easter Island garbage heaps.

Henry Louis Gates Jr. ♠ A GIANT STEP 303

"Pauline," he said to my mother, his voice kindly but amused, "there's not a thing wrong with that child. The problem's psychosomatic. Your son's an overachiever."

Ruth Russell ♠ THE WOUNDS THAT CAN'T BE STITCHED UP 309

Delirious, she cried out for her children and apologized for an accident she neither caused nor could have avoided. An accident that happened when her car was hit head-on by a drunk driver speeding down the wrong side of the road in a half-ton truck with no headlights.

CHAPTER NINE: **ARGUMENT** 314

XXXXXXXXXXXXXXXXXXXXXXXXXXXXXXXXXXXXXXXXXXXXXXXXXXXXXXXXXXXX

We hold these truths to be self-evident, that all men are created equal, that they
are endowed by their Creator with certain unalienable Rights, that among these
are Life, Liberty and the pursuit of Happiness.

The United States should remain an island of plenty in a sea of hunger. The
future of mankind is at stake. We are not responsible for the rest of humanity.

During my research on the effects of radiation on human genes, I noticed that
there were several references to studies of Mormons in Utah. My curiosity piqued,
I studied on. Apparently, the atmospheric bomb tests of the 1950s over Nevada
were performed only when winds were blowing away from Las Vegas toward
Utah.

I've felt the gun in my hand punch psychic holes in my intellectual convictions.
And having felt all that, I do not have much hope that private ownership of
deadly weapons will be at all regulated or controlled in the foreseeable future.

AIDS awareness has become so much a part of the pop culture that not only is it
barely noticeable, it is largely ineffectual. MTV runs programs about safe sex that
are barely distinguishable from documentaries about Madonna.

Let him be just and deal kindly with my people, for the dead are not powerless.
Dead, did I say? There is no death, only a change of worlds.

CHAPTER TEN: **CLASSIC ESSAYS** 358

ᴪᴪᴪ

THEMATIC CONTENTS

MEMORIES OF YOUTH

OVERCOMING DISABILITY

XXXXXXXXXXXXXXXXXXX **PUBLIC POLICY** XXXXXXXXXXXXXXXXXXX

XXXXXXXXXXXXXXXX **SCIENCE AND NATURE** XXXXXXXXXXXXXXXX

XXXXXXXXXXXXXX **SCHOOL AND EDUCATION** XXXXXXXXXXXXXX

XXXXXXXXXX **SOCIOLOGY AND ANTHROPOLOGY** XXXXXXXXXX

XXXXXXXXXXXXXX **SPORTS AND LEISURE** XXXXXXXXXXXXXX

XXXXXXXXXXXXXXXXXX **STUDENT WRITING** XXXXXXXXXXXXXXXXXX

XXXXXXXXXXXXXX **WRITERS AND WRITING** XXXXXXXXXXXXXX

PREFACE

The Norton Sampler is a collection of short essays for composition students. Like the cloth samplers in colonial America that schoolchildren did to learn and perfect their stitches (and their ABCs), *The Norton Sampler* is based on the assumption that writing is a practical art that can be learned by studying some basic patterns.

The rhetorical patterns illustrated by the readings in this *Sampler* include description, narrative, example, classification and division, process analysis, comparison and contrast, definition, cause and effect, and argument. Each chapter focuses on one pattern and includes five or so short essays organized primarily around that pattern. Each essay is followed by a battery—not a deadly one, I hope—of study questions and writing prompts.

Most of the model essays in *The Norton Sampler* are only two to four pages long, and even the longest can be easily read in a single setting. The essays are not only short but complete. I have found that even classic works like Alexander Petrunkevitch's essay about the spider and the wasp are routinely reprinted with unacknowledged amputations. It is the rhetoric of the short piece that our students are learning in beginning composition classes, and we cannot confidently ask them to look at beginnings, middles, and endings or the shape of an author's argument if those forms and shapes are actually the work of an editor. Thus I have taken pains to gather complete essays, or, in a few cases (indicated in the headnotes), complete chapters of books or sections of longer articles.

Though the chapters of the *Sampler* can be taken up in any order, I've provided an Introduction that exposes students to the process that experienced writers tend to follow. This chapter also discusses the four basic modes of writing—description, narration, exposition, and argument—along with how they work together (or apart) to suit a writer's various purposes.

Since many teachers like to begin a course by having students write about their own experiences, the next two chapters of the *Sampler* deal with basic techniques of description and narration, the two modes most essential to personal writing. These are followed by six chapters of exposition, ranging from the simpler techniques of exemplification and classification to the more complex strategies of process analysis, comparison and contrast, definition, and cause and effect. Argumentation and persuasion are addressed in a chapter organized according to the classical divisions of logos, pathos, and ethos (though I have not burdened the student with such terms). A final chapter includes a small collection of classic essays, and there is a Glossary.

Among the many distinctive features of *The Norton Sampler*, those who have used the book before will find much that is familiar, plus a number of features new to the Sixth Edition:

- *Over half the readings are new, most written in the last ten years.* From Sebastian Junger's report of war against the Taliban in Afghanistan to Dave Barry's hilarious essay defining guys (as distinct from men) to an article from *The Onion* reporting on a church bake sale where all seven of the Deadly Sins were committed (repeatedly), the readings in the *Sampler* are selected to interest (and even amuse) today's students. But there are also many classic essays here by writers such as George Orwell, Virginia Woolf, and E. B. White. There are sixty-three essays in all.

- *A new, RealTime writing feature in every chapter shows the modes of writing in everyday, "real world" texts.* Whether descriptive copy from a catalog selling watches or an *Outside* magazine Q&A column explaining what causes old tents to smell like barf, these pieces show students that the techniques and strategies they are being asked to learn are not used just in the writing classroom but in all the writing and thinking that we do. Moreover, these new readings include visual components that make the point that writing in the age of the Internet consists of more than just words.

- *A new Web site offers links to texts written for the Web, showing how the modes of writing play out online.* Each link is introduced by a short headnote with contextual information and is followed by study questions that make the online materials teachable. Go to wwnorton.com/write/sampler.

• *A specially commissioned essay by Annie Dillard looks at the process she went through in writing her famous essay about the death of a moth.* Paired to serve as an introduction to the book, the two essays are explicated to show how Dillard herself uses the various modes of writing to glorious effect.

ACKNOWLEDGEMENTS

There are two people above all whom I want to thank for their work and support on this new edition of *The Norton Sampler:* Barbara Cooley, my patient wife and a skilled technical writer and editor, and the indefatigable Marilyn Moller, editor extraordinaire at Norton, who is chiefly responsible for the *Sampler*'s new look and content. Then there is Nicole Netherton, editor of editors, along with several other people at Norton: Carol Flechner, who copyedited the book; Diane O'Connor, the production manager; Marian Johnson, the managing editor; Eileen Connell, who took charge of the marketing and the Web components; and Nancy Rodwan, the permissions manager. The lovely new interior design and the fanciful new cover design are thanks to Martin Lubin and Anna George respectively.

Among the teachers across the country who read various parts of the manuscript, I wish especially to thank Fred C. Adams, Pennsylvania State University, Fayette Campus; Julie Armstrong, University of South Florida, St. Petersburg; Marian Arkin, LaGuardia Community College; Dorris Brass, University of Maryland, Baltimore County; Linda Breslin, Texas Tech University; Jessica Brown, City College, San Francisco; Tim Bywater, Dixie State College; Karen Clark, The University of Arkansas; Deanna Evans, Bemidji State University; Michael Fisher, South Georgia College; Janet Halbert, Western Texas College; Tom Hallock, University of Tampa; Scott Hathaway, Hudson Valley Community College; Katherine J. Sanchez, Tomball College; George Q. Xu, Clarion University; and Sandra Young, Sacred Heart University.

For their help on this or earlier versions of the *Sampler*, I want also to express my gratitude to Carol Hollar-Zwick, Julia Reidhead, Hugh O'Neill, Kristin Sheerin, Shelly Perron, Kate Lovelady—all formerly or presently of W. W. Norton & Company.

At Ohio State, there are my friends and colleagues over the years, including Lee Abbott, William Allen, Richard Altick, Daniel Barnes, Toni Bates, Morris Beja, Ellen Carter, David Citino, Rebecca Cline, Edward P. J. Corbett, Suellyn Duffey, John Gabel, Kim Gainer, Sara Garnes, Andrea Lunsford, Kitty Locker, Richard Martin, Terence Odlin, Frank O'Hare, Faye Purol, Dennis Quon, Barbara Rigney, Michael Rupright, Arnold Shapiro, Frances Shapiro, Amy Shuman, Clifford Vaida, Eric Walborn, Charles Wheeler, and Christian Zacher.

Thomas Cooley
Columbus, Ohio

THE NORTON SAMPLER

SIXTH EDITION

INTRODUCTION

Writing is a little like sewing or weaving. The end product may be a tight fabric of words, but you must construct it thread by thread through a series of overlapping phases and processes. Since you usually don't know ahead of time exactly what you are going to say, it helps to have some patterns to work with. This is where *The Norton Sampler* comes in. As a collection of short essays for composition, this is a book of prose patterns, a sampler of basic stitches and forms that you can use to make finished designs of your own.

The two essays in this chapter are both written by the Pulitzer Prize-winning writer Annie Dillard, whose work has been compared to that of Henry David Thoreau and Emily Dickinson. The first essay, "The Death of a Moth," originally appeared in *Harper's* and later as part of Dillard's prose NARRATIVE* *Holy the Firm* (1977). As you will soon discover, it is not just about insects, but about writing; and it is the end product of a rigorous composing process that Dillard herself DESCRIBES in the second selection, "How I Wrote the Moth Essay—and Why," written exclusively for *The Norton Sampler*.

These two essays, says Dillard, are "the most personal" ones she's ever written (14). They are her answer to the burning question all writers face when they begin the process of weaving words into a meaningful design: "How do you go from nothing to something? How do you face the blank page without fainting dead away?" (12). Taken together, these two essays will help you begin to answer that question for yourself by introducing you to the basic processes most writers follow to get from nothing to something. After you have studied these essays—and the general processes of writing that they illustrate—we will then turn to specific patterns, or MODES OF WRITING, that you can use in your own work.

*Words printed in SMALL CAPITALS are defined in the Glossary.

ANNIE DILLARD

The Death of a Moth

I live on northern Puget Sound, in Washington State, alone. I have a   1
gold cat, who sleeps on my legs, named Small. In the morning I joke
to her blank face, Do you remember last night? Do you remember? I
throw her out before breakfast, so I can eat.

There is a spider, too, in the bathroom, with whom I keep a sort   2
of company. Her little outfit always reminds me of a certain moth I
helped to kill. The spider herself is of uncertain lineage, bulbous at the
abdomen and drab. Her six-inch mess of a web works, works somehow,
works miraculously, to keep her alive and me amazed. The web itself is
in a corner behind the toilet, connecting tile wall to tile wall and floor,
in a place where there is, I would have thought, scant traffic. Yet under
the web are sixteen or so corpses she has tossed to the floor.

The corpses appear to be mostly sow bugs, those little armadillo   3
creatures who live to travel flat out in houses, and die round. There is
also a new shred of earwig, three old spider skins crinkled and clenched,
and two moth bodies, wingless and huge and empty, moth bodies I drop
to my knees to see.

Today the earwig shines darkly and gleams, what there is of him: a   4
dorsal curve of thorax and abdomen, and a smooth pair of cerci[1] by which
I knew his name. Next week, if the other bodies are any indication, he
will be shrunken and gray, webbed to the floor with dust. The sow bugs
beside him are hollow and empty of color, fragile, a breath away from
brittle fluff. The spider skins lie on their sides, translucent and ragged,
their legs drying in knots. And the moths, the empty moths, stagger
against each other, headless, in a confusion of arching strips of chitin like
peeling varnish, like a jumble of buttresses for cathedral domes, like noth-

[1]Plural of cercus, posterior "feeler" of an insect.

ing resembling moths, so that I should hesitate to call them moths, except that I have had some experience with the figure Moth reduced to a nub.

Two summers ago I was camping alone in the Blue Ridge Mountains in Virginia. I had hauled myself and gear up there to read, among other things, James Ramsey Ullman's *The Day on Fire,* a novel about Rimbaud that had made me want to be a writer when I was sixteen;[2] I was hoping it would do it again. So I read, lost, every day sitting under a tree by my tent, while warblers swung in the leaves overhead and bristle worms trailed their inches over the twiggy dirt at my feet; and I read every night by candlelight, while barred owls called in the forest and pale moths massed round my head in the clearing, where my light made a ring.

Moths kept flying into the candle. They would hiss and recoil, lost upside down in the shadows among my cooking pans. Or they would singe their wings and fall, and their hot wings, as if melted, would stick to the first thing they touched—a pan, a lid, a spoon—so that the snagged moths could flutter only in tiny arcs, unable to struggle free. These I could release by a quick flip with a stick; in the morning I would find my cooking stuff gilded with torn flecks of moth wings, triangles of shiny dust here and there on the aluminum. So I read, and boiled water, and replenished candles, and read on.

One night a moth flew into the candle, was caught, burnt dry, and held. I must have been staring at the candle, or maybe I looked up when a shadow crossed my page; at any rate, I saw it all. A golden female moth, a biggish one with a two-inch wingspan, flapped into the fire, dropped her abdomen into the wet wax, stuck, flamed, frazzled and fried in a second. Her moving wings ignited like tissue paper, enlarging the circle of light in the clearing and creating out of the darkness the sudden blue sleeves of my sweater, the green leaves of jewelweed by my side, the ragged red trunk of a pine. At once the light contracted again and the moth's wings vanished in a fine, foul smoke. At the same time her six legs clawed, curled, blackened, and ceased, disappearing utterly. And her head jerked in spasms, making a spattering noise; her antennae

[2]French poet Arthur Rimbaud (1854–1891) himself began writing at age sixteen and produced his major work before he was twenty. Ullman's novel was published in 1958.

crisped and burned away and her heaving mouth parts crackled like pistol fire. When it was all over, her head was, so far as I could determine, gone, gone the long way of her wings and legs. Had she been new, or old? Had she mated and laid her eggs, had she done her work? All that was left was the glowing horn shell of her abdomen and thorax—a fraying, partially collapsed gold tube jammed upright in the candle's round pool.

And then this moth-essence, this spectacular skeleton, began to act as a wick. She kept burning. The wax rose in the moth's body from her soaking abdomen to her thorax to the jagged hole where her head should be, and widened into flame, a saffron-yellow flame that robed her to the ground like any immolating monk. That candle had two wicks, two flames of identical height, side by side. The moth's head was fire. She burned for two hours, until I blew her out. 8

She burned for two hours without changing, without bending or leaning—only glowing within, like a building fire glimpsed through silhouetted walls, like a hollow saint, like a flame-faced virgin gone to God, while I read by her light, kindled, while Rimbaud in Paris burnt out his brains in a thousand poems, while night pooled wetly at my feet. 9

And that is why I believe those hollow crisps on the bathroom floor are moths. I think I know moths, and fragments of moths, and chips and tatters of utterly empty moths, in any state. How many of you, I asked the people in my class, which of you want to give your lives and be writers? I was trembling from coffee, or cigarettes, or the closeness of faces all around me. (Is this what we live for? I thought; is this the only final beauty: the color of any skin in any light, and living, human eyes?) All hands rose to the question. (You, Nick? Will you? Margaret? Randy? Why do I want them to mean it?) And then I tried to tell them what the choice must mean: you can't be anything else. You must go at your life with a broadax. . . . They had no idea what I was saying. (I have two hands, don't I? And all this energy, for as long as I can remember. I'll do it in the evenings, after skiing, or on the way home from the bank, or after the children are asleep. . . .) They thought I was raving again. It's just as well. 10

I have three candles here on the table which I disentangle from the plants and light when visitors come. Small usually avoids them, although once she came too close and her tail caught fire; I rubbed it out before she noticed. The flames move light over everyone's skin, draw light to the surface of the faces of my friends. When the people leave I never blow the candles out, and after I'm asleep they flame and burn.

XXXXXXXXXXXXXXXXXXXX **FOR DISCUSSION** XXXXXXXXXXXXXXXXXXXX

1. What is Annie Dillard referring to in paragraph 10 when she says, "I'll do it in the evenings, after skiing, or on the way home from the bank . . . "?

2. What is the CLIMACTIC or most dramatic event of Dillard's NARRATIVE? How does she connect it with what she sees in her bathroom?

3. Dillard draws an extended ANALOGY between the burning moth and the writer. What does this analogy imply about the nature of the writer's calling as Dillard sees it?

4. What is "miraculous" about the spider's web in paragraph 2? How would you DESCRIBE Dillard's attitude toward nature and the natural world throughout her essay?

5. What would you say to George, the student who recently posted the following on the www.bookcritics.org Web site: "I need to know the significance of the butterfly in Annie Dillard's 'Death of a Moth.' This essay made absolutely no sense to me so I really need some help."

ANNIE DILLARD

How I Wrote the Moth Essay— and Why

It was November 1975. I was living alone, as described, on an island   1
in Puget Sound, near the Canadian border. I was thirty years old. I
thought about myself a lot (for someone thirty years old), because I
couldn't figure out what I was doing there. What was my life about?
Why was I living alone, when I am gregarious? Would I ever meet someone, or should I reconcile myself to all this solitude? I disliked celibacy;
I dreaded childlessness. I couldn't even think of anything to write. I was
examining every event for possible meaning.

I was then in full flight from success, from the recent fuss over a   2
book of prose I'd published the previous year called *Pilgrim at Tinker
Creek*. There were offers from editors, publishers, and Hollywood and
network producers. They tempted me with world travel, film and TV
work, big bucks. I was there to turn from literary and commercial success
and to rededicate myself to art and to God. That's how I justified my
loneliness to myself. It was a feeble justification and I knew it, because
you certainly don't need to live alone either to write or to pray. Actually
I was there because I had picked the place from an atlas, and I was alone
because I hadn't yet met my husband.

My reading and teaching fed my thoughts. I was reading Simone   3
Weil, *First and Last Notebooks*. Simone Weil was a twentieth-century
French intellectual, born Jewish, who wrote some of the most interesting
Christian theology I've ever read. She was brilliant, but a little nuts; her
doctrines were harsh. "Literally," she wrote, "it is total purity or death."
This sort of fanaticism attracted and appalled me. Weil had deliberately
starved herself to death to call attention to the plight of French workers.
I was taking extensive notes on Weil.

In the classroom I was teaching poetry writing, exhorting myself (in the guise of exhorting my students), and convincing myself by my own rhetoric: commit yourself to a useless art! In art alone is meaning! In sacrifice alone is meaning! These, then, were issues for me at that time: dedication, purity, sacrifice.

4

Early that November morning I noticed the hollow insects on the bathroom floor. I got down on my hands and knees to examine them and recognized some as empty moth bodies. I recognized them, of course, only because I'd seen an empty moth body already—two years before, when I'd camped alone and had watched a flying moth get stuck in a candle and burn.

5

Walking back to my desk, where I had been answering letters, I realized that the burning moth was a dandy visual focus for all my recent thoughts about an empty, dedicated life. Perhaps I'd try to write a short narrative about it.

6

I went to my pile of journals, hoping I'd taken some nice, specific notes about the moth in the candle. What I found disappointed me at first: that night I'd written a long description of owl sounds, and only an annoyed aside about bugs flying into the candle. But the next night, after pages of self-indulgent drivel, I'd written a fuller description, a description of the moth which got stuck in candle wax.

7

The journal entry had some details I could use (bristleworms on the ground, burnt moths' wings sticking to pans), some phrases (her body acted as a wick, the candle had 2 flames, the moth burned until I blew it out), and, especially, some verbs (hiss, recoil, stick, spatter, jerked, crackled).

8

Even in the journals, the moth was female. (From childhood reading I'd learned to distinguish moths by sex.) And, there in the journal, was a crucial detail: on that camping trip, I'd been reading about Rimbaud. Arthur Rimbaud—the French symbolist poet, a romantic, hotheaded figure who attracted me enormously when I was sixteen—had been young and self-destructive. When *he* was sixteen, he ran away from home to Paris, led a dissolute life, shot his male lover (the poet Verlaine), drank absinthe which damaged his brain, deranged his senses with drunkenness

9

Jar B.   Kindling

while R out his furniture

Jan 2

Two summers ago I ~~was camped~~ was camping alone ~~in~~ on
the Blue Ridge mountains in Virginia. I had hauled
myself and gear up there to read, among other things, James Ramsey
Ullman's ~~novel~~ The Day on Fire, a novel about Rimbaud that had
made ~~went the~~ a writer ~~of me~~ when I was sixteen; I was hoping it
would do it again. So I read every ~~all~~ day sitting under a tree
by my tent, ~~pausing to eat~~ four or five times and
~~walk once or twice, and I read~~ every ~~all~~ night while
~~warblers~~ sang in the leaves overhead and bristleworms
trailed their inches over the twiggy ~~ground~~ dirt at my
(side) ~~feet~~, and I read every night by candlelight,
while ~~the~~ barred owls called in the forest and pale
moths ~~near me when my night made~~ massed in the clearing. ~~saying my the words~~ made a ring.
I read,

~~The moths flew on~~ Moths kept flying into the
candle. They would hiss ~~and sputter~~ and recoil, lost
upside down in the darkness shadows among my cooking pans.
Or they would singe their wings and fall, and their
~~burnt~~ hot wings would stick, as if melted, to whatever they
touched, a pan, a lid, a spoon, so that the first thing the moths snagged
could struggle only in tiny arcs, unable to ~~rise~~ free flutter.
These I could release ~~with~~ by a quick flip ~~by~~ with a stick; in
the morning I would find my cooking stuff embossed with torn
flecks of moth wings, little triangles of shiny dust here and
there on the aluminum. So I read, and boiled water,
and replenished candles, and read on.   was caught, burned dry and held

            One night one ~~moth~~ to female flew into the candle, ~~and burned so fast~~ sizzled, dropped ~~down on in to~~ into   ~~caught, burned~~ ~~and held burning.~~
the wet wax, stuck, flamed and fried in a second.
Her wings burnt right off and disappeared in a thin, foul
smoke; her legs ~~crackled~~ spattered and curled, her head ~~jerked~~
crackled and jerked (like small arms fire)
~~Her wings fantwings~~ I must have been staring at
the candle, or maybe I looked up when a shadow
crossed my page; at any rate, I saw ~~the while that~~ it all.

and sleeplessness, and wrote mad vivid poetry which altered the course of Western literature. When he was in his twenties, he turned his back to the Western world and vanished into Abyssinia as a gunrunner.

With my old journal beside me, I took up my current journal and scribbled and doodled my way through an account of my present life and the remembered moth. It went extraordinarily well; it was not typical. It seemed very much "given"—given, I think, because I'd asked, because I'd been looking so hard and so long for connections, meanings. The connections were all there, and seemed solid enough: I saw a moth burnt and on fire; I was reading Rimbaud hoping to rededicate myself to writing (this one bald statement of motive was unavoidable); I live alone. So the writer is like the moth, and like a religious contemplative: emptying himself so he can be a channel for his work. Of course you can reinforce connections with language: the bathroom moths are like a jumble of buttresses for cathedral domes; the female moth is like an immolating monk, like a hollow saint, a flame-faced virgin gone to God; Rimbaud burnt out his brains with poetry while night pooled wetly at my feet.

I liked the piece enough to rewrite it. I took out a couple of paragraphs—one about why I didn't have a dog, another that ran on about the bathroom spider. This is the kind of absurdity you fall into when you write about anything, let alone about yourself. You're so pleased and grateful to be writing at all, especially at the beginning, that you babble. Often you don't know where the work is going, so you can't tell what's irrelevant.

It doesn't hurt much to babble in a first draft, so long as you have the sense to cut out irrelevancies later. If you are used to analyzing texts, you will be able to formulate a clear statement of what your draft turned out to be about. Then you make a list of what you've already written, paragraph by paragraph, and see what doesn't fit and cut it out. (All this requires is nerves of steel and lots of coffee.) Most of the time you'll have to add to the beginning, ensuring that it gives a fair idea of what the point might be, or at least what is about to happen. (Suspense is for mystery writers. The most inept writing has an inadvertent element of

OPPOSITE: *Page from the first draft of "The Death of a Moth."*

suspense: the reader constantly asks himself, where on earth is this going?) Usually I end up throwing away the beginning: the first part of a poem, the first few pages of an essay, the first scene of a story, even the first few chapters of a book. It's not holy writ. The paragraphs and sentences are tesserae—tiles for a mosaic. Just because you have a bunch of tiles in your lap doesn't mean your mosaic will be better if you use them all. In this atypical case, however, there were very few extraneous passages. The focus was tight, probably because I'd been so single-minded before I wrote it.

I added stuff, too, to strengthen and clarify the point. I added some speculation about the burning moth: had she mated and laid her eggs, had she done her work? Near the end I added a passage about writing class: which of you want to give your lives and become writers? [13]

Ultimately I sent it to *Harper*'s magazine, which published it. The early drafts, and the *Harper*'s version, had a different ending, a kind of punch line that was a series of interlocking statements: [14]

> I don't mind living alone. I like eating alone and reading. I don't mind sleeping alone. The only time I mind being alone is when something is funny; then, when I am laughing at something funny, I wish someone were around. Sometimes I think it is pretty funny that I sleep alone.

I took this ending out of the book version, which is the version you have. I took it out because the tone was too snappy, too clever; it reduced everything to celibacy, which was really a side issue; it made the reader forget the moth; and it called too much attention to the narrator. The new ending was milder. It referred back to the main body of the text. [15]

Revising is a breeze if you know what you're doing—if you can look at your text coldly, analytically, manipulatively. Since I've studied texts, I know what I'm doing when I revise. The hard part is devising the wretched thing in the first place. How do you go from nothing to something? How do you face the blank page without fainting dead away? [16]

To start a narrative, you need a batch of things. Not feelings, not opinions, not sentiments, not judgments, not arguments, but specific [17] objects and events: a cat, a spider web, a mess of insect skeletons, a candle, a book about Rimbaud, a burning moth. I try to give the reader a story, or at least a scene (the flimsiest narrative occasion will serve), and something to look at. I try not to hang on the reader's arm and bore him with my life story, my fancy self-indulgent writing, or my opinions. He is my guest; I try to entertain him. Or he'll throw my pages across the room and turn on the television.

I try to say what I mean and not "hide the hidden meaning." "Clarity is the sovereign courtesy of the writer," said J. Henri Fabre, the great French entomologist, "I do my best to achieve it." Actually, it took me about ten years to learn to write clearly. When I was in my twenties, I was more interested in showing off.   18

What do you do with these things? You juggle them. You toss them around. To begin, you don't need a well defined point. You don't need "something to say"—that will just lead you to reiterating clichés. You need bits of the world to toss around. You start anywhere, and join the bits into a pattern by your writing about them. Later you can throw out the ones that don't fit.   19

I like to start by describing something, by ticking off the five senses. Later I go back to the beginning and locate the reader in time and space. I've found that if I take pains to be precise about *things*, feelings will take care of themselves. If you try to force a reader's feelings through dramatic writing ("writhe," "ecstasy," "scream"), you make a fool of yourself, like someone at a party trying too hard to be liked.   20

I have piles of materials in my journals—mostly information in the form of notes on my reading, and to a lesser extent, notes on things I'd seen and heard during the day. I began the journals five or six years after college, finding myself highly trained for taking notes and for little else. Now I have thirty-some journal volumes, all indexed. If I want to write about arctic exploration, say, or star chemistry, or monasticism, I can find masses of pertinent data under that topic. And if I browse I can often find images from other fields that may fit into what I'm writing, if only as metaphor or simile. It's terrific having all these materials handy. It saves and makes available all those years of reading. Otherwise, I'd forget everything, and life wouldn't accumulate, but merely pass.   21

The moth essay I wrote that November day was an "odd" piece— 22 "freighted with heavy-handed symbolism," as I described it to myself just after I wrote it. The reader must be startled to watch this apparently calm, matter-of-fact account of the writer's life and times turn before his eyes into a mess of symbols whose real subject matter is their own relationship. I hoped the reader wouldn't feel he'd been had. I tried to ensure that the actual, historical moth wouldn't vanish into idea, but would stay physically present.

A week after I wrote the first draft I considered making it part of the 23 book *(Holy the Firm)* I had been starting. It seemed to fit the book's themes. (Actually, I spent the next fifteen months fitting the book to *its* themes.) In order to clarify my thinking I jotted down some notes:

> moth in candle:
>
> the poet—	materials of world, of bare earth at feet, sucked up, transformed, subsumed to spirit, to air, to light
>
> the mystic—not through reason but through emptiness
>
> the martyr—virgin, sacrifice, death with meaning.

I prefaced these notes with the comical word "Hothead."

It had been sheer good luck that the different aspects of the histor- 24 ical truth fit together so nicely. It had actually been on that particular solo camping trip that I'd read the Rimbaud novel. If it hadn't been, I wouldn't have hesitated to fiddle with the facts. I fiddled with one fact, for sure: I foully slandered my black cat, Small, by saying she was "gold"—to match the book's moth and little blonde burnt girl. I actually had a gold cat at that time, named Kindling. I figured no one would believe it. It was too much. In the book, as in real life, the cat was spayed.

This is the most personal piece I've ever written—the essay itself, and 25 these notes on it. I don't recommend, or even approve, writing personally. It can lead to dreadful writing. The danger is that you'll get lost in the contemplation of your wonderful self. You'll include things for the lousy reason that they actually happened, or that you feel strongly about them; you'll forget to ensure that the *reader* feels anything whatever. You may hold the popular view that art is self-expression, or a way of understanding the self—in which case the artist need do nothing more than babble uncontrolledly about the self and then congratulate himself that, in addition to all his other wonderfully interesting attributes, he is also an artist. I don't (evidently) hold this view. So I think that this moth piece is a risky one to read: it seems to enforce these romantic and giddy notions of art and the artist. But I trust you can keep your heads.

XXXXXXXXXXXXXXXXXXXX **FOR DISCUSSION** XXXXXXXXXXXXXXXXXXXX

1. Why is Annie Dillard opposed, as a rule, to "writing personally" (25)? What dangers does she advise you to avoid when you write a personal essay? How well do you think she herself avoids these pitfalls? Please point to specific passages in her two essays that support your opinion.

2. According to Dillard, what's the value to a writer of keeping a journal? Again, please point to specific statements in her essays.

3. In which paragraphs does Dillard explicitly DESCRIBE the process of revising the moth essay? What did she omit in the second draft? How and when did she change the ending? What's the nature of the changes? Why did she make them?

4. Think about the ways you generally go about starting to write. Where do you start? What kind of research do you do? How much time do you spend revising? How does your writing process COMPARE with Dillard's?

The Processes of Writing

When a writer plans a new piece of writing, he or she looks for a subject to write about, comes up with ideas about that subject, gathers information, and begins to select details and EXAMPLES. The *planning* phase is thus the "finding" phase of composition; its main business is to "invent" a subject, to "discover" it.

After some time spent planning, the writer begins *drafting*—organizing and presenting information and ideas. The writer busily orders what he or she is discovering into a form that is comprehensible to other people. The writer can describe his or her subject (DESCRIPTION), tell a story about it (NARRATION), compare it with other similar subjects (COMPARISON AND CONTRAST), and ANALYZE how it came about (CAUSE AND EFFECT) or how it works (PROCESS ANALYSIS) or exactly what it is (DEFINITION). In fact, these are a few of the many MODES OF WRITING that you will encounter in the model essays in this book.

In the revising and editing phases of writing, the writer is not so much ordering as reordering what he or she has to say. Ideally, *revision* takes place after getting a response to a draft. Indeed, as the name implies, true "re-vision" is a reseeing of the whole and may require the introduction of new parts and even some starting over again. *Editing* follows revision; it is the phase when the writer looks at words and sentences to be sure his or her writing is clear and makes its points effectively. Revising and editing may be the last phases of writing, but there is nothing "final" about them. This tentative quality of all the processes that go into good writing is suggested by the term *draft*. A draft is a trial; after one or two drafts, one or two or half a dozen more may follow.

In the two sample essays in this chapter—"The Death of a Moth" and "How I Wrote the Moth Essay—and Why"—we watched as a professional writer, Annie Dillard, worked her way through all the basic processes of writing: first finding a subject to write about and taking notes on it; then, after mulling the subject over for a while, writing out a draft; and, afterward, revising it "coldly, analytically" (12).

The Modes of Writing

Suppose that, in addition to keeping a journal and writing an essay about it, Dillard sent a letter to a friend about her camping trip and the moth that turned to flame. Her hypothetical letter might contain the following elements:

a *description* of the campsite, surrounded by mountains, where "warblers swung in the leaves overhead and bristle worms trailed their inches over the twiggy dirt" (3)

a *narrative* about her arrival in camp and what she did there: "hauled myself and gear up there to read"; "one night a moth flew into the candle, was caught, burnt dry, and held" (3, 4)

a *comparison* between the burning moth and the religious ascetic: "like a hollow saint, like a flame-faced virgin gone to God" (4)

reasons why the friend should join her: "when I am laughing at something funny, I wish someone were around" (11)

The four parts of this hypothetical letter are examples of the four traditional *modes of writing* that all writers use—*description, narration, exposition*, and *argument*.

DESCRIPTION tells how something looks, feels, sounds, smells, or tastes. It appeals directly to the senses. Chapter 1 focuses on description.

NARRATION is storytelling. It shows or tells "what happened." Whereas description focuses on sights, sounds, and other sensations, narration focuses on events, actions, adventures—and the narrator's response to them. Chapter 2 focuses on narration.

EXPOSITION is informative writing. The part of our hypothetical letter that gives directions is exposition. It explains by *giving examples* (Chapter 3), by *classifying and dividing* (Chapter 4), by *telling how something is made or works* (Chapter 5), by *comparing and contrasting* (Chapter 6), by *defining* (Chapter 7), or by *analyzing causes and effects* (Chapter 8).

Exposition gets more attention in this book than the other modes because it is the one you are likely to use most often. Examinations, term papers, insurance claims, job and graduate-school applications, sales reports, almost every scrap of practical prose you write over a lifetime, including your last will and testament, will demand expository skills.

ARGUMENT is writing that seeks assent, advises, or moves the reader to action. The last part of our hypothetical letter is argument. In a sense, all writing aims to present an argument because the writer is always trying to convince readers that what he or she says deserves to be heard. Argument is discussed in Chapter 9.

MIXING THE MODES

If you look closely at examples of good writing, however, one thing about the modes becomes clear: they seldom occur alone. Almost all good writing mixes the modes together, although one mode will often dominate the others, as in the sample essays in the different sections of this book. For example, in "The Death of a Moth," Dillard uses description to help us visualize the cluttered scene in the writer's bathroom: "The spider skins lie on their sides, translucent and ragged, their legs drying in knots. And the moths, the empty moths, stagger against each other . . . like a jumble of buttresses for cathedral domes" (4).

Why is Dillard so minutely describing the dry carcasses of insects, particularly ones that catch on fire? Instead of some strange bug fetish, Dillard's essay is working out a dramatic comparison between the writer and the moth drawn to the flame that consumes it "like a hollow saint, like a flame-faced virgin gone to God" (9). The point of this comparison is to explain what being a writer means to her. The writer's calling, she suggests, demands sacrifice and devotion, much as a saint or nun is devoted to her religion.

Describing the writer's raw materials and explaining the nature of the writer's calling are only part of what Dillard's first essay does, however. Besides describing and explaining, the essay also seeks to inspire young writers to take up the torch. "How many of you, I asked the people in my class, which of you want to give your lives and be writers" (10)? These words make an argument.

But here, again, argument is not the primary task of Dillard's essay as a whole. "The Death of a Moth" is first and foremost a personal narrative, like those you will encounter in Chapter 2. Its primary aim is to tell a story—the story of the moth that burns and of the writer who discovers the burning moth and what it signifies. Despite the apparent smallness of the game she hunts, Dillard's narrative is an intellectual adventure story with an emphasis on action, or "plot" (defined in Chapter 2), which is the soul of narrative.

Dillard's second essay is also primarily a personal narrative, although it, too, incorporates the other modes of writing. For example, she explains rather than narrates when she writes, "It doesn't hurt much to babble in a first draft, so long as you have the sense to cut out irrelevancies later" (12). This also is exposition: "If you are used to analyzing texts, you will be able to formulate a clear statement of what your draft turned out to be about" (12). Much of Dillard's essay is written in this mode, which perhaps explains why she refers to her essay as "notes" (25).

To the extent that Dillard's essay explains how to write an essay, it may even be an example, in fact, of process analysis, the mode of exposition presented in Chapter 5. However, Dillard is not just explaining how to write here. She is writing a story about writing a story. The first essay tells what happened on the camping trip. The second tells what happened two years later in the writer's workshop. Like the first moth essay, in other words, the second one is also a personal narrative. It describes and explains, but its primary aim is to tell about something that happened.

Devotion unto death is a stricter standard than most writing courses enforce these days, so as you study and imitate the different kinds and techniques of writing illustrated by the model essays to follow, I hope you won't fall into the trap of trying to keep them entirely separate from one another—either in your reading or your own writing. Incidentally, this book assumes that the two activities, reading and writing, are just as inextricably bound up together as are their respective modes and processes.

A word about the doodles in this chapter: they are facsimiles from the journal Dillard mentions in her two essays and which she graciously permitted the *Sampler* to copy. These artful scribblings afford an intimate visual glimpse into the mind and methods of the writer as she was actually drafting the moth essay. Look closely, and you will notice a cat peering out from the top of the page. This is Dillard's other cat, Kindling. Her name is discernible just to the right of the portrait. Dillard adopted the cat's golden color in her narrative but, in the interest of "truth," omitted the fact of her "incendiary" name. "I figured no one would believe it," she explains. "It was too much."

1. Both "The Death of a Moth" and "How I Wrote the Moth Essay—and Why" are, in part, personal NARRATIVES like the ones you will find in Chapter 2. How would you describe the narrator, the person who is telling each story? Does she seem different in the two essays? If there are differences, how would you account for them?

2. Paragraph 7 of "The Death of a Moth" is largely DESCRIPTIVE, like the essays in the next chapter: "When it was all over, her head was, so far as I could determine, gone, gone the long way of her wings and legs. . . . All that was left was the glowing horn shell of her abdomen and thorax—a fraying, partially collapsed gold tube jammed upright in the candle's round pool." Please point out other places in this essay where Dillard describes the physical world around her. Where she shows or tells what happened to her.

3. Paragraph 17 of "How I Wrote the Moth Essay—and Why" is largely explanatory: "To start a narrative, you need a batch of things. Not feelings, not opinions, not sentiments, not judgments, not arguments, but specific objects and events." Where else in this essay does Dillard explain things, especially the processes of writing? Where is she primarily showing or telling what happened?

4. Personal narratives are told from the vantage point, or POINT OF VIEW, of a narrator. In paragraph 7 of "The Death of a Moth," for example, the narrator (Dillard) looks up "when a shadow crossed my page." How does Dillard give the impression in both of these essays that she is seeing and reporting on the natural world up close, almost as if she were looking through a magnifying glass? Again, please refer to specific passages.

CHAPTER ONE

DESCRIPTION

XXXXXXXXXXXXXXXXXXXXXXXXXXXXXXXXXXXXXXXXXXXXXXXXXXXXXXXXXXXXXXXXXXXX

DESCRIPTION* is the MODE OF WRITING that appeals most directly to the senses by showing or telling us what something looks like, or how it sounds, smells, feels, or tastes. Consider here two descriptions of cemeteries. The first, from *Natural History* magazine, is written in the language of detached observation:

> An old and popular New England tradition for resident and visitor alike is a relaxing walk through one of our historical cemeteries. . . .
> Haphazard rows of slate tablets give way in time to simple marble tablets bearing urn and willow motifs. The latter in turn lose popularity to marble gravestones of a variety of sizes and shapes and often arranged in groups or family plots. The heyday of ornate marble memorials lasted into the 1920s, when measured rows of uniformly sized granite blocks replaced them.
> NATURAL HISTORY

Compare this passage with novelist John Updike's far-from-detached description of the cemetery in the town where he lives:

> The stones are marble, modernly glossy and simple, though I suppose that time will eventually reveal them as another fashion, dated and quaint. Now, the sod is still raw, the sutures of turf are unhealed, the earth still humped, the wreaths scarcely withered. . . . I remember my grandfather's funeral, the hurried cross of sand the minister drew on the coffin lid, the whine of the lowering straps, the lengthening, cleanly cut sides of clay, the

*Words printed in SMALL CAPITALS are defined in the Glossary.

thought of air, the lack of air forever in the close dark space lined
with pink satin. . . .

JOHN UPDIKE, "CEMETERIES"

Our first example relies heavily upon descriptive adjectives: "historical,"
"haphazard," "simple," "ornate," "measured." Many of these adjectives
tend to be ABSTRACT. Indeed, the movement of the entire passage is away
from the particular. No single grave is described in detail. Even the "urn
and willow motifs" adorn a number of tombs. The authors seem interested in the whole sweep of the cemetery, from the haphazard rows
of the oldest section to the ordered ranks of modern headstones in the
newest.

We should remember that description is not limited to things that
can be perceived directly by the physical senses. It may also describe
ideas: the proportions of a building, the style of a baseball player, the
infinitude of space. Our first description of cemeteries, in fact, moves
from the CONCRETE to the abstract because it was written to support an
idea. It is part of a sociological study of cemeteries as they reveal changing
American attitudes toward death, family, and society. The authors take
their "relaxing walk" not because they want to examine individual tomb-
stones, but because they want to generalize from a multitude of physical
evidence. As reporters, they stand between us and the actual objects they
describe.

By contrast, the movement of the Updike passage is from the general to the particular. Starting where the other leaves off—with a field of
glossy modern slabs—it focuses quickly upon newly dug graves and then
narrows even more sharply to a single grave kept fresh in the author's
memory. This time, the adjectives are concrete: "raw," "unhealed,"
"humped," "withered," "hurried," "close," "dark." The nouns are concrete, too: "sod," "turf," and "earth" give way to the "space" lined with
satin. Death is no abstraction for Updike; it is the suffocating loss of
personal life, and he makes us experience the finality of death by describing his own sensations of claustrophobia at his grandfather's funeral.

Different as they are, these two passages illustrate a single peculi-
arity of description as a mode of writing: it seldom stands alone. As in
our first example, scientific description shades easily into exposition. As

in our second, evocative description shades just as easily into narration. The authors of the first example tell us about the changes in a cemetery in order to explain (EXPOSITION) what those changes mean for American culture. After evoking his feelings about a past event, the author of the second example goes on in later lines to *show* us what happened (NARRATION) when his reverie is interrupted by his son, who is learning to ride a bicycle in a peaceful cemetery. Which kind of description is better, scientific or evocative, description that tells or description that shows? Neither is inherently better or worse than the other, although the second kind may be more dramatic. The kind of description that a writer chooses depends upon what he or she wants to do with it.

Updike's reference to the "sutures" of "unhealed" turf suggests how easily description also falls into METAPHOR, SIMILE, and ANALOGY. This is hardly surprising, for we often describe something by telling what it is like. A thump in your closet at night sounds like an owl hitting a haystack. A crowd stirs like a jellyfish. The seams of turf on new graves are like the stitches binding a wound.

The ease with which description shifts into other modes does not mean that a good description has no unity or order of its own, however. When writing description, keep in mind that every detail should contribute to some DOMINANT IMPRESSION. The dominant impression he wanted to convey when describing his grandfather's funeral, says Updike, was "the foreverness, the towering foreverness." Updike creates this impression by moving from the outside to the inside of the grave when he writes "the lack of air forever in the close dark space lined with pink satin. . . ."

Depending on what you are describing, you may want to move from inside out, left to right, top to bottom, or front to back. Whatever arrangement you choose, present the details of your description systematically and from a consistent vantage point, or POINT OF VIEW. In the following example from John Gardner's fairy tale *Freddy's Book*, the order in which the objects in a strange boy's room are described cannot be separated from the point of view of the person who is describing it:

The room was so spare one could see everything at a glance: a closet door with a lock on it, a long table with five perfect constructions—three ships, two dragons—nothing else on the table but a neat stack of stainless-steel razor-blades. What defined all the rest, of course, was that immense desk and chair. They made it seem that the room itself was from a picture book, or better yet, a stage-set, for across one end hung a dark green curtain. Beyond that, presumably, the professor's son crouched, hiding. My gaze stopped and froze on an enormous bare foot that protruded, unbeknownst to its owner, no doubt, from behind the curtain. It was the largest human foot I'd ever seen or imagined. . . .

JOHN GARDNER, *FREDDY'S BOOK*

What makes this description of a fantasy place, the lair of a boy giant, seem real is the systematic way in which it is presented to us by the narrator, or speaker. (Narrators and narrative point of view are discussed more fully in Chapter 2.) The first object the speaker (and we) see in Freddy's room is the closet door, a feature one might expect to find in any boy's bedroom. Then he sees the lock. Why would a boy keep his closet under lock and key? What's he hiding? We are moving here from the near to the far, and from the familiar to the strange.

Next, the narrator sees the "constructions" on the table—model ships and dragons, items any normal, imaginative boy might construct. (Apparently, this boy can be trusted with razor-blades—always good to know when dealing with giants.) But then there is the oversized desk and chair. And the enormous foot. This is no ordinary room and no ordinary boy. The dominant impression here is one of growing wonder. We aren't yet allowed to see the rest of Freddy lurking behind the curtain, however, because the speaker can't see him—not until he crosses the room and throws back the curtain that obscures the boy from his gaze.

What dominant impression, mood, or purpose is your description intended to serve? What specific objects can contribute to it? What do they look, feel, smell, taste, or sound like? Does your object or place suggest any natural order of presentation? If it does, try to follow that order throughout your description, as John Gardner does.

An order of presentation based on the physical characteristics of the thing you are describing will help your reader to see that thing more clearly—and to see *why* you are describing it. Gardner's larger purpose in describing Freddy's room is to tell the story of a boy giant, and his methodical description advances that narrative purpose. As modes of writing, description and narration are so closely related that one seldom occurs without the other. After all, it's hard to tell just what a boy giant (or anyone else) is doing without saying a little about where and how he does it.

When you define something—a watch, for instance—you say what it is: a watch is a timepiece. When you *describe* a particular watch, or other object, you tell what qualities distinguish it from other similar objects: this Chico's watch is said to be "simple and elegant," "versatile," and "rustic-styled." (The rustic styling is further illustrated by displaying it on the end of a log.) Since catalogs abound with descriptive phrases, the ad writer here, whose purpose is to sell watches, adds more descriptive details ("square face," "etched silver metal band," "hinged cuff style closure") to distinguish further this particular watch from others. The finishing touch of this description is to give the watch a name, the Ox Cuff, distinguishing it from others in the catalog—for example, the South Beach Watch. Whereas the ad writer, in describing the Ox Cuff Watch, wants to give a DOMINANT IMPRESSION of simple elegance with rustic details, there is nothing rustic about the impression given in describing the South Beach Watch. Like the Art Deco hotels along Miami's South Beach, it is said to offer "a distinctly vintage appeal" with a mother-of-pearl face and "retro glow" hands. For this added urbanity and nostalgia, you pay $56, instead of $38.

CONSIDER FURTHER . . .

1. "Silver" and "square" are no more or less DESCRIPTIVE terms than "simple" and "elegant"; however, they are more concrete. The concrete and specific details we can use to describe something are not as likely to vary from observer to observer as the more abstract ones. Nobody, for example, is likely to describe Chico's Ox Cuff Watch as round. What other abstract terms, besides "simple," "elegant," or "rustic," might you use to describe the timepiece pictured here?

2. Why do you suppose catalogs, as a rule, spend more time describing the items they picture than defining them or comparing them with other products?

3. Using a favorite catalog, collect descriptions of a few items that you find to be particularly well done. Choose one, and decide what words the writer has used that result in effective description and what dominant impression they give.

Silver Ox Cuff Watch
Simple and elegant are the words that best describe this versatile, rustic-styled watch. Details include a square face, an etched silver metal band, and a hinged cuff style closure. Japanese quartz movement. Imported.
$38 1110102

ALICE STEINBACH

THE MISS DENNIS SCHOOL
OF WRITING

Alice Steinbach (b. 1933) is a freelance writer whose essays and travel sketches often deal with what she calls "lessons from a woman's life." As a reporter for the *Baltimore Sun*, where she won a Pulitzer Prize for feature writing in 1985, Steinbach wrote a column about her ninth-grade creative writing teacher. Revised as an essay—essays are "much more complete" than columns, says Steinbach—it became the title piece in a collection of personal essays, *The Miss Dennis School of Writing* (1996). Here the "lesson" is both a writing lesson and a life lesson. Miss Dennis taught that good descriptive writing (her specialty) makes the reader see what the writer sees. She also taught her students to find their unique personal voices. Steinbach's distinctive voice can be heard in her vivid descriptions of her old teacher. It is a voice, she says, that "tends to look at people with a child's eye."

XXXXXXXXXXXXXXXXXXXXXXXXXXXXXXXXXXXXXXXXXXXXXXXXXXXXXXXXXXXXXX

"What kind of writing do you do?" asked the novelist sitting to my left at a writer's luncheon.   1

"I work for a newspaper in Baltimore," he was told.   2

"Oh, did you go to journalism school?"   3

"Well, yes."   4

"Columbia?" he asked, invoking the name of the most prestigious journalism school in the country.   5

"Actually, no," I heard myself telling him. "I'm one of the lucky ones. I am a graduate of the Miss Dennis School of Writing."   6

Unimpressed, the novelist turned away. Clearly it was a credential that did not measure up to his standards. But why should it? He was not one of the lucky ones. He had never met Miss Dennis, my ninth-   7 grade creative writing teacher, or had the good fortune to be her student. Which meant he had never experienced the sight of Miss Dennis chasing Dorothy Singer around the classroom, threatening her with a yardstick because Dorothy hadn't paid attention and her writing showed it.

"You want to be a writer?" Miss Dennis would yell, out of breath from all the running and yardstick-brandishing. "Then pay attention to what's going on around you. Connect! You are not Switzerland—neutral, aloof, uninvolved. Think Italy!"   8

Miss Dennis said things like this. If you had any sense, you wrote them down.   9

"I can't teach you how to write, but I can tell you how to look at things, how to pay attention," she would bark out at us, like a drill sergeant confronting a group of undisciplined, wet-behind-the-ears Marine recruits. To drive home her point, she had us take turns writing a description of what we saw on the way to school in the morning. Of course, you never knew which morning would be your turn so—just to be on the safe side—you got into the habit of looking things over carefully every morning and making notes: "Saw a pot of red geraniums sitting in the sunlight on a white stucco porch; an orange-striped cat curled like a comma beneath a black van; a dark gray cloud scudding across a silver morning sky."   10

It's a lesson that I have returned to again and again throughout my writing career. To this day, I think of Miss Dennis whenever I write a certain kind of sentence. Or to be more precise, whenever I write a sentence that actually creates in words the picture I want readers to see.   11

Take, for instance, this sentence: Miss Dennis was a small, compact woman, about albatross height—or so it seemed to her students—with short, straight hair the color of apricots and huge eyeglasses that were always slipping down her nose.   12

Or this one: Miss Dennis always wore a variation of one outfit—a dark-colored, flared woolen skirt, a tailored white blouse and a cardigan sweater, usually black, thrown over her shoulders and held together by a little pearl chain.   13

Can you see her? I can. And the image of her makes me smile. Still.   14

But it was not Miss Dennis's appearance or her unusual teaching method—which had a lot in common with an out-of-control terrier—   15 that made her so special. What set her apart was her deep commitment to liberating the individual writer in each student.

"What lies at the heart of good writing," she told us over and over again, "is the writer's ability to find his own unique voice. And then to use it to tell an interesting story." Somehow she made it clear that we were interesting people with interesting stories to tell. Most of us, of course, had never even known we had a story to tell, much less an interesting one. But soon the stories just started bubbling up from some inner wellspring.   16

Finding the material, however, was one thing; finding the individual voice was another.   17

Take me, for instance. I arrived in Miss Dennis's class trailing all sorts of literary baggage. My usual routine was to write like Colette on Monday, one of the Bronte sisters on Wednesday, and Mark Twain on Friday.   18

Right away, Miss Dennis knocked me off my high horse.   19

"Why are you telling other people's stories?" she challenged me, peering up into my face. (At fourteen I was already four inches taller than Miss Dennis.) "You have your own stories to tell."   20

I was tremendously relieved to hear this and immediately proceeded to write like my idol, E. B. White. Miss Dennis, however, wasn't buying.   21

"How will you ever find out what you have to say if you keep trying to say what other people have already said?" was the way she dispensed with my E. B. White impersonation. By the third week of class, Miss Dennis knew my secret. She knew I was afraid—afraid to pay attention to my own inner voice for fear that when I finally heard it, it would have nothing to say.   22

What Miss Dennis told me—and I have carefully preserved these words because they were then, and are now, so very important to me— was this: "Don't be afraid to discover what you're saying in the act of saying it." Then, in her inimitably breezy and endearing way, she added: "Trust me on this one."   23

From the beginning, she made it clear to us that it was not "right" or "wrong" answers she was after. It was thinking.   24

"Don't be afraid to go out on a limb," she'd tell some poor kid struggling to reason his way through an essay on friendship or courage.   25

And eventually—once we stopped being afraid that we'd be chopped off out there on that limb—we needed no encouragement to say what we thought. In fact, after the first month, I can't remember ever feeling afraid of failing in her class. Passing or failing didn't seem to be the point of what she was teaching.

Miss Dennis spent as much time, maybe more, pointing out what was right with your work as she did pointing out what was wrong. I can still hear her critiquing my best friend's incredibly florid essay on nature. "You are a very good observer of nature," she told the budding writer. "And if you just write what you see without thinking so much about adjectives and comparisons, we will see it through your attentive eyes."

By Thanksgiving vacation I think we were all a little infatuated with Miss Dennis. And beyond that, infatuated with the way she made us feel about ourselves—that we were interesting people worth listening to.

I, of course, fancied I had a special relationship with her. It was certainly special to me. And, to tell the truth, I knew she felt the same way.

The first time we acknowledged this was one day after class when I stayed behind to talk to her. I often did that and it seemed we talked about everything—from the latest films to the last issue of the *New Yorker*. The one thing we did not talk about was the sadness I felt about my father's death. He had died a few years before and, although I did not know it then, I was still grieving his absence. Without knowing the details, Miss Dennis somehow picked up on my sadness. Maybe it was there in my writing. Looking back I see now that, without my writing about it directly, my father's death hovered at the edges of all my stories.

But on this particular day I found myself talking not about the movies or about writing but instead pouring out my feelings about the loss of my father. I shall never forget that late fall afternoon: the sound of the vanilla-colored blinds flap, flap, flapping in the still classroom; sun falling in shafts through the windows, each ray illuminating tiny galaxies of chalk dust in the air; the smell of wet blackboards; the teacher, small with apricot-colored hair, listening intently to a young girl blurting out her grief. These memories are stored like vintage photographs.

The words that passed between the young girl and the attentive teacher are harder to recall. With this exception. "One day," Miss Dennis

26

27

28

29

30

31

told me, "you will write about this. Maybe not directly. But you will write about it. And you will find that all this has made you a better writer and a stronger person."

After that day, it was as if Miss Dennis and I shared something. We never talked again about my father but spent most of our time discussing our mutual interests. We both loved poetry and discovered one afternoon that each of us regarded Emily Dickinson with something approaching idolatry. Right then and there, Miss Dennis gave me a crash course in why Emily Dickinson's poems worked. I can still hear her talking about the "spare, slanted beauty" in Dickinson's unique choice of words. She also told me about the rather cloistered life led by this New England spinster, noting that nonetheless Emily Dickinson knew the world as few others did. "She found her world within the word," is the way I remember Miss Dennis putting it. Of course, I could be making that part up.

That night, propped up in bed reading Emily Dickinson's poetry, I wondered if Miss Dennis, a spinster herself, identified in some way with the woman who wrote:

> Wild nights–Wild nights!
> Were I with thee
> Wild Nights should be
> Our luxury!

It seems strange, I know, but I never really knew anything about Miss Dennis' life outside of the classroom. Oh, once she confided in me that the initial "M" in her name stood for Mildred. And I was surprised when I passed by the teachers' lounge one day and saw her smoking a cigarette, one placed in a long, silver cigarette holder. It seemed an exceedingly sophisticated thing to do and it struck me then that she might be more worldly than I had previously thought.

But I didn't know how she spent her time or what she wanted from life or anything like that. And I never really wondered about it. Once I remember talking to some friends about her age. We guessed somewhere around fifty—which seemed really old to us. In reality, Miss Dennis was around forty.

It was Miss Dennis, by the way, who encouraged me to enter some 36
writing contests. To my surprise, I took first place in a couple of them.
Of course, taking first place is easy. What's hard is being rejected. But
Miss Dennis helped me with that, too, citing all the examples of famous
writers who'd been rejected time and time again. "Do you know what
they told George Orwell when they rejected *Animal Farm?*" she would
ask me. Then without waiting for a reply, she'd answer her own question:
"The publisher told him, 'It is impossible to sell animal stories in the
U.S.A.' "

When I left her class at the end of the year, Miss Dennis gave me 37
a present: a book of poems by Emily Dickinson. I have it still. The spine
is cracked and the front cover almost gone, but the inscription remains.
On the inside flyleaf, in her perfect Palmer Method handwriting, she had
written: "Say what you see. Yours in Emily Dickinson, Miss Dennis."

She had also placed little checks next to two or three poems. I took 38
this to mean she thought they contained a special message for me. One
of those checked began this way:

> Hope is the thing with feathers
> That perches in the soul . . .

I can remember carefully copying out these lines onto a sheet of paper,
one which I carried around in my handbag for almost a year. But time
passed, the handbag fell apart and who knows what happened to the
yellowing piece of paper with the words about hope.

The years went by. Other schools and other teachers came and went. 39
But one thing remained constant: My struggle to pay attention to my
own inner life; to hear a voice that I would recognize finally as my own.
Not only in my writing but in my life.

Only recently, I learned that Miss Dennis had died at the age of 40
fifty. When I heard this, it occurred to me that her life was close to being
over when I met her. Neither of us knew this, of course. Or at least I
didn't. But lately I've wondered if she knew something that day we talked
about sadness and my father's death. "Write about it," she said. "It will
help you."

And now, reading over these few observations, I think of Miss Den- 41
nis. But not with sadness. Actually, thinking of Miss Dennis makes me

smile. I think of her and see, with marked clarity, a small, compact woman with apricot-colored hair. She is with a young girl and she is saying something.

She is saying: "Pay attention."   42

XXXXXXXXXXXXXXXXXXX **FOR DISCUSSION** XXXXXXXXXXXXXXXXXXX

1. When some teachers say "Pay attention," they mean "Pay attention to what *I* am saying." According to her former pupil, Alice Steinbach, what did Miss Dennis mean when she told students to pay attention?

2. It was not Miss Dennis's appearance nor her teaching methods that made her so special as a teacher of writing, says Steinbach, but "her deep commitment to liberating the individual writer in each student" (15). How did Miss Dennis accomplish this feat in Steinbach's case?

3. Steinbach poses a direct question to the reader in paragraph 14: "Can you see her?" Well, can you? And if so, what exactly do you see—and hear? For example, what color was Miss Dennis's hair?

4. As a professional writer, Steinbach thinks of her old teacher whenever she writes a sentence "that actually creates in words the picture I want readers to see" (11). This is precisely what good DESCRIPTIVE writing does, although it may appeal to other senses as well as sight. How did Miss Dennis teach this kind of writing?

5. Writing about old teachers who die can be an occasion for sentimentality or excessively emotional writing. Do you think Steinbach's tribute to her former teacher is overly emotional, or does she successfully avoid sentimentality? If she avoids it, in your opinion, please explain how you think she does so. If not, please explain why you think she doesn't. Find places in her essay that support your view.

XXXXXXXXXXXXX **STRATEGIES AND STRUCTURES** XXXXXXXXXXXXX

1. Point out several DESCRIPTIVE passages in Steinbach's essay that follow her principle of creating in words what she wants the reader to see.

2. Why do you think Steinbach, looking back over her recollections of Miss Dennis, refers to them as "observations" (41)?

3. Like the other MODES OF WRITING, description seldom stands alone. Often it shades into NARRATIVE, as here. Thus Miss Dennis, who greatly valued the writer's eye, urged the student, once she found her unique way of look-ing at the world, to use it "to tell an interesting story" (16). Whose story is Steinbach telling besides Miss Dennis's? How interesting do you find *that* narrative?

4. How would *you* describe Steinbach's personal "voice" in this essay? Give EXAMPLES from the essay to demonstrate your description.

5. What DOMINANT IMPRESSION of Miss Dennis do we get from Steinbach's description of her in paragraphs 12 through 14 and 41? Of Steinbach herself?

6. How informative do you find Steinbach's essay as a lesson on how to write, particularly on how to write good description? Where does Steinbach ANALYZE the process? (PROCESS ANALYSIS is discussed in Chapter 5.)

XXXXXXXXXXXXX **WORDS AND FIGURES OF SPEECH** XXXXXXXXXXXXX

1. Which is more CONCRETE, to say that a woman has "hair the color of apricots" or to say that she is a redhead or blonde (12)? Which is more specific?

2. The orange-striped cat in young Steinbach's DESCRIPTION of her walk to school is "curled like a comma" beneath a van (10). Such stated COMPARISONS, frequently using *like* or *as*, are called SIMILES. Implied comparisons, without *like* or *as*, are called METAPHORS. What metaphoric comparison does Steinbach make in the same description? What is she comparing to what?

3. Steinbach compares Miss Dennis to an "albatross" and "an out-of-control terrier" (12, 15). A terrier, you are likely familiar with; but just how tall is an albatross? Does it matter that her reader may never have seen one? Besides describing Miss Dennis, what do these fanciful comparisons tell you about her former writing pupil?

4. Steinbach arrived in Miss Dennis's class "trailing all sorts of literary baggage" (18). To what is she comparing herself here?

5. How would you describe the words that Steinbach uses in paragraph 30 to describe the afternoon? Concrete or ABSTRACT? Specific or general? "Flap," for example, could be both a concrete and a specific term.

XXXXXXXXXXXXXXXXXXX **FOR WRITING** XXXXXXXXXXXXXXXXXXX

1. On your next walk to or around school, pay close attention to your surround-ings. Take notes, as young Steinbach does in paragraph 10. DESCRIBE what you see in a paragraph that "creates in words the picture" you want your reader to see (11). Make it as free of literary or other baggage as you can, and try to select details that contribute to a single, DOMINANT IMPRESSION.

2. Write a profile—a description of a person that not only tells but shows a piece of that person's life story—of one of your favorite (or most despised) teachers or coaches. Try to give your reader a clear sense of what that person looks like; of what he or she wears, says, and does; and of the dominant impression he or she makes on others. Be sure to show how you interact with that person and what he or she has (or has not) taught you.

CHEROKEE PAUL MCDONALD

A VIEW FROM THE BRIDGE

Cherokee Paul McDonald (b. 1949) is a fiction writer and journalist. His latest book, *Into the Green* (2001), recounts his months of combat as an Army lieutenant in Vietnam. (One of the themes of the book, says McDonald, "is hate the war, but don't hate the soldier.") After Vietnam, McDonald served for ten years on the police force of Fort Lauderdale, Florida, an experience that he draws on in numerous crime novels and that he describes graphically in *Blue Truth* (1991). McDonald is also a fisherman and the father of three children, roles that come together in the following descriptive essay about a boy who helps the author see familiar objects in a new light. The essay was first published in *Sunshine*, a Florida sporting magazine.

XXXXXXXXXXXXXXXXXXXXXXXXXXXXXXXXXXXXXXXXXXXXXXXXXXXXXXXXXXXXXXX

I was coming up on the little bridge in the Rio Vista neighborhood of Fort Lauderdale, deepening my stride and my breathing to negotiate the slight incline without altering my pace. And then, as I neared the crest, I saw the kid.   1

He was a lumpy little guy with baggy shorts, a faded T-shirt and heavy sweat socks falling down over old sneakers.   2

Partially covering his shaggy blond hair was one of those blue baseball caps with gold braid on the bill and a sailfish patch sewn onto the peak. Covering his eyes and part of his face was a pair of those stupid-looking '50s-style wrap-around sunglasses.   3

He was fumbling with a beat-up rod and reel, and he had a little bait bucket by his feet. I puffed on by, glancing down into the empty bucket as I passed.   4

"Hey, mister! Would you help me, please?"   5

The shrill voice penetrated my jogger's concentration, and I was determined to ignore it. But for some reason, I stopped.   6

With my hands on my hips and the sweat dripping from my nose 7
I asked, "What do you want, kid?"

"Would you please help me find my shrimp? It's my last one and 8
I've been getting bites and I know I can catch a fish if I can just find
that shrimp. He jumped outta my hand as I was getting him from the
bucket."

Exasperated, I walked slowly back to the kid, and pointed. 9

"There's the damn shrimp by your left foot. You stopped me for 10
that?"

As I said it, the kid reached down and trapped the shrimp. 11

"Thanks a lot, mister," he said. 12

I watched as the kid dropped the baited hook down into the canal. 13
Then I turned to start back down the bridge.

That's when the kid let out a "Hey! Hey!" and the prettiest tarpon 14
I'd ever seen came almost six feet out of the water, twisting and turning
as he fell through the air.

"I got one!" the kid yelled as the fish hit the water with a loud 15
splash and took off down the canal.

I watched the line being burned off the reel at an alarming rate. 16
The kid's left hand held the crank while the extended fingers felt for the
drag setting.

"No, kid!" I shouted. "Leave the drag alone . . . just keep that damn 17
rod tip up!"

Then I glanced at the reel and saw there were just a few loops of 18
line left on the spool.

"Why don't you get yourself some decent equipment?" I said, but 19
before the kid could answer I saw the line go slack.

"Ohhh, I lost him," the kid said. I saw the flash of silver as the fish 20
turned.

"Crank, kid, crank! You didn't lose him. He's coming back toward 21
you. Bring in the slack!"

The kid cranked like mad, and a beautiful grin spread across his 22
face.

"He's heading in for the pilings," I said. "Keep him out of those 23
pilings!"

The kid played it perfectly. When the fish made its play for the 24 pilings, he kept just enough pressure on to force the fish out. When the water exploded and the silver missile hurled into the air, the kid kept the rod tip up and the line tight.

As the fish came to the surface and began a slow circle in the middle of the canal, I said, "Whooee, is that a nice fish or what?"   25

The kid didn't say anything, so I said, "Okay, move to the edge of the bridge and I'll climb down to the seawall and pull him out."   26

When I reached the seawall I pulled in the leader, leaving the fish lying on its side in the water.   27

"How's that?" I said.   28

"Hey, mister, tell me what it looks like."   29

"Look down here and check him out," I said. "He's beautiful."   30

But then I looked up into those stupid-looking sunglasses and it hit me. The kid was blind.   31

"Could you tell me what he looks like, mister?" he said again.   32

"Well, he's just under three, uh, he's about as long as one of your arms," I said. "I'd guess he goes about 15, 20 pounds. He's mostly silver, but the silver is somehow made up of *all* the colors, if you know what I mean." I stopped. "Do you know what I mean by colors?"   33

The kid nodded.   34

"Okay. He has all these big scales, like armor all over his body. They're silver too, and when he moves they sparkle. He has a strong body and a large powerful tail. He has big round eyes, bigger than a quarter, and a lower jaw that sticks out past the upper one and is very tough. His belly is almost white and his back is a gunmetal gray. When he jumped he came out of the water about six feet, and his scales caught the sun and flashed it all over the place."   35

By now the fish had righted itself, and I could see the bright-red gills as the gill plates opened and closed. I explained this to the kid, and then said, more to myself, "He's a beauty."   36

"Can you get him off the hook?" the kid asked. "I don't want to kill him."   37

I watched as the tarpon began to slowly swim away, tired but still alive.   38

By the time I got back up to the top of the bridge the kid had his line secured and his bait bucket in one hand.   39

He grinned and said, "Just in time. My mom drops me off here, and she'll be back to pick me up any minute." 40

He used the back of one hand to wipe his nose. 41

"Thanks for helping me catch that tarpon," he said, "and for helping me to see it." 42

I looked at him, shook my head, and said, "No, my friend, thank you for letting *me* see that fish." 43

I took off, but before I got far the kid yelled again. 44

"Hey, mister!" 45

I stopped. 46

"Someday I'm gonna catch a sailfish and a blue marlin and a giant tuna and *all* those big sportfish!" 47

As I looked into those sunglasses I knew he probably would. I wished I could be there when it happened. 48

XXXXXXXXXXXXXXXXXXXX **FOR DISCUSSION** XXXXXXXXXXXXXXXXXXXXX

1. Which of the five senses does Cherokee Paul McDonald appeal to in his DESCRIPTION of the tarpon in paragraph 35? In "A View from the Bridge" as a whole?

2. How much does McDonald's jogger seem to know about fish and fishing? About boys?

3. What is the attitude of the jogger toward the "kid" before he realizes the boy is blind? As one reader, what is your attitude toward the jogger? Why?

4. How does the jogger feel about the kid when they part? How do you feel about the jogger? What, if anything, changes your view of him?

5. How does meticulously describing a small piece of the world help the grumpy jogger to see the world anew?

XXXXXXXXXXXXXX **STRATEGIES AND STRUCTURES** XXXXXXXXXXXXX

1. McDonald serves as eyes for the boy (and us). Which physical details in his DESCRIPTION of the scene at the bridge do you find to be visually most effective?

2. McDonald's description is part of a NARRATIVE. At first, the narrator seems irritable and in a hurry. What makes him slow down? How does his behavior change? Why?

3. The narrator does not realize the boy is blind until paragraph 31, but we figure it out much sooner. What descriptive details lead us to realize that the boy is blind?

4. McDonald, of course, knew when he wrote this piece that the boy couldn't see. Why do you think he wrote this piece as if he didn't know at first? How does he restrict his POINT OF VIEW in paragraph 6? Elsewhere in the essay?

5. How does the narrator's physical viewpoint change in paragraph 26? Why does this alter the way he sees the boy?

6. "No, my friend," says the jogger, "thank you for letting *me* see that fish" (43). So who is helping whom to see in this essay? How? Cite examples from the essay.

XXXXXXXXXXXX **WORDS AND FIGURES OF SPEECH** XXXXXXXXXXXX

1. *Metonymy* is a FIGURE OF SPEECH in which a word or object stands in for another associated with it. How might the blind boy's cap or sunglasses be seen as examples of metonymy?

2. Point out words and phrases in this essay—for example, "sparkle"—that refer to sights or acts of seeing (35).

3. What possible meanings are suggested by the word "view" in McDonald's title?

4. Besides its literal meaning, how else might we take the word "bridge" here? Who or what is being "bridged"?

XXXXXXXXXXXXXXXXXXXX **FOR WRITING** XXXXXXXXXXXXXXXXXXXX

1. Suppose you had to DESCRIBE a flower, bird, snake, butterfly, or other plant or animal to a blind person. In a paragraph, describe the object—its colors, smell, texture, movement, how the light strikes it—in sufficient physical detail so that the person could form an accurate mental picture of what you are describing.

2. Write an extended description of a scene in which you see a familiar object, person, or place in a new light because of someone else who brings a fresh viewpoint to the picture. For example, you might describe the scene at the dinner table when you bring home a new girlfriend or boyfriend. Or you might take a tour of your campus, home town, neighborhood, or workplace with a friend or relative who has never seen it before.

BEVERLY DIPO

NO RAINBOWS, NO ROSES

Beverly Dipo is a nurse by profession. "No Rainbows, No Roses," which won a Bedford Prize, was written as an assignment for a college writing class. Using the observational method of her profession, Dipo describes a dying woman with clinical detachment—at first. "Right or wrong, it's the way we're trained," she told a fellow writing student. "I frequently observe *things* before I ever speak to a patient or get to know them as human beings." In addition to observing her patient as an object among the other objects in room 309, Dipo goes on to look at the whole person beneath the physical ruin. So sharp and clear are the visual and auditory details of Nurse Dipo's clinical observations, we can picture the woman, too.

xxxxxxxxxxxxxxxxxxxxxxxxxxxxxxxxxxxxxxxxxxxxxxxxxxxxxxxxxxxxxxxx

I have never seen Mrs. Trane before, but I know by the report I received from the previous shift that tonight she will die. Making my rounds, I go from room to room, checking other patients first and saving Mrs. Trane for last, not to avoid her, but because she will require the most time to care for. Everyone else seems to be all right for the time being; they have had their medications, backrubs and are easily settled for the night.

At the door to 309, I pause, adjusting my eyes to the darkness. The only light in the room is coming from an infusion pump, which is flashing its red beacon as if in warning, and the dim hall light that barely confirms the room's furnishings and the shapeless form on the bed. As I stand there, the smell hits my nostrils, and I close my eyes as I remember the stench of rot and decay from past experience. In my mouth I taste the bitter bile churning in the pit of my stomach. I swallow uneasily and cross the room in the dark, reaching for the light switch above the sink, and as it silently illuminates the scene, I return to the bed to observe the patient with a detached, medical routineness.

Mrs. Trane lies motionless: the head seems unusually large on a   3
skeleton frame, and except for a few fine wisps of gray hair around the
ears, is bald from the chemotherapy that had offered brief hope; the skin
is dark yellow and sags loosely around exaggerated long bones that not
even a gown and bedding can disguise; the right arm lies straight out at
the side, taped cruelly to a board to secure the IV fluid its access; the
left arm is across the sunken chest, which rises and falls in the uneven
waves of Cheyne-Stokes respirations; a catheter hanging on the side of
the bed is draining thick brown urine from the bladder, the source of the
deathly smell.

I reach for the long, thin fingers that are lying on the chest. They   4
are ice cold, and I quickly move to the wrist and feel for the weak, thready
pulse. Mrs. Trane's eyes flutter open as her head turns toward me slightly.
As she tries to form a word on her dry, parched lips, I bend close to her
and scarcely hear as she whispers, "Water." Taking a glass of water from
the bedside table, I put my finger over the end of the straw and allow a
few droplets of the cool moisture to slide into her mouth. She makes no
attempt to swallow; there is just not enough strength. "More," the raspy
voice says, and we repeat the procedure. This time she does manage to
swallow and weakly says, "Thank you." I touch her gently in response.
She is too weak for conversation, so without asking, I go about providing
for her needs, explaining to her in hushed tones each move I make.
Picking her up in my arms like a child, I turn her on her side. She is so
very small and light. Carefully, I rub lotion into the yellow skin, which
rolls freely over the bones, feeling perfectly the outline of each vertebrae
in the back and the round smoothness of the ileac crest. Placing a pillow
between her legs, I notice that these too are ice cold, and not until I run
my hand up over her knees do I feel any of the life-giving warmth of
blood coursing through fragile veins. I find myself in awe of the life force
which continues despite such a state of decomposition.

When I am finished, I pull a chair up beside the bed to face her   5
and, taking her free hand between mine, again notice the long, thin fingers. Graceful. There is no jewelry; it would have fallen off long ago. I
wonder briefly if she has any family, and then I see that there are neither
bouquets of flowers, nor pretty plants on the shelves, no brightly crayon-
colored posters of rainbows, nor boastful self-portraits from grand-

children on the walls. There is no hint in the room anywhere that this is a person who is loved. As though she has been reading my mind, Mrs. Trane answers my thoughts and quietly tells me, "I sent . . . my family . . . home . . . tonight . . . didn't want . . . them . . . to see. . . ." She cannot go on, but knowingly, I have understood what it is she has done. I lower my eyes, not knowing what to say, so I say nothing. Again she seems to sense my unease, "You . . . stay. . . ." Time seems to have come to a standstill. In the total silence, I noticeably feel my own heartbeat quicken and hear my breathing as it begins to match hers, stride for uneven stride. Our eyes meet and somehow, together, we become aware that this is a special moment between us, a moment when two human beings are so close we feel as if our souls touch. Her long fingers curl easily around my hand and I nod my head slowly, smiling. Wordlessly, through yellowed eyes, I receive my thank you and her eyes slowly close.

Some unknown amount of time passes before her eyes open again, only this time there is no response in them, just a blank stare. Without warning, her breathing stops, and within a few moments, the faint pulse is also gone. One single tear flows from her left eye, across the cheekbone and down onto the pillow. I begin to cry quietly. There is a tug of emotion within me for this stranger who so quickly came into and went from my life. Her suffering is done, yet so is the life. Slowly, still holding her hand, I become aware that I do not mind this emotional tug of war, that in fact, it was a privilege she has allowed me, and I would do it again, gladly. Mrs. Trane spared her family an episode that perhaps they were not equipped to handle and instead shared it with me, knowing somehow that I would handle it and, indeed, needed it to grow, both privately and professionally. She had not wanted to have her family see her die, yet she did not want to die alone. No one should die alone, and I am glad I was there for her.

Two days later, I read Mrs. Trane's obituary in the paper. She had been a widow for five years, was the mother of seven, grandmother of eighteen, an active member of her church, a leader of volunteer organizations in her community, college-educated in music, a concert pianist, and a piano teacher for over thirty years.

Yes, they were long and graceful fingers.

XXXXXXXXXXXXXXXXXXXX **FOR DISCUSSION** XXXXXXXXXXXXXXXXXXXX

1. How long have the patient and the nurse in Beverly Dipo's DESCRIPTION known each other?

2. Why are there no rainbows or roses in Mrs. Trane's hospital room on her last night?

3. At first Nurse Dipo observes her patient "with a detached, medical routineness" (2). What details does she report? When and where does emotion take over in her description of Mrs. Trane's room and her death? How do her descriptive details change?

4. Does Dipo's expression of emotion make her a better nurse, in your opinion, or is she being unprofessional? Please explain your answer.

XXXXXXXXXXXXXX **STRATEGIES AND STRUCTURES** XXXXXXXXXXXXXX

1. Dipo uses all five senses in her depiction of room 309, leading us to see, hear, smell, feel, and even taste. Point out EXAMPLES of each one at work.

2. Which sense (or senses) dominate(s) in Dipo's DESCRIPTION?

3. Since this is a hospital at night, it is quiet. For what main purpose, then, does the observant nurse in this scene use her sense of hearing?

4. The DOMINANT IMPRESSION in paragraph 5 is of a growing intimacy between the two women. How does the silence contribute to this impression?

5. Why does Dipo prolong her description beyond the night of her patient's death? What important new information (and perspective) does the obituary add to her eyewitness account?

6. An obituary is a NARRATIVE of a person's life, written upon the occasion of his or her death. Dipo's description focuses only upon Mrs. Trane's final hours, but it also has many elements of a narrative, including a narrator. What does this narrator do besides merely observe the scene?

XXXXXXXXXXXX **WORDS AND FIGURES OF SPEECH** XXXXXXXXXXXX

1. What do the rainbows and roses signify in Dipo's DESCRIPTION of room 309?

2. In a phrase like "brief hope," Dipo indicates her true feelings about Mrs. Trane (3). Please give several other examples.

3. Dipo refers several times to her patient's hands and fingers. What aspects of Mrs. Trane and her life does this *metonymy* (see FIGURES OF SPEECH) represent? Why are her hands the last we see of her?

4. Nurse and patient, says Dipo, "feel as if our souls touch" (5). How does Dipo prepare us for this "spiritual" language in her physical description of the scene in room 309?

XXXXXXXXXXXXXXXXXXXXXX **FOR WRITING** XXXXXXXXXXXXXXXXXXXXXX

1. Write a DESCRIPTIVE paragraph or two about a sickroom, sitting room, study, or other personal space that you have visited. Include physical details that allow the reader to visualize both the people in the room and your own presence and purpose there. Do not describe your emotions; instead, describe what you saw, heard, smelled, touched, or tasted that made you feel as you did.

2. Write Mrs. Trane's obituary. Be as fanciful and extravagant in describing her adventures and accomplishments as you please. A real obituary is reprinted on page 59; it might serve as a model.

No Wonder They Call Me a Bitch

Ann Hodgman is a food critic for *Eating Well* magazine. Besides playing goalie on a women's hockey team, she is the author of more than forty children's books, including *My Babysitter Is a Vampire*, and several cookbooks. For reasons soon to be apparent, however, the following "tasteless" essay did not appear in Hodgman's food column, "Sweet and Sour," but in the satiric magazine *Spy*, for which Hodgman was a contributing editor. A spoof on taste testing, it takes a blue ribbon for disgusting description that appeals to the grosser senses.

✗✗

I've always wondered about dog food. Is a Gaines-burger really like a hamburger? Can you fry it? Does dog food "cheese" taste like real cheese? Does Gravy Train actually make gravy in the dog's bowl, or is that brown liquid just dissolved crumbs? And exactly what *are* by-products? 1

Having spent the better part of a week eating dog food, I'm sorry to say that I now know the answers to these questions. While my dachshund, Shortie, watched in agonies of yearning, I gagged my way through can after can of stinky, white-flecked mush and bag after bag of stinky, fat-drenched nuggets. And now I understand exactly why Shortie's breath is so bad. 2

Of course, Gaines-burgers are neither mush nor nuggets. They are, rather, a miracle of beauty and packaging—or at least that's what I thought when I was little. I used to beg my mother to get them for our dogs, but she always said they were too expensive. When I finally bought a box of cheese-flavored Gaines-burgers—after twenty years of longing— I felt deliciously wicked. 3

"Dogs love real beef," the back of the box proclaimed proudly.   4
"That's why Gaines-burgers is the only beef burger for dogs with real
beef and no meat by-products!" The copy was accurate: meat by-
products did not appear in the list of ingredients. Poultry by-products
did, though—right there next to preserved animal fat.

One Purina spokesman told me that poultry by-products consist of   5
necks, intestines, undeveloped eggs and other "carcass remnants," but
not feathers, heads, or feet. When I told him I'd been eating dog food,
he said, "Oh, you're kidding! Oh, *no!*" (I came to share his alarm when,
weeks later, a second Purina spokesman said that Gaines-burgers *do* contain poultry heads and feet—but *not* undeveloped eggs.)

Up close my Gaines-burger didn't much resemble chopped beef.   6
Rather, it looked—and felt—like a single long, extruded piece of redness
that had been chopped into segments and formed into a patty. You could
make one at home if you had a Play-Doh Fun Factory.

I turned on the skillet. While I waited for it to heat up I pulled out   7
a shred of cheese-colored material and palpated it. Again, like Play-Doh,
it was quite malleable. I made a little cheese bird out of it; then I counted
to three and ate the bird.

There was a horrifying rush of cheddar taste, followed immediately   8
by the dull tang of soybean flour—the main ingredient in Gaines-
burgers. Next I tried a piece of red extrusion. The main difference
between the meat-flavored and cheese-flavored extrusions is one of texture. The "cheese" chews like fresh Play-Doh, whereas the "meat" chews
like Play-Doh that's been sitting out on a rug for a couple of hours.

Frying only turned the Gaines-burger black. There was no melting,   9
no sizzling, no warm meat smells. A cherished childhood illusion was
gone. I flipped the patty into the sink, where it immediately began leaking
rivulets of red dye.

As alarming as the Gaines-burgers were, their soy meal began to   10
seem like an old friend when the time came to try some *canned* dog foods.
I decided to try the Cycle foods first. When I opened them, I thought
about how rarely I use can openers these days, and I was suddenly visited
by a long-forgotten sensation of can-opener distaste. *This* is the kind of
unsavory place can openers spend their time when you're not watching!
Every time you open a can of, say, Italian plum tomatoes, you infect
them with invisible particles of by-product.

I had been expecting to see the usual homogeneous scrapple inside, but each can of Cycle was packed with smooth, round, oily nuggets. As if someone at Gaines had been tipped off that a human would be tasting the stuff, the four Cycles really were different from one another. Cycle-1, for puppies, is wet and soyish. Cycle-2, for adults, glistens nastily with fat, but it's passably edible—a lot like some canned Swedish meatballs I once got in a Care package at college. Cycle-3, the "lite" one, for fatties, had no specific flavor; it just tasted like dog food. But at least it didn't make me fat.

Cycle-4, for senior dogs, had the smallest nuggets. Maybe old dogs can't open their mouths as wide. This kind was far sweeter than the other three Cycles—almost like baked beans. It was also the only one to contain "dried beef digest," a mysterious substance that the Purina spokesman defined as "enzymes" and my dictionary defined as "the products of digestion."

Next on the menu was a can of Kal Kan Pedigree with Chunky Chicken. Chunky *chicken*? There were chunks in the can, certainly—big, purplish-brown chunks. I forked one chunk out (by now I was becoming more callous) and found that while it had no discernible chicken flavor, it wasn't bad except for its texture—like meat loaf with ground-up chicken bones.

In the world of canned dog food, a smooth consistency is a sign of low quality—lots of cereal. A lumpy, frightening, bloody, stringy horror is a sign of high quality—lots of meat. Nowhere in the world of wet dog foods was this demonstrated better than in the fanciest I tried—Kal Kan's Pedigree Select Dinners. These came not in a can but in a tiny foil packet with a picture of an imperious Yorkie. When I pulled open the container, juice spurted all over my hand, and the first chunk I speared was trailing a long gray vein. I shrieked and went instead for a plain chunk, which I was able to swallow only after taking a break to read some suddenly fascinating office equipment catalogues. Once again, though, it tasted no more alarming than, say, canned hash.

Still, how pleasant it was to turn to *dry* dog food! Gravy Train was the first I tried, and I'm happy to report that it really does make a "thick, rich, real beef gravy" when you mix it with water. Thick and rich, anyway. Except for a lingering rancid-fat flavor, the gravy wasn't beefy, but since it tasted primarily like tap water, it wasn't nauseating either.

My poor dachshund just gets plain old Purina Dog Chow, but Pur- 16
ina also makes a dry food called Butcher's Blend that comes in Beef,
Bacon & Chicken flavor. Here we see dog food's arcane semiotics at its
best: a red triangle with a *T* stamped into it is supposed to suggest beef;
a tan curl, chicken; and a brown *S*, a piece of bacon. Only dogs understand these messages. But Butcher's Blend does have an endearing slogan:
"Great Meaty Tastes—without bothering the Butcher!" *You know, I
wanted to buy some meat, but I just couldn't bring myself to bother the
butcher* . . .

Purina O.N.E. ("Optimum Nutritional Effectiveness") is targeted 17
at people who are unlikely ever to worry about bothering a tradesperson.
"We chose chicken as a primary ingredient in Purina O.N.E. for several
reasonings," the long, long essay on the back of the bag announces. Chief
among these reasonings, I'd guess, is the fact that chicken appeals to
people who are—you know—*like us.* Although our dogs do nothing but
spend eighteen-hour days alone in the apartment, we still want them to
be *premium* dogs. We want them to cut down on red meat, too. We also
want dog food that comes in a bag with an attractive design, a subtle
typeface, and no kitschy pictures of slobbering golden retrievers.

Besides that, we want a list of the Nutritional Benefits of our dog 18
food—and we get it on O.N.E. One thing I especially like about this list
is its constant references to a dog's "hair coat," as in "Beef tallow is good
for the dog's skin and hair coat." (On the other hand, beef tallow merely
provides palatability, while the dried beef digest in Cycle provides palatability *enhancement.*)

I hate to say it, but O.N.E. was pretty palatable. Maybe that's 19
because it has about 100 percent more fat than, say, Butcher's Blend. Or
maybe I'd been duped by the packaging; that's been known to happen
before.

As with people food, dog snacks taste much better than dog meals. 20
They're better looking too. Take Milk-Bone Flavor Snacks. The loving-
hands-at-home prose describing each flavor is colorful; the writers practically choke on their own exuberance. Of bacon they say, "It's so good,
your dog will think it's hot off the frying pan." Of liver: "The only taste
your dog wants more than liver—is even more liver!" Of poultry: "All
those farm fresh flavors deliciously mixed in one biscuit. Your dog will
bark with delight!" And of vegetable: "Gardens of taste! Specially

blended to give your dog that vegetable flavor he wants—but can rarely get!"

Well, I may be a sucker, but advertising *this* emphatic just doesn't convince me. I lined up all seven flavors of Milk-Bone Flavor Snacks on the floor. Unless my dog's palate is a lot more sensitive than mine—and considering that she steals dirty diapers out of the trash and eats them, I'm loath to think it is—she doesn't detect any more difference in the seven flavors than I did when I tried them.   21

I much preferred Bonz, the hard-baked, bone-shaped snack stuffed with simulated marrow. I liked the bone part, that is; it tasted almost exactly like the cornmeal it was made of. The mock marrow inside was a bit more problematic: in addition to looking like the sludge that collects in the treads of my running shoes, it was bursting with tiny hairs.   22

I'm sure you have a few dog food questions of your own. To save us time, I've answered them in advance.   23

Q. *Are those little cans of Mighty Dog actually branded with the sizzling word* BEEF, *the way they show in the commercials?*   24

A. You should know by now that that kind of thing never happens.   25

Q. *Does chicken-flavored dog food taste like chicken-flavored cat food?*   26

A. To my surprise, chicken cat food was actually a little better—more chickeny. It tasted like inferior canned pâté.   27

Q. *Was there any dog food that you just couldn't bring yourself to try?*   28

A. Alas, it was a can of Mighty Dog called Prime Entree with Bone Marrow. The meat was dark, dark brown, and it was surrounded by gelatin that was almost black. I knew I would die if I tasted it, so I put it outside for the raccoons.   29

XXXXXXXXXXXXXXXXXXXX **For Discussion** XXXXXXXXXXXXXXXXXXX

1. Ann Hodgman's discourse on dog food may be tongue in cheek (or is it lump in throat?), but as DESCRIPTIVE writing do you agree that it is truly disgusting? Which do you find more effectively nauseating, her description of the tastes and textures of dry dog food or canned?

2. Most of Hodgman's "research" is done in her own laboratory kitchen. Where else does she go for information? Do you think her studies qualify her to speak expertly on the subject? How about vividly?

3. How do you suppose Hodgman knows what Play-Doh chews like after it's

been "sitting out on a rug for a couple of hours"—that is, as opposed to fresh Play-Doh (8)?

4. What childhood fantasy does Hodgman fulfill by writing this essay? How does the reality COMPARE with the fantasy?

5. Do you find Hodgman's title in bad taste? Why or why not? How about her entire essay?

6. *Q: Why are you asking these unsavory questions? A:* Somebody has to honor those who do basic research in a new field. What question would you ask about this piece?

XXXXXXXXXXXXXX **STRATEGIES AND STRUCTURES** XXXXXXXXXXXXXX

1. "When I pulled open the container, juice spurted all over my hand, and the first chunk I speared was trailing a long gray vein" (14). Can you see, smell, and taste it? Please cite other horrifying examples of Hodgman's DESCRIPTIVE skills and her direct appeal (if that's the right word) to the senses.

2. Notice the major shift that occurs when the description moves from canned dog food to dry. Where does the shift occur? Why does she find the change so "pleasant"? When does she shift again—to snacks?

3. Why do you suppose Hodgman never tells us why she is describing the ingredients, tastes, and textures of dog food with such scrupulous accuracy and objectivity? What might her reasons be?

4. Why do you think Hodgman shifts to a question-and-answer format at the end of her essay?

5. Hodgman is a professional food critic. What CONCRETE and specific words from her professional vocabulary does she use?

6. What is the DOMINANT IMPRESSION created by Hodgman's description of Bonz in paragraph 22?

7. Hodgman not only describes herself at work in her laboratory kitchen, she ANALYZES the PROCESS of doing basic food research there. Besides tasting, what are some of the other steps in the process (see Chapter 5)?

XXXXXXXXXXXXX **WORDS AND FIGURES OF SPEECH** XXXXXXXXXXXXX

1. Hodgman refers to "some suddenly fascinating office equipment catalogues" that divert her from tasting Kal Kan's best (14). Is this IRONY?

2. How does your dictionary DEFINE "dried beef digest" (12). Where else does Hodgman use the technical language of the industry she is SATIRIZING?

3. Hodgman says her Gaines-burger, when fried and flipped into the sink, "began leaking rivulets of red dye" (9). Is this scientific detachment or HYPERBOLE?

4. The opposite of intentional exaggeration is UNDERSTATEMENT. In Hodgman's ANALYSIS of the simulated marrow in Bonz, would "problematic" qualify as an EXAMPLE (22)?

5. Hodgman says Kal Kan Pedigree with Chunky Chicken tasted "like meat loaf with ground-up chicken bones" (13). Is this a SIMILE, or do you suppose the chicken could be literally chunky because of the bones? Or is Hodgman actually talking about meat loaf and only *likening* the Kal Kan to it? If so, do you think she should change her meat loaf recipe?

XXXXXXXXXXXXXXXXXXXXX **FOR WRITING** XXXXXXXXXXXXXXXXXXXXXX

1. While Hodgman gags her way through sample after sample of premium dog food, her dachshund, Shortie, looks on "in agonies of yearning" (2). DESCRIBE the "data" in Hodgman's taste experiment from Shortie's POINT OF VIEW. How might Gaines-burgers and Kal Kan Pedigree with Chunky Chicken taste to him? Is Hodgman right to say that Shortie cannot distinguish among the seven flavors of Milk-Bone Flavor Snacks? What would Shortie's palate tell us?

2. Conduct a program of research similar to Hodgman's but in the field of junk food. Write an unbiased description of your findings. Or, if you prefer, forget the taste tests, and follow Hodgman's lead in ANALYZING the claims of food advertisers. Choose a category of food products—gummy worms, breath mints, canned soup, frozen pizza, breakfast cereal, cookies—and study the packaging carefully. Write an essay in which you describe how the manufacturers of your samples typically describe their products.

CHAPTER TWO

NARRATIVE

XXXXXXXXXXXXXXXXXXXXXXXXXXXXXXXXXXXXXXXXXXXXXXXXXXXXXXXXXXXX

NARRATIVE* writing tells a story; it reports "what happened." All of the essays in this chapter are narratives, telling about what happened to one New York writer on September 11, for EXAMPLE, and to one African American man when he refused to give up his seat on a bus in North Carolina in the 1940s. There is a big difference, however, between having something "happen" and writing about it, between an event and telling about an event.

In real life, events often occur randomly or chaotically. But in a narrative, they must be told or shown in some orderly sequence (the PLOT), by a particular person (the narrator), from a particular perspective (the POINT OF VIEW), within a definite time and place (the SETTING). Let's look more closely at each of these elements.

Suppose we wanted to tell a story about a young woman sitting alone eating a snack. Our opening line might go something like this:

Little Miss Muffet sat on a tuffet, eating her curds and whey.

Here we have the bare bones of a narrative because we have someone (Miss Muffet) who is doing something (eating) at a particular time (the past) in a particular place (on a tuffet). The problem with our narrative is that it isn't very interesting. We have a character and a setting, but we don't really have a plot.

A good plot requires more than just sitting and eating. Plot can be achieved by introducing a conflict into the action, bringing the tension to a high point (the CLIMAX), then releasing the tension—in other words, by giving it a beginning, middle, and end. In our story about Miss Muf-

---

*Words printed in SMALL CAPITALS are defined in the Glossary.

🍂 54 🍂

fet, we could achieve the necessary conflict in the action by introducing an intruder:

Along came a spider and sat down beside her

You know what's coming next, but I hope you can feel the tension building up and up before we resolve the conflict and release the rising tension in the final line of our story:

And frightened Miss Muffet away.

Well, that's better. We have a sequence of events now. Moreover, those events occur in our narrative in some sort of order—chronologically. Mere time sequence, however, doesn't make a real plot: the events have to be *related* in some meaningful way. In this case, the appearance of the intruder actually *causes* the departure of the heroine. There are many others, but CAUSE AND EFFECT is one meaningful way to relate the events in a narrative (see Chapter 8).

We said earlier that a narrative must have a narrator. That narrator may be directly involved in the action of the narrative or may only report it. Do we have one here? Yes, we do; it is the narrator who refers to Miss Muffet as "her." But this narrator is never identified, and he or she plays no part in the action. Let's look at a narrator who does—Stephen King, in a passage from a narrative about his life-threatening accident:

> Most of the sight lines along the mile-long stretch of Route 5 that I walk are good, but there is one place, a short steep hill, where a pedestrian heading north can see very little of what might be coming his way. I was three-quarters of the way up this hill when the van came over the crest. It wasn't on the road; it was on the shoulder. My shoulder. I had perhaps three-quarters of a second to register this.
> STEPHEN KING, "ON IMPACT"

Notice that the "I" in this piece is King himself, and he is very much involved in the action of the story he is telling. In fact, he is about to be hit by the van coming over the crest of the hill. That would introduce a conflict into his walk along Route 5, wouldn't it?

By narrating this story from a first-person point of view, King is putting himself in the center of the action. If he had said instead "The van was closing in on him fast," we would have a third-person narrative, and the narrator would be reporting the action from the sidelines instead of bearing the brunt of it. What makes a chilling story here is that King is not only showing us what happened to him, he is showing us what he was thinking as he suddenly realized that the van was almost on top of him: "It wasn't on the road; it was on the shoulder. My shoulder." We look in as the narrator goes, in a few swift phrases, from startled disbelief to horrified certainty.

Another way in which King makes a compelling story, rather than just an accident report, out of these events is by using direct speech, or DIALOGUE. When King tells about his first day back at work, instead of writing "My wife, Tabby, said she would get me a table and put it where I could plug in the computer," he lets his wife speak to us directly: "I can rig a table for you in the back hall, outside the pantry. There are plenty of outlets—you can have your Mac, the little printer, and a fan." Quoting direct speech like this shows what the characters in a narrative are thinking and helps readers to imagine them as real people.

But why does King end his narrative back at the writing desk? His encounter with the van might have ended another way, after all—though somebody else would have had to tell *that* story. Fortunately, King survived to write again and so is reporting what actually happened. But a good storyteller like King knows that stories serve a larger purpose than just telling what happened. The larger purpose of King's story (as with Dillard's story about the burning moth in "The Death of a Moth") is to make a point about writing and the writer's life. The van almost killed him, but writing, King demonstrates, helped him to recover and keeps him going.

Well-told stories are almost always told for some reason. The searing tale you heard earlier about Miss Muffet, for example, was told to make a point about narrative structure. A brief, illustrative story like this is called an ANECDOTE. All stories should have a point, but anecdotes in particular are used in all kinds of writing to give examples and to illustrate the greater subject at hand—writing, for instance.

Even a simple narrative may be told for different purposes, however.

An entomologist, for example, might retell the Miss Muffet story as an illustration of popular misconceptions about arachnid behavior, since most spiders are not as aggressive as this one. So when you're using a story to make a point, don't forget to remind the reader exactly what that point is. When Annie Dillard recounts her adventures with spiders and moths in "The Death of a Moth," she explicitly tells us that she is making a point about the profession of writing and the dedication of the writer. That "one bald statement of motive," as Dillard says, "was unavoidable." Don't keep your reader in the dark. Narrative can enliven almost any kind of writing you do. But when your purpose is to explain something, don't get so wound up in the web of telling a good story that you forget to say what the moral is.

Obituaries are public announcements informing readers that someone whom they may know has died. They are also miniature biographies, life stories. This obituary tells us something of Pauline
Schneider Bates's life from beginning (she "was born on June 29, 1914,
. . . in the German immigrant community of Hamburg, Iowa") to end
(she "passed into grace on Sunday, January 20, 2002 at St. Elizabeth's
Hospital"). She is survived by Stanley Bates, whom she first met at a
riding club. As with any good narrative, this one has carefully chosen
details that let us in on important points in Mrs. Bates's life: she attended
a one-room school, drove a horse and buggy, worked for a seed company
to earn money for college. Of the many events in her life, the writer of
her obituary could select but a few. And they must tell the whole story.
Mrs. Bates worked for the navy during the war; she played "a key role"
in the Red Cross, the University Women's club, the First Baptist
Church. She made Christmas wreaths, arranged flowers, invested in the
stock market, put up strawberry jam. Every life has a story—and here
it's the obituary writer's job to tell that story, to choose details of that
life that let us see our heroine in action and form an impression of her
character. No flowers, please. They are pleasant to arrange, but Mrs.
Bates would prefer you to look after someone else.

CONSIDER FURTHER . . .

1. Besides telling us about the important things Mrs. Bates did, the
obituary writer informs us that she arranged flowers and made strawberry jam. What do these details contribute to your impression of her?

2. Mrs. Bates's obituary does not include a detailed physical DESCRIP-
TION of its subject. How would you describe her based on the accompanying photo as well as the text?

Pauline Schneider Bates

Pauline Schneider Bates passed into grace on Sunday, January 20, 2002 at St. Elizabeth's Hospital, Utica, NY after a sudden illness. Mrs. Bates was born on June 29, 1914, the youngest child of Frederick and Augusta Spiegel Schneider in the German immigrant community of Hamburg, Iowa. Growing up on the quarter section family corn farm, she attended a one room school and later drove a horse and buggy four miles to Hamburg Central School. She was the valedictorian of her high school class of 1931 and, after graduation, worked for a local seed company to earn money for college. She attended the University of Iowa and graduated from George Washington University in 1940 with a degree in Business Administration. From 1937 to 1942, she worked as a personnel officer in the Printing Office.

She met Stanley Bates at a riding club in 1940 and they were married in 1942. While her husband served in the 37th Seabee Battalion, Mrs. Bates worked for the Navy, traveling around the country recruiting civilians for the war effort. When her husband returned from the Pacific, they left Washington and settled in Rome. Mrs. Bates assisted and encouraged her husband in establishing his business and helped build the home they designed at 735 N. Jay St.

Mrs. Bates was an active and respected member of the Rome community and played a key role in many organizations. She ran the Red Cross Blood Mobile for over twenty years and served in officer positions with the Wednesday Morning Club, and University Women-Western Division. She was a beloved member of the First Baptist Church, where she was a deacon, Treasurer, active member of the Women's Fellowship and volunteer flower arranger. Every year she took special pride in making the Christmas wreath with her friend Dorothy Updike. She worked enthusiastically with her husband on conservation projects in West Branch and Ava, NY. She was an active investor, passionate gardener and committed parent. Her memberships included the New York Forest Owners, New York Christmas Tree Association, Tug Hill Tomorrow Land Trust, Rome Historical Society and Jervis Public Library Association.

She is survived by her husband, Stanley L. Bates, of Rome, two daughters, Christine and Connie Bates, New York City, and her two grandchildren, Charlotte Bates Greenough and Nicholas Bates Greenough. She was treasured by all who knew her for her selflessness, intelligence, kindness, integrity, faith and strawberry jam. She was especially appreciative of the caring presence of Mae Swaney and many other friends in her final years.

The family will receive friends at the Strong and Burns Funeral Home, Wednesday from 2 to 4 p.m. Memorial contributions may be made to the First Baptist Church Memorial Fund, Rome Salvation Army or Hospice Care, Inc., 4277 Middle Settlement Road, New Hartford, NY 13413. Please omit flowers.

THOMAS BELLER

THE ASHEN GUY: LOWER BROADWAY, SEPTEMBER 11, 2001

Thomas Beller is the author of a collection of short stories, *Seduction Theory* (1995), and a novel, *The Sleep-Over Artist* (2000), and is the Web master of www.mrbellersneighborhood.com, a Web site where New Yorkers can publish "true stories" of life in the big city. Following the events of September 11, 2001, Beller collected many of those personal narratives in a book, *Before & After: Stories from New York* (2002). "The Ashen Guy," written by Beller himself, is an "after" story; it takes place just after the first World Trade Center tower falls down but while the second one is still standing.

XXXXXXXXXXXXXXXXXXXXXXXXXXXXXXXXXXXXXXXXXXXXXXXXXXXXXXXXXXXXXXX

At Broadway and Union Square a woman moved with the crowd talking on her cell phone. "It's a good thing," she began. I biked south. At Tenth Street the bells of Grace Church pealed ten times. Everyone was moving in the same direction, orderly, but with an element of panic and, beneath that, a nervous energy. Their clothes were crisp and unrumpled, their hair freshly combed. Below Houston Street, a fleet of black shiny SUVs with sirens sped south, toward the smoky horizon somewhere south of Canal Street. A messenger biked beside me. I almost asked him if he was making a delivery. 1

At Thomas Street, about six blocks north of the World Trade Center, the nature of the crowd on the street changed. There was more urgency and less mirth. Cop cars parked at odd angles, their red sirens spinning. The policemen were waving their arms, shouting, and amidst the crowd was a guy who had been on the eighty-first floor of Two World Trade Center when the plane hit. It was just after 10 A.M. Two World Trade had just collapsed, and One World Trade stood smoldering behind him. 2

At first glance he looked like a snowman, except instead of snow he   3
was covered in gray, asbestos-colored ash. He was moving along with the
crowd, streaming north, up Broadway. His head and neck and shoulders
and about halfway down his chest were covered in gray ash. You could
make out a pair of bloodshot eyes, and he was running his hand over his
head. A small plume of dust drifted off the top of his head as he walked,
echoing the larger plume of smoke drifting off of One World Trade
behind him.

"There were about 230 people on the eighty-first floor and I was   4
one of the last ones out. We took the stairs. There was smoke, but it
wasn't fire smoke, it was dry wall smoke and dust. The fire was above
us."

He was shaking. His eyes were red from dust and maybe tears. He   5
didn't seem like the sort of man who cried. He had fair skin and a sandy-
colored crew cut. He was wearing chinos and Docksiders and his shirt
was a checked button-down.

He was walking with the crowd, but his body language was a little   6
different. Everyone, even those who weren't looking back, had about
them a certain nervous desire to look behind them, to see, to communicate to their neighbor, but this guy had no interest in anything but in
getting away from where he had just been. It radiated from every muscle
in his body. To get away.

"I was almost out. I got down to the lobby, right near the Borders   7
book store. And then there was this explosion. I don't know, I just got
thrown to the ground and all this stuff fell on top of me."

By now he had dusted his head off and you could see his skin. It   8
was pale and ashen, one of his eyes was very red. At first I thought maybe
it was the dust and perhaps tears that had made his eyes bloodshot;
looking closer I saw that one eye was badly inflamed.

He was joined by another man, a blue oxford shirt with a tie, mid-   9
forties, lawyerly, who worked in the building across the street.

"I watched the whole thing. I saw the second plane hit, the explo-   10
sion. No one told us to evacuate, and then the building just collapsed
and I thought I better get out of here because my building could go too."

On Franklin Street the police were screaming: "There's a package!   11
There's a package! Keep moving!"

They were herding everyone to the left, towards West Broadway.   12
"People! Trust me! Let's go! People let's go! There's an unidentified package across the street!"

The view on West Broadway and Franklin was very good. One   13
tower, gray sky billowing, the sky darkening.

"Do you know which way the tower fell?" a woman asked. A tall   14
man stood behind her, scruffy beard and longish hair, his hand on her shoulder.

"It fell straight down!" someone said.   15

"Because we live one block away and . . . does anyone know which   16
way the building fell?"

The man behind her, her husband, I assumed, had this very sad   17
look on his face, as though he understood something she didn't. It was
as if that consoling hand on her shoulder was there to make sure she
didn't try and make a run for it.

"I don't know what happened," said the ashen guy. "I just hit the   18
ground, don't know if something hit me or . . ."

"It was the force of the building collapsing," said the lawyer.   19

"I got up and just started walking," said the ashen guy.   20

There was a huge rumbling sound accompanied by the sound of   21
people shrieking. Everyone who wasn't already looking turned to see the
remaining building start to crumble in on itself, a huge ball of smoke
rising out from beneath it, a mushroom cloud in reverse. The whole street
paused, froze, screamed, some people broke into tears, many people
brought their hands up to their mouths, everyone was momentarily frozen, except for the ashen guy, who just kept walking.

XXXXXXXXXXXXXXXXXXXXX **FOR DISCUSSION** XXXXXXXXXXXXXXXXXXXXX

1. Who is telling this story? How does he identify himself in his NARRATIVE?
How is he getting around?

2. Why does the narrator single out the ashen guy from the rest of the crowd?
Where was the ashen guy when the first plane hit? When did he get covered
with ash?

3. The ashen guy is walking along with the crowd, "but his body language,"
says the narrator, "was a little different" from everyone else's (6). How and

where does the narrator describe the ashen man's body? What does his body "say?"

4. The identity of the ashen guy is never specified. Who might he be? What might he stand for?

5. The people in Thomas Beller's narrative walk as if they were in a dream. How appropriate do you find this dreamlike account of the events of September 11, 2001?

XXXXXXXXXXXXX **STRATEGIES AND STRUCTURES** XXXXXXXXXXXXX

1. This is a NARRATIVE about mass movement. In which direction is the narrator himself moving at first? When and where does he come closest to ground zero before moving back with the crowd? What role do the police play to move Beller's narrative along?

2. When does the ashen guy first appear? How does the narrator create the impression in paragraph 8 that he is getting closer to this mysterious man who is the focal point of his narrative? In which paragraphs, before and after this close-up, does the narrator give a long perspective to the scene by looking back toward ground zero?

3. DIALOGUE is one of the most dramatic or playlike elements of narrative, introducing multiple POINTS OF VIEW, thus enabling the narrator to show us what other characters are thinking instead of just telling us about their thoughts. How many different speakers does Beller identify? What does each contribute to this narrative?

4. Dialogue also enables the narrator of a story to convey new information to the reader. What crucial details does the ashen guy give us through his dialogue?

5. Why do you think Beller ends this tale of near mass hysteria with the fall of the second tower? What is the significance of his ending with the ashen guy "who just kept walking" (21)?

6. If you left off the first paragraph of Beller's narrative (where the narrator refers to himself in the first person, "I"), it would cease, technically, to be a personal narrative any longer. Why might Beller want his narrator to recede into the background? What's the focus of his story?

7. "At first glance he looked like a snowman, except instead of snow he was covered in gray, asbestos-colored ash" (3). Is this DESCRIPTION or NARRATION? Find some other passages in Beller's narrative where these two MODES OF WRITING shade into one another.

XXXXXXXXXXXXX **WORDS AND FIGURES OF SPEECH** XXXXXXXXXXXXX

1. What are the implications of Beller's use of the word "ashen" in the story of a national nightmare?

2. Why do you suppose Beller calls the person at the center of his NARRATIVE a "guy," rather than a man or a gentleman or a citizen?

3. "A small plume of dust drifted off the top of his head as he walked, echoing the larger plume of smoke drifting off of One World Trade behind him" (3). What do you think of Beller's use of the word "echoing" in this sentence? What are the CONNOTATIONS of "plume"?

4. What are some examples of Beller's figurative linking of "the ashen guy" with the tower? At the end of the NARRATIVE, the second World Trade Center tower falls. What happens to the ashen guy?

XXXXXXXXXXXXXXXXXXXXX **FOR WRITING** XXXXXXXXXXXXXXXXXXXXX

1. In the days and months following the attacks on the World Trade Center, stories of survivors and eyewitnesses abounded. Of all the stories you have heard, which one has affected you most? In a brief NARRATIVE, tell what that survivor or witness did or saw on that fateful day.

2. Where were you on September 11, 2001? Write a personal narrative in which you describe where you were and tell what you and others did and felt. Try to remember the gist of what was said, and quote it directly as DIALOGUE in your NARRATIVE.

SEBASTIAN JUNGER

THE LION IN WINTER

Sebastian Junger (b. 1962) is an award-winning journalist and professional risk-taker. He has worked as a tree climber; fought fires with the smoke jumpers in the Idaho wilderness; reported on armed conflicts in Bosnia, Sierra Leone, and Afghanistan; opened a pub in New York City; and, in *The Perfect Storm* (1997), researched and re-created the storm that swallowed the crew of the *Andrea Gail.* The following narrative, told from both first- and third-person points of view, comprises two complete sections from *Fire* (2001), a book about "people confronting situations that could easily destroy them." Here Junger reports on his five-week visit in 2000 to Afghanistan, where he and renowned Iranian photographer Reza Daghati met in the trenches with Ahmad Shah Massoud, the legendary leader of the Northern Alliance who died from wounds inflicted on September 9, 2001, by suicide bombers posing as journalists. The passages that follow tell about an offensive in the war against the Taliban. The risk of all risks for Junger is writing itself. "Writing is a way to express ideas," he says; but experience comes first. "If you haven't yet acquired the ideas to express," Junger advises, you need to go out and "get dirty."

XXXXXXXXXXXXXXXXXXXXXXXXXXXXXXXXXXXXXXXXXXXXXXXXXXXXXXXXXXXXXXX

The day before the offensive, Massoud decided to go to the front line   1
for a close look at the Taliban. He couldn't tell if the attack, as planned, would succeed in taking their ridgetop positions; he was worried that his men would die in a frontal assault when they could just as easily slip around back. He had been watching the Taliban supply trucks through the binoculars and had determined that there was only one road leading to their forward positions. If his men could take that, the Taliban would have to withdraw.

Massoud goes everywhere quickly, and this time was no exception. He jumped up from a morning meeting with his commanders, stormed out to his white Land Cruiser, and drove off. His commanders and body-guards scrambled into their own trucks to follow him.

The convoy drove through town, raising great plumes of dust, and then turned down toward the river and plowed through the braiding channels, muddy water up to their door handles. One truck stalled in midstream, but they got it going again and tore through no-man's-land while their tanks on Ay Khanom Hill shelled the Taliban to provide cover. They drove up to the forward positions and then got out of the trucks and continued on foot, creeping to within five hundred yards of the Taliban front line. This was the dead zone: Anything that moves gets shot. Dead zones are invariably quiet; there's no fighting, no human noise, just an absolute stillness that can be more frightening than the heaviest gunfire. Into this stillness, as Massoud studied the Taliban positions, a single gunshot rang out.

The bullet barely missed one of his commanders—he felt its wind as it passed—and came to a stop in the dirt between Massoud's feet. Massoud called in more artillery fire, and then he and his men quickly retraced their route to the trucks. The trip had served its purpose, though. Massoud had identified two dirt roads that split in front of the Taliban positions and circled behind them. And he had let himself be seen on the front line, reinforcing the Taliban assumption that this was the focus of his attack.

Late that afternoon Massoud and his commanders went back up to the command post. The artillery exchanges had started up again, and a new Ramadan moon hung delicately in the sunset over the Taliban positions. That night, in the bunker, Massoud gave his commanders their final instructions. The offensive was to be carried out by eight groups of sixty men each, in successive waves. They must not be married or have children; they must not be their families' only sons. They were to take the two roads Massoud had spotted and encircle the Taliban positions on the hill. He told them to cut the supply road and hold their positions while offering the Taliban a way to escape. The idea was not to force the Taliban to fight to the last man. The idea was just to overtake their positions with as few casualties as possible.

The commanders filed out, and Reza and Dr. Abdullah were left   6
alone with Massoud. He was exhausted, and he lay down on his side
with his coat over him and his hands folded under his cheek. He fell
asleep, woke up, asked Reza a question, then fell asleep, over and over
again for the next hour. Occasionally a commander would walk in, and
Massoud would ask if he'd repositioned those mortars or distributed the
fifty thousand rounds of ammunition to the front. At one point, he asked
Reza which country he liked best of all the ones he'd worked in.

"Afghanistan, of course," Reza said.   7
"Have you been to Africa?"   8
"Yes."   9
"Have you been to Rwanda?"   10
"Yes."   11
"What happened there? Why those massacres?"   12

Reza tried to explain. After a few minutes, Massoud sat up. "A few   13
years ago in Kabul, I thought the war was finished, and I started building
a home in Panjshir," he said. "A room for my children, a room for me
and my wife, and a big library for all my books. I've kept all my books.
I've put them in boxes, hoping one day I'll be able to put them on the
shelves and I'll be able to read them. But the house is still unfinished,
and the books are still in their boxes. I don't know when I'll be able to
read my books."

Finally Massoud bade Reza and Dr. Abdullah good night and then   14
lay back down and went to sleep for good. Though he holds the post of
vice-president in Rabbani's deposed government, Massoud is a man with
few aspirations as a political leader, no apparent desire for power. Over
and over he has rejected appeals from his friends and allies to take a more
active role in the politics of his country. The Koran says that war is such
a catastrophe it must be brought to an end as quickly as possible and by
any means necessary. That, perhaps, is why Massoud has devoted himself
exclusively to waging war.

I woke up at dawn. The sky was pale blue and promised a warm, clear   15
day, which meant that the offensive was on. Reza and I ate some bread
and drank tea and then went outside with the fighters. There seemed to
be more of them milling around, and they were talking less than usual.

They stood in tense little groups in the morning sun, waiting for Commander Massoud to emerge from his quarters.

The artillery fire started up in late morning, a dull smattering of explosions on the front line and the occasional heavy boom of a nearby tank. The plan was for Massoud's forces to attack at dusk along the ridge, drawing attention to that part of the front, and then around midnight other attacks would be launched farther south. That was where the front passed close to Taloqan. As the afternoon went by, the artillery fire became more and more regular, and then suddenly at five-fifteen a spate of radio calls came into the bunker. Massoud stood up and went outside. 16

It had begun. Explosions flashed continually against the Taliban positions on the ridge, and rockets started streaking back and forth across the dark valley. We could see the lights from three Taliban tanks that were making their way along the ridgeline to reinforce positions that were getting overrun. A local cameraman named Yusuf had shown me footage of seasoned mujahidin attacking a hill, and I was surprised by how calm and purposeful the process was. In his video the men moved forward at a crouch, stopping to shoot from time to time and then moving forward again until they had reached the top of the hill. They never stopped advancing, and they never went faster than a walk. 17

Unfortunately, I doubted that the battle I was watching was being conducted with such grace. They were just kids up there, mostly, on the hill in the dark with the land mines and the machine-gun fire and the Taliban tanks. Massoud was yelling on the radio a lot, long bursts of Dari and then short silences while whoever he was talking to tried to explain himself. Things were not going well, it seemed. Some of the commanders weren't on the front line, where they belonged, and their men had gone straight up the hill instead of circling. As a result, they had attacked through a minefield. Massoud was in a cold fury. 18

"I never told you to attack from below. I knew it would be mined," he told one commander in the bunker. The man's head tipped backward with the force of Massoud's words. "The plan was not to attack directly. That's why you hit the mines. You made the same mistake last time." 19

The commander suggested that the mistake might have been made by the fighters on the ground. 20

"I don't care. These are my children, your children," Massoud shot 21 back. "When I look at these fighters, they are like lions. The real problem is the commanders. You attacked from below and lost men to land mines. For me, even if you took the position, you lost the war."

The offensive was supposed to continue all night. Reza and I ate dinner with Massoud, then packed up our truck and set out on the long drive back to Khvajeh Baha od Din. We were leaving the front for good, and on the way out of town we decided to check in at the field hospital. It was just a big canvas tent set up in a mud-walled courtyard, lit inside by kerosene lanterns that glowed softly through the fabric. We stopped the truck and walked inside, and we were just wrapping up our conversation with the doctor when an old Soviet flatbed pulled up. 22

It was the first truckload of wounded, the guys who had stepped on mines. They were stunned and quiet, each face blackened by the force of a land mine blast, and their eyes cast around in confusion at the sudden activity surrounding them. The medics lifted the men off the back of the truck, carried them inside, and laid them on metal cots. A soldier standing next to me clucked his disapproval when he saw the wounds. The effect of a land mine on a person is so devastating that it is almost disorienting. It takes several minutes to understand that the sack of bones and blood and shredded cloth that you're looking at used to be a man's leg. One man lost a leg at the ankle; another man lost a leg at the shin; a third lost an entire leg to the waist. This man didn't seem to be in pain, and he didn't seem to have any understanding of what had happened to him. Both would come later. "My back hurts," he kept saying. "There's something wrong with my back." 23

The medics worked quickly and wordlessly in the lamplight, wrapping the stumps of the legs with gauze. The wounded men would be flown out by helicopter the next day and would eventually wind up in a hospital in Tajikistan. "This is the war," Reza hissed over and over again as he shot photos. "This is what war means." 24

Reza had covered a lot of wars and seen plenty of this in his life, but I hadn't. I ducked out of the tent and stood in the cold darkness, leaning against a wall. Dogs were barking in the distance, and a soldier shouted into his radio that the wounded were coming in and they needed more medicine, now. I thought about what Reza had said, and after a while I went back inside. This is the war too, and you have to look 25 straight at it, I told myself. You have to look straight at all of it or you have no business being here at all.

1. According to Sebastian Junger, what was Commander Massoud's main objective in launching the military offensive reported here? What, in particular, did he want to avoid? How well did Massoud succeed in accomplishing his objectives during the part of the battle that Junger reports?

2. For reporting the events of a war, which kind of writing is more authentic in your opinion—impersonal narrative (as in the first part of Junger's account) or personal narrative (the second part)? Please explain your answer.

3. In the last paragraph of his narrative, Junger says that the wounded are part of the war too and that you "have to look straight at all of it" (25). Does Junger's narrative do this in your opinion? How does it do (or fail to do) so?

1. In the first half of his narrative, Junger writes about his subject in the third person ("he," "they"); in the second half, he writes primarily in the first person ("I," "we"). How does this switch in grammatical POINT OF VIEW affect the narrative? Please refer to specific passages in the text to support your answer.

2. Why does Junger picture himself "leaning against a wall" outside the field hospital in the last paragraph of his narrative? What does the physical position of the narrator tell us about his mental attitude? Please explain.

3. Why do you think Junger goes back inside the hospital tent at the end of his narrative? Why doesn't he just end with the picture of himself leaning against the wall?

4. When Junger tells about the bullet that lands harmlessly between Massoud's feet (4), he makes him look almost invincible despite the proximity of the enemy. Find other places in the narrative where Junger creates the impression of Commander Massoud as a heroic figure. Also look for passages where he shows Massoud's humanity, and his vulnerability.

5. What is the purpose of the DIALOGUE in paragraphs 7–13? How objectively is it presented? Where is the narrator in this little scene?

6. Junger does not give us an account of the entire battle in his narrative. Should he have done so? Why—or why not?

XXXXXXXXXXXXX **WORDS AND FIGURES OF SPEECH** XXXXXXXXXXXXX

1. What is Reza, the photographer, referring to literally when he says, *"This* is the war" (24)? What does he mean figuratively?

2. Why does Junger call attention to the "new Ramadan moon" in paragraph 5? If it is a sign or symbol on the eve of battle, what might it signify?

3. Explain the METAPHOR in the title of Junger's narrative. Who or what is being compared to a lion? Why is the lion said to be "in winter" here?

4. What are "mujahidin" (17)? Why does Junger refer to video of "seasoned" mujahidin attacking a hill before he narrates the actual events he is witnessing? What's the IRONY here?

5. *The Lion in Winter* is also the title of a play by James Goldman (1964) about King Henry II of England and Eleanor of Acquitaine. A hit movie, directed by Anthony Harvey and starring Peter O'Toole and Katharine Hepburn (MGM / United Artists, 1968), was based on the play. Why do you think Junger ALLUDES to this particular drama about Christmas in a dysfunctional royal household— and about the division of kingdoms?

XXXXXXXXXXXXXXXXXXXXXX **FOR WRITING** XXXXXXXXXXXXXXXXXXXXXX

1. You probably have not witnessed the war in Afghanistan directly, but you have seen episodes of it and other conflicts on television. As if you were a journalist, write an "objective" narrative of a particular war incident or episode (in Afghanistan or elsewhere) that you recall viewing.

2. Do a little research on the Internet or in the library, and write a short narrative of the life and military career of Ahmad Shah Massoud, or some other military figure whose exploits you have read or heard about.

3. If you yourself have served in the military, write a personal narrative of an experience you had that both captures your involvement in military life and describes the person you were when you had it.

MARY MEBANE

THE BACK OF THE BUS

Mary Mebane (1933–1992) was a member of the last generation of African Americans to endure legal segregation in the South. The daughter of a dirt farmer who sold junk to raise cash, she earned a Ph.D. from the University of North Carolina and became a professor of English. In 1971 on the Op-Ed page of the *New York Times*, Mebane told the story of a bus ride from Durham to Orangeburg, South Carolina, during the 1940s that "realized for me the enormousness of the change" since the Civil Rights Act of 1964. That bus ride was the germ of two autobiographical volumes, *Mary* (1981) and *Mary Wayfarer* (1983). The essay printed here is a complete chapter from the first book. It is a personal narrative of another, earlier bus ride that Mebane took when the segregation laws were still in place. Mebane said she wrote this piece because she "wanted to show what it was like to live under legal segregation *before* the Civil Rights Act of 1964."

XXXXXXXXXXXXXXXXXXXXXXXXXXXXXXXXXXXXXXXXXXXXXXXXXXXXXXXXXXXXXX

Historically, my lifetime is important because I was part of the last generation born into a world of total legal segregation in the Southern United States. When the Supreme Court outlawed segregation in the public schools in 1954, I was twenty-one. When Congress passed the Civil Rights Act of 1964, permitting blacks free access to public places, I was thirty-one. The world I was born into had been segregated for a long time— so long, in fact, that I never met anyone who had lived during the time when restrictive laws were not in existence, although some people spoke of parents and others who had lived during the "free" time. As far as anyone knew, the laws as they then existed would stand forever. They were meant to—and did—create a world that fixed black people at the bottom of society in all aspects of human life. It was a world without options.   1

Most Americans have never had to live with terror. I had had to live with it all my life—the psychological terror of segregation, in which   2 there was a special set of laws governing your movements. You violated them at your peril, for you knew that if you broke one of them, knowingly or not, physical terror was just around the corner, in the form of policemen and jails, and in some cases and places white vigilante mobs formed for the exclusive purpose of keeping blacks in line.

It was Saturday morning, like any Saturday morning in dozens of Southern towns. 3

The town had a washed look. The street sweepers had been busy since six o'clock. Now, at eight, they were still slowly moving down the streets, white trucks with clouds of water coming from underneath the swelled tubular sides. Unwary motorists sometimes got a windowful of water as a truck passed by. As it moved on, it left in its wake a clear stream running in the gutters or splashed on the wheels of parked cars. 4

Homeowners, bent over industriously in the morning sun, were out pushing lawn mowers. The sun was bright, but it wasn't too hot. It was morning and it was May. Most of the mowers were glad that it was finally getting warm enough to go outside. 5

Traffic was brisk. Country people were coming into town early with their produce; clerks and service workers were getting to the job before the stores opened at ten o'clock. Though the big stores would not be open for another hour or so, the grocery stores, banks, open-air markets, dinettes, were already open and filling with staff and customers. 6

Everybody was moving toward the heart of Durham's downtown, which waited to receive them rather complacently, little knowing that in a decade the shopping centers far from the center of downtown Durham would create a ghost town in the midst of the busiest blocks on Main Street. 7

Some moved by car, and some moved by bus. The more affluent used cars, leaving the buses mainly to the poor, black and white, though there were some businesspeople who avoided the trouble of trying to find a parking place downtown by riding the bus. 8

I didn't mind taking the bus on Saturday. It wasn't so crowded. At night or on Saturday or Sunday was the best time. If there were plenty of seats, the blacks didn't have to worry about being asked to move so that a white person could sit down. And the knot of hatred and fear didn't come into my stomach. 9

I knew the stop that was the safety point, both going and coming. 10
Leaving town, it was the Little Five Points, about five or six blocks north
of the main downtown section. That was the last stop at which four or
five people might get on. After the stop, the driver could sometimes pass
two or three stops without taking on or letting off a passenger. So the
number of seats on the bus usually remained constant on the trip from
town to Braggtown. The nearer the bus got to the end of the line, the
more I relaxed. For if a white passenger got on near the end of the line,
often to catch the return trip back and avoid having to stand in the sun
at the bus stop until the bus turned around, he or she would usually
stand if there were not seats in the white section, and the driver would
say nothing, knowing that the end of the line was near and that the
standee would get a seat in a few minutes.

On the trip to town, the Mangum Street A&P was the last point at 11
which the driver picked up more passengers than he let off. These people,
though they were just a few blocks from the downtown section, preferred
to ride the bus downtown. Those getting on at the A&P were usually on
their way to work at the Duke University Hospital—past the downtown
section, through a residential neighborhood, and then past the university,
before they got to Duke Hospital.

So whether the driver discharged more passengers than he took on 12
near the A&P on Mangum was of great importance. For if he took on
more passengers than got off, it meant that some of the newcomers would
have to stand. And if they were white, the driver was going to have to
ask a black passenger to move so that a white passenger could sit down.
Most of the drivers had a rule of thumb, though. By custom the seats
behind the exit door had become "colored" seats, and no matter how
many whites stood up, anyone sitting behind the exit door knew that he
or she wouldn't have to move.

The disputed seat, though, was the one directly opposite the exit 13
door. It was "no-man's-land." White people sat there, and black people
sat there. It all depended on whose section was fuller. If the back section
was full, the next black passenger who got on sat in the no-man's-land
seat; but if the white section filled up, a white person would take the
seat. Another thing about the white people: they could sit anywhere they
chose, even in the "colored" section. Only the black passengers had to
obey segregation laws.

On this Saturday morning Esther[1] and I set out for town for our
music lesson. We were going on our weekly big adventure, all the way
across town, through the white downtown, then across the railroad tracks,
then through the "colored" downtown, a section of run-down dingy
shops, through some fading high-class black neighborhoods, past North
Carolina College, to Mrs. Shearin's house.   14

We walked the two miles from Wildwood to the bus line. Though   15
it was a warm day, in the early morning there was dew on the grass and
the air still had the night's softness. So we walked along and talked and
looked back constantly, hoping someone we knew would stop and pick
us up.

I looked back furtively, for in one of the few instances that I remem-   16
bered my father criticizing me severely, it was for looking back. One day
when I was walking from town he had passed in his old truck. I had
been looking back and had seen him. "Don't look back," he had said.
"People will think that you want them to pick you up." Though he said
"people," I knew he meant men—not the men he knew, who lived in the
black community, but the black men who were not part of the community, and all of the white men. To be picked up meant that something
bad would happen to me. Still, two miles is a long walk and I occasionally
joined Esther in looking back to see if anyone we knew was coming.

Esther and I got to the bus and sat on one of the long seats at the   17
back that faced each other. There were three such long seats—one on
each side of the bus and a third long seat at the very back that faced the
front. I liked to sit on a long seat facing the side because then I didn't
have to look at the expressions on the faces of the whites when they put
their tokens in and looked at the blacks sitting in the back of the bus.
Often I studied my music, looking down and practicing the fingering. I
looked up at each stop to see who was getting on and to check on the
seating pattern. The seating pattern didn't really bother me that day until
the bus started to get unusually full for a Saturday morning. I wondered
what was happening, where all these people were coming from. They got
on and got on until the white section was almost full and the black section
was full.

[1]Mebane's sister.

There was a black man in a blue windbreaker and a gray porkpie   18
hat sitting in no-man's-land, and my stomach tightened. I wondered what
would happen. I had never been on a bus on which a black person was
asked to give a seat to a white person when there was no other seat empty.
Usually, though, I had seen a black person automatically get up and move
to an empty seat farther back. But this morning the only empty seat was
beside a black person sitting in no-man's-land.

The bus stopped at Little Five Points and one black got off. A   19
young white man was getting on. I tensed. What would happen now?
Would the driver ask the black man to get up and move to the empty
seat farther back? The white man had a businessman's air about him:
suit, shirt, tie, polished brown shoes. He saw the empty seat in the "colored" section and after just a little hesitation went to it, put his briefcase
down, and sat with his feet crossed. I relaxed a little when the bus pulled
off without the driver saying anything. Evidently he hadn't seen what
had happened, or since he was just a few stops from Main Street, he
figured the mass exodus there would solve all the problems. Still, I was
afraid of a scene.

The next stop was an open-air fruit stand just after Little Five   20
Points, and here another white man got on. Where would he sit? The
only available seat was beside the black man. Would he stand the few
stops to Main Street or would the driver make the black man move? The
whole colored section tensed, but nobody said anything. I looked at
Esther, who looked apprehensive. I looked at the other men and women,
who studiously avoided my eyes and everybody else's as well, as they
maintained a steady gaze at a far-distant land.

Just one woman caught my eye; I had noticed her before, and I   21
had been ashamed of her. She was a stringy little black woman. She
could have been forty; she could have been fifty. She looked as if she
were a hard drinker. Flat black face with tight features. She was dressed
with great insouciance in a tight boy's sweater with horizontal lines running across her flat chest. It pulled down over a nondescript skirt.
Laced-up shoes, socks, and a head rag completed her outfit. She looked
tense.

The white man who had just gotten on the bus walked to the seat   22
in no-man's-land and stood there. He wouldn't sit down, just stood there.

Two adult males, living in the most highly industrialized, most techno-
logically advanced nation in the world, a nation that had devastated two
other industrial giants in World War II and had flirted with taking on
China in Korea. Both these men, either of whom could have fought for
the United States in Germany or Korea, faced each other in mutual rage
and hostility. The white one wanted to sit down, but he was going to
exert his authority and force the black one to get up first. I watched the
driver in the rearview mirror. He was about the same age as the antag-
onists. The driver wasn't looking for trouble, either.

"Say there, buddy, how about moving back," the driver said, mean-   23
while driving his bus just as fast as he could. The whole bus froze—
whites at the front, blacks at the rear. They didn't want to believe what
was happening was really happening.

The seated black man said nothing. The standing white man said   24
nothing.

"Say, buddy, did you hear me? What about moving on back." The   25
driver was scared to death. I could tell that.

"These is the niggers' seats!" the little lady in the strange outfit   26
started screaming. I jumped. I had to shift my attention from the driver
to the frieze of the black man seated and white man standing to the
articulate little woman who had joined in the fray.

"The government gave us these seats! These is the niggers' seats."   27
I was startled at her statement and her tone. "The president said that
these are the niggers' seats!" I expected her to start fighting at any
moment.

Evidently the bus driver did, too, because he was driving faster and   28
faster. I believe that he forgot he was driving a bus and wanted desperately to pull to the side of the street and get out and run.

"I'm going to take you down to the station, buddy," the driver   29
said.

The white man with the briefcase and the polished brown shoes   30
who had taken a seat in the "colored" section looked as though he might
die of embarrassment at any moment.

As scared and upset as I was, I didn't miss a thing.   31

By that time we had come to the stop before Main Street, and the   32
black passenger rose to get off.

"You're not getting off, buddy. I'm going to take you downtown."   33
The driver kept driving as he talked and seemed to be trying to get
downtown as fast as he could.

"These are the niggers' seats! The government plainly said these   34
are the niggers' seats!" screamed the little woman in rage.

I was embarrassed at the use of the word "nigger" but I was proud   35
of the lady. I was also proud of the man who wouldn't get up.

The bus driver was afraid, trying to hold on to his job but plainly   36
not willing to get into a row with the blacks.

The bus seemed to be going a hundred miles an hour and everybody   37
was anxious to get off, though only the lady and the driver were saying
anything.

The black man stood at the exit door; the driver drove right past   38
the A&P stop. I was terrified. I was sure that the bus was going to the
police station to put the black man in jail. The little woman had her
hands on her hips and she never stopped yelling. The bus driver kept
driving as fast as he could.

Then, somewhere in the back of his mind, he decided to forget the   39
whole thing. The next stop was Main Street, and when he got there, in
what seemed to be a flash of lightning, he flung both doors open wide.
He and his black antagonist looked at each other in the rearview mirror;
in a second the windbreaker and porkpie hat were gone. The little woman
was standing, preaching to the whole bus about the government's gift of
these seats to the blacks; the man with the brown shoes practically fell
out of the door in his hurry; and Esther and I followed the hurrying
footsteps.

We walked about three doors down the block, then caught a bus to   40
the black neighborhood. Here we sat on one of the two long seats facing
each other, directly behind the driver. It was the custom. Since this bus
had a route from a black neighborhood to the downtown section and
back, passing through no white residential areas, blacks could sit where
they chose. One minute we had been on a bus in which violence was
threatened over a seat near the exit door; the next minute we were sitting
in the very front behind the driver.

The people who devised this system thought that it was going to   41
last forever.

XXXXXXXXXXXXXXXXXXXX **FOR DISCUSSION** XXXXXXXXXXXXXXXXXXXX

1. Why does the bus driver threaten to drive to the police station? What was his official duty under segregation?

2. Why does the businessman with the briefcase and brown shoes take the separate seat in the back of the bus instead of the place on the bench across from the exit? Was he upholding or violating segregation customs by doing so?

3. What is the main confrontation of the NARRATIVE? What emotion(s) does it arouse in young Mary Mebane and her sister as witnesses?

4. Who are the "people" to whom Mebane refers in paragraph 41?

5. Why does Mebane claim a national significance for the events of her private life as narrated here? Is her claim justified?

XXXXXXXXXXXXXX **STRATEGIES AND STRUCTURES** XXXXXXXXXXXXXX

1. In which paragraph does Mebane begin telling the story of the bus ride? Why do you think she starts with the routine of the street sweepers and the home-owners doing yard work?

2. What is young Mary's role throughout the story of her wild bus ride? In which paragraph does she DEFINE that role most clearly?

3. List several passages in Mebane's text that seem to be told from young Mary's POINT OF VIEW. Then list others that are told from the point of view of the adult author looking back at an event in her youth. Besides time, what is the main difference in their perspectives?

4. Why does Mebane refer to the black passenger who confronts the bus driver as "the windbreaker and porkpie hat" (39)? Whose point of view is she capturing? Is she showing or telling here—and what difference does it make in her essay?

5. How does Mebane use the increasing speed of the bus to show rather than tell about the precariousness of the segregation system?

6. Mebane interrupts her NARRATIVE of the events of that Saturday morning in paragraphs 10 through 13. What is she explaining to the reader, and why is this information necessary? Where else does she interrupt her NARRATIVE with EXPO-SITION?

XXXXXXXXXXXXXX **WORDS AND FIGURES OF SPEECH** XXXXXXXXXXXXX

1. Why does the narrator refer to the seat across from the exit as a "no-man's-land" (13)? What does this term mean?

2. Mebane compares the seated black man and the standing white man to a "frieze," a decorative horizontal band, often molded or carved, along the upper part of a wall (26). Why is the METAPHOR appropriate here?

3. Look up "insouciance" in your dictionary (21). Does the use of this word prepare you for the rebellious behavior of the "stringy" little woman (21)? How?

4. What are the two possible meanings of "scene" (19)? How might Mebane's personal NARRATIVE be said to illustrate both kinds?

5. Which of the many meanings of "articulate" in your dictionary best fits the woman who screams back at the bus driver (26)?

XXXXXXXXXXXXXXXXXXXXXX **FOR WRITING** XXXXXXXXXXXXXXXXXXXXXX

1. In a brief ANECDOTE, recount a bus, train, plane, roller coaster, boat, or other ride you have taken. Focus on the vehicle itself and the people who were on it with you.

2. Spend a morning in a bus or train station, airport, shopping mall, or other busy intersection of human activity. Write a personal NARRATIVE about the experience. Be sure to DESCRIBE the physical place and tell what you saw and heard and did there. If possible, use the events and sounds you write about to capture a slice of the social or political life of your town, city, or region.

RICHARD RODRIGUEZ

NONE OF THIS IS FAIR

Richard Rodriguez (b. 1944) is an editor for Pacific News Service in his
native San Francisco and a contributing editor for *Harper's, U.S. News
& World Report*, and the *Los Angeles Times*. He is the author of *Hunger
of Memory: The Education of Richard Rodriguez* (1982), from which this
personal narrative is adapted, and *Days of Obligation* (1992), an "argument" with his Mexican father. Although Rodriguez holds a Ph.D. in
English from Berkeley, he has never been an academic. In "None of This
Is Fair" he touches on his reasons for becoming a writer and journalist
instead of a university professor.

XXXXXXXXXXXXXXXXXXXXXXXXXXXXXXXXXXXXXXXXXXXXXXXXXXXXXXXXXXXXXXXXX

My plan to become a professor of English—my ambition during long   1
years in college at Stanford, then in graduate school at Columbia
and Berkeley—was complicated by feelings of embarrassment and guilt.
So many times I would see other Mexican-Americans and know we were
alike only in race. And yet, simply because our race was the same, I was,
during the last years of my schooling, the beneficiary of their situation.
Affirmative Action programs had made it all possible. The disadvantages
of others permitted my promotion; the absence of many Mexican-
Americans from academic life allowed my designation as a "minority
student."

For me opportunities had been extravagant. There were fellowships,   2
summer research grants, and teaching assistantships. After only two years
in graduate school, I was offered teaching jobs by several colleges. Invitations to Washington conferences arrived and I had the chance to travel
abroad as a "Mexican-American representative." The benefits were often,
however, too gaudy to please. In three published essays, in conversations
with teachers, in letters to politicians and at conferences, I worried the
issue of Affirmative Action. Often I proposed contradictory opinions.

Though consistent was the admission that—because of an early, excellent education—I was no longer a principal victim of racism or any other social oppression. I said that but still I continued to indicate on applications for financial aid that I was a Hispanic-American. It didn't really occur to me to say anything else, or to leave the question unanswered.

Thus I complied with and encouraged the odd bureaucratic logic of Affirmative Action. I let government officials treat the disadvantaged condition of many Mexican-Americans with my advancement. Each fall my presence was noted by Health, Education, and Welfare department statisticians. As I pursued advanced literary studies and learned the skill of reading Spenser and Wordsworth and Empson, I would hear myself numbered among the culturally disadvantaged. Still, silent, I didn't object. 3

But the irony cut deep. And guilt would not be evaded by averting my glance when I confronted a face like my own in a crowd. By late 1975, nearing the completion of my graduate studies at Berkeley, I was so wary of the benefits of Affirmative Action that I feared my inevitable success as an applicant for a teaching position. The months of fall— traditionally that time of academic job-searching—passed without my applying to a single school. When one of my professors chanced to learn this in late November, he was astonished, then furious. He yelled at me: Did I think that because I was a minority student jobs would just come looking for me? What was I thinking? Did I realize that he and several other faculty members had already written letters on my behalf? Was I going to start acting like some other minority students he had known? They struggled for success and then, when it was almost within reach, grew strangely afraid and let it pass. Was that it? Was I determined to fail? 4

I did not respond to his questions. I didn't want to admit to him, and thus to myself, the reason I delayed. 5

I merely agreed to write to several schools. (In my letter I wrote: "I cannot claim to represent disadvantaged Mexican-Americans. The very fact that I am in a position to apply for this job should make that clear.") After two or three days, there were telegrams and phone calls, invitations to interviews, then airplane trips. A blur of faces and the murmur of their soft questions. And, over someone's shoulder, the sight of campus 6 buildings shadowing pictures I had seen years before when I leafed through Ivy League catalogues with great expectations. At the end of each visit, interviewers would smile and wonder if I had any questions. A few times I quietly wondered what advantage my race had given me over other applicants. But that was an impossible question for them to answer without embarrassing me. Quickly, several persons insisted that my ethnic identity had given me no more than a "foot inside the door"; at most, I had a "slight edge" over other applicants. "We just looked at your dossier with extra care and we like what we saw. There was never any question of having to alter our standards. You can be certain of that."

In the early part of January, offers arrived on stiffly elegant station- 7
ery. Most schools promised terms appropriate for any new assistant pro- fessor. A few made matters worse—and almost more tempting—by offering more: the use of university housing; an unusually large starting salary; a reduced teaching schedule. As the stack of letters mounted, my hesitation increased. I started calling department chairmen to ask for another week, then 10 more days—"more time to reach a decision"—to avoid the decision I would need to make.

At school, meantime, some students hadn't received a single job 8
offer. One man, probably the best student in the department, did not even get a request for his dossier. He and I met outside a classroom one day and he asked about my opportunities. He seemed happy for me. Faculty members beamed. They said they had expected it. "After all, not many schools are going to pass up getting a Chicano with a Ph.D. in Renaissance literature," somebody said laughing. Friends wanted to know which of the offers I was going to accept. But I couldn't make up my mind. February came and I was running out of time and excuses. (One chairman guessed my delay was a bargaining ploy and increased his offer with each of my calls.) I had to promise a decision by the 10th; the 12th at the very latest.

On the 18th of February, late in the afternoon, I was in the office 9
I shared with several other teaching assistants. Another graduate student was sitting across the room at his desk. When I got up to leave, he looked over to say in an uneventful voice that he had some big news. He had finally decided to accept a position at a faraway university. It was not a job he especially wanted, he admitted. But he had to take it because there

hadn't been any other offers. He felt trapped, and depressed, since his job would separate him from his young daughter.

I tried to encourage him by remarking that he was lucky at least to 10 have found a job. So many others hadn't been able to get anything. But before I finished speaking I realized that I had said the wrong thing. And I anticipated his next question.

"What are your plans?" he wanted to know. "Is it true you've gotten 11 an offer from Yale?"

I said that it was. "Only, I still haven't made up my mind." 12

He stared at me as I put on my jacket. And smiling, then unsmiling, 13 he asked if I knew that he too had written to Yale. In his case, however, no one had bothered to acknowledge his letter with even a postcard. What did I think of that?

He gave me no time to answer. 14

"Damn!" he said sharply and his chair rasped the floor as he pushed 15 himself back. Suddenly, it was to *me* that he was complaining. "It's just not right, Richard. None of this is fair. You've done some good work, but so have I. I'll bet our records are just about equal. But when we look for jobs this year, it's a different story. You get all of the breaks."

To evade his criticism, I wanted to side with him. I was about to 16 admit the injustice of Affirmative Action. But he went on, his voice hard with accusation. "It's all very simple this year. You're a Chicano. And I am a Jew. That's the only real difference between us."

His words stung me: there was nothing he was telling me that I 17 didn't know. I had admitted everything already. But to hear someone else say these things, and in such an accusing tone, was suddenly hard to take. In a deceptively calm voice, I responded that he had simplified the whole issue. The phrases came like bubbles to the tip of my tongue: "new blood"; "the importance of cultural diversity"; "the goal of racial integration." These were all the arguments I had proposed several years ago—and had long since abandoned. Of course the offers were unjustifiable. I knew that. All I was saying amounted to a frantic self-defense. I tried to find an end to a sentence. My voice faltered to a stop.

"Yeah, sure," he said. "I've heard all that before. Nothing you say 18 really changes the fact that Affirmative Action is unfair. You see that, don't you? There isn't any way for me to compete with you. Once there were quotas to keep my parents out of certain schools; now there are quotas to get you in and the effect on me is the same as it was for them."

I listened to every word he spoke. But my mind was really on some-   19
thing else. I knew at that moment that I would reject all of the offers. I stood there silently surprised by what an easy conclusion it was. Having prepared for so many years to teach, having trained myself to do nothing else, I had hesitated out of practical fear. But now that it was made, the decision came with relief. I immediately knew I had made the right choice.

My colleague continued talking and I realized that he was simply   20
right. Affirmative Action programs *are* unfair to white students. But as I listened to him assert his rights, I thought of the seriously disadvantaged. How different they were from white, middle-class students who come armed with the testimony of their grades and aptitude scores and self-confidence to complain about the unequal treatment they now receive. I listen to them. I do not want to be careless about what they say. Their rights are important to protect. But inevitably when I hear them or their lawyers, I think about the most seriously disadvantaged, not simply Mexican-Americans, but of all those who do not ever imagine themselves going to college or becoming doctors: white, black, brown. Always poor. Silent. They are not plaintiffs before the court or against the misdirection of Affirmative Action. They lack the confidence (my confidence!) to assume their right to a good education. They lack the confidence and skills a good primary and secondary education provides and which are prerequisites for informed public life. They remain silent.

The debate drones on and surrounds them in stillness. They are   21
distant, faraway figures like the boys I have seen peering down from freeway overpasses in some other part of town.

XXXXXXXXXXXXXXXXXXXX **FOR DISCUSSION** XXXXXXXXXXXXXXXXXXXX

1. His ambition to become a university professor, says Richard Rodriguez in this NARRATIVE of his graduate school days, "was complicated by feelings of embarrassment and guilt" (1)? What did he feel guilty about? Why, after all that schooling and other training, do you suppose he decided not to take a job in a university?

2. Rodriguez's story leads up to an ARGUMENT between himself and another graduate student. What position does his opponent take on the issue of Affirmative Action? How convincing do you find the opponent's reasoning?

3. What does Rodriguez say he is thinking during this debate? How does he respond to his opponent's argument?

4. Rodriguez ends with a reference to the boys he has seen "peering down from freeway overpasses" (21). Who are these boys? Why do they come to his mind?

5. Do you think someone in Rodriguez's position should have allowed himself to be "guilted" into changing his plans for his life? Why or why not?

6. "Affirmative Action programs *are* unfair to white students" (20), says Rodriguez. Do you agree or disagree? What else is "unfair," in his opinion?

XXXXXXXXXXXXX **STRATEGIES AND STRUCTURES** XXXXXXXXXXXXX

1. How does Rodriguez's NARRATIVE of his search for an academic job use the calendar to build suspense about his future? Where does he resolve that suspense?

2. A key moment in this narrative is when the two fellow graduate students argue. How does Rodriguez show that his own mind is divided and that he struggles with a debate within himself?

3. We might say that the PLOT of this story is about an internal struggle that Rodriguez is trying to resolve. How do his interactions with his professors and potential employers help to advance this plot?

4. How, in the last two paragraphs, does Rodriguez keep his narrative from turning into a speech about the inequities and moral ambiguities of Affirmative Action?

5. In the snippets of DIALOGUE that punctuate Rodriguez's text, various articulate speakers give good reasons both for and against Affirmative Action. What do we hear from the "seriously disadvantaged" (20) in this debate? Why?

6. Rodriguez never explicitly tells us why he decides to give up on becoming a university professor, instead leaving us to DEDUCE the reasons. Why doesn't he just tell us outright? Does choosing to show rather than tell us make his narrative more or less dramatic? Why?

7. What ARGUMENT about Affirmative Action is Rodriguez making in the last two paragraphs of this narrative?

XXXXXXXXXXXX **WORDS AND FIGURES OF SPEECH** XXXXXXXXXXXX

1. What does the pronoun "this" refer to in Rodriguez's title?

2. What are the CONNOTATIONS of the word "drones" (21)? For whom, according to Rodriguez, are the niceties of academic debate over Affirmative Action a droning, essentially meaningless sound?

3. To whom is Rodriguez COMPARING the boys in his last paragraph? What does this SIMILE tell us about those people?

4. Rodriguez speaks of the "logic" of Affirmative Action as both "bureaucratic" and "odd" (3). Why do you think he pairs these two adjectives?

XXXXXXXXXXXXXXXXXXXX **FOR WRITING** XXXXXXXXXXXXXXXXXXXX

1. Have you or anyone you know ever experienced racial, gender, ethnic, or other forms of profiling—whether "affirmative" or negative? If so, write a brief NARRATIVE about that experience.

2. Write a personal narrative about your internal struggle to make some important decision in your life. Lead up to and then focus sharply on the moment of clarity when your mind was made up and you suddenly knew what you were going to do or say or be.

KELLY SIMON

FRANK SINATRA'S GUM

Kelly Simon is a food, mystery, and travel writer. "Frank Sinatra's Gum" appeared in the *Alaska Quarterly* in 1998. Simon interviewed "Frankie, the Voice" many years earlier, when she was a teenager pretending to be a reporter for the *Weequahic High News* in New Jersey. Although Sinatra and the interview are important in this personal narrative, the focus is on young Simon and her efforts not to be a "drooling, moronic, autograph-hunting sheep" at the same time that she desperately wants to be accepted by the other girls in her school.

XXXXXXXXXXXXXXXXXXXXXXXXXXXXXXXXXXXXXXXXXXXXXXXXXXXXXXXXXXXXXXX

It was 1945 and Frankie, the Voice, was singing at the Paramount. Though I pretended to swoon at the mention of his name so I would fit in—a ploy that caused my father to lump me with "the rest of those drooling, moronic, autograph-hunting sheep"—secretly I did not adore him like the other girls in junior high did. Still, I knew if I could get something of his, they might include me in their cliques. 1

I liked that he was Sicilian as many of my father's friends and clients were. Sicilians ate spicy food, waved their arms around, argued in loud voices, and kissed and made up, unlike my mother who did none of these things except argue loudly and wave her arms around. 2

Even though his father was born in Austria and he, himself, was born in America, I thought of my father as Sicilian. He walked like the Sicilian men did—with his hands clasped behind his back. He kissed men on the lips and pinched their cheeks as I had seen Sicilians do. He was a pug like Frankie who—even though he was skinny and wore a bow tie—punched reporters when they got too close. Until my father married my mother he, too, used his fists to settle fights. When he was eighteen he knocked a boy out and when he tried to revive him, the boy just lay there on the sidewalk. Thinking he had killed him, my father 3 skipped town. A month later, when he heard that the fellow was alive, he came back.

I took the train into New York the day that Frankie was to appear at the Paramount. Girls in bobby socks squealed and fainted as they swarmed the box office trying to get in. After standing in line for two hours, I learned that all the tickets were sold out. I had planned for this possibility and I ducked around to the stage door entrance and knocked. A man with a cauliflower nose stuck his head out.   4

"Yeah, what?"   5

"I'm a reporter for the *Weequahic High News.* I came to interview Mr. Sinatra."   6

"Who says?"   7

"I wrote him a letter last month," I lied.   8

"Wait here," he said, and closed the door.   9

Moments later, he came back. "He's in between shows. He says make it snappy."   10

I had thought things out to here, never expecting to get in. Now what? The man brought me to Frankie's dressing room. Frankie was sitting at a small table. He grinned when he saw me and suddenly it occurred to me, Frankie, the Voice, the Crooner, was grinning at me! I stood rooted to the spot, expecting to faint dead away like the shrieking, swooning girls outside who were carted off by the hundreds by the police. I waited to feel light-headed, for my knees to grow weak, but nothing happened.   11

Frankie pointed to a chair opposite him. I sat. He peeled the paper from a stick of Juicy Fruit—very slowly it seemed—crumpling the wrapping and compressing it between his thumb and index finger into a tiny ball the size of a pebble. He tossed it overhand at the wastebasket across the room.   12

"Missed," he said, as it hit the side and fell on the floor.   13

I wrote this in my notebook.   14

Looking directly into my eyes, he folded the gum in half then in half again and placed it on his tongue. I glimpsed the inside of his mouth lined with long almost-colored teeth that rested against the pink wetness of his cheeks. Past the stick of gum that lay upon his tongue like a tiny jelly roll I saw his uvula, pink and tremulous, whose flutter was, in a   15 measure, responsible for his gift of song. I was mesmerized. Like one of those squealing, moronic sheep that my father so despised, I stared into the theater of his mouth at this small pendant of flesh, waiting for inspiration. Then the curtains of his lips closed and he grinned and cracked his gum.

"You got three questions." 16

I tried to think of something to say, but my mind was blank. I saw 17 a *Herald Tribune* lying on the table next to him. "Congress declares that The Lone Ranger and Frank Sinatra are the prime instigators of juvenile delinquency in America," it read.

I took a deep breath. "Is it true you were the ringleader of a gang 18 and your nickname was 'Angles'?"

Caught in mid-chew, his mouth remained open for a moment. Then 19 it closed.

"That was a long time ago," he said. 20

I wrote this in my notebook. 21

"Is it true you were classified 4-F because of a punctured eardrum?" 22

He leaned his elbows on the table. His face was inches from mine. 23 His baby blues twinkled at me. I could smell the Juicy Fruit on his breath.

"I would love to be over there defending my country but someone 24 has to stay home and mind the henhouse." He took his gum from his mouth, parked it under the table and leaned forward. "You got one more question." My hand under the table worked his gum loose. Anyone could get an autograph, but Frankie's gum!

I said, "Is it true you gave Ava Gardner a $10,000 emerald necklace 25 while you were married to Nancy Barbato?"

"The only present I ever gave Ava was a six-pack of Coke." 26

I wrote this in my notebook. 27

When he wasn't looking, I put his gum in my mouth. It tasted 28 chewed out, unsugary. In the hallway as I was leaving, the man minding the door looked sidewise at me when I spit it into the trash.

XXXXXXXXXXXXXXXXXXXXX **FOR DISCUSSION** XXXXXXXXXXXXXXXXXXXXX

1. As the CLIMACTIC incident in a NARRATIVE about meeting "Frankie, the Voice, the Crooner" (11), how effective is Kelly Simon's theft of the chewed gum (21)?

2. Simon spits out Sinatra's gum because "it tasted chewed out" (28). Why do you think she put it in her mouth in the first place?

3. In paragraph 28, "the man minding the door" gives young Simon a "sidewise" look. Might he, in any sense, be considered a stand-in for the reader? How appropriate do you find his response to Simon's actions?

4. Simon lied about having written Sinatra in advance (8). Do you think she actually took his gum and put it in her mouth or that she interviewed him at all? Could these just be more lies? How does she establish her reliability as a narrator (if she does)?

5. How much difference would it make to the "truth" of her story if Simon had not really chewed Sinatra's gum but only said she did to make a good tale? If she had not actually interviewed him? Please explain.

XXXXXXXXXXXXXX **STRATEGIES AND STRUCTURES** XXXXXXXXXXXXXX

1. Why do you think Simon begins her NARRATIVE about meeting Frank Sinatra with a DESCRIPTION of her "Sicilian" father and his opinions about "drooling, moronic autograph-hunting" girls (1–3)? How does this beginning affect the way we read the essay?

2. At times Simon refers to teenage girls who faint at the sight of their idol. How does she distance herself from them? Under what circumstances does she almost succumb to the singer's mesmerizing influence? Give EXAMPLES from the text.

3. Why do you think Simon tells us that Sinatra's mouth closes "in mid-chew" (19)? What kinds of questions does she ask him?

4. If young Simon is not really interested in Sinatra as a matinee idol, why does she pretend to be? Whom *is* she trying to impress by getting in to see him?

5. As you follow the surface events of Simon's narrative, do you have the sense that more is going on here than at first meets the eye (or mouth)? How does the remarkable physical description in paragraph 15 go beyond the ingenious-teenage-girl-reporter story that Simon is telling?

xxxxxxxxxxxxx **WORDS AND FIGURES OF SPEECH** xxxxxxxxxxxxx

1. Simon interviews Sinatra backstage at the Paramount in New York City. In paragraph 15, she compares his mouth to a theater. Entering the Paramount by subterfuge through the back door, she is invading Sinatra's privacy. What else does the parallel suggest that, in a figurative sense at least, she might also be invading?

2. Explain the METAPHOR that Simon uses to COMPARE Sinatra's lips to curtains (15). What is the reporter supposed to do to these "curtains?"

3. Though Franz Mesmer (1734–1815) did not actually practice hypnotism, it is often associated with his notions of animal magnetism. What are the implications of Simon saying that she was "mesmerized" when she peered into Sinatra's mouth (15)?

4. Simon twice refers to Sinatra's swooning fans as "sheep." Does she have any reason to feel "sheepish" as she says, repeatedly, "I wrote this in my notebook" (14, 21, 27)? Sheepish in what sense?

xxxxxxxxxxxxxxxxxxxxxxx **FOR WRITING** xxxxxxxxxxxxxxxxxxxxxxx

1. In your opinion, who would be the equivalent today of a Sinatra in his prime? Suppose you were granted an interview with that person (or persons) but were given only three questions to ask. What would they be? What answers do you think you would get? Compile your imaginary interview in question-and-answer form: YOU: "Good afternoon, Bono. Thanks for agreeing to speak to me." BONO: "You got three questions."

2. Conduct an interview with someone—a public official, musician, writer, journalist, teacher, family member, or local (or national) personality. Unlike young Simon, you will probably want to prepare at least some of your questions in advance. Take careful notes during the interview, or, better still, if the interviewee agrees, use a tape recorder. Instead of simply compiling your notes and transcripts in question-and-answer form, however, write a personal NARRATIVE about the whole experience of conducting the interview. Be sure to characterize the interviewee, to describe where and how the interview took place, and to reflect on what you learned about your subject.

CHAPTER THREE

EXAMPLE

XXXXXXXXXXXXXXXXXXXXXXXXXXXXXXXXXXXXXXXXXXXXXXXXXXXXXXXXXXXXXXXXX

EXAMPLES* are used in all kinds of writing. They help to make general statements more specific and ABSTRACT ideas more CONCRETE. In their *Nuclear Waste Primer*, for example, the League of Women Voters makes the following statement about our exposure to nuclear radiation:

> Most people have received only small amounts of radiation from nuclear weapons production and testing. Some activities, occupations, and geographic areas, however, expose a person to greater-than-average radiation. For example, a person living at an altitude of 5,000 feet in Denver, Colorado, receives nearly twice as much cosmic radiation from outer space as a person living at sea level in Washington, D.C.

By using the specific examples of Denver and Washington, the League of Women Voters is narrowing down what it means by the general term "geographic areas." The other general terms in the league's statement about increased exposure to radiation are "activities" and "occupations." The first of these might be narrowed down by citing as examples the use of cell phones and microwave ovens; the second, by citing X-ray technicians and atomic scientists. Narrowing down like this—by substituting a specific term for a more general one—is what it means, logically, to specify.

All specific examples are members of a general group ("areas," "activities," "occupations") that are taken out to represent the whole. (The prefix *ex-* in the word *example*, you may remember, means "from" or "out of.") When the whole to be exemplified is an abstract idea

---

*Words printed in SMALL CAPITALS are defined in the Glossary.

or concept, the examples taken out are said to be concrete rather than specific.

The abstract concept behind the League of Women Voters' statement about radiation is "risk," which the league measures as "a combination of the chance that exposure will occur and the consequences or harm that could result." No discussion of important issues, especially in science and technology, can get far without abstract ideas like these. But two things are likely to happen—speaking of risk—if the authors of such a statement do not soon supply us with concrete examples: we are not going to understand what they mean, and we are likely to fall asleep before we do.

Good examples clarify by making general statements more specific and abstract statements more concrete. They also vivify—in the sense of making writing more intense and alive in the reader's mind. The League of Women Voters is not actually suggesting that the inhabitants of Denver leave their homes, come down from the mountains, and migrate to Washington and the sea. Since cosmic rays account for only a fraction of the total radiation to which the U.S. population is exposed, "the harm that could result" from living in Denver, as with the use of cell phones and microwave ovens, is probably not very great. Apparently, the Denver example is intended mainly to get the reader's attention.

The same could be said of this (potentially) striking example from "Math Can Resolve Toilet-Seat Feuds" by Paul Marantz, an epidemiologist and statistician who claims to have "heard once too often that men should be putting the seat down whenever we left the bathroom":

> There are very few things in life that are absolutes, but this one is clear: Leaving the seat down is patently unfair to men; leaving the seat where it is when you're done still favors women, but it's at least fairer to the unfair sex.

Whether a particular example is specific or concrete depends upon what it exemplifies. As an example of items in the plumbing department, a toilet seat would be highly specific. In an essay on probabilities like this one, it would be coldly concrete. Interesting examples, whether concrete or specific, have yet another standard to meet, however: they must be truly *representative* of the group or idea they purport to exemplify. What about Marantz's toilet seat?

Like the League of Women Voters, Marantz has a serious point to make. As an epidemiologist specializing in population-based medicine, he is interested in such issues of public health (to give a few examples) as "how much salt people should eat, what age women should start getting mammograms, or whether we should ban cellphones." Whether the toilet seat should be left up or down would not appear to be in the same CLASS as these complex issues and so, at first glance, would seem a poor choice of an example, however concrete, to represent the whole class.

We'll come back to Marantz's attention-grabbing toilet-seat example in a moment. But first let's look at one that clearly *is* representative of the class it exemplifies. In "The Price of Power" (Chapter 9), Kori Quintana writes about a different population from the one represented by the League of Women Voters:

> Apparently, the atmospheric bomb tests of the 1950s over Nevada were performed only when winds were blowing away from Las Vegas toward Utah. Subsequent studies of residents of towns with high nuclear fallout showed that various illnesses, especially leukemia, had stricken people who had no family history of them.

Two overlapping groups are represented here: residents of towns in Utah with a high incidence of nuclear fallout in the 1950s and Utah families stricken mysteriously with such illnesses as leukemia.

Quintana's mother and grandmother were both residents of Utah in the fifties, when nuclear weapons were being tested, and they both lived downwind of the Nevada test site. Thus both of them would make good, representative examples of the first group because they possess all the features that define that group. Since they have also been diagnosed with mysterious illnesses—her mother with allergies and thyroid problems, her grandmother with bone cancer—the two women would also qualify as representatives of the second group. Again they possess all of the distinguishing characteristics of the group: this is what "representative" means.

Quintana herself was diagnosed at age seventeen with Lupus, a disease of the autoimmune system. But she is not as good a representative of the genetically damaged group because, by the time her generation came along, her family had developed a "history" of illnesses with unknown causes. And while Quintana was born and raised in Utah, she is not as good a representative of the nuclear-radiated group as either her mother and grandmother, since she was born after the 1950s. (Although Quintana admits that any link between the two groups may be "purely coincidental," she believes that the radiation *caused* the genetic damage. CAUSE AND EFFECT arguments like this one are discussed in Chapter 8.)

Compared with the suffering of Quintana and her family, the great toilet-seat debate may seem trivial. And even Marantz, whose "solution" is to leave the seat as you used it, admits the whole thing is "a little silly." (Left as used, the more the seat is used by both men and women, the closer, Marantz calculates, it will approach being in the right place for either sex 50 percent of the time.) The placement of a toilet seat, a clean one anyway, would not seem to be a representative example of a serious public health issue even when put forth by a professor of preventive medicine. So why does Marantz use it?

Marantz feels that the great toilet-seat debate is representative "of a wider issue: the resistance of passionate argument to rational thought." Marantz's statistical solution to the up-versus-down question is thus intended as an example of how scientists approach problems in general. "Not all problems are amenable to such clear, straightforward solutions," he says. "But most of the time, a little unbiased reflection can . . . help decisions be made according to their actual probabilities and consequences."

Marantz's toilet seat is not only a concrete example that represents an abstract idea in an amusing way; it is also a convenient organizing device for his entire essay. (Which is probably the main reason he chose it.) Marantz begins by asserting that the fiercest battles of "the gender wars" are not being fought in the bedroom, but in the bathroom. Then, having introduced the comic toilet-seat question, he slowly, over the next dozen paragraphs, redefines the problem as a serious contest between "passionate argument" and "rational thought." The scientist's solution to the problem is "scientific scrutiny" of even the most "hotly contested" of personal issues. In a concluding paragraph that is still, shall we say, firmly seated by his single unifying example, Marantz raises a now merely rhetorical question. "How can we hope to make rational decisions about . . . issues that really matter," he asks, "if we can't even speak clearly about toilet seats?"

Examples clarify and vivify; they also unify. As one further example of how examples help to organize our writing—whether on the level of the sentence, the paragraph, or an entire essay—consider the lurid tale of J. P. Morgan's nose. In her introduction to *Morgan, American Financier* (1999), the prize-winning biographer Jean Strouse discusses the difficulties she faced in writing a life of the banker who almost single-handedly ran the American economy a hundred years ago. First, there was the sheer bulk of biographical material to be pulled together somehow. "The Pierpont Morgan Library in New York," writes Strouse, "had vaults of uncatalogued biographical documents, including Morgan's childhood diaries and schoolbooks, his adult letters and cables, volumes of business correspondence, hundreds of photographs, and extensive files on his purchases of art." Besides the documentary evidence, there were also countless stories and legends that had grown up around the great man—or "vile capitalist," depending on which stories the biographer took to be truly representative of the man behind them.

Strouse did not solve the problem of organizing all this material by focusing on Morgan's unusual nose; but she did use it effectively to introduce the scope of the problem to her readers:

> Even Morgan's personal appearance gave rise to legend. He had a skin disease called rhinophyma that in his fifties turned his nose into a hideous purple bulb. One day the wife of his partner Dwight Morrow reportedly invited him to tea. She wanted her daughter Anne to meet the great man, and for weeks coached the girl about what would happen. Anne would come into the room and say good afternoon; she would not stare at Mr. Morgan's nose, she would not say anything about his nose, and she would leave.

The appointed day came, as Strouse tells the story, and the Morrows' young daughter, Anne, played her part flawlessly. Mrs. Morrow herself, however, had more difficulty:

> Mrs. Morrow and Mr. Morgan sat on a sofa by the tea tray. Anne came in, said hello, did not look at Morgan's nose, did not say anything about his nose, and left the room. Sighing in relief, Mrs. Morrow asked, "Mr. Morgan, do you take one lump or two in your nose?"

The usefulness of this story as an example of how examples can be used to organize and focus our writing is only enhanced by the fact that it never happened.

When she grew up, Anne Morrow went on to become the writer Anne Morrow Lindbergh, wife of aviator Charles Lindbergh, who made the first solo transatlantic flight. "This ridiculous story has not a grain of truth in it," Mrs. Lindbergh told Morgan's biographer many years later; but "it is so funny I am sure it will continue."

Brief NARRATIVES, or anecdotes, such as the story of Mrs. Morrow and J. P. Morgan's nose, often make good, unifying examples because they link generalities or abstractions—populations at risk from nuclear radiation, basic issues of public health, principles of biography—to specific people and concrete events. By citing just this one story among the many inspired by Morgan's appearance and personality, Strouse accomplishes several things at a stroke: she paints a clear picture of how his contemporaries regarded the man whose life story she is introducing; she shows how difficult it was to see her controversial subject through the legends that enshrouded him; and she finds a focal point for organizing the introduction to her entire book. Evidently, Strouse has a good nose for examples.

Examples—they're all around us, even on our food packages. Consider the statement on the Girl Scout cookie box on the following page that "You'd be surprised what a Girl Scout Cookie can build." Such a general statement needs to be backed up with some specifics. The Girl Scouts of America are prepared to meet this RHETORICAL and logical need, as you should always be in your own writing. Thus they give eight particular examples of what a Girl Scout cookie can "build": strong values, strong minds, strong bodies, strong spirit, and so on. Of course, these examples also serve as an ARGUMENT for why you should purchase a box of cookies. For more examples of how cookie revenue benefits the Girl Scouts, go to www.girlscouts.org/about/cookie.html.

CONSIDER FURTHER . . .

1. The eight examples of what Girl Scout Cookies can build are somewhat abstract. How do the icons beside each of the examples help to make them more concrete?

2. Many products use examples on their labels and in their ads. Find one or two with examples you find especially interesting. What general qualities do they exemplify?

You'd be surprised
what a Girl Scout
Cookie can build:

Strong Values

Strong Minds

Strong Bodies

Strong Spirit

Strong Friendships

Strong Skills

Strong Leadership

Strong Community

Thin Mints • Thin
Thin Mints • Thin

THE ONION

ALL SEVEN DEADLY SINS COMMITTED AT CHURCH BAKE SALE

The *Onion* is a SATIRICAL newspaper that originated in Madison, home of the University of Wisconsin. In a typical issue, the paper pokes fun at everything from politics ("Bush Extremely Proud of New Suit") and American lifestyles ("TV Helps Build Valuable Looking Skills") to medicine ("Colonoscopy Offers Non-Fantastic Voyage through Human Body") and religion (which is what this selection is about—sort of). According to the Catholic Church, there are basically two types of sins: "venial" ones that are easily forgiven and "deadly" ones that, well, are not. In the fifth century, Pope Gregory the Great identified what he, and the Church ever since, took to be the seven worst of the worst: pride, envy, wrath, sloth, avarice (or greed), gluttony, and lust. As originally conceived, the seven deadlies are highly abstract concepts. In this tongue-in-cheek news release from a church bake sale in Gadsden, Alabama, the roving *Onion* reporter, who knows sin when he sees it, finds concrete, specific examples of each of them. The down-to-earth acts of sin reported here actually took place. In accordance with *Onion* editorial policy, however, the names of the sinners have been changed to protect the not-so-innocent. Additional examples can be reported to www.theonion.com.

XXXXXXXXXXXXXXXXXXXXXXXXXXXXXXXXXXXXXXXXXXXXXXXXXXXXXXXXXXXXXX

GADSDEN, AL—The seven deadly sins—avarice, sloth, envy, lust, gluttony, pride, and wrath—were all committed Sunday during the twice-annual bake sale at St. Mary's of the Immaculate Conception Church.   1

   In total, 347 individual acts of sin were committed at the bake sale, with nearly every attendee committing at least one of the seven deadly sins as outlined by Gregory the Great in the Fifth Century.   2

♠ 101 ♠

Patti George (far right) commits the sin of envy as she eyes fellow parishioner Mary Hoechst's superior strawberry rhubarb pie.

"My cookies, cakes, and brownies are always the highlight of our church bake sales, and everyone says so," said parishioner Connie Barrett, 49, openly committing the sin of pride. "Sometimes, even I'm amazed by how well my goodies turn out."

Fellow parishioner Betty Wicks agreed.

"Every time I go past Connie's table, I just have to buy something," said the 245-pound Wicks, who commits the sin of gluttony at every St. Mary's bake sale, as well as most Friday nights at Old Country Buffet. "I simply can't help myself—it's all so delicious."

The popularity of Barrett's mouth-watering wares elicited the sin of envy in many of her fellow vendors.

"Connie has this fantastic book of recipes her grandmother gave her, and she won't share them with anyone," church organist Georgia Brandt said. "This year, I made white-chocolate blondies and thought they'd be a big hit. But most people just went straight to Connie's table, got what they wanted, and left. All the while, Connie just stood there with this look of smug satisfaction on her face. It took every ounce of strength in my body to keep from going over there and really telling her off."

While the sins of wrath and avarice were each committed dozens of times at the event, Barrett and longtime bake-sale rival Penny Cox brought them together in full force.

8

"Penny said she wanted to make a bet over whose table would make the most money," said Barrett, exhibiting avarice. "Whoever lost would have to sit in the dunk tank at the St. Mary's Summer Fun Festival. I figured it's for such a good cause, a little wager couldn't hurt. Besides, I always bring the church more money anyway, so I couldn't possibly lose."

9

Moments after agreeing to the wager, Cox became wrathful when Barrett, the bake sale's co-chair, grabbed the best table location under the pretense of having to keep the coffee machine full. Cox attempted to exact revenge by reporting an alleged Barrett misdeed to the church's priest.

10

"I mentioned to Father Mark [O'Connor] that I've seen candles at Connie's house that I wouldn't be surprised one bit if she stole from the church's storage closet," said Cox, who also committed the sin of sloth by forcing her daughter to set up and man her booth while she gossiped with friends. "Perhaps if he investigates this, by this time next year, Connie won't be co-chair of the bake sale and in her place we'll have someone who's willing to rotate the choice table spots."

11

The sin of lust also reared its ugly head at the bake sale, largely due to the presence of Melissa Wyckoff, a shapely 20-year-old redhead whose family recently joined the church. While male attendees ogled Wyckoff, the primary object of lust for females was the personable, boyish Father Mark.

12

Though attendees' feelings of lust for Wyckoff and O'Connor were never acted on, they did not go unnoticed.

13

"There's something not right about that Melissa Wyckoff," said envious and wrathful bake-sale participant Jilly Brandon, after her husband Craig offered Wyckoff one of her Rice Krispie treats to "welcome [her] to the parish." "She might have just moved here from California, but that red dress of hers should get her kicked out of the church."

14

According to St. Mary's treasurer Beth Ellen Coyle, informal

15

church-sponsored events are a notorious breeding ground for the seven deadly sins.

"Bake sales, haunted houses, pancake breakfasts . . . such church events are rife with potential for sin," Coyle said. "This year, we had to eliminate the 'Guess Your Weight' booth from the annual church carnival because the envy and pride had gotten so out of hand. Church events are about glorifying God, not violating His word. If you want to do that, you're no better than that cheap strumpet Melissa Wyckoff."

16

XXXXXXXXXXXXXXXXXXX **For Discussion** XXXXXXXXXXXXXXXXXXX

1. The *Onion* reporter gives bake-sale-specific EXAMPLES for each of the Deadly Sins. What general concept did Pope Gregory intend the deadly sins to exemplify?

2. Statistics is the science of analyzing numerical examples. In all, says the *Onion* reporter, parishioners at the St. Mary's bake sale committed "347 individual acts of sin" (2). Anything suspicious about these stats? How do you suppose they were determined?

3. All of the seven deadly sins are identified in the first paragraph of the *Onion's* spoof. In what order are they explained after that? Which one does the watchful reporter come back to at the end?

4. Which specific deadly sin is the only one unacted upon at the bake sale? Who inspired it?

XXXXXXXXXXXXX **Strategies and Structures** XXXXXXXXXXXXX

1. Pope Gregory might object to the *Onion's* EXAMPLES as being too trivial. How about *his* examples as instances of the broad category "deadly" sins? How CONCRETE and specific are they?

2. SATIRE is writing that makes fun of vice or folly in order to expose and correct it. To the extent that the *Onion* is satirizing the behavior of people at "church-sponsored events," what less-than-truly-deadly "sins" is the paper actually making fun of (15)?

3. A *spoof* is a gentle parody or mildly satirical imitation. What kind of writing or reporting is the *Onion* spoofing here?

4. As a "news" story, this one has elements of NARRATIVE. What are some of them, specifically?

5. As a Catholic priest, "boyish Father Mark" would probably say that all the other deadly sins are examples of pride (12). How might pride be thought of as the overarchingly general "deadly sin"?

XXXXXXXXXXXXX **WORDS AND FIGURES OF SPEECH** XXXXXXXXXXXXX

1. What, exactly, is a "strumpet" (16)?

2. *Deadly* (or *mortal*) sins are to be distinguished from *venial* sins. According to your dictionary, what kind of sins would these be? Please give several EXAMPLES.

3. Give a synonym for each of the following words: "avarice," "sloth," "gluttony," and "wrath" (1).

4. Another word for *pride* is *hubris*. What language does it derive from? What's the distinction between the two?

5. *Hypocrisy* is not one of the seven deadly sins, but how would you DEFINE it? Which of the St. Mary's parishioners might be said to commit *this* sin?

XXXXXXXXXXXXXXXXXXXXXXX **FOR WRITING** XXXXXXXXXXXXXXXXXXXXXXX

1. Imagine a strip mall called the Seven Deadly Sins Shopping Center, where each item on Pope Gregory's list is represented by a store selling ordinary products and services. Draw up a list of store names that would EXEMPLIFY each of the seven deadlies—for example, Big Joe's Eats. You might also compose some signs or other advertising to place in the windows of each shop.

2. Using examples, write an essay entitled "All Seven Deadly Sins Committed at _____." Fill in the blank with any venue you choose—"School Cafeteria," for example, or "College Library." Give at least one example for each offense.

3. According to somebody's critical theory, the characters on Gilligan's Island each represent one of the seven deadly sins. If you've seen enough reruns of the show to have an opinion, write an essay either questioning or supporting this reading.

MALCOLM BROWNE

THE INVISIBLE FLYING CAT

Malcolm Browne (b. 1931) is a science writer for the *New York Times*. He began his journalism career in the U.S. Army, later winning a Pulitzer Prize for his reporting from Vietnam. As a foreign correspondent, he has covered Southeast Asia, South America, and eastern Europe. This essay from the *Times* is about getting "The Feel" for science. Browne illustrates this highly abstract notion by proposing, among other unscientific examples, the possibility "that the world is infested by invisible flying cats." Shooting them down is not cruel to animals, he says, but a matter of intellectual survival.

XXXXXXXXXXXXXXXXXXXXXXXXXXXXXXXXXXXXXXXXXXXXXXXXXXXXXXXXXXXXXXXXXX

The late Paul Gallico, a distinguished sports journalist and writer of 1
short stories, believed in the vital importance of something he called "The Feel." To acquire "The Feel" of one aspect of prizefighting, for instance, Gallico once went into the ring with Jack Dempsey and got knocked flat. As a result, he wrote, "I knew all that there was to know about being hit." The season for valedictory pronouncements is at hand and a few parting thoughts about science come to mind. The main one has to do with Gallico's "Feel."

Getting a kick out of science does not necessarily require the feel of 2
the practicing researcher (although it helps). Because science touches every aspect of human existence from sewer mains to symphonic composition, it offers something for everyone.

Even those with no real interest in its techniques and insights may 3
take comfort from the fact that science can lengthen life, improve health, defend us against enemies and make existence more comfortable.

For others, the outlandish curiosities science turns up—cloned mice, 4
black holes, pigeons psychologically reinforced to play Ping-Pong, and

so on—offer the same class of amusement as circus freak shows. The discovery and identification of dinosaur fossils during the last century touched off a furious race to unearth more of the old monsters, and for a time the scientific investigation of paleontology was shouldered aside by the likes of P. T. Barnum.

But for some lucky people, science is fun for its own sake. For them, watching a good television program about some aspect of science can be at least as absorbing as a Saturday football game or a Shakespeare play. They find deep satisfaction in reading of discoveries about our genetic codes, about the exotic atmospheres of outer planets, about our complex relations with the parasites living within us, and all the other things science examines. 5

But there is an even more satisfying stratum of science to be mined, and it has to do with the feel. A cook who has experimented with a recipe by changing the amount of some ingredient and comparing the result with the original knows something about scientific feel. The gardener who sets up controlled experiments with seed varieties, soil conditions and hybrids encounters the feel. 6

It's hard for most of us to capture the feel of today's frontiers of science. Contemporary experimental science generally requires paraphernalia costing tens of millions of dollars and big teams of researchers. 7

Nevertheless, the personal act of reaffirming a known scientific principle can impart a warm glow in itself. There is a pleasurable feel in retracing Archimedes' steps, as one discovers how to estimate the gold content of a wedding ring with a weighing balance, a glass of water and some thread. Jupiter's moons glitter through ordinary binoculars, and even household chemicals can reveal the heart of nature. 8

There are good books about the feel derived from home experiments, one of the best of which is *The Flying Circus of Physics*, by Jearl Walker. 9

But many of the world's greatest scientists have foregone laboratory research completely, relying instead on what Einstein called "thought experiments." And anyone can profit from thought experiments. 10

In simplest terms, a thought experiment examines the logical consequences of some hypothetical action or assumption, comparing them 11 with observed reality. A thought experiment comparing the timekeeping of a clock hurtling through space with an identical clock resting on Earth helped lead Einstein to his special theory of relativity.

The reasoning techniques of thought experiments are not necessarily difficult. To test the statement that the world is infested by invisible flying cats which invariably avoid human beings, we would consider the consequences of such a situation. It would seem, for instance, that invisible flying cats would have such advantages as predators that they must quickly bring about the extinction of sparrows. But since we continue to see lots of sparrows, the invisible flying cat hypothesis becomes improbable.   12

In a world enveloped by the cant of the propagandist—commercial, political, ideological and religious—the scientific feel for shooting down invisible flying cats becomes an attribute of survival.   13

Like Gallico after a blow from Dempsey's glove, the amateur may go down under the impact of an encounter with molecular biology or quantum mechanics. But the mind needs to jump in the ring sometimes, even against the most impenetrable ideas of science. The Feel alone makes it worth the bruises.   14

ᗿᗿᗿᗿᗿᗿᗿᗿᗿᗿᗿᗿᗿᗿᗿᗿ **FOR DISCUSSION** ᗿᗿᗿᗿᗿᗿᗿᗿᗿᗿᗿᗿᗿᗿᗿᗿ

1. Malcolm Browne never actually DEFINES "The Feel" (1). How, then, does he explain what it is?

2. What general principle is Browne illustrating with his "invisible flying cat" EXAMPLE?

3. According to Browne, why is it important to learn to "shoot down" invisible flying cats (13)? Give several examples of the threat he is talking about.

4. According to Browne, what specific "thought experiment" did Einstein conduct when developing his theory of special relativity (11)? What other example of a "thought experiment" does Browne give (12)?

ᗿᗿᗿᗿᗿᗿᗿᗿᗿᗿᗿᗿᗿ **STRATEGIES AND STRUCTURES** ᗿᗿᗿᗿᗿᗿᗿᗿᗿᗿᗿᗿᗿ

1. What is Browne illustrating with the EXAMPLE of Paul Gallico and Jack Dempsey in paragraph 1? How does he use this example again in his essay?

2. What other examples of acquiring "The Feel" does Browne cite?

3. Science, says Browne, turns up "outlandish curiosities" (4). What three specific examples does he give? What larger general principle do these examples illustrate? What other examples can you find in this essay?

4. Besides ARGUING that "the scientific feel" helps us to fight faulty reasoning, Browne is also arguing that "science is fun for its own sake" (5, 13). What examples does he give to support this conclusion?

XXXXXXXXXXXXXX **WORDS AND FIGURES OF SPEECH** XXXXXXXXXXXX

1. Look up *valediction* in a dictionary. When would be "the season for valedictory pronouncements" (1)?

2. Define "cant" (13). What EXAMPLES does Browne cite?

3. Give several synonyms for "The Feel" (1).

4. The basic meaning of *hypothetical* is "contrary to fact" (11). What do Browne and his fellow scientists mean by the term?

5. The human mind doesn't literally "jump in the ring" with a tough idea (14). What does Browne mean by this METAPHOR?

XXXXXXXXXXXXXXXXXXXXX **FOR WRITING** XXXXXXXXXXXXXXXXXXXXXX

1. Write a paragraph explaining how you would disprove the HYPOTHESIS that the world is infested with invisible flying cats. Give some EXAMPLES other than the presence of sparrows.

2. Compose an essay illustrating the idea that science can be fun (or, if you prefer, that science can be duller than shooting down nonexistent flying cats). Give specific examples of developments, activities, and / or experiments that have influenced your opinion. For inspiration, you might consult the book Browne mentions—Jearl Walker's *The Flying Circus of Physics*. If you cite any words or ideas from this or another source, be sure to provide appropriate documentation.

RICHARD LEDERER

ENGLISH IS A CRAZY LANGUAGE

Richard Lederer (b. 1938) taught for many years at St. Paul's, a boarding school in New Hampshire. He retired in 1989 to carry on his "mission as a user-friendly English teacher" by writing extensively and humorously about the peculiarities of the English language. Lederer is the author of *Anguished English* (1987) and *Adventures of a Verbivore* (1994). This essay, made up of one rapid-fire example after another, is the opening chapter of his best-selling *Crazy English* (1989).

XXXXXXXXXXXXXXXXXXXXXXXXXXXXXXXXXXXXXXXXXXXXXXXXXXXXXXXXXXXXXXX

English is the most widely spoken language in the history of our planet, used in some way by at least one out of every seven human beings around the globe. Half of the world's books are written in English, and the majority of international telephone calls are made in English. English is the language of over sixty percent of the world's radio programs, many of them beamed, ironically, by the Russians, who know that to win friends and influence nations, they're best off using English. More than seventy percent of international mail is written and addressed in English, and eighty percent of all computer text is stored in English. English has acquired the largest vocabulary of all the world's languages, perhaps as many as two million words, and has generated one of the noblest bodies of literature in the annals of the human race.

Nonetheless, it is now time to face the fact that English is a crazy language.

In the crazy English language, the blackbird hen is brown, blackboards can be blue or green, and blackberries are green and then red before they are ripe. Even if blackberries were really black and blueberries really blue, what are strawberries, cranberries, elderberries, huckleberries, raspberries, boysenberries, mulberries, and gooseberries supposed to look like?

To add to the insanity, there is no butter in buttermilk, no egg in   4
eggplant, no grape in grapefruit, neither worms nor wood in wormwood,
neither pine nor apple in pineapple, neither peas nor nuts in peanuts,
and no ham in a hamburger. (In fact, if somebody invented a sandwich
consisting of a ham patty in a bun, we would have a hard time finding
a name for it.) To make matters worse, English muffins weren't invented
in England, french fries in France, or danish pastries in Denmark. And
we discover even more culinary madness in the revelations that sweetmeat
is candy, while sweetbread, which isn't sweet, is made from meat.

In this unreliable English tongue, greyhounds aren't always grey (or   5
gray); panda bears and koala bears aren't bears (they're marsupials); a
woodchuck is a groundhog, which is not a hog; a horned toad is a lizard;
glowworms are fireflies, but fireflies are not flies (they're beetles); ladybugs and lightning bugs are also beetles (and to propagate, a significant
proportion of ladybugs must be male); a guinea pig is neither a pig nor
from Guinea (it's a South American rodent); and a titmouse is neither
mammal nor mammaried.

Language is like the air we breathe. It's invisible, inescapable, indis-   6
pensable, and we take it for granted. But when we take the time, step
back, and listen to the sounds that escape from the holes in people's faces
and explore the paradoxes and vagaries of English, we find that hot dogs
can be cold, darkrooms can be lit, homework can be done in school,
nightmares can take place in broad daylight, while morning sickness and
daydreaming can take place at night, tomboys are girls, midwives can be
men, hours—especially happy hours and rush hours—can last longer
than sixty minutes, quicksand works *very* slowly, boxing rings are square,
silverware can be made of plastic and tablecloths of paper, most telephones are dialed by being punched (or pushed?), and most bathrooms
don't have any baths in them. In fact, a dog can go to the bathroom
under a tree—no bath, no room; it's still going to the bathroom. And
doesn't it seem at least a little bizarre that we go to the bathroom in order
to go to the bathroom?

Why is it that a woman can man a station but a man can't woman   7
one, that a man can father a movement but a woman can't mother one,
and that a king rules a kingdom but a queen doesn't rule a queendom?

How did all those Renaissance men reproduce when there don't seem to have been any Renaissance women?

A writer is someone who writes, and a stinger is something that stings. But fingers don't fing, grocers don't groce, hammers don't ham, and humdingers don't humding. If the plural of *tooth* is *teeth*, shouldn't the plural of *booth* be *beeth*? One goose, two geese—so one moose, two meese? One index, two indices—one Kleenex, two Kleenices? If people ring a bell today and rang a bell yesterday, why don't we say that they flang a ball? If they wrote a letter, perhaps they also bote their tongue. If the teacher taught, why isn't it also true that the preacher praught? Why is it that the sun shone yesterday while I shined my shoes, that I treaded water and then trod on soil, and that I flew out to see a World Series game in which my favorite player flied out? 8

If we conceive a conception and receive at a reception, why don't we grieve a greption and believe a beleption? If a horsehair mat is made from the hair of horses and a camel's hair brush from the hair of camels, from what is a mohair coat made? If a vegetarian eats vegetables, what does a humanitarian eat? If a firefighter fights fire, what does a freedom fighter fight? If a weightlifter lifts weights, what does a shoplifter lift? If *pro* and *con* are opposites, is congress the opposite of progress? 9

Sometimes you have to believe that all English speakers should be committed to an asylum for the verbally insane. In what other language do people drive in a parkway and park in a driveway? In what other language do people recite at a play and play at a recital? In what other language do privates eat in the general mess and generals eat in the private mess? In what other language do men get hernias and women get hysterectomies? In what other language do people ship by truck and send cargo by ship? In what other language can your nose run and your feet smell? 10

How can a slim chance and a fat chance be the same, "what's going on?" and "what's coming off?" be the same, and a bad licking and a good licking be the same, while a wise man and a wise guy are opposites? How can sharp speech and blunt speech be the same and *quite a lot* and *quite a few* the same, while *overlook* and *oversee* are opposites? How can the weather be hot as hell one day and cold as hell the next? 11

If *button* and *unbutton* and *tie* and *untie* are opposites, why are *loosen*   12
and *unloosen* and *ravel* and *unravel* the same? If *bad* is the opposite of
good, *hard* the opposite of *soft,* and *up* the opposite of *down,* why are
badly and *goodly, hardly* and *softly,* and *upright* and *downright* not opposing pairs? If harmless actions are the opposite of harmful actions, why
are shameless and shameful behavior the same and pricey objects less
expensive than priceless ones? If appropriate and inappropriate remarks
and passable and impassable mountain trails are opposites, why are flammable and inflammable materials, heritable and inheritable property, and
passive and impassive people the same and valuable objects less treasured
than invaluable ones? If *uplift* is the same as *lift up,* why are *upset*
and *set up* opposite in meaning? Why are *pertinent* and *impertinent, canny*
and *uncanny,* and *famous* and *infamous* neither opposites nor the same?
How can *raise* and *raze* and *reckless* and *wreckless* be opposites when each
pair contains the same sound?

Why is it that when the sun or the moon or the stars are out, they   13
are visible, but when the lights are out, they are invisible, and that when
I wind up my watch, I start it, but when I wind up this essay, I shall
end it?

English is a crazy language.   14

✗✗✗✗✗✗✗✗✗✗✗✗✗✗✗✗✗✗✗✗ **FOR DISCUSSION** ✗✗✗✗✗✗✗✗✗✗✗✗✗✗✗✗✗✗✗✗

1. Most of the time, Richard Lederer is illustrating the "craziness" of English.
But what does he say about its widespread influence? What EXAMPLES does he
give?

2. Do you think English is as crazy as Lederer says it is? Why or why not?
Please give several examples to support your opinion.

3. How seriously do you think Lederer actually intends for us to take the general
proposition of his essay? Why do you think he gives so many crazy examples?

4. Linguists hold that the meanings of words are arbitrary, determined by con-
vention rather than by any innate qualities. What do the examples in Lederer's
essay say about this principle? Refer to specific passages in his essay that support
your position.

5. List several examples of your own of the craziness of the English language.

✗✗✗✗✗✗✗✗✗✗✗✗✗✗ **STRATEGIES AND STRUCTURES** ✗✗✗✗✗✗✗✗✗✗✗✗✗

1. How does the opening paragraph of Lederer's essay color the rest of what he says about the craziness of the English language?

2. Lederer's essay is made up almost entirely of clusters of EXAMPLES. What do the examples in paragraph 3 have in common? Are the examples in paragraph 4 more like those in paragraph 3 or paragraph 5? Please explain.

3. In paragraph 8, Lederer pretends to be upset with irregular verbs and irregular plurals of nouns. Which are examples of which? Make a list of his examples for both categories.

4. Which examples have to do primarily with gender? What connects all the examples in paragraph 12?

5. In paragraph 6, Lederer refers to two related aspects of the English language that all of his examples might be said to illustrate. What are these aspects? Where else in his essay does Lederer actually name the aspects of English he is exemplifying?

6. Lederer gives his essay the form of a logical ARGUMENT. The proposition he intends to prove is stated in paragraph 2. Where does he state it again as a conclusion? Is the argument in between primarily INDUCTIVE (reasoning from specific examples to a general conclusion) or DEDUCTIVE (reasoning from general principles to a more specific conclusion)? Please explain your answer.

✗✗✗✗✗✗✗✗✗✗✗✗ **WORDS AND FIGURES OF SPEECH** ✗✗✗✗✗✗✗✗✗✗✗

1. In American English (speaking of contradictions), a *rant* is a form of vehement speech, a rave; in British English (speaking of redundancies), a *rant* can also mean an outburst of wild merriment. Which meaning or meanings apply to Lederer's essay?

2. *Rant* and *rave* are synonyms for "fly into a rage." But if a book or play gets a *rave* review, people praise it wildly. How is this possible?

3. How does your dictionary DEFINE the word "vagaries" (6)? How is it related to the word *vagabonds*?

4. Lederer "winds up" his essay in paragraph 13. Could he be said, just as accurately, to "wind it down?"

XXXXXXXXXXXXXXXXXXXXXXX **FOR WRITING** XXXXXXXXXXXXXXXXXXXXXXX

1. Write an essay illustrating the craziness of some language other than English that you have studied. For EXAMPLE, one way to say you're welcome in French is "Je vous en prie," which means, literally, "I beg of you."

2. For all its "craziness," Lederer asserts that "English is the most widely spoken language in the history of our planet" (1). Giving lots of examples of who uses it, where, and for what purposes, write an essay in support of (or contesting) this proposition.

NAT HENTOFF

Jazz: Music beyond Time and Nations

Nat Hentoff (b. 1925) is a columnist for the *Village Voice* and a frequent contributor to the *Wall Street Journal* and the *New York Times*. He has written many books on politics, civil liberties, and jazz, as well as numerous novels, biographies, children's books, and liner notes for jazz recordings. In this essay from *America and the World at the End of the Century*, Hentoff gives numerous examples of why jazz is "a common language throughout the world" (4). His examples take the form of anecdotes, or brief narratives, about Dizzy Gillespie, Louis Armstrong, John Coltrane, Charles Mingus, Charlie ("Bird") Parker, and other great jazz players and composers he has known.

✕✕

At Gestapo headquarters in Paris, Charles Delaunay, under suspicion 1
of being a member of the Maquis, was brought in for questioning. Delaunay, an expert on jazz, was the author of the first definitive jazz discography—listings of full personnel on jazz labels.

As the interrogation began, the first thing the German officer said 2
to Delaunay was, "You have the wrong personnel on the 1928 Fletcher Henderson recording." They argued the point for a while, and Delaunay was eventually released after routine questioning. "There are jazz aficionados everywhere," Delaunay, who had a quick sense of irony, told me years later.

In Nazi Germany, jazz was forbidden as a mongrel black-and- 3
Jewish music, but recordings were still played behind closed doors. And in Russia, under the Communists, jazz was declared an enemy of the people, but there too it could not be entirely suppressed. Some of my

liner notes for a John Coltrane recording were surreptitiously distributed to jazz lovers in Moscow as *samizdats*.[1]

What is it that makes this music a common language throughout the world—as it so transcends popular fads that recordings made seventy years ago are played again and again, continually beyond the ordinary boundaries of time?

    4

A vivid sense of the jazz experience is a 1998 New York play, *Side Man*, by Warren Leight. This is a key scene, described by Peter Marks in the *New York Times*: "Three musicians . . . sit around a cassette player listening to the tape of a fervent, wrenching trumpet solo. The jazz man on the tape is dead, but his instrument remains feverishly alive."

    5

The essential attraction of jazz throughout time is its "sound of surprise"—a term invented by the *New Yorker*'s critic Whitney Balliett. Because the music is largely improvised, the listener is often startled by a sound, a phrasing, a turn of rhythm that is so deeply emotional that he or she may shout aloud in pleasure.

    6

I was eleven when I first heard jazz. Walking down a street in Boston, I was stopped by the sound coming out of a public address system attached to a record store. I was so exhilarated that I yelled in delight— something I had never done before on the proper streets of Boston. The music was Artie Shaw's "Nightmare."

    7

I was soon working in a candy store and expanded my jazz horizons by buying recordings of Duke Ellington, Billie Holiday, Lester Young, Bessie Smith and blues singer Peetie Wheatstraw ("the Devil's son-in-law").

    8

A few years later, I came upon the very essence of jazz. It was late on a winter afternoon when I walked past the Savoy Cafe, in a black neighborhood of Boston. The club was closed, but the blues coming from inside stopped me. I looked through the glass in the door and saw, as in a fantasy, several of the legends of jazz. Sitting in a chair that was leaning back against a table was a saxophonist with a huge, swaggering sound. It was Coleman Hawkins, who had invented the jazz tenor saxophone. The pianist was Count Basie, whose bands were the very definition of

    9

[1]Banned literature published illegally and distributed secretly in the former Soviet Union.

swinging, and he had created a precisely economical way of improvising. Each of his notes was exactly placed to give the big tenor a further lift. And on the drums was Jo Jones, whom his colleagues in the Basie band described as "the man who plays like the wind." Uncommonly subtle, his eyes darting from player to player, Jo's brushes were dancing on the drumhead, punctuated by an occasionally deep sigh from a cymbal.

Every night, in many clubs in many countries throughout the world, this ceaselessly intriguing interplay between improvising musicians creates new patterns of melody, harmony and rhythm for an audience that knows no generational divide. Youngsters are drawn to the depth of feeling that can't be found in popular music and older listeners relive their own musical adventures while learning more about the further dimensions of this music. 10

There is also the spirit of the jazz musician that attracts lay enthusiasts. Since the music is largely improvised and risk-taking, those qualities also usually define jazz musicians off the stand. They tend to be self-confident, irreverent and unflinchingly independent. 11

An incandescent illustration of that spirit was Dizzy Gillespie. On one of his trips for the U.S. State Department, he had been scheduled to play at a lawn party in Ankara, arranged by the American ambassador to Turkey. The climax was to be a Jam session with Dizzy in charge. 12

"While I was signing autographs," Dizzy recalled, "I happened to look at the fence surrounding the grounds. A lot of street kids were pressed against the fence. They wanted to come in and hear the music. One of them actually climbed over the fence and a guard threw him right back over it. 13

"I asked what was going on. 'Why did they do that?' And some official said, 'This party is for select people—local dignitaries and important Americans in the city.' I said, 'Select people! We're not over here for no select people! We're over here to show these people that Americans are all kinds of people!' I had a girl in the band, and almost as many whites as blacks. We had a good mix. 14

"The ambassador comes over and asks, 'Are you going to play?' I say, 'No! I saw that guard throw a little kid over the fence. Those are the people we're trying to get close to—the people outside the fence.' So 15 the ambassador said, 'Let them in, let them all in!' " That is the spirit of jazz.

Dizzy Gillespie was an original, and so are—and have been—many 16 other conjugators of the forms and feelings of the music. Part of the originality of the music consists of how players have expanded the capacities of their instruments—from the gypsy guitarist Django Reinhardt to the first and never entirely surpassed jazz soloist, Louis Armstrong.

In the early 1930s, a delegation of the leading brass players in the 17 Boston Symphony Orchestra made a journey to Louis Armstrong's dressing room in a theater in the city. They had heard of his almost unbelievable technique and range and asked him to play a passage they had heard in his act. Armstrong picked up his horn and obliged, performing the requested passage and then improvising a dazzling stream of variations. Shaking their heads, these "legitimate" trumpet players left the room, one of them saying, "I watched his fingers and I still don't know how he does it. I also don't know how it is that, playing there all by himself, he sounded as if a whole orchestra was behind him. I never heard a musician like this, and I thought he was just a colored entertainer."

The older players, though very serious about their musicianship and 18 the quality of their instruments, were also entertainers. In the years before there was a reasonably sizable number of jazz admirers, the players worked before all kinds of audiences, and so they had to entertain them between improvisations.

In time, younger musicians, playing by then before musically 19 sophisticated listeners, declined to entertain in the traditional sense. And their music began to reflect their interests outside of music. Max Roach and Julian "Cannonball" Adderley, for instance, composed pieces dealing with the Civil Rights Movement. Duke Ellington, of course, had been writing about black music and culture long before the Civil Rights Movement had begun ("Black Beauty," "Black, Brown and Beige," et al.).

Revealingly, in one of the more dramatic events in jazz history, 20 Louis Armstrong also inserted himself into the struggle for black equality. Before then he hadn't done this explicitly in his music, and there were younger musicians who, accordingly, called him an "Uncle Tom." Armstrong proved them decidedly wrong when, in the 1950s, Governor

Orville Faubus of Arkansas defied the orders of the Supreme Court of the United States to integrate the public schools of Little Rock. When then President Dwight Eisenhower delayed and delayed intervening, Armstrong declared: "The way they are treating my people in the South, the government can go to hell! The president has no guts."

In 1965, when Martin Luther King's march on Selma, Alabama, was brutally attacked by local and state police, Armstrong told the nation: "They would beat Jesus if he was black and marched."   21

At one point Armstrong's manager, the powerful and forceful Joe Glaser, sent an emissary to find Armstrong on the road and order him to stop saying such controversial things, for they would cause him to lose bookings. Louis Armstrong threw Glaser's emissary out of his dressing room. That, too, is the spirit of jazz!   22

It is an unavoidably personal music. John Coltrane, who created new ways of hearing as well as playing jazz, told me, "The music is the whole question of life itself." Other players have also emphasized that what you live—and how you live—becomes an integral part of what you play each night. Jazz, then, is a continual autobiography, or, rather, a continuum of intersecting autobiographies—one's own and those of the musicians with whom one plays. As the prodigious bassist and bold composer Charles Mingus told me: "I'm trying to play the truth of what I am. The reason it's difficult is because I'm changing all the time."   23

Then there was Charlie "Bird" Parker, who changed music fundamentally, as Louis Armstrong had before him. Describing Parker, as he evolved into a dominant musician of his time, bassist Gene Ramey was also describing the acute sensitivity of other jazz players to the sounds all around them: "Everything had a musical significance for Bird—the swish of a car speeding down a highway, the hum of the wind as it goes through the leaves. If he heard a dog bark, he would say the dog was speaking. . . . And maybe some girl would walk past on the dance floor while he was playing, and something she might do, or an expression on her face, would give him an idea for something to play on his solo."   24

And Duke Ellington would tell me how, at a dance, a sigh of pleasure from a dancer would float back to the bandstand and enter into the music. One of his sidemen told me how, after a long, wearying bus trip,   25 the musicians would be regenerated by the dancers: "You're giving them something to move by, but you're giving them something back. You can tell whether you're really cooking by how they move on the floor, and when they groove, they make you groove more."

It's harder for these physical and emotional messages to be sent and received in a concert hall, where more and more jazz is played. But the interactions between musicians and listeners take place there too, because jazz is a music in which both the player and the audience are continually in conversation. 26

I once asked the flawless pianist Hank Jones whether he agreed with Dizzy Gillespie that music is so vast that no one can get more than a small piece of it. "That's exactly right," Jones said. "That's why every night, I begin again." 27

Duke Ellington resisted the very idea of ending. Trumpeter Clark Terry said of him, "He wants life and music to be always in a state of becoming. He doesn't even like to write definitive endings to a piece. He always likes to make the end of a song sound as if it's still going somewhere." 28

And that's the story of jazz. 29

ⵉⵉⵉⵉⵉⵉⵉⵉⵉⵉⵉⵉⵉⵉⵉⵉⵉⵉⵉⵉⵉ **FOR DISCUSSION** ⵉⵉⵉⵉⵉⵉⵉⵉⵉⵉⵉⵉⵉⵉⵉⵉⵉⵉⵉⵉⵉ

1. What aspect of jazz does Nat Hentoff EXEMPLIFY when he tells about his first reaction to it?

2. What aspect of jazz is Hentoff illustrating in paragraph 9 with the EXAMPLE of hearing a jam session with Coleman Hawkins, Count Basie, and Jo Jones?

3. The story of Dizzy Gillespie and the ambassador in paragraphs 12 through 16, says Hentoff, is an "incandescent illustration" (12). Of what?

4. Hentoff is quick to ARGUE that early jazz players were not just entertainers, but great musicians. Why might he insist on this point? What examples does he use to make it?

ⵉⵉⵉⵉⵉⵉⵉⵉⵉⵉⵉⵉⵉⵉⵉ **STRATEGIES AND STRUCTURES** ⵉⵉⵉⵉⵉⵉⵉⵉⵉⵉⵉⵉⵉ

1. Why do you think Hentoff starts his essay with the EXAMPLE of the Nazi officer interrogating a jazz expert instead of the example of his own first exposure to jazz on the streets of Boston?

2. Hentoff says that jazz is a not only a musical genre beyond nations, but "beyond . . . time" (4). What examples does he use to substantiate this claim? How well do you think his examples prove his point?

3. If jazz is beyond time and nations, is it also "beyond" race? In which examples does Hentoff address racial issues? What conclusions does he come to?

4. Many of Hentoff's examples are ANECDOTES, little stories about particular jazz musicians. How do these stories contribute to his essay? How successful would the essay be without the stories?

XXXXXXXXXXXXXX WORDS AND FIGURES OF SPEECH XXXXXXXXXXXXX

1. What are the CONNOTATIONS of "mongrel" (3)? Why would the Nazis use such a term?

2. Though Hentoff is recounting the history of jazz, he never explains the history of the word *jazz*. Should he? What difficulties might he face in doing so?

3. "Incandescent" means, literally, "emitting bright light as a result of being heated" (12). How can an illustration be incandescent? Why might a writer use this word in connection with jazz?

4. What is an "aficionado" (2)? What language does the word come from, and how is it pronounced?

5. If someone is "the Devil's son-in-law," to whom is he married (8)?

XXXXXXXXXXXXXXXXXXXXXXX FOR WRITING XXXXXXXXXXXXXXXXXXXXXX

1. Who was Fletcher Henderson (2)? Do a little research on this great band-leader, and write up an ANECDOTE that EXEMPLIFIES one of Henderson's contributions to jazz.

2. Who is your favorite musician? Collect a number of illustrative facts and stories about him or her, and write an essay that explains through EXAMPLES and anecdotes the role of that person as a musician.

JANET WU

HOMEWARD BOUND

Janet Wu (b. 1966), a reporter for Boston television, was twelve years old when she first met her Chinese grandmother. Wu's father had escaped China during the communist revolution at the end of World II, and for the next twenty-five years, because of strained relations between the two countries, Chinese Americans were not allowed to return to their homeland. "Homeward Bound," first published in the *New York Times Magazine* in 1999, is about Wu's visits with an ancestor she did not know she had. In this essay, Wu looks at the vast differences between two cultures through a single, extended example—the ancient practice, now outlawed, of breaking and binding the feet of young, upper-class Chinese girls. These "lotus feet" were a symbol of status and beauty.

XXXXXXXXXXXXXXXXXXXXXXXXXXXXXXXXXXXXXXXXXXXXXXXXXXXXXXXXXXXXXXXXX

My grandmother has bound feet. Cruelly tethered since her birth, they are like bonsai trees, miniature versions of what should have been. She is a relic even in China, where foot binding was first banned more than 80 years ago when the country could no longer afford a population that had to be carried. Her slow, delicate hobble betrays her age and the status she held and lost. 1

My own size 5 feet are huge in comparison. The marks and callouses they bear come from running and jumping, neither of which my grandmother has ever done. The difference between our feet reminds me of the incredible history we hold between us like living bookends. We stand like sentries on either side of a vast gulf. 2

For most of my childhood, I didn't even know she existed. My father was a young man when he left his family's village in northern China, disappearing into the chaos of the Japanese invasion and the Communist revolution that followed. He fled to Taiwan and eventually made his way to America, alone. To me, his second child, it seemed he had no family or his- 3 tory other than his American-born wife and four children. I didn't know that he had been writing years of unanswered letters to China.

I was still a young girl when he finally got a response, and with it the news that his father and six of his seven siblings had died in those years of war and revolution. But the letter also contained an unexpected blessing: somehow his mother had survived. So 30 years after he left home, and in the wake of President Nixon's visit, my father gathered us up and we rushed to China to find her.

4

I saw my grandmother for the very first time when I was 12. She was almost 80, surprisingly alien and shockingly small. I searched her wrinkled face for something familiar, some physical proof that we belonged to each other. She stared at me the same way. Did she feel cheated, I wondered, by the distance, by the time we had not spent together? I did. With too many lost years to reclaim, we had everything and nothing to say. She politely listened as I struggled with scraps of formal Chinese and smiled as I fell back on "Wo bu dong" ("I don't understand you"). And yet we communicated something strange and beautiful. I found it easy to love this person I had barely met.

5

The second time I saw her I was 23, arriving in China on an indulgent post-graduate-school adventure, with a Caucasian boyfriend in tow. My grandmother sat on my hotel bed, shrunken and wise, looking as if she belonged in a museum case. She stroked my asymmetrically cropped hair. I touched her feet, and her face contorted with the memory of her childhood pain. "You are lucky," she said. We both understood that she was thinking of far more than the bindings that long ago made her cry. I wanted to share even the smallest part of her life's journey, but I could not conceive of surviving a dynasty and a revolution, just as she could not imagine my life in a country she had never seen. In our mutual isolation of language and experience, we could only gaze in wonder, mystified that we had come to be sitting together.

6

I last saw her almost five years ago. At 95, she was even smaller, and her frailty frightened me. I was painfully aware that I probably would never see her again, that I would soon lose this person I never really had. So I mentally logged every second we spent together and jockeyed with my siblings for the chance to hold her hand or touch her shoulder. Our departure date loomed like some kind of sentence. And when it came,

7

she broke down, her face bowed into her gnarled hands. I went home, and with resignation awaited the inevitable news that she was gone.

But two months after that trip, it was my father who died. For me, his loss was doubly cruel: his death deprived me of both my foundation and the bridge to my faraway grandmother. For her, it was the second time she had lost him. For the 30 years they were separated, she had feared her son was dead. This time, there was no ambiguity, no hope. When she heard the news, my uncle later wrote us, she wept quietly.

When I hear friends complain about having to visit their nearby relatives, I think of how far away my grandmother is and how untouched our relationship remains by the modern age. My brief handwritten notes are agonizingly slow to reach her. When they do arrive, she cannot read them. I cannot call her. I cannot see, hear or touch her.

But last month my mother called to tell me to brush up on my Chinese. Refusing to let go of our tenuous connection to my father's family, she has decided to take us all back to China in October for my grandmother's 100th birthday. And so every night, I sit at my desk and study, thinking of her tiny doll-like feet, of the miles and differences that separate us, of the moments we'll share when we meet one last time. And I beg her to hold on until I get there.

XXXXXXXXXXXXXXXXXXXXX **FOR DISCUSSION** XXXXXXXXXXXXXXXXXXXXX

1. Janet Wu's feet are calloused from exercise. What does this difference between her feet and her grandmother's show about the differences in their lives?

2. Why does Wu touch her grandmother's feet in paragraph 6? What is her grandmother's response? What has happened to the "vast gulf" between them (2)?

3. What is the CONCRETE EXAMPLE Wu's essay is organized around? How does this example illustrate the differences between her and her grandmother, and their connection as family? Refer to particular passages in her essay to explain your answer.

XXXXXXXXXXXXXX **STRATEGIES AND STRUCTURES** XXXXXXXXXXXXXX

1. Where does Wu mention her grandmother's feet for the last time in her essay? How does it serve as an EXAMPLE of bridging two disparate thoughts?

2. Wu is separated from her grandmother by culture, physical distance, and *time*. Point out several of the many references to time and the passage of time in her essay. How do these references help Wu to organize her essay?

3. Wu's NARRATIVE takes an unexpected turn in paragraph 8. What is it? How does the physical frailty of her grandmother contribute to the IRONY of this turn of events?

4. A big part of the cultural difference that separates Wu and her grandmother is *language*. List some of the examples Wu gives of this separation. Why do you think Wu ends her essay by saying that "every night, I sit at my desk and study" (10)?

5. Wu uses the example of her grandmother's bound feet as the basis of an extended COMPARISON AND CONTRAST (Chapter 6). Besides feet, what is she comparing to what? What specific similarities and differences does she exemplify? What other examples does she use?

XXXXXXXXXXXXX **WORDS AND FIGURES OF SPEECH** XXXXXXXXXXXX

1. Explain the pun(s), or play(s) on words, in Wu's title.

2. Wu COMPARES her grandmother's feet to "bonsai trees" (1). What is a bonsai, and what do the grandmother's feet have in common with one?

3. Wu says her wrinkled, shrunken grandmother looks like she belongs in "a museum case" (6). Why? To what is she comparing her grandmother?

4. If Wu and her grandmother are "living bookends," what do they hold between them (2)? What connection(s) between books and "history" does Wu's use of this METAPHOR imply (2)?

5. When is Wu using her grandmother's bound feet as a METAPHOR, and when are the feet simply serving her as a literal EXAMPLE? Please cite specific passages.

XXXXXXXXXXXXXXXXXXXXXX **FOR WRITING** XXXXXXXXXXXXXXXXXXXXXX

1. In a paragraph or two, give several EXAMPLES of distinctive traits, gestures, or physical features shared by members of your family.

2. Write a personal NARRATIVE about a meeting between you and a relative or family friend that exemplifies both the differences separating you and the ties binding you together. Use lots of examples to illustrate those similarities and differences.

CHAPTER FOUR

CLASSIFICATION AND DIVISION

XXXXXXXXXXXXXXXXXXXXXXXXXXXXXXXXXXXXXXXXXXXXXXXXXXXXXXXXXXXXXX

When we DIVIDE* a group of similar things, we separate them from one another. A physiologist, for EXAMPLE, divides human beings according to body types: mesomorphs (muscular and bony), ectomorphs (skinny), and endomorphs (soft and fleshy). When we CLASSIFY something, we group it with similar things. A zoologist might classify a monkey and a person as primates because both are mammals and have nails and opposable thumbs. Although classification and division can be defined as two different operations, they are often used together.

Classification systems divide things into those that exhibit certain distinguishing features and those that do not. The features should not overlap. Suppose, for example, that we classified all birds according to the following categories: flightless, nocturnal, flat-billed, web-footed. Our system might work well enough for owls (nocturnal), but where would a duck (flat-billed, web-footed) fit? Or a penguin (flightless, web-footed)? A system of classifying birds must have one and only one pigeonhole for pigeons. Our faulty system would put a penguin and an ostrich in the same category since both are flightless, but anyone can see significant differences between the two.

The distinguishing features of any classification system will vary with who is doing the classifying and for what purpose. A teacher divides a group of thirty students according to scholarship: A, B, C, D, and F. A basketball coach might divide the same group of students into for-

---

*Words printed in SMALL CAPITALS are defined in the Glossary.

wards, guards, and centers. The director of a student drama group would have entirely different criteria. All three systems are valid for the purposes they are intended to serve. And classification must serve some purpose, or it becomes an empty game.

Systems of classification and division can help us organize our thoughts about the world around us. They can also help us organize our thoughts, in writing, whether in a single paragraph or a whole essay. For example, you might organize a paragraph by introducing your topic, dividing it into types, and then giving the distinguishing features of each type. Here is a paragraph that follows such a pattern. Its subject is familiar (but still mystifying).

> There are several types of lightning named according to where the discharge takes place. Among them are intracloud lightning, by far the most common type, in which the flash occurs within the thundercloud; air-discharge lightning, in which the flash occurs between the cloud and the surrounding air; and cloud-to-ground lightning, in which the discharge takes place between the cloud and the ground.
>
> RICHARD ORVILLE, "BOLTS FROM THE BLUE"

This short paragraph could be the opening of an essay that goes on to discuss each of the three types of lightning in order, devoting a paragraph or more to each type. Or, having introduced all three, it could focus on a single type of lightning, further dividing it into discharges that are positive and discharges that are negative, positively charged lightning being the more powerful subtype. If the writer's purpose were to ANALYZE weather conditions in general, then intracloud lightning might be the one to take up since it is "by far the most common type."

In this case, however, the author, a meteorologist at Texas A&M University, chooses to develop his essay further by writing several paragraphs on the third type of lightning, "in which the discharge takes place between the cloud and the ground," since this is the most dangerous kind—to property, natural resources such as forests, and people who are not in airplanes. Meteorologists classify storms—especially hurricanes, tornadoes, and thunderstorms—not only to understand them, but also to predict where they are most likely to occur next. "Being able to look into a storm system and see where the most dangerous lightning is occurring," Richard Orville writes, "means you can tell what parts on the ground will be most threatened by the lightning activity." Meteorologists have a still larger purpose than this for classing storms, however.

Classification and division, we have said, must serve some larger purpose if they are to be more than just an exercise. Classifying lightning into one of three categories—each "according to where the discharge takes place"—can help us better understand an important part of the world we live in as well as help us organize our knowledge in writing. But the meteorologist's ultimate reason for classifying and predicting severe weather conditions based on those classification systems is to warn people to seek shelter. And to warn the power companies. Then, says Orville, they can deploy power crews more effectively, even rerouting electricity away from a plant before that plant is hit.

Whenever you turn on a computer, you are using the most fundamental of all classification systems—the simple binary: 0/1, on/off, yes/no, plus/minus, this/that. No matter how sophisticated your computer, it uses the same basic system as does the kid in a candy store who chooses from items displayed in various bins or categories. So do the home pages of most Web sites, including the one pictured here, www.dailycandy.com, which is dedicated to providing "the latest need-to-know information" about fashion and shopping in New York City. Notice how the commodity it's selling—DailyCandy's latest scoop on a wide range of consumer goods and services—is classified into six basic categories (drinks & food, fun, fashion, beauty, arts & culture, service). Within each of DailyCandy's electronic bins, the subscriber is invited to select "bite-size scoops" of information on restaurant openings, new fashion trends, sample sales, and other such events. As with any system of classification, dividing the site's wares into smaller and smaller categories like this makes for easier consumption by the user. In addition, says DailyCandy, each "newsy, concise tidbit of info" in this electronic candy store is "sugar-coated" with illustrations, presumably to make every bit of information as sweet as can be.

CONSIDER FURTHER . . .

1. Classification systems usually serve some larger RHETORICAL purpose than mere pigeonholing. Check out www.dailycandy.com, starting with About Us. Besides providing information, what kind of ARGUMENT do you think DailyCandy makes about shopping in general? How does its classification of urban living as a set of goods and services contribute to this argument?

2. The electronic auction house eBay (www.ebay.com) is essentially a vast classification system of interlocking categories, almost like nesting boxes or Russian dolls. What are some of its categories? How does eBay's virtual system for organizing its goods compare with the classification systems in department, record, book, or other "real" stores?

3. Apart from computers, where else in your ordinary experience do you find classification systems at work? What purposes do they serve?

DAILY
CANDY NYC

HOME | TODAY'S CANDY | SUBSCRIBE | SEND TO A FRIEND | CONTRIBUTE | GENERAL ARCHIVE | MY ARCHIVE

NEW YORK CITY   LOS ANGELES   LONDON

SIGN UP FOR YOUR
FREE DAILY
E-MAIL

TODAY'S CANDY 08.12.02
Step on It

DRINKS & FOOD

BEAUTY

FASHION

ASK DAILY CANDY

FUN

ARTS & CULTURE

SERVICE

HOME | ASK DAILY CANDY | DRINKS & FOOD | FUN | BEAUTY | ARTS & CULTURE | FASHION | SERVICE | WIRELESS
MAKE DAILY CANDY MY HOMEPAGE | CONTACT US | SETTINGS / UNSUBSCRIBE | THE ADVISORY COUNCIL | OUR PRIVACY POLICY

AMY TAN

MOTHER TONGUE

Amy Tan (b. 1952) is a native of California. In her best-selling first novel, *The Joy Luck Club* (1989), Tan used all of the different forms of the English language she had spoken since childhood with her mother, whose native language was Chinese. In "Mother Tongue," which first appeared in the *Threepenny Review* (1990), Tan not only *uses* her family's different "Englishes," she classifies them into their various kinds and explains how each type lends itself to a different form of communication. Tan's latest novel is *The Bonesetter's Daughter* (2001).

XXXXXXXXXXXXXXXXXXXXXXXXXXXXXXXXXXXXXXXXXXXXXXXXXXXXXXXXXXXX

I am not a scholar of English or literature. I cannot give you much more than personal opinions on the English language and its variations in this country or others. 1

I am a writer. And by that definition, I am someone who has always loved language. I am fascinated by language in daily life. I spend a great deal of my time thinking about the power of language—the way it can evoke an emotion, a visual image, a complex idea, or a simple truth. Language is the tool of my trade. And I use them all—all the Englishes I grew up with. 2

Recently, I was made keenly aware of the different Englishes I do use. I was giving a talk to a large group of people, the same talk I had already given to half a dozen other groups. The nature of the talk was about my writing, my life, and my book, *The Joy Luck Club*. The talk was going along well enough, until I remembered one major difference that made the whole talk sound wrong. My mother was in the room. And it was perhaps the first time she had heard me give a lengthy speech, using the kind of English I have never used with her. I was saying things like, "The intersection of memory upon imagination" and "There is an aspect of my fiction that relates to thus-and-thus"—a speech filled with carefully wrought grammatical phrases, burdened, it suddenly seemed to 3 me, with nominalized forms, past perfect tenses, conditional phrases, all the forms of standard English that I had learned in school and through books, the forms of English I did not use at home with my mother.

Just last week, I was walking down the street with my mother, and I again found myself conscious of the English I was using, the English I do use with her. We were talking about the price of new and used furniture and I heard myself saying this: "Not waste money that way." My husband was with us as well, and he didn't notice any switch in my English. And then I realized why. It's because over the twenty years we've been together I've often used the same kind of English with him, and sometimes he even uses it with me. It has become our language of intimacy, a different sort of English that relates to family talk, the language I grew up with.

So you'll have some idea of what this family talk I heard sounds like, I'll quote what my mother said during a recent conversation which I videotaped and then transcribed. During this conversation, my mother was talking about a political gangster in Shanghai who had the same last name as her family's, Du, and how the gangster in his early years wanted to be adopted by her family, which was rich by comparison. Later, the gangster became more powerful, far richer than my mother's family, and one day showed up at my mother's wedding to pay his respects. Here's what she said in part:

"Du Yusong having business like fruit stand. Like off the street kind. He is Du like Du Zong—but not Tsung-ming Island people. The local people call putong, the river east side, he belong to that side local people. That man want to ask Du Zong father take him in like become own family. Du Zong father wasn't look down on him, but didn't take seriously, until that man big like become a mafia. Now important person, very hard to inviting him. Chinese way, came only to show respect, don't stay for dinner. Respect for making big celebration, he shows up. Mean gives lots of respect. Chinese custom. Chinese social life that way. If too important won't have to stay too long. He come to my wedding. I didn't see, I heard it. I gone to boy's side, they have YMCA dinner. Chinese age I was nineteen."

You should know that my mother's expressive command of English belies how much she actually understands. She reads the *Forbes* report, listens to *Wall Street Week*, converses daily with her stockbroker, reads all of Shirley MacLaine's books with ease—all kinds of things I can't begin to understand. Yet some of my friends tell me they understand 50 percent of what my mother says. Some say they understand 80 to 90 percent. Some say they understand none of it, as if she were speaking pure Chinese. But to me, my mother's English is perfectly clear, perfectly natural. It's my mother tongue. Her language, as I hear it, is vivid, direct, full of observation and imagery. That was the language that helped shape the way I saw things, expressed things, made sense of the world.

Lately, I've been giving more thought to the kind of English my mother   8 speaks. Like others, I have described it to people as "broken" or "fractured" English. But I wince when I say that. It has always bothered me that I can think of no way to describe it other than "broken," as if it were damaged and needed to be fixed, as if it lacked a certain wholeness and soundness. I've heard other terms used, "limited English," for example. But they seem just as bad, as if everything is limited, including people's perceptions of the limited English speaker.

I know this for a fact, because when I was growing up, my mother's   9 "limited" English limited *my* perception of her. I was ashamed of her English. I believed that her English reflected the quality of what she had to say. That is, because she expressed them imperfectly her thoughts were imperfect. And I had plenty of empirical evidence to support me: the fact that people in department stores, at banks, and at restaurants did not take her seriously, did not give her good service, pretended not to understand her, or even acted as if they did not hear her.

My mother has long realized the limitations of her English as well.   10 When I was fifteen, she used to have me call people on the phone to pretend I was she. In this guise, I was forced to ask for information or even to complain and yell at people who had been rude to her. One time it was a call to her stockbroker in New York. She had cashed out her small portfolio and it just so happened we were going to go to New York the next week, our very first trip outside California. I had to get on the phone and say in an adolescent voice that was not very convincing, "This is Mrs. Tan."

And my mother was standing in the back whispering loudly, "Why he don't send me check, already two weeks late. So mad he lie to me, losing me money." 11

And then I said in perfect English, "Yes, I'm getting rather concerned. You had agreed to send the check two weeks ago, but it hasn't arrived." 12

Then she began to talk more loudly. "What he want, I come to New York tell him front of his boss, you cheating me?" And I was trying to calm her down, make her be quiet, while telling the stockbroker, "I can't tolerate any more excuses. If I don't receive the check immediately, I am going to have to speak to your manager when I'm in New York next week." And sure enough, the following week there we were in front of this astonished stockbroker, and I was sitting there red-faced and quiet, and my mother, the real Mrs. Tan, was shouting at his boss in her impeccable broken English. 13

We used a similar routine just five days ago, for a situation that was far less humorous. My mother had gone to the hospital for an appointment, to find out about a benign brain tumor a CAT scan had revealed a month ago. She said she had spoken very good English, her best English, no mistakes. Still, she said, the hospital did not apologize when they said they had lost the CAT scan and she had come for nothing. She said they did not seem to have any sympathy when she told them she was anxious to know the exact diagnosis, since her husband and son had both died of brain tumors. She said they would not give her any more information until the next time and she would have to make another appointment for that. So she said she would not leave until the doctor called her daughter. She wouldn't budge. And when the doctor finally called her daughter, me, who spoke in perfect English—lo and behold— we had assurances the CAT scan would be found, promises that a conference call on Monday would be held, and apologies for any suffering my mother had gone through for a most regrettable mistake. 14

I think my mother's English almost had an effect on limiting my possibilities in life as well. Sociologists and linguists probably will tell you that a person's developing language skills are more influenced by peers. But I do think that the language spoken in the family, especially 15 in immigrant families which are more insular, plays a large role in shaping the language of the child. And I believe that it affected my results on achievement tests, IQ tests, and the SAT. While my English skills were never judged as poor, compared to math, English could not be considered my strong suit. In grade school I did moderately well, getting perhaps B's, sometimes B-pluses, in English and scoring perhaps in the sixtieth or seventieth percentile on achievement tests. But those scores were not good enough to override the opinion that my true abilities lay in math and science, because in those areas I achieved A's and scored in the ninetieth percentile or higher.

This was understandable. Math is precise; there is only one correct 16 answer. Whereas, for me at least, the answers on English tests were always a judgment call, a matter of opinion and personal experience. Those tests were constructed around items like fill-in-the-blank sentence completion, such as, "Even though Tom was _____, Mary thought he was _____." And the correct answer always seemed to be the most bland combinations of thoughts, for example, "Even though Tom was shy, Mary thought he was charming," with the grammatical structure "even though" limiting the correct answer to some sort of semantic opposites, so you wouldn't get answers like, "Even though Tom was foolish, Mary thought he was ridiculous." Well, according to my mother, there were very few limitations as to what Tom could have been and what Mary might have thought of him. So I never did well on tests like that.

The same was true with word analogies, pairs of words in which 17 you were supposed to find some sort of logical, semantic relationship— for example, *"Sunset* is to *nightfall* as _____ is to _____." And here you would be presented with a list of four possible pairs, one of which showed the same kind of relationship: *red* is to *stoplight, bus* is to *arrival, chills* is to *fever, yawn* is to *boring.* Well, I could never think that way. I knew what the tests were asking, but I could not block out of my mind the images already created by the first pair, *"sunset* is to *nightfall"*—and I would see a burst of colors against a darkening sky, the moon rising, the lowering of a curtain of stars. And all the other pairs of words—red, bus, stoplight, boring—just threw up a mass of confusing images, making it impossible for me to sort out something as logical as saying: "A sunset precedes nightfall" is the same as "a chill precedes a fever." The only way I would have gotten that answer right would have been to imagine an associative situation, for example, my being disobedient and staying out past sunset, catching a chill at night, which turns into feverish pneumonia as punishment, which indeed did happen to me.

I have been thinking about all this lately, about my mother's English, about achievement tests. Because lately I've been asked, as a writer, why there are not more Asian Americans represented in American literature. Why are there few Asian Americans enrolled in creative writing programs? Why do so many Chinese students go into engineering? Well, these are broad sociological questions I can't begin to answer. But I have noticed in surveys—in fact, just last week—that Asian students, as a whole, always do significantly better on math achievement tests than in English. And this makes me think that there are other Asian-American students whose English spoken in the home might also be described as "broken" or "limited." And perhaps they also have teachers who are steering them away from writing and into math and science, which is what happened to me.   18

Fortunately, I happen to be rebellious in nature and enjoy the challenge of disproving assumptions made about me. I became an English major my first year in college, after being enrolled as pre-med. I started writing nonfiction as a freelancer the week after I was told by my former boss that writing was my worst skill and I should hone my talents toward account management.   19

But it wasn't until 1985 that I finally began to write fiction. And at first I wrote using what I thought to be wittily crafted sentences, sentences that would finally prove I had mastery over the English language. Here's an example from the first draft of a story that later made its way into *The Joy Luck Club,* but without this line: "That was my mental quandary in its nascent state." A terrible line, which I can barely pronounce.   20

Fortunately, for reasons I won't get into today, I later decided I should envision a reader for the stories I would write. And the reader I decided upon was my mother, because these were stories about mothers. So with this reader in mind—and in fact she did read my early drafts—I began to write stories using all the Englishes I grew up with: the English   21

I spoke to my mother, which for lack of a better term might be described as "simple"; the English she used with me, which for lack of a better term might be described as "broken"; my translation of her Chinese, which could certainly be described as "watered down"; and what I imagined to be her translation of her Chinese if she could speak in perfect English, her internal language, and for that I sought to preserve the essence, but neither an English nor a Chinese structure. I wanted to capture what language ability tests can never reveal: her intent, her passion, her imagery, the rhythms of her speech and the nature of her thoughts.

Apart from what any critic had to say about my writing, I knew I had succeeded where it counted when my mother finished reading my book and gave me her verdict: "So easy to read."   22

XXXXXXXXXXXXXXXXXXX **FOR DISCUSSION** XXXXXXXXXXXXXXXXXXX

1. Into what two basic categories does Amy Tan DIVIDE all the Englishes that she uses in writing and speaking (3)?

2. How many Englishes did Tan learn at home from conversing with her mother, a native speaker of Chinese? How does she distinguish among them?

3. How does Tan DEFINE "standard" English (3)? How and where did she learn it?

4. How would you CLASSIFY the English Tan uses most of the time in this essay?

5. As a writer of many kinds of English, how does Tan decide which to use in various situations? What standard does she apply?

XXXXXXXXXXXXX **STRATEGIES AND STRUCTURES** XXXXXXXXXXXXX

1. Why do you think Tan begins her essay with the disclaimer that she is "not a scholar" of the English language (1)? How does she otherwise establish her authority on the subject? Does she do it well, in your opinion?

2. Tan first gives EXAMPLES of "family talk" and only later CLASSIFIES them (4, 21). Why do you think she follows this order? Why not give the categories first, then the specific examples?

3. What specific kind of English, by Tan's classification, is represented by paragraph 6 of her essay?

4. Besides classifying and DIVIDING Englishes, Tan is also telling stories about using them. What do the stories contribute to her essay? How would it be different without the stories?

5. In which paragraphs is Tan advancing an ARGUMENT about achievement tests? How does she use her different Englishes to show the limitations she finds in the tests?

XXXXXXXXXXXXXX **WORDS AND FIGURES OF SPEECH** XXXXXXXXXXXXX

1. What are some of the implications of using such terms as "broken" or "fractured" to refer to "nonstandard" forms of speech or writing (8)?

2. Do you find "simple" to be better or worse than "broken"? How about "watered down" (21)? Please explain your answer.

3. Tan does not give a term for the kind of English she uses to represent her mother's "internal language" (21). What name would you give it? Why?

4. Explain the PUN in Tan's title. What does it tell us about the essay?

5. By what standards, according to Tan, is "standard" English to be established and measured (3)?

XXXXXXXXXXXXXXXXXXXXXXX **FOR WRITING** XXXXXXXXXXXXXXXXXXXXXXX

1. Many families have private jokes, code words, gestures, even family whistles. In a paragraph or two, give EXAMPLES of your family's private speech or language. How does each function within the family? In relation to the family and the outside world?

2. How many different Englishes (and other languages) do you use at home, at school, among friends, and elsewhere? Write an essay CLASSIFYING them, DESCRIBING what each is like, and explaining how and when each is used.

ERIC A. WATTS

THE COLOR OF SUCCESS

Eric A. Watts grew up in Springfield, Massachusetts, and attended
Brown University, graduating in 1995. He wrote this essay about racial
typing for the Brown *Alumni Monthly* when he was a sophomore. In it,
Watts argues that African Americans who criticize each other for "acting
white" and who say that success based on academic achievement is "not
black" are making a false distinction because they are misclassifying
themselves as victims. Responding to an article on campus diversity in
the Brown *Daily Herald* in 2000, Watts added that the real question for
him was not whether his alma mater and other schools encouraged diversity, but whether they encouraged "harmony and understanding among
the diverse communities in place there" already.

XXXXXXXXXXXXXXXXXXXXXXXXXXXXXXXXXXXXXXXXXXXXXXXXXXXXXXXXXXXXXXX

W hen I was a black student at a primarily white high school, I occa- 1
sionally confronted the stereotypes and prejudice that some whites
aimed at those of my race. These incidents came as no particular surprise—after all, prejudice, though less prevalent than in the past, is ages
old.

What did surprise me during those years was the profound disap- 2
proval that some of my black peers expressed toward my studious behavior. "Hitting the books," expressing oneself articulately, and, at times,
displaying more than a modest amount of intelligence—these traits were
derided as "acting white."

Once, while I was traveling with other black students, a young 3
woman asked me what I thought of one of our teachers. My answer,
phrased in what one might call "standard" English, caused considerable
discomfort among my audience. Finally, the young woman exploded:
"Eric," she said, "stop talking like a white boy! You're with us now!"

Another time, again in a group of black students, a friend asked 4
how I intended to spend the weekend. When I answered that I would

study, my friend's reaction was swift: "Eric, you need to stop all this studying; you need to stop acting so white." The others laughed in agreement.

Signithea Fordham's 1986 ethnographic study of a mostly black high school in Washington, D.C., *Black Students' School Success,* concluded that many behaviors associated with high achievement—speaking standard English, studying long hours, striving to get good grades—were regarded as "acting white." Fordham further concluded that "many black students limit their academic success so their peers won't think they are 'acting white'." 5

Frankly, I never took the "acting white" accusation seriously. It seemed to me that certain things I valued—hard work, initiative, articulateness, education—were not solely white people's prerogative. 6

Trouble begins, however, when students lower their standards in response to peer pressure. Such a retreat from achievement has potentially horrendous effects on the black community. 7

Even more disturbing is the rationale behind the "acting white" accusation. It seems that, on a subconscious level, some black students wonder whether success—in particular, academic success—is a purely white domain. 8

In his essay "On Being Black and Middle Class," in *The Content of Our Character* (1990), Shelby Steele, a black scholar at San Jose State University, argues that certain "middle-class" values—the work ethic, education, initiative—by encouraging "individualism," encourage identification with American society, rather than with race. The ultimate result is integration. 9

But, Steele argues, the racial identification that emerged during the 1960s, and that still persists, urges middle-class blacks to view themselves as an embattled minority: to take an adversarial stance toward the mainstream. It emphasizes ethnic consciousness over individualism. 10

Steele says that this form of black identification emerged in the civil-rights effort to obtain full racial equality, an effort that demanded that blacks present themselves (by and large) as a racial monolith: a single mass with the common experience of oppression. So blackness became virtually synonymous with victimization and the characteristics associated with it: lack of education and poverty. 11

I agree with Steele that a monolithic form of racial identification   12
persists. The ideas of the black as a victim and the black as inferior have
been too much entrenched in cultural imagery and too much enforced
by custom and law not to have damaged the collective black psyche.

This damage is so severe that some black adolescents still believe   13
that success is a white prerogative—the white "turf." These young people
view the turf as inaccessible, both because (among other reasons) they
doubt their own abilities and because they generally envision whites as,
if not outspoken racists, people who are mildly interested in "keeping
blacks down."

The result of identifying oneself as a victim can be, "Why even   14
try? It's a white man's world."

Several years ago I was talking to an old friend, a black male. He   15
justified dropping out of school and failing to look for a job on the basis
of one factor: the cold, heartless, white power structure. When I suggested that such a power structure might indeed exist, but that opportunity for blacks was at an unprecedented level, he laughed. Doomed, he
felt, to a life of defeat, my friend soon eased his melancholy with crack.

The most frustrating aspect of the "acting white" accusation is that its   16
main premise—that academic and subsequent success are "white"—is
demonstrably false. And so is the broader premise: that blacks are the
victims of whites.

That academic success is "not black" is easily seen as false if one   17
takes a brisk walk through the Brown University campus and looks at
the faces one passes. Indeed, the most comprehensive text concerning
blacks in decades, *A Common Destiny* (1989), states, "Despite large gaps
. . . whether the baseline is the 1940s, 1950s, or 1960s, the achievement
outcomes . . . of black schooling have greatly improved." That subsequent success in the world belongs to blacks as well as whites is exemplified today by such blacks as Jesse Jackson, Douglas Wilder, Norman
Rice, Anne Wortham, Sara Lawrence Lightfoot, David Dinkins, August
Wilson, Andrew Young. . . .

The idea of a victimized black race is slowly becoming outdated.   18
Today's black adolescents were born after the *Brown v. Board of Education*
decision of 1954; after the passage of the Civil Rights Act; after the
Economic Opportunity Act of 1964. With these rulings and laws, whites'

attitudes toward blacks have also greatly improved. Although I cannot say that my life has been free of racism on the part of whites, good racial relations in my experience have far outweighed the bad. I refuse to apologize for or retreat from this truth.

The result of changes in policies and attitudes has been to provide more opportunities for black Americans than at any other point in their history. As early as 1978, William Julius Wilson, in *The Declining Significance of Race,* concluded that "the recent mobility patterns of blacks lend strong support to the view that economic class is clearly more important than race in predetermining . . . occupational mobility." 19

There are, of course, many factors, often socioeconomic, that still impede the progress of blacks. High schools in black neighborhoods receive less local, state, and federal support than those in white areas; there is evidence that the high school diplomas of blacks are little valued by employers. 20

We should rally against all such remaining racism, confronting particularly the economic obstacles to black success. But we must also realize that racism is not nearly as profound as it once was, and that opportunities for blacks (where opportunity equals jobs and acceptance for the educated and qualified) have increased. Furthermore, we should know that even a lack of resources is no excuse for passivity. 21

As the syndicated columnist William Raspberry (who is black) says, it is time for certain black adolescents to "shift their focus": to move from an identity rooted in victimization to an identity rooted in individualism and hard work. 22

Simply put, the black community must eradicate the "you're-acting-white" syndrome. Until it does, black Americans will never realize their potential. 23

ⵉⵉⵉⵉⵉⵉⵉⵉⵉⵉⵉⵉⵉⵉⵉⵉⵉ **FOR DISCUSSION** ⵉⵉⵉⵉⵉⵉⵉⵉⵉⵉⵉⵉⵉⵉⵉⵉⵉ

1. CLASSIFYING human behavior strictly by race, says Eric A. Watts, is invalid. What reasons does he give for making this assertion? How valid do you find them?

2. In his high school, what specific behaviors did Watts's black peers associate with "acting white" (2, 5)?

3. Watts says that he personally never took the accusation of "acting white" too seriously when he was in high school (2). Why not? Did he change his mind when he went to college?

4. According to Watts (and the columnist William Raspberry, whom he quotes), what is the worst potential danger of "identifying oneself as a victim" (14)?

XXXXXXXXXXXXXX **STRATEGIES AND STRUCTURES** XXXXXXXXXXXXXX

1. As an essay that CLASSIFIES (or, rather, declassifies), is "The Color of Success" about race or success or both? How?

2. Watts does not deny that people come in different colors. How, then, do his frequent references to color help him to call into question stereotypical ways of categorizing human beings?

3. Why do you think Watts refers to the work of such scholars and researchers as Signithea Fordham and Shelby Steele?

4. What, according to Watts, *is* the color of success? What system of classifying people does he use to ARGUE against "black and white" distinctions?

5. Watts uses CLASSIFICATION AND DIVISION to argue about the significance of race in determining individual success. What is his position?

XXXXXXXXXXXX **WORDS AND FIGURES OF SPEECH** XXXXXXXXXXXX

1. One of Watts's key terms is "success." How does he DEFINE it?

2. What does Watts mean by "standard" English (3)? Cite several of his phrases that help to define "standard."

3. How does Watts's own use of language in this essay confirm (or deny) what he is saying about acting "white" or "black"?

4. What is a "syndrome" (23)? How well does the term fit the feelings of being victimized that Watts DESCRIBES?

XXXXXXXXXXXXXXXXXXXXX **FOR WRITING** XXXXXXXXXXXXXXXXXXXXX

1. "Success" is a relative term. What different kinds are there? Make a list of the different kinds that occur to you and of the traits that distinguish each kind.

2. Watts is especially concerned with racial stereotyping, but race is only one of the grounds on which people can falsely CLASSIFY each other's behavior. In an all-girls' school, for EXAMPLE, female students frequently do better in math and science than female students in schools with a mixed student body. Apparently, acting "feminine" and acting "masculine" are socially conditioned. Write an essay about your own high-school experience in which you classify the socially acceptable and socially unacceptable ways in which students pressured one another to behave.

ISAAC ASIMOV

WHAT DO YOU CALL A PLATYPUS?

Isaac Asimov (1920–1992) was born in Petrovichi, Russia, entered the United States at age three, and became a naturalized citizen in 1928. He wrote almost 500 books dealing with an astounding range of subjects: biochemistry, the human body, ecology, mathematics, physics, astronomy, genetics, history, the Bible, and Shakespeare—to name only a few. Asimov is best known, however, for his science fiction, including *I, Robot* (1950) and the *Foundation* trilogy (1951–53). "What Do You Call a Platypus?" (1973) is an essay in taxonomy, the science of classifying plants and animals. Is the duckbill platypus (*Ornithorhynchus anatinus*) to be classified as a mammal? a reptile? a bird? There are good anatomical reasons for placing it in any of these categories, and Asimov's playful exercise in scientific classification shows both the limitations of classification systems in general and how they can help us to organize our knowledge of the world—or even to discover new knowledge.

XXXXXXXXXXXXXXXXXXXXXXXXXXXXXXXXXXXXXXXXXXXXXXXXXXXXXXXXXXXXXXXX

1   In 1800, a stuffed animal arrived in England from the newly discovered continent of Australia.

2   The continent had already been the source of plants and animals never seen before—but this one was ridiculous. It was nearly two feet long, and had a dense coating of hair. It also had a flat rubbery bill, webbed feet, a broad flat tail, and a spur on each hind ankle that was clearly intended to secrete poison. What's more, under the tail was a single opening.

3   Zoologists stared at the thing in disbelief. Hair like a mammal! Bill and feet like an aquatic bird! Poison spurs like a snake! A single opening in the rear as though it laid eggs!

4   There was an explosion of anger. The thing was a hoax. Some unfunny jokester in Australia, taking advantage of the distance and

strangeness of the continent, had stitched together parts of widely different creatures and was intent on making fools of innocent zoologists in England.

Yet the skin seemed to hang together. There were no signs of artificial joining. Was it or was it not a hoax? And if it wasn't a hoax, was it a mammal with reptilian characteristics, or a reptile with mammalian characteristics, or was it partly bird, or *what?*

The discussion went on heatedly for decades. Even the name emphasized the ways in which it didn't seem like a mammal despite its hair. One early name was *Platypus anatinus* which is Graeco-Latin[1] for "Flat-foot, ducklike." Unfortunately, the term, platypus, had already been applied to a type of beetle and there must be no duplication in scientific names. It therefore received another name, *Ornithorhynchus paradoxus*, which means "Birdbeak, paradoxical."

Slowly, however, zoologists had to fall into line and admit that the creature was real and not a hoax, however upsetting it might be to zoological notions. For one thing, there were increasingly reliable reports from people in Australia who caught glimpses of the creature alive. The *paradoxus* was dropped and the scientific name is now *Ornithorhynchus anatinus*.

To the general public, however, it is the "duckbill platypus," or even just the duckbill, the queerest mammal (assuming it is a mammal) in the world.

When specimens were received in such condition as to make it possible to study the internal organs, it appeared that the heart was just like those of mammals and not at all like those of reptiles. The egg-forming machinery in the female, however, was not at all like those of mammals, but like those of birds or reptiles. It seemed really and truly to be an egg-layer.

It wasn't till 1884, however, that the actual eggs laid by a creature with hair were found. Such creatures included not only the platypus, but another Australian species, the spiny anteater. That was worth an excited announcement. A group of British scientists were meeting in Montreal

[1]Combination of Greek and Latin; many scientific names put Latin endings on the Greek roots.

at the time, and the egg-discoverer, W. H. Caldwell, sent them a cable to announce the finding.

It wasn't till the twentieth century that the intimate life of the duck-bill came to be known. It is an aquatic animal, living in Australian fresh water at a wide variety of temperatures—from tropical streams at sea level to cold lakes at an elevation of a mile. 11

The duckbill is well adapted to its aquatic life, with its dense fur, its flat tail, and its webbed feet. Its bill has nothing really in common with that of the duck, however. The nostrils are differently located and the platypus bill is different in structure, rubbery rather than duckishly horny. It serves the same function as the duck's bill, however, so it has been shaped similarly by the pressures of natural selection. 12

The water in which the duckbill lives is invariably muddy at the bottom and it is in this mud that the duckbill roots for its food supply. The bill, ridged with horny plates, is used as a sieve, dredging about sensitively in the mud, filtering out the shrimps, earthworms, tadpoles and other small creatures that serve it as food. 13

When the time comes for the female platypus to produce young, she builds a special burrow, which she lines with grass and carefully plugs. She then lays two eggs, each about three quarters of an inch in diameter and surrounded by a translucent, horny shell. 14

These the mother platypus places between her tail and abdomen and curls up about them. It takes two weeks for the young to hatch out. The new-born duckbills have teeth and very short bills, so that they are much less "birdlike" than the adults. They feed on milk. The mother has no nipples, but milk oozes out of pore openings in the abdomen and the young lick the area and are nourished in this way. As they grow, the bills become larger and the teeth fall out. 15

Yet despite everything zoologists learned about the duckbills, they never seemed entirely certain as to where to place them in the table of animal classification. On the whole, the decision was made because of hair and milk. In all the world, only mammals have true hair and only mammals produce true milk. The duckbill and spiny anteater have hair and produce milk, so they have been classified as mammals. 16

Just the same, they are placed in a very special position. All the mammals are divided into two subclasses. In one of these subclasses ("Prototheria" or "first-beasts") are the duckbill and five species of the 17 spiny anteater. In the other ("Theria" or just "beast") are all the other 4,231 known species of mammals.

But all this is the result of judging only living species of mammals. Suppose we could study extinct species as well. Would that help us decide on the place of the platypus? Would it cause us to confirm our decision— or change it? 18

Fossil remnants exist of mammals and reptiles of the far past, but these remnants are almost entirely of bones and teeth. Bones and teeth give us interesting information but they can't tell us everything. 19

For instance, is there any way of telling, from bones and teeth alone, whether an extinct creature is a reptile or a mammal? 20

Well, all living reptiles have legs splayed out so that the upper part above the knee is horizontal (assuming they have legs at all). All mammals, on the other hand, have legs that are vertical all the way down. Again, reptiles have teeth that all look more or less alike, while mammals have teeth that have different shapes, with sharp incisors in front, flat molars in back, and conical incisors and premolars in between. 21

As it happens, there are certain extinct creatures, to which have been given the name "therapsids," which have their leg bones vertical and their teeth differentiated just as in the case of mammals.—And yet they are considered reptiles and not mammals. Why? Because there is another bony difference to be considered. 22

In living mammals, the lower jaw contains a single bone; in reptiles, it is made up of a number of bones. The therapsid lower jaw is made up of seven bones and because of that those creatures are classified as reptiles. And yet in the therapsid lower jaw, the one bone making up the central portion of the lower jaw is by far the largest. The other six bones, three on each side, are crowded into the rear angle of the jaw. 23

There seems no question, then, that if the therapsids are reptiles they are nevertheless well along the pathway towards mammals. 24

But how far along the pathway are they? For instance, did they have hair? It might seem that it would be impossible to tell whether an extinct animal had hair or not just from the bones, but let's see— 25

Hair is an insulating device. It keeps body heat from being lost too rapidly. Reptiles keep their body temperature at about that of the outside environment. They don't have to be concerned over loss of heat and hair would be of no use to them. 26

Mammals, however, maintain their internal temperature at nearly 27
100° F. regardless of the outside temperature; they are "warm-blooded."
This gives them the great advantage of remaining agile and active in cold
weather, when the chilled reptile is sluggish. But then the mammal must
prevent heat loss by means of a hairy covering. (Birds, which also are
warm-blooded, use feathers as an insulating device.)

With that in mind, let's consider the bones. In reptiles, the nostrils 28
open into the mouth just behind the teeth. This means that reptiles can
only breathe with their mouths empty. When they are biting or chewing,
breathing must stop. This doesn't bother a reptile much, for it can sus-
pend its need for oxygen for considerable periods.

Mammals, however, must use oxygen in their tissues constantly, in 29
order to keep the chemical reactions going that serve to keep their body
temperature high. The oxygen supply must not be cut off for more than
very short intervals. Consequently mammals have developed a bony palate, a roof to the mouth. When they breathe, air is led above the mouth
to the throat. This means they can continue breathing while they bite
and chew. It is only when they are actually in the act of swallowing that
the breath is cut off and this is only a matter of a couple of seconds at
a time.

The later therapsid species had, as it happened, a palate. If they 30
had a palate, it seems a fair deduction that they needed an uninterrupted
supply of oxygen that makes it look as though they were warm-blooded.
And if they were warm-blooded, then very likely they had hair, too.

The conclusion, drawn from the bones alone, would seem to be that 31
some of the later therapsids had hair, even though, judging by their
jawbones, they were still reptiles.

The thought of hairy reptiles is astonishing. But that is only because 32
the accident of evolution seems to have wiped out the intermediate
forms. The only therapsids alive seem to be those that have developed
all the mammalian characteristics, so that we call them mammals.
The only reptiles alive are those that developed *none* of the mammalian
characteristics.

Those therapsids that developed some but not others seem to be 33
extinct.

Only the duckbill and the spiny anteater remain near the border 34
line. They have developed the hair and the milk and the singleboned

lower jaw and the four-chambered heart, but not the nipples or the ability to bring forth live young.

For all we know, some of the extinct therapsids, while still having their many-boned lower jaw (which is why we call them reptiles instead of mammals), may have developed even beyond the duckbill in other ways. Perhaps some late therapsids had nipples and brought forth living young. We can't tell from the bones alone. 35

If we had a complete record of the therapsids, flesh and blood, as well as teeth and bone, we might decide that the duckbill was on the therapsid side of the line and not on the mammalian side.—Or are there any other pieces of evidence that can be brought into play? 36

An American zoologist, Giles T. MacIntyre, of Queens College, has taken up the matter of the trigeminal nerve, which leads from the jaw muscles to the brain. 37

In all reptiles, without exception, the trigeminal nerve passes through the skull at a point that lies between two of the bones making up the skull. In all mammals that bring forth living young, without exception, the nerve actually passes *through* a particular skull bone. 38

Suppose we ignore all the matter of hair and milk and eggs, and just consider the trigeminal nerve. In the duckbill, does the nerve pass through a bone, or between two bones? It has seemed in the past that the nerve passed through a bone and that put the duckbill on the mammalian side of the dividing line. 39

Not so, says MacIntyre. The study of the trigeminal nerve was made in adult duckbills, where the skull bones are fused together and the boundaries are hard to make out. In young duckbills, the skull bones are more clearly separated and in them it can be seen, MacIntyre says, that the trigeminal nerve goes between two bones. 40

In that case, there is a new respect in which the duckbill falls on the reptilian side of the line and MacIntyre thinks it ought not to be considered a mammal, but as a surviving species of the otherwise long-extinct therapsid line. 41

And so, a hundred seventy years after zoologists began to puzzle out the queer mixture of characteristics that go to make up the duckbill platypus—there is still argument as to what to call it. 42

Is the duckbill platypus a mammal? A reptile? Or just a duckbill platypus? 43

XXXXXXXXXXXXXXXXXX **FOR DISCUSSION** XXXXXXXXXXXXXXXXXX

1. Taxonomists place individual specimens, such as the stuffed platypus that first arrived in England in 1800 from the strange land of Australia, into categories based on certain distinguishing features. As reported by Asimov, what are the chief distinguishing features of mammals? Of reptiles?

2. Which mammalian features does the platypus lack? Which reptilian CHARACTERISTICS does it possess?

3. How does the EXAMPLE of the platypus show the limitations of the zoological CLASSIFICATION system? Of classification systems in general?

4. What new evidence does Asimov cite in favor of reclassifying the platypus? How convincing do you find this ARGUMENT?

XXXXXXXXXXXXX **STRATEGIES AND STRUCTURES** XXXXXXXXXXXX

1. Why do you think Asimov begins his case for reclassifying the platypus by recounting the confused history of how the animal got its name?

2. Why does it matter what we *call* a platypus? For what ultimate purpose is Asimov concerned with the creature's name and formal CLASSIFICATION?

3. What is Asimov's purpose in referring to extinct creatures, beginning in paragraph 18? What is the function of the therapsids in his line of reasoning (22)?

4. This essay for reclassification ends with three alternatives (43). Why three instead of just two?

5. The logic of paragraph 32 depends upon an unstated assumption about the order of evolution. Which does Asimov assume came first, reptiles or mammals? How does this assumption influence his entire ARGUMENT?

XXXXXXXXXXXX **WORDS AND FIGURES OF SPEECH** XXXXXXXXXXX

1. Why was the term "paradoxical" an appropriate part of the platypus's early scientific name (6)? How does it differ in meaning from *ambiguous* and *ambivalent*?

2. Asimov refers to the "egg-forming machinery" of the female platypus (9). How technically scientific is this term? What does his use of such terms suggest about the nature of the audience for whom he is writing?

3. What is meant by "the pressures of natural selection" (12)?

4. Asimov's essay is an exercise in taxonomy, although he does not use the word. What does it mean, according to a dictionary?

XXXXXXXXXXXXXXXXXXXXXX **FOR WRITING** XXXXXXXXXXXXXXXXXXXXXX

1. In a paragraph or two, explain why a whale is CLASSIFIED as a mammal instead of a fish.

2. What's the scientific background for the notion that humans belong in the great-ape category? Recent DNA studies indicate that the genes of gorillas differ from those of both humans and chimpanzees by about 2.3 percent. Humans and chimps, however, share 98.4 percent of their genes—a difference of only 1.6 percent. Science writer David Quammen addresses this evidence in "Beast in the Mirror: Science Uncovers Another Chimpanzee." Write an essay that classifies human beings within the animal kingdom, taking into account these newly determined facts. If you cite Quammen's article, be sure to document those facts accordingly.

FREEMAN J. DYSON

SCIENCE, GUIDED BY ETHICS, CAN LIFT UP THE POOR

Freeman J. Dyson (b. 1933) is Professor Emeritus of physics at Princeton. Born in England and trained as a mathematician, he has worked in the fields of quantum electrodynamics, condensed-matter physics, statistical mechanics, nuclear engineering, climate studies, astrophysics, and biology. Outside of these technical fields, he has written extensively on technology and human society in such books as *Weapons and Hope* (1984) and *The Sun, the Genome and the Internet* (1999). In this essay, Dyson classifies the technology of the last 10,000 years into two basic types, each with a "dark" side and a "light" side. Which side, he wonders, will prevail as the older type of technology takes on aspects of the newer? Originally part of a speech that Dyson delivered at the Washington National Cathedral in 2000, this version of his essay was published in *The Best American Science Writing, 2001.*

XXXXXXXXXXXXXXXXXXXXXXXXXXXXXXXXXXXXXXXXXXXXXXXXXXXXXXXXXXXXXXX

Throughout history, people have used technology to change the world. Our technology has been of two kinds, green and gray. Green technology is seeds and plants, gardens and vineyards and orchards, domesticated horses and cows and pigs, milk and cheese, leather and wool. Gray technology is bronze and steel, spears and guns, coal and oil and electricity, automobiles and airplanes and rockets, telephones and computers. Civilization began with green technology, with agriculture and animal-breeding, 10,000 years ago. Then, beginning about 3,000 years ago, gray technology became dominant, with mining and metallurgy and machinery. For the last 500 years, gray technology has been racing ahead and has given birth to the modern world of cities and factories and supermarkets.

The dominance of gray technology is coming to an end. During the last 50 years, we have achieved a fundamental understanding of the processes in living cells. With understanding comes the ability to exploit and control. Out of the knowledge acquired by modern biology, modern biotechnology is growing. The new green technology will give us the power, using only sunlight as a source of energy, and air and water and soil as materials, to manufacture and recycle chemicals of all kinds. Our gray technology of machines and computers will not disappear, but green technology will be moving ahead even faster. Green technology can be cleaner, more flexible and less wasteful than our existing chemical industries. A great variety of manufactured objects could be grown instead of made. Green technology could supply human needs with far less damage to the natural environment. And green technology could be a great equalizer, bringing wealth to the tropical areas of the planet, which have most of the world's sunshine, people and poverty. I am saying that green technology could do all these good things, not that green technology will do all these good things.

To make these good things happen, we need not only the new technology but the political and economic conditions that will give people all over the world a chance to use it. To make these things happen, we need a powerful push from ethics. We need a consensus of public opinion around the world that the existing gross inequalities in the distribution of wealth are intolerable. In reaching such a consensus, religions must play an essential role. Neither technology alone nor religion alone is powerful enough to bring social justice to human societies, but technology and religion working together might do the job.

We all know that green technology has a dark side, just as gray technology has a dark side. Gray technology brought us hydrogen bombs as well as telephones. Green technology brought us anthrax bombs as well as antibiotics. Besides the dangers of biological weapons, green technology brings other dangers having nothing to do with weapons. The ultimate danger of green technology comes from its power to change the nature of human beings by the application of genetic engineering to human embryos. If we allow a free market in human genes, wealthy parents will be able to buy what they consider superior genes for their babies. This could cause a splitting of humanity into hereditary castes.

Within a few generations, the children of rich and poor could become separate species. Humanity would then have regressed all the way back to a society of masters and slaves. No matter how strongly we believe in the virtues of a free market economy, the free market must not extend to human genes.

I see two tremendous goods coming from biotechnology: first, the alleviation of human misery through progress in medicine, and second, the transformation of the global economy through green technology spreading wealth more equitably around the world. The two great evils to be avoided are the use of biological weapons and the corruption of human nature by buying and selling genes. I see no scientific reason why we should not achieve the good and avoid the evil. The obstacles to achieving the good are political rather than technical. Unfortunately, a large number of people in many countries are strongly opposed to green technology, for reasons having little to do with the real dangers. It is important to treat the opponents with respect, to pay attention to their fears, to go gently into the new world of green technology so that neither human dignity nor religious conviction is violated. If we can go gently, we have a good chance of achieving within a hundred years the goals of ecological sustainability and social justice that green technology brings within our reach.

The great question for our time is how to make sure that the continuing scientific revolution brings benefits to everybody rather than widening the gap between rich and poor. To lift up poor countries, and poor people in rich countries, from poverty, technology is not enough. Technology must be guided and driven by ethics if it is to do more than provide new toys for the rich. Scientists and business leaders who care about social justice should join forces with environmental and religious organizations to give political clout to ethics. Science and religion should work together to abolish the gross inequalities that prevail in the modern world. That is my vision, and it is the same vision that inspired Francis Bacon[1] 400 years ago, when he prayed that through science God would "endow the human family with new mercies."

---

[1]Sir Francis Bacon (1561–1626), English philosopher and essayist who first proposed the system of scientific observation that came to be known as the INDUCTIVE method.

XXXXXXXXXXXXXXXXXXXX **FOR DISCUSSION** XXXXXXXXXXXXXXXXXXXX

1. Freeman J. Dyson DIVIDES human technology into two basic kinds, "green" and "gray" (1). Make a list of the distinguishing features of the two kinds.

2. Which kind of technology, according to Dyson, has dominated human society in the past? Which kind dominates now? Which does he say will dominate?

3. What advantages does Dyson see in the new green technology, as opposed to the old gray kind?

4. Both categories of technology have "a dark side," says Dyson (4). What EXAMPLES does he give of the dark side of both types of technology?

5. In paragraph 4, Dyson envisions humanity splitting into "separate species" within a few generations. What would have to happen for such a revolution in human taxonomy to occur so quickly? How likely do you think this scenario is? Why?

6. How does Dyson propose to reap the advantages of green technology in the future without unleashing its harmful consequences? Dyson seems cautiously optimistic about our ability to do one and avoid the other. How about you?

XXXXXXXXXXXXXX **STRATEGIES AND STRUCTURES** XXXXXXXXXXXXXX

1. Dyson DIVIDES all human technology into two basic categories. Are these divisions significant? Are they mutually exclusive? Are they sufficient? How well does Dyson's scheme meet each of these criteria for a good CLASSIFICATION system?

2. What other categories, if any, would you add to Dyson's classification scheme?

3. Where does Dyson's essay shift from classifying human technology to advancing an ARGUMENT based on that classification? Please point out specific passages in which you see such a shift taking place.

4. Classification and division should serve some larger purpose than mere pigeonholing. What is Dyson's main purpose in this essay? What great social changes would he like to see come about? How does Dyson link those changes to the different kinds of technology he identifies?

5. In paragraph 5, Dyson is dividing the "goods" that can come from biotechnology into two basic categories. What are they? Is biotechnology itself a subdivision of green technology or gray technology?

6. Into what basic categories is Dyson dividing all human populations? Where does he identify their distinguishing features, and what are some of them?

7. How does Dyson use his classification of human populations to support the ARGUMENT that "technology must be guided and driven by ethics" (6)?

XXXXXXXXXXXXX **WORDS AND FIGURES OF SPEECH** XXXXXXXXXXXX

1. Although it is one of his key terms, Dyson does not explicitly DEFINE *ethics*. What does he seem to mean by it?

2. Dyson gets his designation for "green" technology from the color of nature, of "seeds and plants, gardens and vineyards" (1). Where does his designation for "gray" technology come from?

3. As Dyson uses them, which are the broader terms, *science* and *religion* or *technology* and *ethics*? Please explain.

4. What are "castes" (4)? How do they differ from systems of CLASSIFICATION based on scientific principles?

5. Why does Dyson end his essay with an ALLUSION to Francis Bacon?

XXXXXXXXXXXXXXXXXXXXXXX **FOR WRITING** XXXXXXXXXXXXXXXXXXXXXXX

1. "Gray technology," says Dyson, "brought us hydrogen bombs as well as telephones" (4). What else did it bring? Write a brief essay in which you DIVIDE the fruits of conventional technology into good and bad, "dark" and "light."

2. Stephen Jay Gould ("In Praise of Stem Cells and Lifesaving Knowledge") observes that "all new and truly important ideas must pass through three stages: first dismissed as nonsense, then rejected as against religion, and finally acknowledged as true." In the field of biotechnology, especially genetic engineering, Dyson advises caution, whereas Gould says, "may this third stage come soon." Who's right, in your opinion? Write an essay agreeing or disagreeing with Dyson's contention that the gap between the rich and the poor can be closed. You may want to read Johnson C. Montgomery's "The Island of Plenty" (Chapter 9) as well.

JEFF JACOBY

THE RISE OF THE BLENDED AMERICAN

Jeff Jacoby (b. 1958) is a columnist for the *Boston Globe*. As a self-proclaimed conservative, he has played devil's advocate on such traditionally liberal issues as gun control, federally funded antismoking campaigns, and the lifting of economic sanctions against Cuba. In this essay from the *International Herald Tribune*, Jacoby attacks as "laughably obsolete" the lingering notion "that people can be scientifically classified by race." Thus he believes that the U.S. census, which last time included 63 separate categories for race on its questionnaire, should "go from 63 choices to zero." As such, this essay argues *against* one classification system. Jacoby is not arguing that all classification systems are invalid, however, only that racial divisions based on such characteristics as skin color are invalid because their distinguishing features don't distinguish anything. They are distinctions without a difference. A longer version of this essay appeared in the *Globe* in 2001 under the title "Defeated in the Bedroom."

XXXXXXXXXXXXXXXXXXXXXXXXXXXXXXXXXXXXXXXXXXXXXXXXXXXXXXXXXXXXXXXX

Writing recently in *National Review*, Ward Connerly[1] described meeting a woman who supported his efforts to abolish racial preferences and promote colorblind government.   1

"What you're doing," she told him, "is also best for your people."   2

At the words "your people," Mr. Connerly flinched. He loathes the   3
mind-set that sorts human beings into racial categories. He decided he owed her the honesty of explaining why her words set his teeth on edge. So he confronted her.

"What did you mean when you referred to my people?"   4

---

[1] A regent of the University of California and a leader in the campaign against Affirmative Action.

🏵 159 🏵

"The black race," she said.   5

"What is your race?" Mr. Connerly inquired.   6

"I'm Irish and German."   7

"Would it affect your concept of my race," he asked, "if I told you   8
that one of my grandparents was Irish and American Indian, another
French Canadian, another of African descent, and the other Irish? Aren't
they all my people?"

The woman was taken aback, Mr. Connerly records, but the   9
exchange led to "one of the richest conversations about race I have ever
had."

If only Mr. Connerly could have that conversation with everyone.   10
Too many Americans still believe that people can be scientifically classified by race, a 17th-century notion more closely related to myth than
to science. By now racial taxonomy should have been shelved with phlogiston and phrenology as laughably obsolete explanations of the way the
world works. Indeed, it should be reviled, since race-mindedness has led
to incalculable cruelty, sorrow and strife.

That was why the giants of the civil rights movement argued so   11
forcefully for a government blind to color. "Distinctions by race are so
evil, so arbitrary and insidious," Thurgood Marshall[2] argued in 1954,
"that a state bound to defend the equal protection of the laws must not
allow them in any public sphere."

Yet the government still draws and values those distinctions—more   12
obsessively than ever, to judge from last year's census questionnaire,
which offered 63 racial options. Respondents for the first time were
invited to choose "one or more" racial categories. The federal government
was finally acknowledging that a growing number of Americans are multiracial. Now it ought to take the next step and go from 63 choices to
zero. For as people like Mr. Connerly demonstrate, racial labels grow
more meaningless by the day.

Almost 7 million Americans identified themselves as multiracial on   13
last year's census, proof, if any were needed, that love doesn't stop at the
color line. And if that was true for couples like the Connerlys or the
parents of Tiger Woods, who married and had children at a time when

[2]First African American justice on the U.S. Supreme Court (1967–1991).

the taboo against interracial families still ran deep, how much more will it be true of those falling in love today?

Many minority interest groups fear that fewer people identifying 14 themselves as black or Hispanic or Asian will mean a drop in their own political power. Some of them push a separatist line, urging minorities to resist assimilation into the mainstream.

But in the piquant phrase of the demographics expert Ben Watten- 15 berg, the separatists are being "defeated in the bedroom." The population of blended citizens is soaring, and with it the realization that racial divisions are only skin deep. Tens of millions of Americans have learned to think outside the racial box. It's time the government followed suit.

XXXXXXXXXXXXXXXXXXXXXXXX **FOR DISCUSSION** XXXXXXXXXXXXXXXXXXXXXXXX

1. Taxonomy is the science of CLASSIFICATION, particularly of plants and animals. What, then, is "racial taxonomy" (10)? How "scientific" does Jeff Jacoby consider this classification to be? What reasons does he give for his position?

2. Why does Jacoby think classifications by race should be "reviled" (10)? Do you agree or disagree with his position? Why?

3. According to Jacoby, many groups perpetuate a "separatist" system of racial classification (14). What alternative to such a system does he offer?

4. Although it offered 63 racial categories, the census of 2000 was different from all earlier national head counts. In what way? Why does Jacoby think this difference is so important?

XXXXXXXXXXXXXX **STRATEGIES AND STRUCTURES** XXXXXXXXXXXXXX

1. Jacoby begins his essay about racial CLASSIFYING with a brief NARRATIVE. Where does the narrative end and his EXPOSITION begin? What purpose does the narrative serve in his essay as a whole?

2. In scientific classification systems, the categories into which things can be DIVIDED do not overlap. What's wrong with the system advanced by the woman quoted in paragraphs 5 and 7, where categories are "black," "Irish," and "German"?

3. How is the classification system set forth in paragraphs 7 and 8 different from that set forth in paragraph 5?

4. U.S. Supreme Court justice Thurgood Marshall gave three reasons for distrusting distinctions based on race, saying they are "evil," "arbitrary," and "insidious" (11). With which of these charges was Justice Marshall attacking racial classification on moral and ethical grounds? On scientific grounds? Please explain your answer.

5. Are Jacoby's own objections to "race-mindedness" based more on morality or on science and logic (10)? In your view, has he included sufficient proof for his ARGUMENT? What additional proof *could* he offer? Please cite specific passages to explain your answer.

ⅩⅩⅩⅩⅩⅩⅩⅩⅩⅩⅩ WORDS AND FIGURES OF SPEECH ⅩⅩⅩⅩⅩⅩⅩⅩⅩⅩⅩ

1. Phrenology was the nineteenth-century pseudoscience of reading a person's character from the bumps and valleys on his or her head (10). How is this COMPARABLE, in Jacoby's view, to DEFINING racial categories based on skin color?

2. Phlogiston was a mythological essence once thought to be released in combustion as flame (10). What ANALOGY is Jacoby making by comparing it to race?

3. Race has often been defined in terms of genetically transmitted traits, such as skin color and hair texture. What elements usually define a person's ethnicity?

4. Is Hispanic a racial or an ethnic distinction (14)? How about Asian (14)?

5. Is Jacoby using the term "colorblind" in a literal or a METAPHORIC sense (1)? Please explain.

ⅩⅩⅩⅩⅩⅩⅩⅩⅩⅩⅩⅩⅩⅩⅩ FOR WRITING ⅩⅩⅩⅩⅩⅩⅩⅩⅩⅩⅩⅩⅩⅩⅩ

1. One system of CLASSIFICATION on some college campuses is "Greeks" vs. "Independents." How are students classified, socially or otherwise, at your school today? Using any system that fits, write an essay classifying your classmates. Or, if fraternities and sororities interest you (positively or negatively), write an essay classifying some of the Greek or other social organizations on your campus.

2. "Love," says Jacoby, "doesn't stop at the color line" (13). Write an essay agreeing or disagreeing with the THESIS that racial distinctions are diminishing in America as more people become racially "blended."

CHAPTER FIVE

PROCESS ANALYSIS

XXXXXXXXXXXXXXXXXXXXXXXXXXXXXXXXXXXXXXXXXXXXXXXXXXXXXXXXXXXXXXX

The essays in this chapter are examples of PROCESS ANALYSIS,* writing that explains *how*. Process analysis breaks down a process into the sequence of actions that leads to an end result. Basically, there are two kinds of process analysis: *directive* and *explanatory*. Directive process analysis explains how to make or do something—how to throw a boomerang, for instance. Explanatory process analysis explains how something works; it tells you what makes the boomerang come back.

Here is an example of the how-to-do-it kind:

> Hold the boomerang . . . with the V-point, called the elbow, pointing toward you, and with the flat side facing out. . . . Bring the boomerang back behind you and snap it forward as if you were throwing a baseball.
>
> www.howstuffworks.com

This kind of process analysis is often addressed to the second person (*you*) because the author is giving instructions directly to the reader. Sometimes the *you* is understood, as in a recipe: [you] combine the milk with the eggs; then add a pinch of salt and the juice of one lemon.

Here is an example of the how-it-works kind of process analysis. In this kind, the third-person pronoun (*he, she, it, they*) is usually used because the author is giving information to the reader *about* something.

> The uneven force caused by the difference in speed between the two wings applies a constant force at the top of the spinning boomerang. . . . Like a leaning bicycle wheel, the boomerang is

*Words printed in SMALL CAPITALS are defined in the Glossary.

constantly turning to the left or right, so that it travels in a circle
and comes back to its starting point.
www.howstuffworks.com

Most processes that you ANALYZE will be linear rather than cyclical. Even
if the process is repeatable, your analysis will proceed chronologically step
by step, stage by stage to an end result that is different from the starting
point. Consider this explanatory analysis of how fresh oranges are turned
into orange juice concentrate:

> As the fruit starts to move along a concentrate plant's assembly
> line, it is first culled. . . . Moving up a conveyer belt, oranges
> are scrubbed with detergent before they roll on into juicing
> machines. There are several kinds of juicing machines, and they
> are something to see. One is called the Brown Seven Hundred.
> Seven hundred oranges a minute go into it and are split and
> reamed on the same kind of rosettes that are in the centers of
> ordinary kitchen reamers. The rinds that come pelting out the
> bottom are integral halves, just like the rinds of oranges squeezed
> in a kitchen. Another machine is the Food Machinery Corpo-
> ration's FMC In-line Extractor. It has a shining row of aluminum
> teeth. When an orange tumbles in, the upper jaw comes crunch-
> ing down on it while at the same time the orange is penetrated
> from below by a perforated steel tube. As the jaws crush the
> outside, the juice goes through the perforations in the tube and
> down into the plumbing of the concentrate plant. All in a second,
> the juice has been removed and the rind has been crushed and
> shredded beyond recognition.
>   From either machine, the juice flows on into a thing called
> the finisher, where seeds, rag, and pulp are removed. The fin-
> isher has a big stainless-steel screw that steadily drives the juice
> through a fine-mesh screen. From the finisher, it flows on into
> holding tanks.
> JOHN MCPHEE, *ORANGES*

John McPhee divides the process of making orange juice concentrate
from fresh fruit into five stages: (1) culling, (2) scrubbing, (3) extracting,
(4) straining, (5) storing. When you plan an essay that analyzes a process,

make a list of all the stages or phases in the process you are analyzing. Make sure that they are separate and distinct and that you haven't left any out. When you are satisfied that your list is complete, you are ready to decide upon the order in which you will present the steps.

The usual order of process analysis is chronological, beginning with the earliest stage of the process (the culling of the split and rotten oranges from the rest) and ending with the last, or with the finished product (concentrated orange juice in holding tanks). Notice that after they leave the conveyer belt, McPhee's oranges come to a fork in the road. They can go in different directions, depending upon what kind of juicing machine is being used. McPhee briefly follows the oranges into one kind of juicer and then comes back to the other. He has stopped time and forward motion for a moment. Now he picks them up again and proceeds down the line: "from either machine, the juice flows on into a thing called the finisher" where it is strained. From the straining stage, the orange concentrate goes into the fifth (and final) holding stage, where it is stored in large tanks.

Another lesson to take away here: if the order of the process you are analyzing is controlled by a piece of machinery or other mechanism, let it work for you. The first two stages of McPhee's analysis are organized as much by that conveyor belt—"moving up a conveyer belt, the oranges are scrubbed"—as by time. The third stage is organized by the operations of the extractor, and the last two stages are controlled by the finisher, which is connected to the extractor by the "plumbing" of the plant.

Some stages in a process analysis may be more complicated than others. Suppose you are explaining to someone how to replace a light switch. You might break the process down into six stages: (1) select and purchase the new switch; (2) turn off the power at the breaker box; (3) remove the switch plate; (4) disconnect the old switch and install the new one; (5) replace the switch plate; (6) turn the power back on. Obviously, one of these stages—"disconnect the old switch and install the new one"—is more complicated than the others. When this happens, you can break down the more complicated stage into its constituent steps, as McPhee does with his analysis of the production of orange juice concentrate.

The most complicated stage in McPhee's process analysis is the third one, extracting. He breaks it into the following steps: (1) an orange enters the extractor; (2) it is crushed by the extractor's steel jaws; (3) at the same time, the orange is "penetrated from below by a perforated steel tube"; (4) the extracted juice flows on to the next stage of the process. All of this happens "in a second," says McPhee; but for purposes of analysis and explanation, the steps must be presented in sequence, using such indicators of time and motion as "when," "while at the same time," "all in a second," "from . . . to," "next," and "then."

McPhee's process analysis is explanatory; it tells how orange juice concentrate is made. When you are telling someone how to do something (a directive process analysis), the method of breaking the process into steps and stages is the same. Here's how our analysis of how to change a light switch might break down the most complicated step in the process, the one where the old switch is removed and replaced. The words and phrases that signal the order and timing of the steps *within* this stage are printed in italics:

> To remove the old switch, *first* unscrew the two terminal screws on the sides. *If* the wires are attached to the back of the switch, *instead* clip off the old wires as closely to the switch as possible. *As* necessary, strip the insulation from the ends of the wires *until* approximately half an inch is exposed. *Next*, unscrew the green grounding screw, *and* disconnect the bare wire attached to it. You are *now* ready to remove the old switch and *replace* it with the new one. *Either* insert the ends of the insulated wires into the holes on the back of the new switch, *or* bend the ends of the wires around the terminal screws *and* tighten the screws. *Reattach* the bare wire to the green terminal. *Finally*, secure the new switch by tightening the two long screws at top and bottom into the ears on the old switch box.

Explaining this stage in our analysis is further complicated because we have to stop the flow of information (with "if . . . instead"; "either . . . or . . . and") to go down a fork in the road—the wires can be attached either to the screws on the sides of the switch or to holes in the rear—before getting back on track. And we now have to signal a move on to the next stage: "Once the new switch is installed, replacing the switch plate is a snap."

Actually, this simple next-to-last stage (don't forget to turn the power back on) requires a *twist* of the little screw in the center of the switch plate, which can serve to remind us that the forward movement of a process analysis, step by step, from beginning to end, is much like the twisting and turning of the plot in a NARRATIVE. Like plot in narrative, a process is a sequence of events or actions. You are the narrator, and you are telling the exciting story of how something is made or done or how it works.

You may simply conclude your story with the product or end result of the process you've been analyzing. But you may want to round out your account by summarizing the stages you have just gone through or by encouraging the reader to follow your directions—"changing a light switch yourself is easy, and it can save money"—or by explaining why the process is important. The production of orange juice concentrate, for example, transformed Florida's citrus industry. In what is called "the old fresh-fruit days," 40 percent of the oranges grown in Florida were left to rot in the fields because they couldn't travel well. "Now," as McPhee notes, "with the exception of split and rotten fruit, all of Florida's orange crop is used." This is not exactly the end product of the process McPhee is analyzing, but it is an important consequence and one that makes technical advances in the citrus industry seem more worth reading about.

One other detail, though a minor one, in McPhee's analysis that you may find interesting: when all that fresh fruit was left to rot on the ground because it couldn't be shipped and local people couldn't use it all, the cows stepped in to help. Thus McPhee notes that in the days before orange juice concentrate, "Florida milk tasted like orangeade." Details like this may not make the process you are analyzing clearer or more accurate, but they may well make the reader more interested in the process itself.

Recipes such as this one for Razzleberry Lemonade are common examples of process analysis. Notice that even in this simple form, the analysis (or breakdown) of the process being explained (how to make a special kind of lemonade) is divided into steps or stages. This is a pattern you can use to explain operations as complex as how to use an FMC In-line Extractor to turn citrus fruit into concentrate or as simple as how to make orange juice from concentrate (directions: add water). Most complicated problems, however, are easier to solve if you break them down into a series of smaller problems. Once you have solved a problem, the pieces of the puzzle may fit together seamlessly in your mind. But if you are explaining the solution in writing to other people, they can grasp it better if you re-create the process step by step, stage by stage, in more or less chronological order.

CONSIDER FURTHER . . .

1. Write out a favorite recipe for someone who has never prepared the dish before. Be sure to include a list of ingredients and to break the process down into steps.

2. Without diagrams or gestures, using only words, write out directions telling how to do one of the following simple tasks: sharpen a pencil with a knife; tie a necktie or a pair of shoelaces or a square knot; use chopsticks.

Razzleberry Lemonade

On a hot day, nothing beats a cold, frosty glass of sweet-tart lemonade. Our version includes the kick of tangy raspberries. If fresh berries are available, they make a slightly better puree, although frozen unsweetened berries will do.

- 10 cups water
- 1 cup sugar
- 1 cup fresh or frozen unsweetened raspberries
- 1¼ cups fresh lemon juice (about 9 lemons)
- Grated zest of 1 lemon

1. Combine 2 cups of the water and the sugar in a non-aluminum 3½-quart saucepan over high heat. When the mixture comes to a boil, remove from the heat and set aside to cool.

2. Puree the raspberries in a blender. Strain into a small bowl to remove the seeds. Add the lemon juice, the lemon zest, and the raspberry puree to the cooled sugar water. Stir in the remaining 8 cups water.

3. Pour into a glass pitcher. Chill and serve over ice.

Serves 8 to 10

JOSHUA PIVEN AND DAVID BORGENICHT

How to Fend Off a Shark

Joshua Piven and David Borgenicht are the authors of the best-selling *Worst-Case Scenario Survival Handbook* (1999), a section of which is reprinted here. You never know when you may need to deliver a baby in a taxi, identify a bomb, or escape from a mountain lion. Piven and Borgenicht's survival guide analyzes how experts perform these and other alarming feats. Process-analysis writing often involves problem solving, remember. So if you do not happen to have an expert on hand the next time you are attacked by a shark or need to jump from a bridge, you may want to pull out Piven and Borgenicht's manual for an instant analysis of the problem—and its solution.

XXXXXXXXXXXXXXXXXXXXXXXXXXXXXXXXXXXXXXXXXXXXXXXXXXXXXXXXXXXXXXXX

1 Hit back.

If a shark is coming toward you or attacks you, use anything you have in your possession—a camera, probe, harpoon gun, your fist—to hit the shark's eyes or gills, which are the areas most sensitive to pain.

2 Make quick, sharp, repeated jabs in these areas.

Sharks are predators and will usually only follow through on an attack if they have the advantage, so making the shark unsure of its advantage in any way possible will increase your chances of survival. Contrary to popular opinion, the shark's nose is not the area to attack, unless you cannot reach the eyes or gills. Hitting the shark simply tells it that you are not defenseless.

How to Avoid an Attack

- Always stay in groups—sharks are more likely to attack an individual.
- Do not wander too far from shore. This isolates you and creates the additional danger of being too far from assistance.

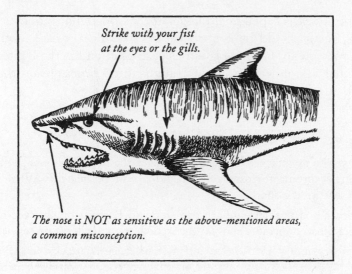

Strike with your fist at the eyes or the gills.

The nose is NOT as sensitive as the above-mentioned areas, a common misconception.

- Avoid being in the water during darkness or twilight hours, when sharks are most active and have a competitive sensory advantage. 7
- Do not enter the water if you are bleeding from an open wound or if you are menstruating—a shark is drawn to blood and its olfactory ability is acute. 8
- Try not to wear shiny jewelry, because the reflected light resembles the sheen of fish scales. 9
- Avoid waters with known effluents or sewage and those being used by sport or commercial fishermen, especially if there are signs of bait fish or feeding activity. Diving seabirds are good indicators of such activity. 10
- Use extra caution when waters are murky and avoid showing any uneven tan lines or wearing brightly colored clothing—sharks see contrast particularly well. 11
- If a shark shows itself to you, it may be curious rather than predatory and will probably swim on and leave you alone. If you are under the surface and lucky enough to see an attacking shark, then you do have a good chance of defending yourself if the shark is not too large. 12
- Scuba divers should avoid lying on the surface, where they may look like a piece of prey to a shark, and from where they cannot see a shark approaching. 13

- A shark attack is a potential danger for anyone who frequents marine   14
waters, but it should be kept in perspective. Bees, wasps, and snakes
are responsible for far more fatalities each year, and in the United States
the annual risk of death from lightning is thirty times greater than from
a shark attack.

XXXXXXXXXXXXXXXXXXXXXX **FOR DISCUSSION** XXXXXXXXXXXXXXXXXXXXX

1. If you are being attacked by a shark, what is the first thing you should do to
fend it off, according to Joshua Piven and David Borgenicht? What message
does this send to the shark?

2. It is a common misconception, say Piven and Borgenicht, that the nose of a
shark is its most vulnerable spot. Which parts are actually more sensitive?

3. Besides explaining how to fend off a shark once it attacks you, Piven and
Borgenicht also explain how to avoid an attack in the first place. Which of their
recommendations seem most valuable to you? Why?

4. How likely is it that you or anyone else who frequents marine waters will
actually be attacked by a shark? Does this mean you don't need to take the
precautions the authors advise?

XXXXXXXXXXXXXX **STRATEGIES AND STRUCTURES** XXXXXXXXXXXXX

1. PROCESS ANALYSIS typically tells the reader how to do something or how
something works or is made. Which do we have here? Please explain.

2. Piven and Borgenicht tell how to fight off a shark before they explain how to
avoid a fight in the first place. Why do you think they chose this order for
presenting the parts of their ANALYSIS rather than the other way around?

3. How is item 2 in Piven and Borgenicht's first list related to item 1? Please
explain.

4. Both sections of this how-to selection take the form of lists. How effective do
you find such listing as a means of organizing the information conveyed here?
Why do you think Piven and Borgenicht chose this method rather than putting
their advice in paragraphs?

5. Are the items in the second part of this selection listed in any particular order
that you can discern—for EXAMPLE, from more to less important? If so, what is
that order? If not, should they be? Or are they all more or less equally important?

XXXXXXXXXXXX **WORDS AND FIGURES OF SPEECH** XXXXXXXXXXXX

1. The language in this selection is simple and direct. What would be the justification for using such plain language in an essay listing procedures for dealing with an emergency?

2. "Contrary to popular opinion" is a CLICHÉ. Should the authors have avoided such a well-worn phrase here, or might there be a justification for it?

3. What part of a fish's anatomy are the gills (2)? What are they used for? To what anatomical function does the word "olfactory" refer (8)?

4. If you were to study the *nomenclature* of shark anatomy, what would you be studying? Why do you think Piven and Borgenicht give a simplified nomenclature in their diagram rather than a full-scale version?

XXXXXXXXXXXXXXXXXXXX **FOR WRITING** XXXXXXXXXXXXXXXXXXXX

1. Piven and Borgenicht's scenarios are all "worst-case." Make a short list of the steps you would take to avoid a more likely danger such as an auto collision on an icy road, running over a deer, having your pocket picked, having your identity stolen, or paying too much for something—an article of clothing or a bad meal at a restaurant, for instance.

2. Develop your list into a step-by-step essay. List procedures as appropriate, but also try to give your reader a sense of priorities: which steps are crucial? which ones are important but not vital? which are subordinate parts of a larger whole?

HOW BOYS BECOME MEN

Jon Katz (b. 1947) is a mystery writer and media critic. A former executive producer for CBS *Morning News*, he has written columns about the Internet for *Rolling Stone, HotWired*, and slashdot.org, a Web site dedicated to "News for Nerds." For Katz, the Internet is different from other, more traditional media, such as books and newspapers, because it is interactive. Interactivity, however, is not a trait that most men come by naturally in their personal lives, says Katz. Why? Because "sensitivity" has been beaten out of them as boys. Katz analyzes this male maturation process in "How Boys Become Men," first published in 1993 in *Glamour*, a magazine for young women.

xxxxxxxxxxxxxxxxxxxxxxxxxxxxxxxxxxxxxxxxxxxxxxxxxxxxxxxxxxxxxxxxx

Two nine-year-old boys, neighbors and friends, were walking home 1
from school. The one in the bright blue windbreaker was laughing and swinging a heavy-looking book bag toward the head of his friend, who kept ducking and stepping back. "What's the matter?" asked the kid with the bag, whooshing it over his head. "You chicken?"

His friend stopped, stood still and braced himself. The bag slammed 2
into the side of his face, the thump audible all the way across the street where I stood watching. The impact knocked him to the ground, where he lay mildly stunned for a second. Then he struggled up, rubbing the side of his head. "See?" he said proudly. "I'm no chicken."

No. A chicken would probably have had the sense to get out of the 3
way. This boy was already well on the road to becoming a *man*, having learned one of the central ethics of his gender: Experience pain rather than show fear.

Women tend to see men as a giant problem in need of solution. 4
They tell us that we're remote and uncommunicative, that we need to demonstrate less machismo and more commitment, more humanity. But

🖤 174 🖤

if you don't understand something about boys, you can't understand why men are the way we are, why we find it so difficult to make friends or to acknowledge our fears and problems.

Boys live in a world with its own Code of Conduct, a set of ruthless,   5
unspoken, and unyielding rules:

Don't be a goody-goody.

Never rat. If your parents ask about bruises, shrug.

Never admit fear. Ride the roller coaster, join the fistfight, do what you have to do. Asking for help is for sissies.

Empathy is for nerds. You can help your best buddy, under certain circumstances. Everyone else is on his own.

Never discuss anything of substance with anybody. Grunt, shrug, dump on teachers, laugh at wimps, talk about comic books. Anything else is risky.

Boys are rewarded for throwing hard. Most other activities—read-   6
ing, befriending girls, or just thinking—are considered weird. And if there's one thing boys don't want to be, it's weird.

More than anything else, boys are supposed to learn how to handle   7
themselves. I remember the bitter fifth-grade conflict I touched off by elbowing aside a bigger boy named Barry and seizing the cafeteria's last carton of chocolate milk. Teased for getting aced out by a wimp, he had to reclaim his place in the pack. Our fistfight, at recess, ended with my knees buckling and my lip bleeding while my friends, sympathetic but out of range, watched resignedly.

When I got home, my mother took one look at my swollen face and   8
screamed. I wouldn't tell her anything, but when my father got home I cracked and confessed, pleading with them to do nothing. Instead, they called Barry's parents, who restricted his television for a week.

The following morning, Barry and six of his pals stepped out from   9
behind a stand of trees. "It's the rat," said Barry.

I bled a little more. *Rat* was scrawled in crayon across my desk.   10

They were waiting for me after school for a number of afternoons   11
to follow. I tried varying my routes and avoiding bushes and hedges. It usually didn't work.

I was as ashamed for telling as I was frightened. "You did ask for   12
it," said my best friend. Frontier Justice has nothing on Boy Justice.

In panic, I appealed to a cousin who was several years older. He   13
followed me home from school, and when Barry's gang surrounded me,
he came barreling toward us. "Stay away from my cousin," he shouted,
"or I'll kill you."

After they were gone, however, my cousin could barely stop laugh-   14
ing. "You were afraid of *them?*" he howled. "They barely came up to my
waist."

Men remember receiving little mercy as boys; maybe that's why it's   15
sometimes difficult for them to show any.

"I know lots of men who had happy childhoods, but none who have   16
happy memories of the way other boys treated them," says a friend. "It's
a macho marathon from third grade up, when you start butting each
other in the stomach."

"The thing is," adds another friend, "you learn early on to hide   17
what you feel. It's never safe to say, 'I'm scared.' My girlfriend asks me
why I don't talk more about what I'm feeling. I've gotten better at it,
but it will *never* come naturally."

You don't need to be a shrink to see how the lessons boys learn   18
affect their behavior as men. Men are being asked, more and more, to
show sensitivity, but they dread the very word. They struggle to build
their increasingly uncertain work lives but will deny they're in trouble.
They want love, affection, and support but don't know how to ask for
them. They hide their weaknesses and fears from all, even those they
care for. They've learned to be wary of intervening when they see others
in trouble. They often still balk at being stigmatized as weird.

Some men get shocked into sensitivity—when they lose their jobs,   19
their wives, or their lovers. Others learn it through a strong marriage, or
through their own children.

It may be a long while, however, before male culture evolves to the   20
point that boys can learn more from one another than how to hit curve
balls. Last month, walking my dog past the playground near my house,
I saw three boys encircling a fourth, laughing and pushing him. He was
skinny and rumpled, and he looked frightened. One boy knelt behind

him while another pushed him from the front, a trick familiar to any former boy. He fell backward.

When the others ran off, he brushed the dirt off his elbows and walked toward the swings. His eyes were moist and he was struggling for control. 21

"Hi," I said through the chain-link fence. "How ya doing?" 22

"Fine," he said quickly, kicking his legs out and beginning his swing. 23

XXXXXXXXXXXXXXXXXXXX **FOR DISCUSSION** XXXXXXXXXXXXXXXXXXXX

1. In order to explain how boys become men, Jon Katz must first explain how boys become boys. By what specific "rules" does this process occur, according to him (5)?

2. Is Katz right, do you think, in his ANALYSIS of how boys are brought up? Why or why not?

3. The end result of how they learn to behave as boys, says Katz, is that men find it difficult "to make friends or to acknowledge our fears and problems" (4). They lack "sensitivity" (19). Do you agree? In your experience, is Katz's analysis accurate or inaccurate? Please explain.

4. According to Katz, women are puzzled by "male culture" (20). How, in his view, do women regard men? Do you agree or disagree with this analysis? Why?

5. What evidence, if any, can you find in Katz's essay to indicate that the author has learned as an adult male to behave in ways he was not taught as a boy? By what processes, according to Katz, do men sometimes learn such new kinds of behavior?

XXXXXXXXXXXXXX **STRATEGIES AND STRUCTURES** XXXXXXXXXXXXXX

1. Katz tells the story in paragraphs 1 and 2 of a boy who prefers to get knocked down rather than be called a "chicken." Why do you think he begins with this incident? What stage or aspect of the boy-training process is he illustrating?

2. The longest of the ANECDOTES that Katz tells to show how boys learn to behave is the one about himself. Where does it begin and end? By what process or processes is he being taught here?

3. What is the role of the older cousin in the NARRATIVE Katz tells about himself as a boy? How does the cousin's response in paragraph 14 illustrate the process Katz is analyzing?

4. Where else in his essay does Katz tell a brief story to illustrate what he is saying about how boys are trained? How important are these stories to his ARGUMENT? What would the essay be like without any of the stories?

5. "If you don't understand something about boys, you can't understand why men are the way we are . . ." (4). To whom is Katz speaking here? What purposes might he have for explaining the male maturation process to this particular audience?

6. Besides ANALYZING the processes by which boys learn to behave according to a rigid "Code of Conduct," Katz's essay also analyzes the lasting EFFECTS caused by this early training (5). What are some of these effects?

XXXXXXXXXXXXX **WORDS AND FIGURES OF SPEECH** XXXXXXXXXXXXX

1. How does your dictionary define "machismo" (4)? What language(s) does it derive from?

2. To feel *sympathy* for someone means to have feelings and emotions similar to theirs. What does "empathy" mean (5)?

3. A "dead" METAPHOR, such as "table leg," is so familiar we forget it is making a figurative COMPARISON. How about "shrink" in paragraph 18? What's the comparison here?

4. Verbal IRONY is the use of one word or phrase to imply another with a quite different meaning. What's ironic about the boy's reply to Katz's question in paragraph 23?

XXXXXXXXXXXXXXXXXXXXXXX **FOR WRITING** XXXXXXXXXXXXXXXXXXXXXXX

1. Write a brief Code of Conduct like the one in paragraph 5 that lays out the unspoken rules of the "culture," male or female, in which you grew up.

2. Write an ANALYSIS of the process of how boys become men, as you see it. Or, alternatively, write an analysis of the process(es) by which *girls* are typically socialized to become women in America or somewhere else. Draw on your own personal experience, or what you know from others, or both. Feel free to use ANECDOTES and other elements of NARRATIVE as appropriate to illustrate your analysis.

ALEXANDER PETRUNKEVITCH

The Spider and the Wasp

Alexander Petrunkevitch (1875–1964), a native of Russia who came to the United States in his late twenties, was a world-renowned expert on spiders. Beginning in 1911 with an index to the spiders of Central and South America, he studied and wrote about arachnids for more than fifty years. In "The Spider and the Wasp," first published in *Scientific American* in 1952, Petrunkevitch analyzes the process by which a female digger wasp converts a living tarantula into food for her young. The process, he says, is "a classic example of what looks like intelligence pitted against instinct."

XXXXXXXXXXXXXXXXXXXXXXXXXXXXXXXXXXXXXXXXXXXXXXXXXXXXXXXXXXXXXXXXX

To hold its own in the struggle for existence, every species of animal must have a regular source of food, and if it happens to live on other animals, its survival may be very delicately balanced. The hunter cannot exist without the hunted; if the latter should perish from the earth, the former would, too. When the hunted also prey on some of the hunters, the matter may become complicated. 1

This is nowhere better illustrated than in the insect world. Think of the complexity of a situation such as the following: There is a certain wasp, *Pimpla inquisitor*, whose larvae feed on the larvae of the tussock moth. *Pimpla* larvae in turn serve as food for the larvae of a second wasp, and the latter in their turn nourish still a third wasp. What subtle balance between fertility and mortality must exist in the case of each of these four species to prevent the extinction of all of them! An excess of mortality over fertility in a single member of the group would ultimately wipe out all four. 2

This is not a unique case. The two great orders of insects, Hymenoptera and Diptera, are full of such examples of interrelationship. And the spiders (which are not insects but members of a separate order of arthropods) also are killers and victims of insects. 3

The picture is complicated by the fact that those species which are 4
carnivorous in the larval stage have to be provided with animal food by
a vegetarian mother. The survival of the young depends on the mother's
correct choice of a food which she does not eat herself.

In the feeding and safeguarding of their progeny the insects and 5
spiders exhibit some interesting analogies to reasoning and some crass
examples of blind instinct. The case I propose to describe here is that of
the tarantula spiders and their arch-enemy, the digger wasps of the genus
Pepsis. It is a classic example of what looks like intelligence pitted against
instinct—a strange situation in which the victim, though fully able to
defend itself, submits unwittingly to its destruction.

Most tarantulas live in the Tropics, but several species occur in the tem- 6
perate zone and a few are common in the southern U.S. Some varieties
are large and have powerful fangs with which they can inflict a deep
wound. These formidable looking spiders do not, however, attack man;
you can hold one in your hand, if you are gentle, without being bitten.
Their bite is dangerous only to insects and small mammals such as mice;
for a man it is no worse than a hornet's sting.

Tarantulas customarily live in deep cylindrical burrows, from which 7
they emerge at dusk and into which they retire at dawn. Mature males
wander about after dark in search of females and occasionally stray into
houses. After mating, the male dies in a few weeks, but a female lives
much longer and can mate several years in succession. In a Paris museum
is a tropical specimen which is said to have been living in captivity for
25 years.

A fertilized female tarantula lays from 200 to 400 eggs at a time; 8
thus it is possible for a single tarantula to produce several thousand
young. She takes no care of them beyond weaving a cocoon of silk to
enclose the eggs. After they hatch, the young walk away, find convenient
places in which to dig their burrows and spend the rest of their lives in
solitude. Tarantulas feed mostly on insects and millepedes. Once their
appetite is appeased, they digest the food for several days before eating
again. Their sight is poor, being limited to sensing a change in the intensity of light and to the perception of moving objects. They apparently
have little or no sense of hearing, for a hungry tarantula will pay no

attention to a loudly chirping cricket placed in its cage unless the insect happens to touch one of its legs.

But all spiders, and especially hairy ones, have an extremely delicate 9 sense of touch. Laboratory experiments prove that tarantulas can distinguish three types of touch: pressure against the body wall, stroking of the body hair and riffling of certain very fine hairs on the legs called trichobothria. Pressure against the body, by a finger or the end of a pencil, causes the tarantula to move off slowly for a short distance. The touch excites no defensive response unless the approach is from above where the spider can see the motion, in which case it rises on its hind legs, lifts its front legs, opens its fangs and holds this threatening posture as long as the object continues to move. When the motion stops, the spider drops back to the ground, remains quiet for a few seconds and then moves slowly away.

The entire body of a tarantula, especially its legs, is thickly clothed 10 with hair. Some of it is short and woolly, some long and stiff. Touching this body hair produces one of two distinct reactions. When the spider is hungry, it responds with an immediate and swift attack. At the touch of a cricket's antennae the tarantula seizes the insect so swiftly that a motion picture taken at the rate of 64 frames per second shows only the result and not the process of capture. But when the spider is not hungry, the stimulation of its hairs merely causes it to shake the touched limb. An insect can walk under its hairy belly unharmed.

The trichobothria, very fine hairs growing from disk-like mem- 11 branes on the legs, were once thought to be the spider's hearing organs, but we now know that they have nothing to do with sound. They are sensitive only to air movement. A light breeze makes them vibrate slowly without disturbing the common hair. When one blows gently on the trichobothria, the tarantula reacts with a quick jerk of its four front legs. If the front and hind legs are stimulated at the same time, the spider makes a sudden jump. This reaction is quite independent of the state of its appetite.

These three tactile responses—to pressure on the body wall, to 12 moving of the common hair and to flexing of the trichobothria—are so different from one another that there is no possibility of confusing them. They serve the tarantula adequately for most of its needs and enable it to avoid most annoyances and dangers. But they fail the spider completely when it meets its deadly enemy, the digger wasp *Pepsis*.

These solitary wasps are beautiful and formidable creatures. Most   13
species are either a deep shiny blue all over, or deep blue with rusty
wings. The largest have a wing span of about four inches. They live on
nectar. When excited, they give off a pungent odor—a warning that they
are ready to attack. The sting is much worse than that of a bee or common wasp, and the pain and swelling last longer. In the adult stage the
wasp lives only a few months. The female produces but a few eggs, one
at a time at intervals of two or three days. For each egg the mother must
provide one adult tarantula, alive but paralyzed. The tarantula must be
of the correct species to nourish the larva. The mother wasp attaches the
egg to the paralyzed spider's abdomen. Upon hatching from the egg, the
larva is many hundreds of times smaller than its living but helpless victim. It eats no other food and drinks no water. By the time it has finished
its single gargantuan meal and become ready for wasphood, nothing
remains of the tarantula but its indigestible chitinous skeleton.

The mother wasp goes tarantula-hunting when the egg in her ovary   14
is almost ready to be laid. Flying low over the ground late on a sunny
afternoon, the wasp looks for its victim or for the mouth of a tarantula
burrow, a round hole edged by a bit of silk. The sex of the spider makes
no difference, but the mother is highly discriminating as to species. Each
species of *Pepsis* requires a certain species of tarantula, and the wasp will
not attack the wrong species. In a cage with a tarantula which is not its
normal prey the wasp avoids the spider, and is usually killed by it in the
night.

Yet when a wasp finds the correct species, it is the other way about.   15
To identify the species the wasp apparently must explore the spider with
her antennae. The tarantula shows an amazing tolerance to this exploration. The wasp crawls under it and walks over it without evoking any
hostile response. The molestation is so great and so persistent that the
tarantula often rises on all eight legs, as if it were on stilts. It may stand
this way for several minutes. Meanwhile the wasp, having satisfied itself
that the victim is of the right species, moves off a few inches to dig the
spider's grave. Working vigorously with legs and jaws, it excavates a hole
8 to 10 inches deep with a diameter slightly larger than the spider's girth.

Now and again the wasp pops out of the hole to make sure that the spider is still there.

When the grave is finished, the wasp returns to the tarantula to complete her ghastly enterprise. First she feels it all over once more with her antennae. Then her behavior becomes more aggressive. She bends her abdomen, protruding her sting, and searches for the soft membrane at the point where the spider's leg joins its body—the only spot where she can penetrate the horny skeleton. From time to time, as the exasperated spider slowly shifts ground, the wasp turns on her back and slides along with the aid of her wings, trying to get under the tarantula for a shot at the vital spot. During all this maneuvering, which can last for several minutes, the tarantula makes no move to save itself. Finally the wasp corners it against some obstruction and grasps one of its legs in her powerful jaws. Now at last the harassed spider tries a desperate but vain defense. The two contestants roll over and over on the ground. It is a terrifying sight and the outcome is always the same. The wasp finally manages to thrust her sting into the soft spot and holds it there for a few seconds while she pumps in the poison. Almost immediately the tarantula falls paralyzed on its back. Its legs stop twitching; its heart stops beating. Yet it is not dead, as is shown by the fact that if taken from the wasp it can be restored to some sensitivity by being kept in a moist chamber for several months. [16]

After paralyzing the tarantula, the wasp cleans herself by dragging her body along the ground and rubbing her feet, sucks the drop of blood oozing from the wound in the spider's abdomen, then grabs a leg of the flabby, helpless animal in her jaws and drags it down to the bottom of the grave. She stays there for many minutes, sometimes for several hours, and what she does all that time in the dark we do not know. Eventually she lays her egg and attaches it to the side of the spider's abdomen with a sticky secretion. Then she emerges, fills the grave with soil carried bit by bit in her jaws, and finally tramples the ground all around to hide any trace of the grave from prowlers. Then she flies away, leaving her descendant safely started in life. [17]

In all this the behavior of the wasp evidently is qualitatively different from that of the spider. The wasp acts like an intelligent animal. This is [18] not to say that instinct plays no part or that she reasons as man does. But her actions are to the point; they are not automatic and can be modified to fit the situation. We do not know for certain how she identifies the tarantula—probably it is by some olfactory or chemo-tactile sense— but she does it purposefully and does not blindly tackle a wrong species.

On the other hand, the tarantula's behavior shows only confusion. Evidently the wasp's pawing gives it no pleasure, for it tries to move away. That the wasp is not simulating sexual stimulation is certain, because male and female tarantulas react in the same way to its advances. That the spider is not anesthetized by some odorless secretion is easily shown by blowing lightly at the tarantula and making it jump suddenly. What, then, makes the tarantula behave as stupidly as it does? 19

No clear, simple answer is available. Possibly the stimulation by the wasp's antennae is masked by a heavier pressure on the spider's body, so that it reacts as when prodded by a pencil. But the explanation may be much more complex. Initiative in attack is not in the nature of tarantulas; most species fight only when cornered so that escape is impossible. Their inherited patterns of behavior apparently prompt them to avoid problems rather than attack them. For example, spiders always weave their webs in three dimensions, and when a spider finds that there is insufficient space to attach certain threads in the third dimension, it leaves the place and seeks another, instead of finishing the web in a single plane. This urge to escape seems to arise under all circumstances, in all phases of life and to take the place of reasoning. For a spider to change the pattern of its web is as impossible as for an inexperienced man to build a bridge across a chasm obstructing his way. 20

In a way the instinctive urge to escape is not only easier but more efficient than reasoning. The tarantula does exactly what is most efficient in all cases except in an encounter with a ruthless and determined attacker dependent for the existence of her own species on killing as many tarantulas as she can lay eggs. Perhaps in this case the spider follows its usual pattern of trying to escape, instead of seizing and killing the wasp, because it is not aware of its danger. In any case, the survival of the tarantula species as a whole is protected by the fact that the spider is much more fertile than the wasp. 21

XXXXXXXXXXXXXXXXXXXXXX **FOR DISCUSSION** XXXXXXXXXXXXXXXXXXXXXX

1. The first half of paragraph 8 of "The Spider and the Wasp" is a miniature PROCESS ANALYSIS. What process does it ANALYZE?

2. Alexander Petrunkevitch begins his main process analysis with its end result and then returns to the wasp's hunt for her prey. That end result is DESCRIBED in paragraph 13. What is it?

3. Petrunkevitch describes the process by which the wasp converts the spider into food as a case of "intelligence pitted against instinct" (5). What does the spider do (or not do) that seems merely instinctive? What is there in the wasp's behavior that looks like intelligence at work?

4. If a digger wasp's favorite kind of tarantula always loses the deadly struggle between them, why don't tarantulas die out as a species?

5. What might happen to the digger wasp as a species if it were a more prolific breeder? If the tarantula were less prolific? What delicate natural balance do spider and wasp together illustrate?

XXXXXXXXXXXXXX **STRATEGIES AND STRUCTURES** XXXXXXXXXXXXXX

1. By what "process of capture" does the tarantula get its food in paragraph 10? Petrunkevitch observes "the result" of the process here. Why doesn't he also ANALYZE the process itself into steps?

2. Point out the six stages—from hunting to burying—into which Petrunkevitch analyzes the process by which the wasp conquers the spider.

3. How does Petrunkevitch's account of the other wasp larvae in paragraph 2 prepare us for the case of the spider and the digger wasp?

4. Petrunkevitch refers to the wasp as the spider's "arch-enemy" (5). How else does he give their struggle human characteristics and a human scale? Give several EXAMPLES from the text.

5. Paragraphs 12 and 19 are transition paragraphs. Which sentences look backward? Which look forward? With what single sentence in paragraph 19 does Petrunkevitch set up the remainder of his essay?

6. Petrunkevitch's PROCESS ANALYSIS incorporates elements of the COMPARISON AND CONTRAST essays discussed in Chapter 6. Which does he stress: the differences between spiders and wasps, or their similarities? Please point to specific passages to support your answer.

1. "Gargantuan" means "gigantic" (13). Who is Gargantua?

2. In addition to scientific terms ("Hymenoptera," "Diptera," "trichobothria"), Petrunkevitch uses such nontechnical terms as "wasphood" and "prowlers" (3, 9, 11, 13, 17). Point out additional EXAMPLES of both kinds of language. What does Petrunkevitch's "mixed" vocabulary tell you about the readers of *Scientific American*?

3. Choose four of the following words with which you are least familiar, and look up their exact meanings in your dictionary: "subtle" (2), "carnivorous" (4), "progeny" (5), "formidable" (6, 13), "appeased" (8), "tactile" (12), "pungent" (13), "chitinous" (13), "olfactory" (18), "simulating" (19), "anesthetized" (19), "chasm" (20).

1. Make a list of the steps you went through to master some complex activity, perhaps one in which instinct eventually took over from conscious intelligence. Examples might be swimming, sailing, driving a car, riding a bike, or playing a musical instrument.

2. ANALYZE the process by which an insect or animal or bird you have observed meets its basic needs. Examples might be getting food; building a nest or burrow; or producing, looking after, or training its young. Alternatively, if you have trained an animal to do something that goes beyond mere instinct, analyze the training process that you (and the animal) went through.

GARRISON KEILLOR

How to Write a Letter

Garrison Keillor (b. 1942), is the father of public radio's "A Prairie Home Companion" and sole proprietor of the mythical Lake Wobegon, "where all the men are good looking, all the women are strong, and all the children are above average." "How to Write a Letter" comes from *We Are Still Married* (1989), a collection dedicated to Keillor's "classmate" Corinne Guntzel (1942–1986), whom he addresses in the opening paragraphs. Meditating on the person you're writing to "until you can almost see her or him in the room with you" is just one of the steps into which Keillor breaks down the complexities of the writing process.

XXXXXXXXXXXXXXXXXXXXXXXXXXXXXXXXXXXXXXXXXXXXXXXXXXXXXXXXXXXXXX

We shy persons need to write a letter now and then, or else we'll dry up and blow away. It's true. And I speak as one who loves to reach for the phone, dial the number, and talk. I say, "Big Bopper here—what's shakin', babes?" The telephone is to shyness what Hawaii is to February, it's a way out of the woods, *and yet*: a letter is better. 1

Such a sweet gift—a piece of handmade writing, in an envelope that is not a bill, sitting in our friend's path when she trudges home from a long day spent among wahoos and savages, a day our words will help repair. They don't need to be immortal, just sincere. She can read them twice and again tomorrow: *You're someone I care about, Corinne, and think of often and every time I do you make me smile.* 2

We need to write, otherwise nobody will know who we are. They will have only a vague impression of us as A Nice Person, because, frankly, we don't shine at conversation, we lack the confidence to thrust our faces forward and say, "Hi, I'm Heather Hooten; let me tell you about my week." Mostly we say "Uh-huh" and "Oh, really." People smile and look over our shoulder, looking for someone else to meet. 3

So a shy person sits down and writes a letter. To be known by another person—to meet and talk freely on the page—to be close despite 4 distance. To escape from anonymity and be our own sweet selves and express the music of our souls.

Same thing that moves a giant rock star to sing his heart out in front of 123,000 people moves us to take ballpoint in hand and write a few lines to our dear Aunt Eleanor. *We want to be known.* We want her to know that we have fallen in love, that we quit our job, that we're moving to New York, and we want to say a few things that might not get said in casual conversation: *Thank you for what you've meant to me, I am very happy right now.*

The first step in writing letters is to get over the guilt of *not* writing. You don't "owe" anybody a letter. Letters are a gift. The burning shame you feel when you see unanswered mail makes it harder to pick up a pen and makes for a cheerless letter when you finally do. *I feel bad about not writing, but I've been so busy*, etc. Skip this. Few letters are obligatory, and they are *Thanks for the wonderful gift* and *I am terribly sorry to hear about George's death* and *Yes, you're welcome to stay with us next month*, and not many more than that. Write those promptly if you want to keep your friends. Don't worry about the others, except love letters, of course. When your true love writes, *Dear Light of My Life, Joy of My Heart, O Lovely Pulsating Core of My Sensate Life*, some response is called for.

Some of the best letters are tossed off in a burst of inspiration, so keep your writing stuff in one place where you can sit down for a few minutes and *(Dear Roy, I am in the middle of a book entitled* We Are Still Married *but thought I'd drop you a line. Hi to your sweetie, too)* dash off a note to a pal. Envelopes, stamps, address book, everything in a drawer so you can write fast when the pen is hot.

A blank white eight-by-eleven sheet can look as big as Montana if the pen's not so hot—try a smaller page and write boldly. Or use a note card with a piece of fine art on the front; if your letter ain't good, at least they get the Matisse. Get a pen that makes a sensuous line, get a comfortable typewriter, a friendly word processor—whichever feels easy to the hand.

Sit for a few minutes with the blank sheet in front of you, and meditate on the person you will write to, let your friend come to mind until you can almost see her or him in the room with you. Remember the last time you saw each other and how your friend looked and what you said and what perhaps was unsaid between you, and when your friend becomes real to you, start to write.

Write the salutation—*Dear* You—and take a deep breath and plunge in. A simple declarative sentence will do, followed by another and another and another. Tell us what you're doing and tell it like you were talking to us. Don't think about grammar, don't think about lit'ry style, don't try to write dramatically, just give us your news. Where did you go, who did you see, what did they say, what do you think?   10

If you don't know where to begin, start with the present moment: *I'm sitting at the kitchen table on a rainy Saturday morning. Everyone is gone and the house is quiet.* Let your simple description of the present moment lead to something else, let the letter drift gently along.   11

The toughest letter to crank out is one that is meant to impress, as we all know from writing job applications; if it's hard work to slip off a letter to a friend, maybe you're trying too hard to be terrific. A letter is only a report to someone who already likes you for reasons other than your brilliance. Take it easy.   12

Don't worry about form. It's not a term paper. When you come to the end of one episode, just start a new paragraph. You can go from a few lines about the sad state of pro football to the fight with your mother to your fond memories of Mexico to your cat's urinary-tract infection to a few thoughts on personal indebtedness and on to the kitchen sink and what's in it. The more you write, the easier it gets, and when you have a True True Friend to write to, a *compadre*, a soul sibling, then it's like driving a car down a country road, you just get behind the keyboard and press on the gas.   13

Don't tear up the page and start over when you write a bad line— try to write your way out of it. Make mistakes and plunge on. Let the letter cook along and let yourself be bold. Outrage, confusion, love— whatever is in your mind, let it find a way to the page. Writing is a means of discovery, always, and when you come to the end and write *Yours ever* or *Hugs and kisses*, you'll know something you didn't when you wrote *Dear Pal*.   14

Probably your friend will put your letter away, and it'll be read again a few years from now—and it will improve with age. And forty years from now, your friend's grandkids will dig it out of the attic and   15 read it, a sweet and precious relic of the ancient eighties that gives them a sudden clear glimpse of you and her and the world we old-timers knew. You will then have created an object of art. Your simple lines about where you went, who you saw, what they said, will speak to those children and they will feel in their hearts the humanity of our times.

You can't pick up a phone and call the future and tell them about our times. You have to pick up a piece of paper.   16

XXXXXXXXXXXXXXXXXXXXXX **FOR DISCUSSION** XXXXXXXXXXXXXXXXXXXXXX

1. If you don't know where to begin a letter, how does Garrison Keillor suggest you get going once you've said *"Dear* You" (10)? How might you apply this advice to other kinds of writing?

2. According to Keillor, what's the hardest kind of letter to write? What advice does he give for avoiding this kind of letter when writing to a friend?

3. "A letter is better," says Keillor, than a phone call (1). Why? For what specific purposes does he suggest we write a letter? Which ones(s) can *only* be accomplished by writing?

4. Except for a few "obligatory" kinds, a letter is a gift, says Keillor (6). What are the obligatory kinds? What happens if we don't write them?

5. When does a personal letter written from one ordinary person to another become, in Keillor's view, "an object of art" (15)? Would the same be true of an e-mail message? Why or why not?

XXXXXXXXXXXXXX **STRATEGIES AND STRUCTURES** XXXXXXXXXXXXX

1. Freewriting is a technique of finding something to write about by freely writing down whatever pops into your head as you are trying to think about a topic. What does Keillor say about the process of freewriting?

2. Getting over the guilt of not writing a letter says Keillor, is often the "first step" in writing one (6). What are the other steps he gives before getting to the salutation?

3. Keillor's essay imitates the process he is ANALYZING. Where does he tell us how to begin actually writing a letter? In which of the paragraphs that follow does he deal more with the beginning and early stages of letter writing? With the middle stages? Why do you think he has so little to say about preparing for the ending?

4. In which paragraphs of his essay does Keillor deal most explicitly with the recipient, or audience, of a letter? How might the advice he gives here carry over to other kinds of writing?

5. Most of Keillor's essay explains how to write a good letter. Where and why does he analyze how not to? Among his letter-writing don'ts, which do you think are most important?

6. At first glance, the EXAMPLES that Keillor gives in paragraph 13 don't seem to have much to do with one another. How do these examples work to tie together his ARGUMENT about letter writing?

7. How would you DESCRIBE the TONE of this essay? What personality does Keillor assume?

XXXXXXXXXXXXXX **WORDS AND FIGURES OF SPEECH** XXXXXXXXXXXXX

1. The "Big Bopper" was fifties rock star Jape Richardson (1). How does this ALLUSION anticipate the "precious relic" of paragraph 15?

2. What do you think of Keillor's rhyming "letter" with "better" in paragraph 1? How does this fit in with his personality of letter writer?

3. Why does Keillor contract "literary" into "lit'ry" (10)?

4. In what sense is any piece of writing "handmade" (2)?

5. How does the comic METAPHOR in the last sentence of paragraph 13 EXEMPLIFY what Keillor says about yoking ideas?

XXXXXXXXXXXXXXXXXXXXX **FOR WRITING** XXXXXXXXXXXXXXXXXXXXXXX

1. Write an e-mail message to Keillor explaining the process of composing an e-mail and why e-mail is better than old-fashioned letter writing.

2. Write an essay ANALYZING the process of one of the following: how to talk on a cell phone in a public place, how to make a good (or bad) impression on a friend's parents, how to change a tire, how to buy or sell a used car, how to train a dog.

PHILIP WEISS

How to Get Out of
a Locked Trunk

Philip Weiss is a columnist for the *New York Observer* and for the *Jewish World Review* (www.jewishworldreview.com). He is also a contributing editor for *Esquire* and for *Harper's*, in which "How to Get Out of a Locked Trunk" was first published (1992). Weiss's political novel, *Cock-A-Doodle-Doo*, appeared in 1995. About to be married when he wrote this essay, Weiss obsessively analyzes his way out of the trunks of locked cars, a strange fixation that suggests his bachelor self may be carrying some extra baggage. The essay also analyzes how Weiss got out of his condition.

XXXXXXXXXXXXXXXXXXXXXXXXXXXXXXXXXXXXXXXXXXXXXXXXXXXXXXXXXXXX

On a hot Sunday last summer my friend Tony and I drove my rental car, a '91 Buick, from St. Paul to the small town of Waconia, Minnesota, forty miles southwest. We each had a project. Waconia is Tony's boyhood home, and his sister had recently given him a panoramic postcard of Lake Waconia as seen from a high point in the town early in the century. He wanted to duplicate the photograph's vantage point, then hang the two pictures together in his house in Frogtown. I was hoping to see Tony's father, Emmett, a retired mechanic, in order to settle a question that had been nagging me: Is it possible to get out of a locked car trunk?

We tried to call ahead to Emmett twice, but he wasn't home. Tony thought he was probably golfing but that there was a good chance he'd be back by the time we got there. So we set out.

I parked the Buick, which was a silver sedan with a red interior, by the graveyard near where Tony thought the picture had been taken. He took his picture and I wandered among the headstones, reading the epitaphs. One of them was chillingly anti-individualist. It said, "Not to do my will, but thine."

Trunk lockings had been on my mind for a few weeks. It seemed to me that the fear of being locked in a car trunk had a particular hold on the American imagination. Trunk lockings occur in many movies and books—from *Goodfellas* to *Thelma and Louise* to *Humboldt's Gift*. And while the highbrow national newspapers generally shy away from trunk lockings, the attention they receive in local papers suggests a widespread anxiety surrounding the subject. In an afternoon at the New York Public Library I found numerous stories about trunk lockings. A Los Angeles man is discovered, bloodshot, banging the trunk of his white Eldorado following a night and a day trapped inside; he says his captors went on joyrides and picked up women. A forty-eight-year-old Houston doctor is forced into her trunk at a bank ATM and then the car is abandoned, parked near the Astrodome. A New Orleans woman tells police she gave birth in a trunk while being abducted to Texas. Tests undermine her story, the police drop the investigation. But so what if it's a fantasy? That only shows the idea's hold on us.

Every culture comes up with tests of a person's ability to get out of a sticky situation. The English plant mazes. Tropical resorts market those straw finger-grabbers that tighten their grip the harder you pull on them, and Viennese intellectuals gave us the concept of childhood sexuality— figure it out, or remain neurotic for life.

At least you could puzzle your way out of those predicaments. When they slam the trunk, though, you're helpless unless someone finds you. You would think that such a common worry should have a ready fix, and that the secret of getting out of a locked trunk is something we should all know about.

I phoned experts but they were very discouraging.

"You cannot get out. If you got a pair of pliers and bat's eyes, yes. But you have to have a lot of knowledge of the lock," said James Foote at Automotive Locksmiths in New York City.

Jim Frens, whom I reached at the technical section of *Car and Driver* in Detroit, told me the magazine had not dealt with this question. But he echoed the opinion of experts elsewhere when he said that the best hope for escape would be to try and kick out the panel between the trunk and the backseat. That angle didn't seem worth pursuing. What if your enemies were in the car, crumpling beer cans and laughing at your fate? It didn't make sense to join them.

The people who deal with rules on auto design were uncomfortable with my scenarios. Debra Barclay of the Center for Auto Safety, an organization founded by Ralph Nader, had certainly heard of cases, but she was not aware of any regulations on the matter. "Now, if there was a defect involved—" she said, her voice trailing off, implying that trunk locking was all phobia. This must be one of the few issues on which she and the auto industry agree. Ann Carlson of the Motor Vehicle Manufacturers Association became alarmed at the thought that I was going to play up a non-problem: "In reality this very rarely happens. As you say, in the movies it's a wonderful plot device," she said. "But in reality apparently this is not that frequent an occurrence. So they have not designed that feature into vehicles in a specific way." 10

When we got to Emmett's one-story house it was full of people. Tony's sister, Carol, was on the floor with her two small children. Her husband, Charlie, had one eye on the golf tournament on TV, and Emmett was at the kitchen counter, trimming fat from meat for lunch. I have known Emmett for fifteen years. He looked better than ever. In his retirement he had sharply changed his diet and lost a lot of weight. He had on shorts. His legs were tanned and muscular. As always, his manner was humorous, if opaque. 11

Tony told his family my news: I was getting married in three weeks. Charlie wanted to know where my fiancée was. Back East, getting everything ready. A big-time hatter was fitting her for a new hat. 12

Emmett sat on the couch, watching me. "Do you want my advice?" 13

"Sure." 14

He just grinned. A gold tooth glinted. Carol and Charlie pressed him to yield his wisdom. 15

Finally he said, "Once you get to be thirty, you make your own mistakes." 16

He got out several cans of beer, and then I brought up what was on my mind. 17

Emmett nodded and took off his glasses, then cleaned them and   18
put them back on.

We went out to his car, a Mercury Grand Marquis, and Emmett   19
opened the trunk. His golf clubs were sitting on top of the spare tire in
a green golf bag. Next to them was a toolbox and what he called his
"burglar tools," a set of elbowed rods with red plastic handles he used
to open door locks when people locked their keys inside.

Tony and Charlie stood watching. Charlie is a banker in Minne-   20
apolis. He enjoys gizmos and is extremely practical. I would describe him
as unflappable. That's a word I always wanted to apply to myself, but
my fiancée had recently informed me that I am high-strung. Though that
surprised me, I didn't quarrel with her.

For a while we studied the latch assembly. The lock closed in much   21
the same way that a lobster might clamp on to a pencil. The claw portion,
the jaws of the lock, was mounted inside the trunk lid. When you shut
the lid, the jaws locked on to the bend of a U-shaped piece of metal
mounted on the body of the car. Emmett said my best bet would be to
unscrew the bolts. That way the U-shaped piece would come loose and
the lock's jaws would swing up with it still in their grasp.

"But you'd need a wrench," he said.   22

It was already getting too technical. Emmett had an air of endless   23
patience, but I felt defeated. I could only imagine bloodied fingers,
cracked teeth. I had hoped for a simple trick.

Charlie stepped forward. He reached out and squeezed the lock's   24
jaws. They clicked shut in the air, bound together by heavy springs.
Charlie now prodded the upper part of the left-hand jaw, the thicker
part. With a rough flick of his thumb, he was able to force the jaws to
snap open. Great.

Unfortunately, the jaws were mounted behind a steel plate the size   25
of your palm in such a way that while they were accessible to us, standing
outside the car, had we been inside the trunk the plate would be in our
way, blocking the jaws.

This time Emmett saw the way out. He fingered a hole in the plate.   26
It was no bigger than the tip of your little finger. But the hole was close
enough to the latch itself that it might be possible to angle something

through the hole from inside the trunk and nudge the jaws apart. We tried with one of my keys. The lock jumped open.

It was time for a full-dress test. Emmett swung the clubs out of the trunk, and I set my can of Schmidt's on the rear bumper and climbed in. Everyone gathered around, and Emmett lowered the trunk on me, then pressed it shut with his meaty hands. Total darkness. I couldn't hear the people outside. I thought I was going to panic. But the big trunk felt comfortable. I was pressed against a sort of black carpet that softened the angles against my back.

I could almost stretch out in the trunk, and it seemed to me I could make them sweat if I took my time. Even Emmett, that sphinx, would give way to curiosity. Once I was out he'd ask how it had been and I'd just grin. There were some things you could only learn by doing.

It took a while to find the hole. I slipped the key in and angled it to one side. The trunk gasped open.

Emmett motioned the others away, then levered me out with his big right forearm. Though I'd only been inside for a minute, I was dis-oriented—as much as anything because someone had moved my beer while I was gone, setting it down on the cement floor of the garage. It was just a little thing, but I could not be entirely sure I had gotten my own beer back.

Charlie was now raring to try other cars. We examined the latch on his Toyota, which was entirely shielded to the trunk occupant (i.e., no hole in the plate), and on the neighbor's Honda (ditto). But a 1991 Dodge Dynasty was doable. The trunk was tight, but its lock had a feature one of the mechanics I'd phoned described as a "tailpiece": a finger-like extension of the lock mechanism itself that stuck out a half inch into the trunk cavity; simply by twisting the tailpiece I could free the lock. I was even faster on a 1984 Subaru that had a little lever device on the latch.

We went out to my rental on Oak Street. The Skylark was in direct sun and the trunk was hot to the touch, but when we got it open we could see that its latch plate had a perfect hole, a square in which the edge of the lock's jaw appeared like a face in a window.

The trunk was shallow and hot. Emmett had to push my knees down before he could close the lid. This one was a little suffocating. I imagined being trapped for hours, and even before he had got it closed

I regretted the decision with a slightly nauseous feeling. I thought of Edgar Allan Poe's live burials, and then about something my fiancée had said more than a year and a half before. I had been on her case to get married. She was divorced, and at every opportunity I would reissue my proposal—even during a commercial. She'd interrupted one of these chirps to tell me, in a cold, throaty voice, that she had no intention of ever going through another divorce: "This time, it's death out." I'd carried those words around like a lump of wet clay.

As it happened, the Skylark trunk was the easiest of all. The hole 34
was right where it was supposed to be. The trunk popped open, and I felt great satisfaction that we'd been able to figure out a rule that seemed to apply about 60 percent of the time. If we publicized our success, it might get the attention it deserved. All trunks would be fitted with such a hole. Kids would learn about it in school. The grip of the fear would relax. Before long a successful trunk-locking scene would date a movie like a fedora dates one today.

When I got back East I was caught up in wedding preparations. I live 35
in New York, and the wedding was to take place in Philadelphia. We set up camp there with five days to go. A friend had lent my fiancée her BMW, and we drove it south with all our things. I unloaded the car in my parents' driveway. The last thing I pulled out of the trunk was my fiancée's hat in its heavy cardboard shipping box. She'd warned me I was not allowed to look. The lid was free but I didn't open it. I was willing to be surprised.

When the trunk was empty it occurred to me I might hop in and 36
give it a try. First I looked over the mechanism. The jaws of the BMW's lock were shielded, but there seemed to be some kind of cable coming off it that you might be able to manipulate so as to cause the lock to open. The same cable that allowed the driver to open the trunk remotely . . .

I fingered it for a moment or two but decided I didn't need to test 37
out the theory.

XXXXXXXXXXXXXXXXXXX **FOR DISCUSSION** XXXXXXXXXXXXXXXXXXX

1. So, according to Philip Weiss, how *do* you get out of a locked trunk? How, according to his fiancée, do you get out of a marriage? What is the implication of Weiss's addressing these two problems in the same essay?

2. Why does Weiss say, "There were some things you could only learn by doing" (28)? What might some of them be?

3. Of the cars he tests, which one alarms Weiss most yet turns out to be the easiest to get out of? Why is he so alarmed, do you think? Why is he so anxious to find a "simple trick" that will fit all instances (23)?

4. Why do you think Weiss refrains from taking a peek at his fiancée's new hat, since the lid is "free" and the box would be so easy to open (35)? Incidentally, how does Weiss know that the lid is free?

XXXXXXXXXXXXXX **STRATEGIES AND STRUCTURES** XXXXXXXXXXXXX

1. Weiss's essay is divided into three parts—paragraphs 1 through 10, 11 through 34, and 35 through 37. In which section does Weiss most fully ANALYZE the process of getting out of a locked car trunk? How clear and precise do you find his analysis?

2. Why do you think the last section of Weiss's essay is the shortest? How—and how effectively—does it bring the essay to a satisfying conclusion?

3. What is Weiss's purpose in citing several "experts" in paragraphs 7 through 10? What is Emmett's role in the big experiment?

4. "It's a wonderful plot device," Weiss quotes one expert as saying about being locked in a car trunk (10). Is she right? Where in his essay is Weiss telling a story, and where is he analyzing a process? Give specific EXAMPLES, from the text.

5. Like NARRATIVES, which often report events chronologically, PROCESS ANALYSES are often organized in the chronological order of the steps or stages of the process that is being analyzed. Where does Weiss use chronology either to tell a story or to analyze a process? Give specific examples from the text.

XXXXXXXXXXXXX **WORDS AND FIGURES OF SPEECH** XXXXXXXXXXXX

1. The lock on the trunk of Emmett's Mercury Grand Marquis, says Weiss, "closed in much the same way that a lobster might clamp on to a pencil" (21).

How effective do you find this SIMILE for explaining how this particular trunk locks? Where else does Weiss use FIGURES OF SPEECH as a tool of ANALYSIS?

2. A phobia is an irrational fear (10). Point out specific EXAMPLES in his essay where Weiss (or his persona) might be said to exhibit phobic behavior. What's he afraid of?

3. To whom is Weiss referring when he mentions "Viennese intellectuals" (5)? Why is he ALLUDING to them? Why does he allude to Poe in paragraph 33?

4. "Not to do my will, but thine" (3). What are the implications of this inscription, which Weiss reads on a tombstone at the beginning of his essay?

5. "Case," "reissue," "chirp," and "death out" (33): why does Weiss use these words in the ANECDOTE about his proposals? What about "willing" (35)?

XXXXXXXXXXXXXXXXXXXXX **FOR WRITING** XXXXXXXXXXXXXXXXXXXXX

1. Has anyone you know ever exhibited phobic behavior? Explain how the phobia manifested itself and what specific steps the victim took to deal with it.

2. "Every culture," writes Weiss, "comes up with tests of a person's ability to get out of a sticky situation" (5). Have you ever been in such a situation? How did you get out of it? Write an essay ANALYZING the process.

CHAPTER SIX

COMPARISON AND CONTRAST

XXXXXXXXXXXXXXXXXXXXXXXXXXXXXXXXXXXXXXXXXXXXXXXXXXXXXXXXXXXXX

If you are thinking of buying a new car, you will want to do some COMPARISON* shopping. You might compare the Mazda Miata to the Mitsubishi Spider, for example: both are sporty convertibles with similar features in about the same price range. If you're in the market for a convertible, you would be wasting your time getting a second quote on a van or pickup. That would be comparing apples to oranges, and true comparisons can only be made among like kinds. Your final decision, however, will be based more on differences (in acceleration, fuel economy, trunk space) than on the similarities. Your comparison, that is, will also entail CONTRAST.

Drawing comparisons in writing is a lot like comparison shopping. It points out similarities in different subjects and differences in similar ones. Consider the following comparison between two items we might normally think of as identical:

> The common yo-yo is crudely made, with a thick shank between two widely spaced wooden disks. The string is knotted or stapled to the shank. With such an instrument nothing can be done except the simple up-down movement. My yo-yo, on the other hand, was a perfectly balanced construction of hard wood, slightly weighted, flat, with only a sixteenth of an inch between the halves. The string was not attached to the shank, but looped over it in such a way as to allow the wooden part to spin freely

*Words printed in SMALL CAPITALS are defined in the Glossary.

on its own axis. The gyroscopic effect thus created kept the yo-yo stable in all attitudes.

FRANK CONROY, *STOP TIME*

Why is Frank Conroy comparing yo-yos here? He is not going to buy one, nor is he telling the reader what kind to buy. Conroy is a man with a message: all yo-yos are not created equal. They may look alike and they may all go up and down on a string, but he points out meaningful (if you are interested in yo-yos) differences between them. There are good yo-yos, Conroy is saying, and bad yo-yos.

Once Conroy has brought together like kinds (apples to apples, yo-yos to yo-yos) and established in his own mind a basis for comparing them (the "common" kind versus "my" kind), he can proceed in one of two ways. He can dispense his information in "chunks" or in "slices" (as when selling bologna). These basic methods of organizing a comparison or contrast are sometimes called the subject-by-subject and the point-by-point methods. The subject-by-subject method treats several aspects of one subject, then discusses the same aspects of the other. So the author provides chunks of information all about one subject before moving on to the other subject. Point-by-point organization shifts back and forth between each subject, treating each point of similarity and difference before going on to the next one.

In his comparison, Conroy uses the subject-by-subject method. He first gives several traits of the inferior, "common" yo-yo ("crudely made", string fixed to the shank, only goes up and down); then he gives contrasting traits of his superior yo-yo ("perfectly balanced," string loops over the shank, spins freely at all levels). Now let's look at an example of a comparison that uses the point-by-point method to compare two great basketball players, Wilt ("the Stilt") Chamberlain and Bill Russell:

Russell has been above all a team player—a man of discipline, self-denial and killer instinct; in short, a *winner*, in the best American Calvinist tradition. Whereas Russell has been able somehow to squeeze out his last ounce of ability, Chamberlain's performances have been marked by a seeming nonchalance—as if, recognizing his Gigantistic fate, he were more concerned with personal style than with winning. "I never want to set records. The only thing I strive for is perfection," Chamberlain has said.

JAMEY LARNER, "DAVID VS. GOLIATH"

Paragraph by paragraph, Jamey Larner goes on like this, alternating "slices" of information about each player: Chamberlain's free throws are always uncertain; Russell's are always accurate in the clutch. Chamberlain is efficient; Russell is more so. Chamberlain is fast; Russell is faster. Chamberlain is Goliath at 7-feet-3-inches tall; Russell is David at 6-feet-9. The fans expect Chamberlain to lose; they expect Russell to win.

Point by point, Larner goes back and forth between his two subjects, making one meaningful (to basketball fans) distinction after another. But why, finally, is he bringing these two giants together? What's his reason for comparing them at all? Larner has a point to make, just as Conroy does when he compares two yo-yos and just as you should when you compare something in your writing. The author compares these two to ARGUE that although the giant Chamberlain was "typecast" by the fans to lose to Russell the giant-killer, Wilt "the Stilt," defying all expectations, was the one who (arguably) became the greatest basketball player ever. (This decision was made without consulting Michael Jordan.)

Whether you use chunks or slices, you can take a number of other hints from Conroy and Larner. First, choose subjects that belong to the same general CLASS or category: two toys, two athletes, two religions, two mammals. You might point out many differences between a mattress and motorcycle, but any distinctions you make between them are not likely to be meaningful because there is no logical basis for comparing these two items. (If you can establish one, then that's another matter.)

Even more important, you need to have a good reason for bringing your subjects together in the first place. Then, whether you proceed subject by subject or point by point, stick to two and only two subjects at a time.

And, finally, don't feel that you must always give equal weight to similarities and differences. You might want to pay more attention to the similarities if you wish to convince your parents that a two-seater with a rag top actually has a lot in common (wheels, headlights, engine) with the big, safe sedan they want you to consider. But you might want to emphasize the differences between your two subjects if the similarities are readily apparent, as between two yo-yos and two basketball giants.

The writer of this paragraph from the *New York Times* is doing to his subjects—Dave Winfield of the San Diego Padres and New York Yankees, among other teams, and Kirby Puckett of the Minnesota Twins— what they did so well to the baseball: he's making connections between them. This is what any comparison does, whether in pictures, numbers, words, or (as here) all three. The main point of contact between the two men, and the reason for the story, is that they were the two top vote-getters in the 2001 balloting for baseball's Hall of Fame. Both men were elected in their first year of eligibility, and both once played together on the same team (Minnesota). So the writer's two subjects are in the same ballpark. If they weren't, he would have no real basis of comparison and, thus, no reason to look for differences between them (such as Kirby's short career with a single team and Winfield's long career with half a dozen). In other words, if his gazelle and his fire hydrant didn't both play major league baseball, the writer's comparison wouldn't have a pogo stick to stand on.

CONSIDER FURTHER . . .

1. Sports pages abound in comparisons and contrasts. Scout out a few, and bring them to class. How are your examples effective at making connections between their subjects?

2. We are told not to compare apples to oranges. Why not? What logical faults are we being asked to avoid?

3. What about comparing apples to tomatoes? On what basis might they be logically compared and contrasted? What other familiar items might be well explained by comparing and contrasting?

Dave Winfield and Kirby Puckett Elected to Hall of Fame

One looked like a loping gazelle in the outfield. The other looked like a fire hydrant on a pogo stick. One played for six teams in a 22-year career. The other played for one team in a 12-year career. One played until he was 44 years old. The other stopped playing when he contracted glaucoma at age 35. One is Dave Winfield, the other is Kirby Puckett and they are now both in baseball's Hall of Fame.

Winfield's stats		Puckett's stats	
Seasons	22	Seasons	12
Average	.318	Average	.318
At bats	11,003	At bats	7,244
Hits	3,110	Hits	2,304
Home Runs	465	Home Runs	207
RBI	1,833	RBI	1,085
Stolen Bases	223	Stolen Bases	134
Walks	1,216	Walks	450
Strikeouts	1,686	Strikeouts	965

DEBORAH DALFONSO

GRAMMY REWARDS

Deborah Dalfonso is a contributor to *Down East, Yankee,* and other magazines, including *Body and Soul,* where she writes a column on spiritual practice. "Grammy Rewards" appeared in *Newsweek* in 1990. It compares two grandmothers "who are as different as chalk and cheese" and who influence her then six-year-old daughter Jill in wildly different ways. The daughter is puzzled by the contrasts, but Dalfonso herself finds a common ground between them.

XXXXXXXXXXXXXXXXXXXXXXXXXXXXXXXXXXXXXXXXXXXXXXXXXXXXXXXXXXXXXX

Our daughter, Jill, has two grandmothers who are as different as chalk and cheese.

One grandmother taught her to count cards and make her face as blank as a huge, white Kleenex when she bluffed at blackjack. They practiced in the bathroom mirror. The other grandmother taught her where to place the salad forks. When Jill was three, this grandmother taught her not to touch anything until invited to do so. The other grandmother taught her to slide down four carpeted stairs on a cookie sheet.

They are both widows, these grandmothers, and one lives in a trailer park in Florida from October until May, then moves north to an old lakefront camp in Maine for the summer. This is a leaning discouraged-looking structure filled with furniture impervious to wet swimsuits. Raccoons sleep on the deck every night. The other grandmother resides in a townhouse at the Best Address in the City—a brick, regal-looking building boasting a security system and plants in the hallways that are tended by florists who arrive weekly in green vans.

One grandmother plays Lotto America, Tri-State Megabucks, and bingo at the Penobscot Indian Reservation. The other grandmother plays bridge every Tuesday afternoon with monogrammed playing cards. One wears primary colors, favoring fluorescents when she has a tan; the other wears Leslie Fay suits, largely taupe or black.

They both take Jill on adventures, these grandmothers. One took her to a Bonnie Raitt concert, and the other to a Monet exhibit at a fine arts museum.

One grandmother believes in magic; the other believes in the stock market. They both believe in security. To one, security means plenty of white mushrooms, Vermont cheddar, and fresh limes in the refrigerator when the meteorologist says, "We're gonna have some weather." The other thinks security refers to a financial planner with solid references. 6

Both grandmothers are near 70 and have hair the color of good wood smoke. One wears her hair long and braided, and pins her plaits into a crown around her head. Sometimes in the evening she lets Jill loosen all of that heavy hair and fluff it free with an ancient hairbrush. The other grandmother has her hair done twice a week by Cyril, who wears silk shirts with shoulder pads and discourses on the art world. 7

One grandmother would be delighted to learn that many people think of her as eccentric. The other hopes that people will refer to her as "correct." This grandmother, when startled, says "Oh, my word," her strongest expletive. The other one says "Jesus, Mary, and Joseph" or "hot damn," or both, or worse. 8

Before entertaining, one grandmother hires help to come in for an extra half day to polish the silver and attend to the table setting. From this grandmother, Jill will learn about civility and elegance and the gleam of things well cared for. The other gram kills the lights, burns candles, smiles, and says, "They're coming to see me, not my house." 9

During Hurricane Bob, one of Jill's grandmothers bought her a duckling-yellow slicker and took her to Higgins Beach to watch the wind kicking up the surf. She believes that the ocean throws off positive ions, excellent for growth and peace of mind. While they were experiencing the elements, Jill's other grandmother called to make certain that we were safely down in the cellar. 10

"Are there many ways to live?" my puzzled six-year-old asked me after a recent overnight visit to the Best Address in the City, where she was expected to bathe and dress for dinner. 11

"Yes," I said gently. "There are many, many ways, and you may choose which feels right for you." And, I promised myself silently, I will let her make her own choice. 12

Two grandmothers, two different worlds. Both want for Jill no less than the lion's share. One will be her anchor; the other will be her mainsail. 13

XXXXXXXXXXXXXXXXXXXX **FOR DISCUSSION** XXXXXXXXXXXXXXXXXXXX

1. Deborah Dalfonso COMPARES each of the grandmothers to parts of a sailboat. What parts? Which grandmother is which? How effective is the comparison?

2. Dalfonso's daughter is puzzled by the CONTRASTING behavior of her two grandmothers (11). What lesson does she learn from their differences?

3. Which of the two grandmothers do you suppose is Dalfonso's own mother? Why do you think so? Which grandmother would you prefer to have? Why?

XXXXXXXXXXXXXX **STRATEGIES AND STRUCTURES** XXXXXXXXXXXXX

1. When you COMPARE and CONTRAST two subjects in writing, you can go back and forth between them a trait at a time (point-by-point), as Dalfonso does in paragraph 2. Or you can lay out all the traits of one subject, then all the traits of the other (subject-by-subject), as in paragraph 3. Label the paragraphs in Dalfonso's essay according to which of the two organizational methods she uses.

2. Dalfonso's essay is largely made up of specific details about the appearance and behavior of the two older women she is comparing. Which details do you find most interesting and revealing? Why?

3. Dalfonso finds more differences between the two grandmothers than similarities, yet she also compares the two women in the sense of discovering a common ground between them. How does she achieve this?

XXXXXXXXXXXXX **WORDS AND FIGURES OF SPEECH** XXXXXXXXXXXXX

1. Just how different are chalk and cheese (1)? anchors and mainsails (13)? What's different about these two CONTRASTING pairs of words as Dalfonso uses them?

2. What is "lion's share" (13)? What are the implications of this METAPHOR?

3. Explain the PUN, or play on words, in Dalfonso's title.

XXXXXXXXXXXXXXXXXXXX **FOR WRITING** XXXXXXXXXXXXXXXXXXXX

1. "Two grandmothers, two different worlds" (13). Make a subject-by-subject or point-by-point outline of CHARACTERISTICS of your own grandmothers (or grandfathers) as you know or remember them.

2. Write an essay COMPARING and CONTRASTING two people or places you know well. Use specific details and EXAMPLES as Dalfonso does. And let the details speak for themselves—avoid explicitly judging your two subjects.

DEBI DAVIS

BODY IMPERFECT

Debi Davis wrote "Body Imperfect" for a writing class at Wayne County Community College in Detroit. Nominated by her writing teacher, Marjorie Oliver, it won first place in 1992 in the *Norton Textra Extra* contest, sponsored by the publisher of this book. Since then, Davis has pioneered the use of small dogs as service animals for people with disabilities. In 2002, she and Peek, her prize-winning Papillon, helped to carry the Olympic torch through Tucson. Written soon after Davis lost her legs to a rare vascular disease, "Body Imperfect" compares and contrasts the reactions of adults to her disability (they often look away) with those of children (who are fascinated by her physical appearance).

XXXXXXXXXXXXXXXXXXXXXXXXXXXXXXXXXXXXXXXXXXXXXXXXXXXXXXXXXXXXX

When I became a double amputee at the age of 29, I was forced to shed many misconceptions I had unknowingly embraced regarding the importance of physical perfection. In the space of one hour I changed from an acceptably attractive female to an object of pity and fear.

I was not aware of this at first. I was too busy dealing with the physical pain and new limitations in mobility I now faced. Yet I was determined to succeed and proud of my progress on a daily basis. My contact with physicians, rehabilitation specialists, close friends and family only enhanced my perceptions of myself as a "winner."

My new status in society, however, was brought to my attention on my first excursion outside the hospital walls. Jubilant to be free of confinement, I rolled through the shopping mall in my wheelchair with the inimitable confidence of a proud survivor, a war hero anticipating a ticker-tape reception. As I glanced around, I sensed that all eyes were upon me, yet no one dared to make eye contact. Their downcast glances made me realize that they did not see the triumph in my eyes, only my missing limbs.

I noticed that shoppers gave me a wide berth, walking far around 4
me as if I were contagious. Mothers held their children closer as I passed,
and elderly women patted me on the head saying, "Bless you!" Men,
who might normally wink and smile, now looked away. Like bruised fruit
on a produce stand, I existed, but was bypassed for a healthier looking
specimen.

Children, in contrast, found my appearance clearly fascinating. One 5
small girl came up to me and stared with unabashed curiosity at my
empty pantlegs. She knelt down and put her arm up one pantleg as far
as she could reach, and finding nothing there, looked up at me with
bewilderment. "Lady, where did your legs go?" she innocently inquired.
I explained to her that my legs had been very sick, that they hadn't been
strong and healthy like hers, and that my doctor removed my legs so that
I could be healthy again. Tilting her head up she chirped, "But lady, did
they go to 'Leg Heaven'?"

That incident made me think about how differently children and 6
adults react to the unknown. To a child, an odd appearance is an interesting curiosity and a learning experience, while adults often view the
unusual with fear and repulsion. I began to realize that prior to my disability I had been guilty of the same inappropriate reactions.

From observing children, I learned to reach out and reassure adults 7
of my humanness and to reaffirm the genuine worth of all human beings.
To accentuate the wholeness of my mind and spirit, I smile warmly,
coerce eye contact, and speak in a confident manner. By using a positive
approach, I attempt to enlighten society that having a perfect body is not
synonymous with quality of life.

XXXXXXXXXXXXXXXXXXXX **FOR DISCUSSION** XXXXXXXXXXXXXXXXXXXX

1. According to Debi Davis, children react with curiosity to physical disabilities
in other people, whereas adults react with "repulsion" (6). What explanation
does she give, or imply, for the difference?

2. How does Davis attempt to change not only the way people look at her, but
the way they look at other people with disabilities?

3. According to Davis, what valuable lesson about difference do physically
"imperfect" people have to teach the physically "perfect"?

1. What is Davis's point in COMPARING the reactions of adults and children to her disability?

2. How would you CHARACTERIZE Davis's TONE as she DESCRIBES the children and adults she meets? Is there a difference? And if so, compare.

3. As Davis compares the way people react to her disability, she is also telling a story. What is the PLOT of that story?

1. Comment on the IRONY of Davis's COMPARING herself to a "war hero" in paragraph 3.

2. What are the implications of the word "coerce" (7)?

3. How effective do you find Davis's "bruised fruit" METAPHOR in paragraph 4?

1. Revisit a town, building, shopping mall, park, or other place that has changed a lot since you were last there. Using the subject-by-subject method, write a paragraph on the place "then" and the place "now." Or, using the point-by-point method, write one paragraph on the aspects of the place that have remained the same and one paragraph on the main differences.

2. Davis implies that children see the world differently than adults do. What's your opinion? Write an essay COMPARING the two.

BRUCE CATTON

GRANT AND LEE: A STUDY IN CONTRASTS

Bruce Catton (1899–1979) was a noted historian of the Civil War, winner of both the Pulitzer Prize and the National Book Award for *A Stillness at Appomattox* (1953). Among Catton's many other Civil War books are *This Hallowed Ground* (1956), *The Army of the Potomac* (1962), *Terrible Swift Sword* (1963), and *Grant Takes Command* (1969). It was not, said Catton, "the strategy or political meanings" that most fascinated him, but the "almost incomprehensible emotional experience which this war brought to our country." "Grant and Lee: A Study in Contrasts" looks at two great Americans—one "the modern man emerging," the other from "the age of chivalry."

XXXXXXXXXXXXXXXXXXXXXXXXXXXXXXXXXXXXXXXXXXXXXXXXXXXXXXXXXXXXXXXXX

When Ulysses S. Grant and Robert E. Lee met in the parlor of a modest house at Appomattox Court House, Virginia, on April 9, 1865, to work out the terms for the surrender of Lee's Army of Northern Virginia, a great chapter in American life came to a close, and a great new chapter began.   1

These men were bringing the Civil War to its virtual finish. To be sure, other armies had yet to surrender, and for a few days the fugitive Confederate government would struggle desperately and vainly, trying to find some way to go on living now that its chief support was gone. But in effect it was all over when Grant and Lee signed the papers. And the little room where they wrote out the terms was the scene of one of the poignant, dramatic contrasts in American history.   2

They were two strong men, these oddly different generals, and they represented the strengths of two conflicting currents that, through them, had come into final collision.   3

Back of Robert E. Lee was the notion that the old aristocratic con- 4
cept might somehow survive and be dominant in American life.

Lee was tidewater Virginia, and in his background were family, cul- 5
ture, and tradition . . . the age of chivalry transplanted to a New World
which was making its own legends and its own myths. He embodied a
way of life that had come down through the age of knighthood and the
English country squire. America was a land that was beginning all over
again, dedicated to nothing much more complicated than the rather hazy
belief that all men had equal rights and should have an equal chance in
the world. In such a land Lee stood for the feeling that it was somehow
of advantage to human society to have a pronounced inequality in the
social structure. There should be a leisure class, backed by ownership of
land; in turn, society itself should be keyed to the land as the chief source
of wealth and influence. It would bring forth (according to this ideal) a
class of men with a strong sense of obligation to the community; men
who lived not to gain advantage for themselves, but to meet the solemn
obligations which had been laid on them by the very fact that they were
privileged. From them the country would get its leadership; to them it
could look for the higher values—of thought, of conduct, of personal
deportment—to give it strength and virtue.

Lee embodied the noblest elements of this aristocratic ideal. 6
Through him, the landed nobility justified itself. For four years, the
Southern states had fought a desperate war to uphold the ideals for which
Lee stood. In the end, it almost seemed as if the Confederacy fought for
Lee; as if he himself was the Confederacy . . . the best thing that the way
of life for which the Confederacy stood could ever have to offer. He had
passed into legend before Appomattox. Thousands of tired, underfed,
poorly clothed Confederate soldiers, long since past the simple enthusiasm of the early days of the struggle, somehow considered Lee the symbol of everything for which they had been willing to die. But they could
not quite put this feeling into words. If the Lost Cause, sanctified by so
much heroism and so many deaths, had a living justification, its justification was General Lee.

Grant, the son of a tanner on the Western frontier, was everything 7
Lee was not. He had come up the hard way and embodied nothing in
particular except the eternal toughness and sinewy fiber of the men who

grew up beyond the mountains. He was one of a body of men who owed reverence and obeisance to no one, who were self-reliant to a fault, who cared hardly anything for the past but who had a sharp eye for the future.

These frontier men were the precise opposites of the tidewater aristocrats. Back of them, in the great surge that had taken people over the Alleghenies and into the opening Western country, there was a deep, implicit dissatisfaction with a past that had settled into grooves. They stood for democracy, not from any reasoned conclusion about the proper ordering of human society, but simply because they had grown up in the middle of democracy and knew how it worked. Their society might have privileges, but they would be privileges each man had won for himself. Forms and patterns meant nothing. No man was born to anything, except perhaps to a chance to show how far he could rise. Life was competition. 8

Yet along with this feeling had come a deep sense of belonging to a national community. The Westerner who developed a farm, opened a shop, or set up in business as a trader, could hope to prosper only as his own community prospered—and his community ran from the Atlantic to the Pacific and from Canada down to Mexico. If the land was settled, with towns and highways and accessible markets, he could better himself. He saw his fate in terms of the nation's own destiny. As its horizons expanded, so did his. He had, in other words, an acute dollars-and-cents stake in the continued growth and development of his country. 9

And that, perhaps, is where the contrast between Grant and Lee becomes most striking. The Virginia aristocrat, inevitably, saw himself in relation to his own region. He lived in a static society which could endure almost anything except change. Instinctively, his first loyalty would go to the locality in which that society existed. He would fight to the limit of endurance to defend it, because in defending it he was defending everything that gave his own life its deepest meaning. 10

The Westerner, on the other hand, would fight with an equal tenacity for the broader concept of society. He fought so because everything he lived by was tied to growth, expansion, and a constantly widening horizon. What he lived by would survive or fall with the nation itself. He could not possibly stand by unmoved in the face of an attempt to destroy the Union. He would combat it with everything he had, because he could only see it as an effort to cut the ground out from under his feet. 11

So Grant and Lee were in complete contrast, representing two dia-   12
metrically opposed elements in American life. Grant was the modern man
emerging; beyond him, ready to come on the stage, was the great age of
steel and machinery, of crowded cities and a restless burgeoning vitality.
Lee might have ridden down from the old age of chivalry, lance in hand,
silken banner fluttering over his head. Each man was the perfect cham-
pion of his cause, drawing both his strengths and his weaknesses from
the people he led.

Yet it was not all contrast, after all. Different as they were—in   13
background, in personality, in underlying aspiration—these two great soldiers had much in common. Under everything else, they were marvelous
fighters. Furthermore, their fighting qualities were really very much alike.

Each man had, to begin with, the great virtue of utter tenacity and   14
fidelity. Grant fought his way down the Mississippi Valley in spite of
acute personal discouragement and profound military handicaps. Lee
hung on in the trenches at Petersburg after hope itself had died. In each
man there was an indomitable quality . . . the born fighter's refusal to
give up as long as he can still remain on his feet and lift his two fists.

Daring and resourcefulness they had, too; the ability to think faster   15
and move faster than the enemy. These were the qualities which gave
Lee the dazzling campaigns of Second Manassas and Chancellorsville and
won Vicksburg for Grant.

Lastly, and perhaps greatest of all, there was the ability, at the end,   16
to turn quickly from war to peace once the fighting was over. Out of the
way these two men behaved at Appomattox came the possibility of a
peace of reconciliation. It was a possibility not wholly realized, in the
years to come, but which did, in the end, help the two sections to become
one nation again . . . after a war whose bitterness might have seemed to
make such a reunion wholly impossible. No part of either man's life
became him more than the part he played in this brief meeting in the
McLean house at Appomattox. Their behavior there put all succeeding
generations of Americans in their debt. Two great Americans, Grant and
Lee—very different, yet under everything very much alike. Their
encounter at Appomattox was one of the great moments of American
history.

XXXXXXXXXXXXXXXXXX **FOR DISCUSSION** XXXXXXXXXXXXXXXXXXX

1. Bruce Catton writes that Generals Lee and Grant represented two conflicting currents of American culture. What were these currents? What CONTRASTING qualities and ideals does Catton associate with each man?

2. What qualities, according to Catton, did Grant and Lee have in common? How does this "study in contrasts" actually lead us to recognize these important commonalities?

3. With Lee's surrender, says Catton, "a great new chapter of American history began" (1). What CHARACTERISTICS of the new era does Catton anticipate in his DESCRIPTION of Grant?

4. Catton does not describe, in any detail, how Grant and Lee behaved as they worked out the terms of peace at Appomattox. What does he imply about the conduct of the two men in general?

5. Catton does not really give specific reasons for the Confederacy's defeat. What general explanation does he hint at, however, when he associates Lee with a "static society" and Grant with a society of "restless burgeoning vitality" (10, 12)? Why is Catton drawing this extensive COMPARISON?

XXXXXXXXXXXXXX **STRATEGIES AND STRUCTURES** XXXXXXXXXXXXX

1. Beginning with paragraph 3, Catton gets down to the particulars of his CONTRAST between the two generals. Where does the contrast end? In which paragraph does he begin to list similarities between the two men?

2. Which sentence in the final paragraph brings together both the differences and the similarities outlined in the preceding paragraphs? How does this paragraph recall the opening paragraphs of the essay? Why might Catton end with an echo of his beginning?

3. In COMPARING and contrasting the two generals in this essay, Catton also DESCRIBES two regional types. What are some of the specific personal CHARACTERISTICS Catton ascribes to Grant and Lee that, at the same time, make them representative figures?

XXXXXXXXXXXXX **WORDS AND FIGURES OF SPEECH** XXXXXXXXXXXX

1. Catton DESCRIBES the parlor where Grant and Lee met as the "scene" of a "dramatic" CONTRAST, and he says that a new era was "ready to come on stage" (2). What view of history is suggested by these METAPHORS?

2. What does Catton mean by "the Lost Cause" in paragraph 6?

3. What is the precise meaning of "obeisance" (7)? Why might Catton choose this term instead of the more common *obedience* when describing General Grant?

4. Look up any of the following words with which you are not on easy terms: "fugitive" (2), "poignant" (2), "chivalry" (5), "sinewy" (7), "implicit" (8), "tenacity" (11), "diametrically" (12), "acute" (14), "profound" (14), "indomitable" (14). What words would you substitute to help make the TONE of the essay less formal?

XXXXXXXXXXXXXXXXXXXXXX **FOR WRITING** XXXXXXXXXXXXXXXXXXXXXX

1. Write an essay COMPARING and CONTRASTING a pair of important historical figures with whom you are familiar—Thomas Jefferson and Alexander Hamilton, perhaps, or Yasir Arafat and Saddam Hussein, Hillary Clinton and Janet Reno.

2. Compare and contrast two other Civil War generals—for example, William Tecumseh Sherman and Thomas Jonathan "Stonewall" Jackson—or two battles of the Civil War or of some more recent conflict.

GARY SOTO

LIKE MEXICANS

Gary Soto (b. 1952), who grew up in Fresno, California, teaches Chi-
cano studies and English literature at the University of California at
Riverside. He is the author of ten books of poetry, numerous stories for
children and young adults, and two novels: *Nickel and Dime* (2000) and
Poetry Lover (2001). Soto's memoir, *Living up the Street* (1985), won an
American Book Award. In "Like Mexicans," from *Small Faces* (1986),
another collection of reminiscences about growing up in the barrio,
Soto compares his future wife's Japanese American family with his own
Mexican American one. They are pretty much the same, he concludes,
only different.

ⵝⵝⵝ

My grandmother gave me bad advice and good advice when I was   1
in my early teens. For the bad advice, she said that I should
become a barber because they made good money and listened to the radio
all day. "Honey, they don't work como burros," she would say every time
I visited her. She made the sound of donkeys braying. "Like that, honey!"
For the good advice, she said that I should marry a Mexican girl. "No
Okies, hijo"—she would say—"Look, my son. He marry one and they
fight every day about I don't know what and I don't know what." For
her, everyone who wasn't Mexican, black, or Asian were Okies. The
French were Okies, the Italians in suits were Okies. When I asked about
Jews, whom I had read about, she asked for a picture. I rode home on
my bicycle and returned with a calendar depicting the important races
of the world. "Pues si, son Okies tambien!"[1] she said, nodding her head.
She waved the calendar away and we went to the living room where she
lectured me on the virtues of the Mexican girl: first, she could cook and,

[1]Well yes, they're Okies too.

second, she acted like a woman, not a man, in her husband's home. She said she would tell me about a third when I got a little older.

I asked my mother about it—becoming a barber and marrying Mexican. She was in the kitchen. Steam curled from a pot of boiling beans, the radio was on, looking as squat as a loaf of bread. "Well, if you want to be a barber—they say they make good money." She slapped a round steak with a knife, her glasses slipping down with each strike. She stopped and looked up. "If you find a good Mexican girl, marry her of course." She returned to slapping the meat and I went to the backyard where my brother and David King were sitting on the lawn feeling the inside of their cheeks.

"This is what girls feel like," my brother said, rubbing the inside of his cheek. David put three fingers inside his mouth and scratched. I ignored them and climbed the back fence to see my best friend, Scott, a second-generation Okie. I called him and his mother pointed to the side of the house where his bedroom was, a small aluminum trailer, the kind you gawk at when they're flipped over on the freeway, wheels spinning in the air. I went around to find Scott pitching horseshoes.

I picked up a set of rusty ones and joined him. While we played, we talked about school and friends and record albums. The horseshoes scuffed up dirt, sometimes ringing the iron that threw out a meager shadow like a sundial. After three argued-over games, we pulled two oranges apiece from his tree and started down the alley still talking school and friends and record albums. We pulled more oranges from the alley and talked about who we would marry. "No offense, Scott," I said with an orange slice in my mouth, "but I would never marry an Okie." We walked in step, almost touching, with a sled of shadows dragging behind us. "No offense, Gary," Scott said, "but I would *never* marry a Mexican." I looked at him: a fang of orange slice showed from his munching mouth. I didn't think anything of it. He had his girl and I had mine. But our seventh-grade vision was the same: to marry, get jobs, buy cars and maybe a house if we had money left over.

We talked about our future lives until, to our surprise, we were on the downtown mall, two miles from home. We bought a bag of popcorn at Penneys and sat on a bench near the fountain watching Mexican and Okie girls pass. "That one's mine," I pointed with my chin when a girl with eyebrows arched into black rainbows ambled by. "She's cute," Scott said about a girl with yellow hair and a mouthful of gum. We dreamed aloud, our chins busy pointing out girls. We agreed that we couldn't wait to become men and lift them onto our laps.

But the woman I married was not Mexican but Japanese. It was a surprise to me. For years, I went about wide-eyed in my search for the brown girl in a white dress at a dance. I searched the playground at the baseball diamond. When the girls raced for grounders, their hair bounced like something that couldn't be caught. When they sat together in the lunchroom, heads pressed together, I knew they were talking about us Mexican guys. I saw them and dreamed them. I threw my face into my pillow, making up sentences that were good as in the movies.

6

But when I was twenty, I fell in love with this other girl who worried my mother, who had my grandmother asking once again to see the calendar of the Important Races of the World. I told her I had thrown it away years before. I took a much-glanced-at snapshot from my wallet. We looked at it together, in silence. Then grandma reclined in her chair, lit a cigarette, and said, "Es pretty." She blew and asked with all her worry pushed up to her forehead: "Chinese?"

7

I was in love and there was no looking back. She was the one. I told my mother who was slapping hamburger into patties. "Well, sure if you want to marry her," she said. But the more I talked, the more concerned she became. Later I began to worry. Was it all a mistake? "Marry a Mexican girl," I heard my mother say in my mind. I heard it at breakfast. I heard it over math problems, between Western Civilization and cultural geography. But then one afternoon while I was hitchhiking home from school, it struck me like a baseball in the back: my mother wanted me to marry someone of my own social class—a poor girl. I considered my fiancee, Carolyn, and she didn't look poor, though I knew she came from a family of farm workers and pull-yourself-up-by-your-bootstraps ranchers. I asked my brother, who was marrying Mexican poor that fall, if I should marry a poor girl. He screamed "Yeah" above his terrible guitar playing in his bedroom. I considered my sister who had married Mexican. Cousins were dating Mexican. Uncles were remarrying poor women. I asked Scott, who was still my best friend, and he said, "She's too good for you, so you better not."

8

I worried about it until Carolyn took me home to meet her parents.   9
We drove in her Plymouth until the houses gave way to farms and
ranches and finally her house fifty feet from the highway. When we
pulled into the drive, I panicked and begged Carolyn to make a U-turn
and go back so we could talk about it over a soda. She pinched my cheek,
calling me a "silly boy." I felt better, though, when I got out of the car
and saw the house: the chipped paint, a cracked window, boards for a
walk to the back door. There were rusting cars near the barn. A tractor
with a net of spiderwebs under a mulberry. A field. A bale of barbed
wire like children's scribbling leaning against an empty chicken coop.
Carolyn took my hand and pulled me to my future mother-in-law who
was coming out to greet us.

We had lunch: sandwiches, potato chips, and iced tea. Carolyn and   10
her mother talked mostly about neighbors and the congregation at the
Japanese Methodist Church in West Fresno. Her father, who was in
khaki work clothes, excused himself with a wave that was almost a salute
and went outside. I heard a truck start, a dog bark, and then the truck
rattle away.

Carolyn's mother offered another sandwich, but I declined with a   11
shake of my head and a smile. I looked around when I could, when I
was not saying over and over that I was a college student, hinting that I
could take care of her daughter. I shifted my chair. I saw newspapers
piled in corners, dusty cereal boxes and vinegar bottles in corners. The
wallpaper was bubbled from rain that had come in from a bad roof. Dust.
Dust lay on lamp shades and window sills. These people are just like
Mexicans, I thought. Poor people.

Carolyn's mother asked me through Carolyn if I would like a *sushi*.   12
A plate of black and white things were held in front of me. I took one,
wide-eyed, and turned it over like a foreign coin. I was biting into one
when I saw a kitten crawl up the window screen over the sink. I chewed
and the kitten opened its mouth of terror as she crawled higher, wanting
in to paw the leftovers from our plates. I looked at Carolyn who said
that the cat was just showing off. I looked up in time to see it fall. It
crawled up, then fell again.

We talked for an hour and had apple pie and coffee, slowly. Finally,   13
we got up with Carolyn taking my hand. Slightly embarrassed, I tried to

pull away but her grip held me. I let her have her way as she led me down the hallway with her mother right behind me. When I opened the door, I was startled by a kitten clinging to the screen door, its mouth screaming "cat food, dog biscuits, *sushi*. . . ." I opened the door and the kitten, still holding on, whined in the language of hungry animals. When I got into Carolyn's car, I looked back: the cat was still clinging. I asked Carolyn if it were possibly hungry, but she said the cat was being silly. She started the car, waved to her mother, and bounced us over the rain-poked drive, patting my thigh for being her lover baby. Carolyn waved again. I looked back, waving, then gawking at a window screen where there were now three kittens clawing and screaming to get in. Like Mexicans, I thought. I remembered the Molinas and how the cats clung to their screens—cats they shot down with squirt guns. On the highway, I felt happy, pleased by it all. I patted Carolyn's thigh. Her people were like Mexicans, only different.

XXXXXXXXXXXXXXXXXXXX **FOR DISCUSSION** XXXXXXXXXXXXXXXXXXXX

1. After COMPARING his future wife's family to his own, Gary Soto concludes that they are much alike, "only different" (13). What are the implications of this afterthought for his comparison as a whole?

2. How does Soto's grandmother define an "Okie" (1)? Why doesn't she want him to marry one?

3. "It was a surprise to me," says Soto about marrying a girl of Japanese descent (6). Why didn't he marry a Mexican girl, as his grandmother advised?

4. Why does Soto say that his grandmother gave him bad advice and good advice (1)? Which is which, and why?

5. What does Soto imply about ethnic and racial stereotypes when he refers to the calendar showing the "Important Races of the World" (1, 7)? Why does his grandmother ask for the calendar again?

XXXXXXXXXXXXX **STRATEGIES AND STRUCTURES** XXXXXXXXXXXXX

1. Before COMPARING them with Japanese Americans, Soto explains what Mexican Americans are "like." What are some of the specifics by which he CHARACTERIZES himself and his family? What is his purpose for citing these particular traits?

2. We meet Carolyn's family in paragraph 10. How has Soto already prepared us to expect more similarities than differences between the two families? Cite details by which Soto explains what Carolyn's people are "like."

3. Why does Soto refer several times in this essay to kittens?

4. Besides giving advice, Soto's grandmother, like all the other adult women in "Like Mexicans," is engaged in what activity? Why do you think Soto focuses on this?

5. Soto's comparison of two American families has many elements of NARRATIVE. Who is the narrator: a young man growing up in a Mexican American neighborhood, an older man looking back at him, or both? Please explain your answer.

XXXXXXXXXXXXX **WORDS AND FIGURES OF SPEECH** XXXXXXXXXXXX

1. What is the effect of Soto's DESCRIPTION of the orange slice in Scott's mouth as a "fang" (4)? Why do you think he says, "I didn't think anything of it" (4)?

2. What does Soto mean by the term "social class" in paragraph 8?

3. Why do you think Soto COMPARES *sushi* to a foreign coin (12)? Give EXAMPLES of other SIMILES like this one in his essay.

4. What is the derivation of Soto's grandmother's favorite ethnic slur, "Okies"?

5. When Soto mentions Jews to his grandmother, she calls for the calendar of the races. Is this a racial or an ethnic category? What's the difference? How about "Hispanic" or "Japanese American?"?

XXXXXXXXXXXXXXXXXXXXX **FOR WRITING** XXXXXXXXXXXXXXXXXXXXXXX

1. Write a paragraph COMPARING and CONTRASTING your girlfriend's or boyfriend's (or wife's or husband's) family with your own in one specific way—how or what they eat, how they interact within their family, how they celebrate special occasions, and so forth. Be creative.

2. Whether or not you grew up in a racially or ethnically diverse neighborhood, you may recall friends and acquaintances who differed from each other in social, economic, physical, religious, or other ways. Write an essay comparing and contrasting several of these friends.

DEBORAH TANNEN

GENDER IN THE CLASSROOM

Deborah Tannen (b. 1945) is a linguist at Georgetown University. She specializes, she says, in "the language of everyday conversation." "Gender in the Classroom," which originally appeared in the *Chronicle of Higher Education*, grew out of her research for *You Just Don't Understand* (1990), a book about the various conversational styles of men and women. In the United States, says Tannen, the sexes bond differently. Women do it by talking with each other about their troubles; men do it by exchanging "playful insults." In this essay, Tannen compares and contrasts the various behaviors that result from gender-related styles of talking and then explains how she changes her teaching methods to accommodate these behaviors.

XXXXXXXXXXXXXXXXXXXXXXXXXXXXXXXXXXXXXXXXXXXXXXXXXXXXXXXXXXXXX

When I researched and wrote my latest book, *You Just Don't Understand: Women and Men in Conversation*, the furthest thing from my mind was reevaluating my teaching strategies. But that has been one of the direct benefits of having written the book.

The primary focus of my linguistic research always has been the language of everyday conversation. One facet of this is conversational style: how different regional, ethnic, and class backgrounds, as well as age and gender, result in different ways of using language to communicate. *You Just Don't Understand* is about the conversational styles of women and men. As I gained more insight into typically male and female ways of using language, I began to suspect some of the causes of the troubling facts that women who go to single-sex schools do better in later life, and that when young women sit next to young men in classrooms, the males talk more. This is not to say that all men talk in class, nor that no women do. It is simply that a greater percentage of discussion time is taken by men's voices.

The research of sociologists and anthropologists such as Janet Lever, Marjorie Harness Goodwin, and Donna Eder has shown that girls and boys learn to use language differently in their sex-separate peer groups. Typically, a girl has a best friend with whom she sits and talks, frequently telling secrets. It's the telling of secrets, the fact and the way that they talk to each other, that makes them best friends. For boys, activities are central: Their best friends are the ones they do things with. Boys also tend to play in larger groups that are hierarchical. High-status boys give orders and push low-status boys around. So boys are expected to use language to seize center stage: by exhibiting their skill, displaying their knowledge, and challenging and resisting challenges.

These patterns have stunning implications for classroom interaction. Most faculty members assume that participating in class discussion is a necessary part of successful performance. Yet speaking in a classroom is more congenial to boys' language experience than to girls', since it entails putting oneself forward in front of a large group of people, many of whom are strangers and at least one of whom is sure to judge speakers' knowledge and intelligence by their verbal display.

Another aspect of many classrooms that makes them more hospitable to most men than to most women is the use of debate-like formats as a learning tool. Our educational system, as Walter Ong argues persuasively in his book *Fighting for Life* (Cornell University Press, 1981), is fundamentally male in that the pursuit of knowledge is believed to be achieved by ritual opposition: public display followed by argument and challenge. Father Ong demonstrates that ritual opposition—what he calls "adversativeness" or "agonism"—is fundamental to the way most males approach almost any activity. (Consider, for example, the little boy who shows he likes a little girl by pulling her braids and shoving her.) But ritual opposition is antithetical to the way most females learn and like to interact. It is not that females don't fight, but that they don't fight for fun. They don't *ritualize* opposition.

Anthropologists working in widely disparate parts of the world have found contrasting verbal rituals for women and men. Women in completely unrelated cultures (for example, Greece and Bali) engage in ritual laments: spontaneously produced rhyming couplets that express their pain, for example, over the loss of loved ones. Men do not take part in laments. They have their own, very different verbal ritual: a contest, a war of words in which they vie with each other to devise clever insults.

When discussing these phenomena with a colleague, I commented 7
that I see these two styles in American conversation: Many women bond by talking about troubles, and many men bond by exchanging playful insults and put-downs, and other sorts of verbal sparring. He exclaimed: "I never thought of this, but that's the way I teach: I have students read an article, and then I invite them to tear it apart. After we've torn it to shreds, we talk about how to build a better model."

This contrasts sharply with the way I teach: I open the discussion 8
of readings by asking, "What did you find useful in this? What can we use in our own theory building and our own methods?" I note what I see as weaknesses in the author's approach, but I also point out that the writer's discipline and purposes might be different from ours. Finally, I offer personal anecdotes illustrating the phenomena under discussion and praise students' anecdotes as well as their critical acumen.

These different teaching styles must make our classrooms wildly 9
different places and hospitable to different students. Male students are more likely to be comfortable attacking the readings and might find the inclusion of personal anecdotes irrelevant and "soft." Women are more likely to resist discussion they perceive as hostile, and, indeed, it is women in my classes who are most likely to offer personal anecdotes.

A colleague who read my book commented that he had always taken 10
for granted that the best way to deal with students' comments is to challenge them: this, he felt it was self-evident, sharpens their minds and helps them develop debating skills. But he had noticed that women were relatively silent in his classes, so he decided to try beginning discussion with relatively open-ended questions and letting comments go unchallenged. He found, to his amazement and satisfaction, that more women began to speak up.

Though some of the women in his class clearly liked this better, per- 11
haps some of the men liked it less. One young man in my class wrote in a questionnaire about a history professor who gave students questions to think about and called on people to answer them: "He would then play devil's advocate . . . i.e., he debated us. . . . That class *really* sharpened me intellectually. . . . We as students do need to know how to defend our-

selves." This young man valued the experience of being attacked and challenged publicly. Many, if not most, women would shrink from such a "challenge," experiencing it as a public humiliation.

A professor at Hamilton College told me of a young man who was upset because he felt his class presentation had been a failure. The professor was puzzled because he had observed that class members had listened attentively and agreed with the student's observations. It turned out that it was this very agreement that the student interpreted as failure: Since no one had engaged his ideas by arguing with him, he felt they had found them unworthy of attention. 12

So one reason men speak in class more than women is that many of them find the "public" classroom setting more conducive to speaking, whereas most women are more comfortable speaking in private to a small group of people they know well. A second reason is that men are more likely to be comfortable with the debate-like form that discussion may take. Yet another reason is the different attitudes toward speaking in class that typify women and men. 13

Students who speak frequently in class, many of whom are men, assume that it is their job to think of contributions and try to get the floor to express them. But many women monitor their participation not only to get the floor but to avoid getting it. Women students in my class tell me that if they have spoken up once or twice, they hold back for the rest of the class because they don't want to dominate. If they have spoken a lot one week, they will remain silent the next. These different ethics of participation are, of course, unstated, so those who speak freely assume that those who remain silent have nothing to say, and those who are reining themselves in assume that the big talkers are selfish and hoggish. 14

When I looked around my classes, I could see these differing ethics and habits at work. For example, my graduate class in analyzing conversation had twenty students, eleven women and nine men. Of the men, four were foreign students: two Japanese, one Chinese, and one Syrian. With the exception of the three Asian men, all the men spoke in class at least occasionally. The biggest talker in the class was a woman, but there were also five women who never spoke at all, only one of whom was Japanese. I decided to try something different. 15

I broke the class into small groups to discuss the issues raised in the readings and to analyze their own conversational transcripts. I devised 16 three ways of dividing the students into groups: one by the degree program they were in, one by gender, and one by conversational style, as closely as I could guess it. This meant that when the class was grouped according to conversational style, I put Asian students together, fast talkers together, and quiet students together. The class split into groups six times during the semester, so they met in each grouping twice. I told students to regard the groups as examples of interactional data and to note the different ways in which they participated in the different groups. Toward the end of the term, I gave them a questionnaire asking about their class and group participation.

I could see plainly from my observation of the groups at work that women who never opened their mouths in class were talking away in the small groups. In fact, the Japanese woman commented that she found it particularly hard to contribute to the all-woman group she was in because "I was overwhelmed by how talkative the female students were in the female-only group." This is particularly revealing because it highlights that the same person who can be "oppressed" into silence in one context can become the talkative "oppressor" in another. No one's conversational style is absolute; everyone's style changes in response to the context and others' styles.

Some of the students (seven) said they preferred the same-gender groups; others preferred the same-style groups. In answer to the question "Would you have liked to speak in class more than you did?" six of the seven who said yes were women; the one man was Japanese. Most startlingly, this response did not come only from quiet women; it came from women who had indicated they had spoken in class never, rarely, sometimes and often. Of the eleven students who said the amount they had spoken was fine, seven were men. Of the four women who checked, "fine," two added qualifications indicating it wasn't completely fine: One wrote in "maybe more," and one wrote, "I have an urge to participate often but feel I should have something more interesting/relevant/wonderful/intelligent to say!"

I counted my experiment a success. Everyone in the class found the small groups interesting, and no one indicated he or she would have preferred that the class not break into groups. Perhaps most instructive, however, was the fact that the experience of breaking into groups, and of talking about participation in class, raised everyone's awareness about classroom participation. After we had talked about it, some of the quietest women in the class made a few voluntary contributions, though sometimes I had to insure their participation by interrupting the students who were exuberantly speaking out.

Americans are often proud that they discount the significance of cultural differences: "We're all individuals," many people boast. Ignoring such issues as gender and ethnicity becomes a source of pride: "I treat everyone the same." But treating people the same is not equal treatment if they are not the same. 20

The classroom is a different environment for those who feel comfortable putting themselves forward in a group than it is for those who find the prospect of doing so chastening, or even terrifying. When a professor asks, "Are there any questions?," students who can formulate statements the fastest have the greatest opportunity to respond. Those who need significant time to do so have not really been given a chance at all, since by the time they are ready to speak, someone else has taken the floor. 21

In a class where some students speak out without raising hands, those who feel they must raise their hands and wait to be recognized do not have equal opportunity to speak. Telling them to feel free to jump in will not make them feel free; one's sense of timing, of one's rights and obligations in a classroom, are automatic, learned over years of interaction. They may be changed over time, with motivation and effort, but they cannot be changed on the spot. And everyone assumes his or her own way is best. When I asked my students how the class could be changed to make it easier for them to speak more, the most talkative woman said she would prefer it if no one had to raise hands, and a foreign student said he wished people would raise their hands and wait to be recognized. 22

My experience in this class has convinced me that small-group interaction should be part of any class that is not a small seminar. I also am convinced that having the students become observers of their own interaction is a crucial part of their education. Talking about ways of talking in class makes students aware that their ways of talking affect other students, that the motivations they impute to others may not truly 23 reflect others' motives, and that the behaviors they assume to be self-evidently right are not universal norms.

The goal of complete equal opportunity in class may not be attainable, but realizing that one monolithic classroom-participation structure is not equal opportunity is itself a powerful motivation to find more diverse methods to serve diverse students—and every classroom is diverse.

XXXXXXXXXXXXXXXXXXX **FOR DISCUSSION** XXXXXXXXXXXXXXXXXXX

1. According to Deborah Tannen, speaking up in class is typically more "congenial" to whom, women or men (4)? What accounts for this difference, according to her COMPARISON of "the language experience" (4)?

2. Men, says Tannen, "ritualize opposition"; women don't (5). Why not? What is the difference, according to the authorities she cites, between how men fight and how women fight? Do you agree?

3. One of Tannen's colleagues teaches by asking students to read an article and then "tear it apart" (7). How does Tannen say this compares with the way she teaches?

4. Tannen CONTRASTS the "ethics of [class] participation" by men with those of women (14). What differences does she find? What are the consequences of their being "unstated" (14)?

5. Tannen, in paragraph 18, presents the results of her questionnaire about class and group participation. What are some of those results? What do you think of her findings?

6. Tannen says that her research in the conversation of men and women caused her to change her classroom teaching strategies. What are some of the changes she made? How compelling do you find her reasons for making them?

XXXXXXXXXXXXXX **STRATEGIES AND STRUCTURES** XXXXXXXXXXXXX

1. Tannen's title announces that she is COMPARING men and women, and that the basis on which she compares them is their classroom behavior. Where does she first indicate what particular aspects of this behavior she will focus on? What are some of them?

2. In paragraph 13, Tannen sums up two of the points of comparison that she has previously made. What are they, and why do you think she summarizes them here? What new point of comparison does she then introduce, and how does she develop it in the next paragraph(s)?

3. "No one's conversational style is absolute," says Tannen; "everyone's style changes in response to the context and others' styles" (17). How does the EXAMPLE of the Japanese woman in her class illustrate the principle that people have different styles of conversation in different situations?

4. Besides comparing and CONTRASTING the behavior of men and women, Tannen is advancing an ARGUMENT about equal opportunity in the classroom (24). What is the conclusion of her argument? What does she argue *for*?

5. "I broke the class into small groups," says Tannen in paragraph 16. Where else in her essay do you find Tannen telling a brief, illustrative story or ANECDOTE of what she did or said? How do the NARRATIVE elements in her essay fit in with her primary purpose of comparing and contrasting?

XXXXXXXXXXXX **WORDS AND FIGURES OF SPEECH** XXXXXXXXXXXX

1. Roughly speaking, one's "sex" is biological while one's "gender" is not, or not entirely. Why do you think Tannen uses the second term in her essay rather than the first one?

2. "Behavior" is usually a collective noun, as in the sentence "Their behavior last night was atrocious." Why do you suppose social scientists like Tannen often use the plural form, "behaviors," in their writing (23)? What is the significance of this difference in terminology?

3. Like that of other social scientists, Tannen's writing style is peppered with compound nouns and nouns used as adjectives—for example "single-sex schools" and "sex-separate peer groups" (2, 3). Point out other expressions like these throughout her essay.

4. What is the meaning of the word "hierarchical," (3) and why does Tannen use it to refer to boys?

5. What is the difference between "ritual opposition" as Tannen uses the term and just plain opposition (5)? What other behaviors does Tannen cite that might be considered rituals?

XXXXXXXXXXXXXXXXXXXXXX **FOR WRITING** XXXXXXXXXXXXXXXXXXXXXXX

1. How do Tannen's observations on gender in the classroom COMPARE with your own? Write a paragraph comparing and CONTRASTING some aspect of the classroom behaviors of the two genders.

2. Commenting on the differences in the ways girls and boys use language to make friends, Tannen writes: "Typically, a girl has a best friend with whom she sits and talks, frequently telling secrets" (3). Talking together makes them best friends. Boys, she says, make friends through "activities" (3). Consequently, they "use language to seize center stage," to take control (3). How do Tannen's observations square with your experience of making friends while growing up? Write an essay in which you compare and contrast how you made same-sex friends with the way, as you recall, the "opposite" gender did so. Please give specific EXAMPLES and include ANECDOTES when possible.

DAVID SEDARIS

REMEMBERING MY CHILDHOOD ON THE CONTINENT OF AFRICA

David Sedaris (b. 1957) is a satirist and playwright who contributes to *Esquire* and other magazines, and whose voice can be heard regularly on NPR's *This American Life*. Named humorist of the year in 2001 by *Time* magazine, he is the author of *Barrel Fever* (1994), *Naked* (1997), and *Me Talk Pretty One Day* (2000), from which this selection is taken. Although Sedaris once worked as a Christmas elf for Macy's department store, he did not grow up in the exotic settings he remembers here. In this essay, Sedaris steals memories from his friend Hugh, the son of a career diplomat, who actually grew up in Africa. Point by point, Sedaris compares his childhood with his friend's. "Certain events are parallel," he says: for example, they both saw the same movie about a talking Volkswagen. But by comparison with his friend's early years in the Congo and Ethiopia, Sedaris's own childhood in North Carolina was "unspeakably dull."

XXXXXXXXXXXXXXXXXXXXXXXXXXXXXXXXXXXXXXXXXXXXXXXXXXXXXXXXXXXXXXXXX

When Hugh was in the fifth grade, his class took a field trip to an Ethiopian slaughterhouse. He was living in Addis Ababa at the time, and the slaughterhouse was chosen because, he says, "it was convenient." 1

This was a school system in which the matter of proximity outweighed such petty concerns as what may or may not be appropriate for a busload of eleven-year-olds. "What?" I asked. "Were there no autopsies scheduled at the local morgue? Was the federal prison just a bit too far out of the way?" 2

Hugh defends his former school, saying, "Well, isn't that the whole point of a field trip? To see something new?" 3

"Technically yes, but . . ." 4

"All right then," he says. "So we saw some new things."   5

One of his field trips was literally a trip to a field where the class   6
watched a wrinkled man fill his mouth with rotten goat meat and feed it
to a pack of waiting hyenas. On another occasion they were taken to
examine the bloodied bedroom curtains hanging in the palace of the former dictator. There were tamer trips, to textile factories and sugar refin-
eries, but my favorite is always the slaughterhouse. It wasn't a big
company, just a small rural enterprise run by a couple of brothers operating out of a low-ceilinged concrete building. Following a brief lecture
on the importance of proper sanitation, a small white piglet was herded
into the room, its dainty hooves clicking against the concrete floor. The
class gathered in a circle to get a better look at the animal, who seemed
delighted with the attention he was getting. He turned from face to face
and was looking up at Hugh when one of the brothers drew a pistol from
his back pocket, held it against the animal's temple, and shot the piglet,
execution-style. Blood spattered, frightened children wept, and the man
with the gun offered the teacher and bus driver some meat from a freshly
slaughtered goat.

When I'm told such stories, it's all I can do to hold back my feelings   7
of jealousy. An Ethiopian slaughterhouse. Some people have all the luck.
When I was in elementary school, the best we ever got was a trip to Old
Salem or Colonial Williamsburg, one of those preserved brick villages
where time supposedly stands still and someone earns his living as a town
crier. There was always a blacksmith, a group of wandering patriots, and
a collection of bonneted women hawking corn bread or gingersnaps made
"the ol'-fashioned way." Every now and then you might come across a
doer of bad deeds serving time in the stocks, but that was generally as
exciting as it got.

Certain events are parallel, but compared with Hugh's, my child-   8
hood was unspeakably dull. When I was seven years old, my family
moved to North Carolina. When he was seven years old, Hugh's family
moved to the Congo. We had a collie and a house cat. They had a
monkey and two horses named Charlie Brown and Satan. I threw stones
at stop signs. Hugh threw stones at crocodiles. The verbs are the same,
but he definitely wins the prize when it comes to nouns and objects. An
eventful day for my mother might have involved a trip to the dry cleaner

or a conversation with the potato-chip deliveryman. Asked one ordinary Congo afternoon what she'd done with her day, Hugh's mother answered that she and a fellow member of the Ladies' Club had visited a leper colony on the outskirts of Kinshasa. No reason was given for the expedition, though chances are she was staking it out for a future field trip.

Due to his upbringing, Hugh sits through inane movies never realizing that they're often based on inane television shows. There were no poker-faced sitcom martians in his part of Africa, no oil-rich hillbillies or aproned brides trying to wean themselves from the practice of witchcraft. From time to time a movie would arrive packed in a dented canister, the film scratched and faded from its slow trip around the world. The theater consisted of a few dozen folding chairs arranged before a bedsheet or the blank wall of a vacant hangar out near the airstrip. Occasionally a man would sell warm soft drinks out of a cardboard box, but that was it in terms of concessions.

When I was young, I went to the theater at the nearby shopping center and watched a movie about a talking Volkswagen. I believe the little car had a taste for mischief but I can't be certain, as both the movie and the afternoon proved unremarkable and have faded from my memory. Hugh saw the same movie a few years after it was released. His family had left the Congo by this time and were living in Ethiopia. Like me, Hugh saw the movie by himself on a weekend afternoon. Unlike me, he left the theater two hours later, to find a dead man hanging from a telephone pole at the far end of the unpaved parking lot. None of the people who'd seen the movie seemed to care about the dead man. They stared at him for a moment or two and then headed home, saying they'd never seen anything as crazy as that talking Volkswagen. His father was late picking him up, so Hugh just stood there for an hour, watching the dead man dangle and turn in the breeze. The death was not reported in the newspaper, and when Hugh related the story to his friends, they said, "You saw the movie about the talking car?"

I could have done without the flies and the primitive theaters, but I wouldn't have minded growing up with a houseful of servants. In North Carolina it wasn't unusual to have a once-a-week maid, but Hugh's family had houseboys, a word that never fails to charge my imagination. They had cooks and drivers, and guards who occupied a gatehouse, armed with machetes. Seeing as I had regularly petitioned my parents for an electric fence, the business with the guards strikes me as the last word in quiet sophistication. Having protection suggests that you are important. Having that protection paid for by the government is even better, as it suggests your safety is of interest to someone other than yourself.

Hugh's father was a career officer with the U.S. State Department, and every morning a black sedan carried him off to the embassy. I'm told it's not as glamorous as it sounds, but in terms of fun for the entire family, I'm fairly confident that it beats the sack race at the annual IBM picnic. By the age of three, Hugh was already carrying a diplomatic passport. The rules that applied to others did not apply to him. No tickets, no arrests, no luggage search: he was officially licensed to act like a brat. Being an American, it was expected of him, and who was he to deny the world an occasional tantrum?

12

They weren't rich, but what Hugh's family lacked financially they more than made up for with the sort of exoticism that works wonders at cocktail parties, leading always to the remark "That sounds fascinating." It's a compliment one rarely receives when describing an adolescence spent drinking Icees at the North Hills Mall. No fifteen-foot python ever wandered onto my school's basketball court. I begged, I prayed nightly, but it just never happened. Neither did I get to witness a military coup in which forces sympathetic to the colonel arrived late at night to assassinate my next-door neighbor. Hugh had been at the Addis Ababa teen club when the electricity was cut off and soldiers arrived to evacuate the building. He and his friends had to hide in the back of a jeep and cover themselves with blankets during the ride home. It's something that sticks in his mind for one reason or another.

13

Among my personal highlights is the memory of having my picture taken with Uncle Paul, the legally blind host of a Raleigh children's television show. Among Hugh's is the memory of having his picture taken with Buzz Aldrin on the last leg of the astronaut's world tour. The man who had walked on the moon placed his hand on Hugh's shoulder and offered to sign his autograph book. The man who led Wake County schoolchildren in afternoon song turned at the sound of my voice and asked, "So what's your name, princess?"

14

When I was fourteen years old, I was sent to spend ten days with   15
my maternal grandmother in western New York State. She was a small
and private woman named Billie, and though she never came right out
and asked, I had the distinct impression she had no idea who I was. It
was the way she looked at me, squinting through her glasses while chewing on her lower lip. That, coupled with the fact that she never once
called me by name. "Oh," she'd say, "are you still here?" She was just
beginning her long struggle with Alzheimer's disease, and each time I
entered the room, I felt the need to reintroduce myself and set her at
ease. "Hi, it's me. Sharon's boy, David. I was just in the kitchen admiring
your collection of ceramic toads." Aside from a few trips to summer
camp, this was the longest I'd ever been away from home, and I like to
think I was toughened by the experience.

About the same time I was frightening my grandmother, Hugh   16
and his family were packing their belongings for a move to Somalia.
There were no English-speaking schools in Mogadishu, so, after a few
months spent lying around the family compound with his pet monkey,
Hugh was sent back to Ethiopia to live with a beer enthusiast his father
had met at a cocktail party. Mr. Hoyt installed security systems in foreign embassies. He and his family gave Hugh a room. They invited him
to join them at the table, but that was as far as they extended themselves. No one ever asked him when his birthday was, so when the day
came, he kept it to himself. There was no telephone service between
Ethiopia and Somalia, and letters to his parents were sent to Washington
and then forwarded on to Mogadishu, meaning that his news was more
than a month old by the time they got it. I suppose it wasn't much different than living as a foreign-exchange student. Young people do it all
the time, but to me it sounds awful. The Hoyts had two sons about
Hugh's age who were always saying things like "Hey that's *our* sofa
you're sitting on" and "Hands off that ornamental stein. It doesn't
belong to you."

He'd been living with these people for a year when he overheard   17
Mr. Hoyt tell a friend that he and his family would soon be moving to
Munich, Germany, the beer capital of the world.

"And that worried me," Hugh said, "because it meant I'd have to   18
find some other place to live."

Where I come from, finding shelter is a problem the average teen-   19
ager might confidently leave to his parents. It was just something that
came with having a mom and a dad. Worried that he might be sent to
live with his grandparents in Kentucky, Hugh turned to the school's guid-
ance counselor, who knew of a family whose son had recently left for
college. And so he spent another year living with strangers and not mentioning his birthday. While I wouldn't have wanted to do it myself, I
can't help but envy the sense of fortitude he gained from the experience.
After graduating from college, he moved to France knowing only the
phrase "Do you speak French?"—a question guaranteed to get you
nowhere unless you also speak the language.

While living in Africa, Hugh and his family took frequent vaca-   20
tions, often in the company of their monkey. The Nairobi Hilton, some
suite of high-ceilinged rooms in Cairo or Khartoum: these are the places
his people recall when gathered at a common table. "Was that the summer we spent in Beirut or, no, I'm thinking of the time we sailed from
Cyprus and took the *Orient Express* to Istanbul."

Theirs was the life I dreamt about during my vacations in eastern   21
North Carolina. Hugh's family was hobnobbing with chiefs and sultans
while I ate hush puppies at the Sanitary Fish Market in Morehead City,
a beach towel wrapped like a hijab around my head. Someone unknown
to me was very likely standing in a muddy ditch and dreaming of an
evening spent sitting in a clean family restaurant, drinking iced tea and
working his way through an extra-large seaman's platter, but that did not
concern me, as it meant I should have been happy with what I had.
Rather than surrender to my bitterness, I have learned to take satisfaction
in the life that Hugh has led. His stories have, over time, become my
own. I say this with no trace of a kumbaya. There is no spiritual sym-
biosis; I'm just a petty thief who lifts his memories the same way I'll
take a handful of change left on his dresser. When my own experiences
fall short of the mark, I just go out and spend some of his. It is with
pleasure that I sometimes recall the dead man's purpled face or the report
of the handgun ringing in my ears as I studied the blood pooling beneath
the dead white piglet. On the way back from the slaughterhouse, we
stopped for Cokes in the village of Mojo, where the gas-station owner
had arranged a few tables and chairs beneath a dying canopy of vines. It

was late afternoon by the time we returned to school, where a second bus carried me to the foot of Coffeeboard Road. Once there, I walked through a grove of eucalyptus trees and alongside a bald pasture of starving cattle, past the guard napping in his gatehouse, and into the waiting arms of my monkey.

XXXXXXXXXXXXXXXXXXXXX **FOR DISCUSSION** XXXXXXXXXXXXXXXXXXXXX

1. When he was in elementary school, David Sedaris went on field trips to places like Old Salem and Colonial Williamsburg (7). How do these experiences COMPARE with the typical field trips that his friend Hugh took as a child? What is his point in comparing the two experiences?

2. When they were growing up, both Sedaris and Hugh saw the same "unremarkable" movie about a talking Volkswagen (10). How, then, was Hugh's experience different from Sedaris's?

3. Sedaris says that he has learned "to take satisfaction" in Hugh's experience rather than "surrender to my bitterness" (21). What does he claim to be "bitter" about? How seriously are we supposed to take this claim?

4. After comparing and CONTRASTING their adventures for several pages, how does Sedaris finally "take" satisfaction from the life of his friend?

5. On the whole, whose childhood would you prefer to remember having lived, Sedaris's or his friend Hugh's? Why?

XXXXXXXXXXXXXX **STRATEGIES AND STRUCTURES** XXXXXXXXXXXXXX

1. In COMPARING his childhood with Hugh's, Sedaris obviously stresses the CONTRASTS. What similarities does he nonetheless mention?

2. In paragraph 8, Sedaris constructs a point-by-point mini-essay in comparison and contrast. How does the order of his sentences and their grammatical structure help to heighten the contrasts he draws between "parallel" events in his life and Hugh's?

3. Parallel lines run along together but never intersect. Point out examples in this essay where Sedaris shows events in the two boys' lives as parallel but contrasting.

4. Paragraph 10 recalls a rare common experience in the two boys' lives—going to the movie about the talking Volkswagen. How—and why—does Sedaris turn this identical experience into another contrast between them?

5. What specific details does Sedaris use to give the impression in his final paragraph that he has "stolen" (or stolen into) his friend's memories?

6. Even though Sedaris's essay is organized as a comparison of events in his childhood and that of his friend, it has many elements of personal NARRATIVE. What are some of them? Cite specific examples from the text. (Imagine this essay *without* any narrative. How would it be different?)

XXXXXXXXXXXX **WORDS AND FIGURES OF SPEECH** XXXXXXXXXXX

1. What does Sedaris mean when he says that his life and Hugh's shared the same verbs but different nouns and objects (8)?

2. Explain the IRONY in Sedaris's use of this phrase: "Among my personal high-lights is the memory of having my picture taken with Uncle Paul, the legally blind host of a Raleigh children's television show" (14).

3. A "hijab" is a sort of veil (21). Why does Sedaris use this term in the context of the Sanitary Fish Market in Morehead City?

4. Sedaris uses the African word "kumbaya" in paragraph 21. How does he DEFINE it?

5. On what basis is Sedaris drawing an ANALOGY between himself and a "petty thief" in paragraph 21?

XXXXXXXXXXXXXXXXXXXXX **FOR WRITING** XXXXXXXXXXXXXXXXXXXXXX

1. Have you and a friend or a family member ever had entirely different recollections of the same event? Ask that person to write out (or tape) his or her recollection, and you do the same—separately. Then, in a list or a paragraph or two, make a point-by-point COMPARISON of the two versions.

2. Write an essay comparing and CONTRASTING your childhood with that of someone whose childhood you know (or imagine) to be very different from your own. Your counterpart can be someone you are personally acquainted with or whom you only know about.

CHAPTER SEVEN

DEFINITION

XXXXXXXXXXXXXXXXXXXXXXXXXXXXXXXXXXXXXXXXXXXXXXXXXXXXXXXXXXXXXXXXXXXX

When you DEFINE* something, you tell what it is—and what it is not. The most basic definitions take the form of simple declarative sentences, often with the word *is*, as in the following famous definitions:

> Happiness is a warm puppy.
> SNOOPY

> Man is a biped without feathers.
> PLATO

> Hope is the thing with feathers.
> EMILY DICKINSON

> Home is where the heart is.
> EPES SARGENT

All of these model definitions, you'll notice, work in the same way. They place the thing to be defined (happiness, man, hope, home) into a general category (puppy, biped, thing, place) and then add QUALIFIERS (warm, without feathers, with feathers, where the heart is) that distinguish it from others in the same category.

This is the kind of defining—by general category and qualifiers—that dictionaries do. *The American Heritage Dictionary*, for example, defines the word *scepter* as "a staff held by a sovereign . . . as an emblem of authority." Here the general category is "staff," and the qualifiers—the CHARACTERISTICS that differentiate it from other staffs, such as those carried by shepherds—are "held by a sovereign" and "as an emblem of authority."

*Words printed in SMALL CAPITALS are defined in the Glossary.

The problem with basic dictionary definitions like this is that they often don't tell us everything we need to know. You might begin an essay with one, but you are not going to get very far with a subject unless you *extend* your definition. One way to give an *extended definition* is to name other similar items in the same category as the item you are defining.

Take the term *folklore*, for example. A standard definition of *folklore* is "the study of traditional materials." This simple definition is not likely to enlighten anyone who is not already familiar with what those "materials" are, however. So one folklorist defines his field by listing a host of similar items that all belong to it:

> Folklore includes myths, legends, folktales, jokes, proverbs, riddles, chants, charms, blessings, curses, oaths, insults, retorts, taunts, teases, toasts, tongue-twisters, and greeting and leave-taking formulas (e.g., See you later, alligator). It also includes folk costumes, folk dance, folk drama (and mime), folk art, folk belief (or superstition), folk medicine, folk instrumental music (e.g., fiddle tunes), folksongs (e.g., lullabies, ballads), folk speech (e.g., to paint the town red), and names (e.g., nicknames and place names).
>
> ALAN DUNDES, *THE STUDY OF FOLKLORE*

Dundes's extended definition does not stop here; it goes on to include "latrinalia (writings on the walls of public bathrooms)," "envelope sealers (e.g., SWAK—Sealed With A Kiss)," "comments made after body emissions (e.g., after burps or sneezes)," and many others items that populate the field he is defining.

Another way to extend a basic definition is to specify additional qualities of the item or idea you are defining. *Hydroponic tomatoes*, for example, are tomatoes grown mostly in water. Food expert Raymond Sokolov further defines this kind of tomato as one that is "mass-produced, artificially ripened, mechanically picked, and long-hauled." "It has no taste," he says, "and it won't go splat" (all additional negative qualities or attributes). *Organic tomatoes*, by contrast, says Sokolov, are to be defined as "squishable, blotchy, tart, and sometimes green-dappled."

To extend your definition further, you might give synonyms for the word or concept you're defining, or trace its ETYMOLOGY, or word history.

Tomatoes, for example, are commonly defined as "vegetables," but an extended definition might point out that they are actually synonymous with "berries" or "fleshy fruits" and that they derive their name from the Nahuatl word *tomatl*. How do I know this last obscure fact? Because my dictionary, like yours, includes etymologies along with many basic definitions. Etymologies trace the origins of a word and sometimes can help organize an entire essay.

For example, here is the beginning of an essay by biologist Stephen Jay Gould on the concept of evolution:

> The exegesis [interpretation] of evolution as a concept has occu-pied the lifetimes of a thousand scientists. In this essay, I present something almost laughably narrow in comparison—an exegesis of the word itself. I shall trace how organic change came to be called *evolution*. The tale is complex and fascinating as a pure antiquarian exercise in etymological detection. But more is at stake, for a past usage of this word has contributed to the most common, current misunderstanding among laymen of what sci-entists mean by evolution.
>
> STEPHEN JAY GOULD, *EVER SINCE DARWIN*

The misunderstanding to which this paragraph refers is the idea that *evolution* means "progress." To scientists, says Gould, *evolution* simply signifies change, adaptation—with no implication of improvement.

Gould is writing to correct what he perceives as a grave error. There is more at stake for him here than just defining a word or idea—as there should be for you when you write an essay that defines something. Good definitions have good reasons for introducing and defining their key terms. When Langston Hughes, for example, defines "Bop" music in one of the essays in this chapter, he has something to say about racism. Or when physicist John Archibald Wheeler defines the quantum principle, he is not indulging in an antiquarian exercise, but challenging a new generation to solve one of the great unsolved mysteries in his field.

There is no set formula for writing good definitions, but there are some questions to keep in mind when you are working on one: What is the essential nature or main use of the thing you are defining? What are its most important qualities? How is it different from other things like it? And, perhaps most important, why do we need to know about it?

What is the *peduncle* of a manatee? It's the spot where the tail of the animal joins the body. But what is a manatee? These are questions about definitions and, like all such questions, the best way to start answering them is to identify the unique category to which such a beast belongs. Christopher Columbus, upon encountering the manatee in the New World, mistakenly put it in the same category as mermaids: human-like, aquatic mammals with long hair. The Save the Manatee Club (SMC) defines manatees as "large, gray-brown aquatic mammals." This is a simple definition. To define anything fully, however, we must go beyond simply identifying the fundamental CLASS or category to which it belongs and provide distinguishing features of that class or category. For example, the SMC tells us that manatees have "bodies that taper to a flat, paddle-shaped tail." Or we can link the thing we're defining with other kinds of things: "The manatee's closest relatives are the elephant and hyrax." Or we can describe its typical behavior ("gentle and slow-moving") and identify other unusual attributes, such as its ability to consume 10 to 15 percent of its weight in vegetation daily. Another thing to remember: definitions are seldom ends in themselves. The people at www.savethemanatee.org, for example, already know what manatees are. But they have good reasons for defining them anyway: they want to educate other people, particularly boaters, about these gentle, endangered animals; and they want to raise money to protect them.

CONSIDER FURTHER . . .

1. What are sirenians? Besides the manatee, what other creatures of the world belong to this order? How are they defined? Any relation to the sirens who called to Ulysses? Here, www.savethemanatee.org can help.

2. Name several improbable or imaginary beings that you would like more clearly defined. Where would you go for more information on them? Practice writing your own definitions of a few—for example, a unicorn, phoenix, elf, or ogre.

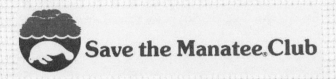

Save the Manatee® Club

West Indian manatees are large, gray-brown aquatic mammals with bodies that taper to a flat, paddle-shaped tail. They have two flippers with three to four nails on each, and their head and face are wrinkled with whiskers on the snout. The manatee's closest relative is the elephant and hyrax (a small furry animal that resembles a rodent). Manatees are believed to have evolved from a wading, plant-eating animal. The West Indian manatee is related to the West African manatee, the Amazonian manatee, the dugong, and Steller's sea cow, which was hunted to extinction in 1768. The average adult manatee is about 10 feet long and weighs about 1,000 pounds.

Behavior: Manatees are gentle and slow-moving. Most of their time is spent eating, resting, and in travel. Manatees are completely herbivorous. They eat aquatic plants and can consume 10–15% of their body weight daily in vegetation. They graze for food along water bottoms and on the surface. They may rest submerged at the bottom or just below the surface, coming up to breathe on the average of every three to five minutes. When manatees are using a great deal of energy, they may surface to breathe as often as every 30 seconds.

DAVE BARRY

GUYS VS. MEN

Dave Barry (b. 1947) is a syndicated columinist for the *Miami Herald*, where he won a Pulitzer Prize for commentary in 1988. He is the author of twenty-three humor books, including *Dave Barry's Complete Guide to Guys* (1995), the introduction of which is included here. Despite its title, "Guys vs. Men" is not a comparative study of these two basic types of males. Men and manhood have been written about far too much already, says Barry. But guys and guyhood are neglected topics, and even though he "can't define exactly what it means to be a guy," Barry's essay lays out "certain guy characteristics" that distinguish his quarry from other warm-blooded animals in the field.

XXXXXXXXXXXXXXXXXXXXXXXXXXXXXXXXXXXXXXXXXXXXXXXXXXXXXXXXXXXX

This is a book about guys. It's *not* a book about men. There are
already way too many books about men, and most of them are *way* too serious. 1

Men itself is a serious word, not to mention *manhood* and *manly*. Such words make being male sound like a very important activity, as opposed to what it primarily consists of, namely, possessing a set of minor and frequently unreliable organs. 2

But men tend to attach great significance to Manhood. This results in certain characteristically masculine, by which I mean stupid, behavioral patterns that can produce unfortunate results such as violent crime, war, spitting, and ice hockey. These things have given males a bad name.[1] And the "Men's Movement," which is supposed to bring out the more positive aspects of Manliness, seems to be densely populated with loons and goobers. 3

[1]Specifically, "asshole."

So I'm saying that there's another way to look at males: not as   4
aggressive macho dominators; not as sensitive, liberated, hugging drummers; but as *guys*.

And what, exactly, do I mean by "guys"? I don't know. I haven't   5
thought that much about it. One of the major characteristics of guyhood
is that we guys don't spend a lot of time pondering our deep innermost
feelings. There is a serious question in my mind about whether guys
actually *have* deep innermost feelings, unless you count, for example,
loyalty to the Detroit Tigers, or fear of bridal showers.

But although I can't define exactly what it means to be a guy, I can   6
describe certain guy characteristics, such as:

Guys Like Neat Stuff

By "neat," I mean "mechanical and unnecessarily complex." I'll give you   7
an example. Right now I'm typing these words on an *extremely* powerful
computer. It's the latest in a line of maybe ten computers I've owned,
each one more powerful than the last. My computer is chock full of RAM
and ROM and bytes and megahertzes and various other items that enable
a computer to kick data-processing butt. It is probably capable of supervising the entire U.S. air-defense apparatus while simultaneously processing the tax return of every resident of Ohio. I use it mainly to write
a newspaper column. This is an activity wherein I sit and stare at the
screen for maybe ten minutes, then, using only my forefingers, slowly
type something like:

Henry Kissinger* looks like a big wart.   8

I stare at this for another ten minutes, have an inspiration, then amplify   9
the original thought as follows:

Henry Kissinger looks like a big fat wart.   10

Then I stare at that for another ten minutes pondering whether I   11
should try to work in the concept of "hairy."

*Henry Kissinger (b. 1923), U.S. Secretary of State 1973–77 [Editor's note].

This is absurdly simple work for my computer. It sits there, hum-   12
ming impatiently, bored to death, passing the time between keystrokes
via brain-teaser activities such as developing a Unified Field Theory of
the universe and translating the complete works of Shakespeare into rap.[2]

In other words, this computer is absurdly overqualified to work for   13
me, and yet soon, I guarantee, I will buy an *even more powerful* one. I
won't be able to stop myself, I'm a guy.

Probably the ultimate example of the fundamental guy drive to have   14
neat stuff is the Space Shuttle. Granted, the guys in charge of this program *claim* it has a Higher Scientific Purpose, namely to see how humans
function in space. But of course we have known for years how humans
function in space: They float around and say things like: "Looks real
good, Houston!"

No, the real reason for the existence of the Space Shuttle is that it   15
is one humongous and spectacularly gizmo-intensive item of hardware.
Guys can tinker with it practically forever, and occasionally even get it
to work, and use it to place *other* complex mechanical items into orbit,
where they almost immediately break, which provides a great excuse to
send the Space Shuttle up *again*. It's Guy Heaven.

Other results of the guy need to have stuff are Star Wars, the rec-   16
reational boating industry, monorails, nuclear weapons, and wristwatches
that indicate the phase of the moon. I am not saying that women haven't
been involved in the development or use of this stuff. I'm saying that,
without guys, this stuff probably would not exist; just as, without women,
virtually every piece of furniture in the world would still be in its original
position. Guys do not have a basic need to rearrange furniture. Whereas
a woman who could cheerfully use the same computer for fifty-three
years will rearrange her furniture on almost a weekly basis, sometimes in
the dead of night. She'll be sound asleep in bed, and suddenly, at 2 A.M.,
she'll be awakened by the urgent thought: *The blue-green sofa needs to go
perpendicular to the wall instead of parallel, and it needs to go there RIGHT
NOW.* So she'll get up and move it, which of course necessitates moving
other furniture, and soon she has rearranged her entire living room, shift-

[2]To be or not? I got to *know.*
Might kill myself by the end of the *show.*

ing great big heavy pieces that ordinarily would require several burly men to lift, because there are few forces in Nature more powerful than a woman who needs to rearrange furniture. Every so often a guy will wake up to discover that, because of his wife's overnight efforts, he now lives in an entirely different house.

(I realize that I'm making gender-based generalizations here, but my feeling is that if God did not want us to make gender-based generalizations, She would not have given us genders.)

Guys Like a Really Pointless Challenge

Not long ago I was sitting in my office at the *Miami Herald*'s Sunday magazine, *Tropic*, reading my fan mail[3] when I heard several of my guy coworkers in the hallway talking about how fast they could run the forty-yard dash. These are guys in their thirties and forties who work in journalism, where the most demanding physical requirement is the ability to digest vending-machine food. In other words, these guys have absolutely no need to run the forty-yard dash.

But one of them, Mike Wilson, was writing a story about a star high-school football player who could run it in 4.38 seconds. Now if Mike had written a story about, say, a star high-school poet, none of my guy coworkers would have suddenly decided to find out how well they could write sonnets. But when Mike turned in his story, they became *deeply* concerned about how fast they could run the forty-yard dash. They were so concerned that the magazine editor, Tom Shroder, decided that they should get a stopwatch and go out to a nearby park and find out. Which they did, a bunch of guys taking off their shoes and running around barefoot in a public park on company time.

This is what I heard them talking about, out in the hall. I heard Tom, who was thirty-eight years old, saying that his time in the forty had been 5.75 seconds. And I thought to myself: This is ridiculous. These are middle-aged guys, supposedly adults, and they're out there *bragging* about their performance in this stupid juvenile footrace. Finally I couldn't stand it anymore.

---

[3]Typical fan letter: "Who cuts your hair? Beavers?"

"Hey!" I shouted. "*I could beat 5.75 seconds.*"   21

So we went out to the park and measured off forty yards, and the   22
guys told me that I had three chances to make my best time. On the first
try my time was 5.78 seconds, just three-hundredths of a second slower
than Tom's, even though, at forty-five, I was seven years older than he.
So I just *knew* I'd beat him on the second attempt if I ran really, really
hard, which I did for a solid ten yards, at which point my left hamstring
muscle, which had not yet shifted into Spring Mode from Mail-Reading
Mode, went, and I quote, "pop."

I had to be helped off the field. I was in considerable pain, and I   23
was obviously not going to be able to walk right for weeks. The other
guys were very sympathetic, especially Tom, who took the time to call
me at home, where I was sitting with an ice pack on my leg and twenty-
three Advil in my bloodstream, so he could express his concern.

"Just remember," he said, "*you didn't beat my time.*"   24

There are countless other examples of guys rising to meet pointless   25
challenges. Virtually all sports fall into this category, as well as a large
part of U.S. foreign policy ("I'll bet you can't capture Manuel Noriega!"*
"Oh YEAH??")

Guys Do Not Have a Rigid and Well-Defined Moral Code

This is not the same as saying that guys are bad. Guys *are* capable of   26
doing bad things, but this generally happens when they try to be Men
and start becoming manly and aggressive and stupid. When they're being
just plain guys, they aren't so much actively *evil* as they are *lost*. Because
guys have never really grasped the Basic Human Moral Code, which I
believe was invented by women millions of years ago when all the guys
were out engaging in some other activity, such as seeing who could burp
the loudest. When they came back, there were certain rules that they
were expected to follow unless they wanted to get into Big Trouble, and
they have been trying to follow these rules ever since, with extremely
irregular results. Because guys have never *internalized* these rules. Guys

---

*Manuel Noriega (b. 1934), Panamanian dictator removed from power by armed U.S.
intervention in 1989 [Editor's note].

are similar to my small auxiliary backup dog, Zippy, a guy dog[4] who has been told numerous times that he is *not* supposed to (1) get into the kitchen garbage or (2) poop on the floor. He knows that these are the rules, but he has never really understood *why*, and sometimes he gets to thinking: Sure, I am *ordinarily* not supposed to get into the garbage, but obviously this rule is not meant to apply when there are certain extenuating[5] circumstances, such as (1) somebody just threw away some perfectly good seven-week-old Kung Pao Chicken, and (2) I am home alone.

And so when the humans come home, the kitchen floor has been transformed into Garbage-Fest USA, and Zippy, who usually comes rushing up, is off in a corner disguised in a wig and sunglasses, hoping to get into the Federal Bad Dog Relocation Program before the humans discover the scene of the crime.   27

When I yell at him, he frequently becomes so upset that he poops on the floor.   28

Morally, most guys are just like Zippy, only taller and usually less hairy. Guys are *aware* of the rules of moral behavior, but they have trouble keeping these rules in the forefronts of their minds at certain times, especially the present. This is especially true in the area of faithfulness to one's mate. I realize, of course, that there are countless examples of guys being faithful to their mates until they die, usually as a result of being eaten by their mates immediately following copulation. Guys outside of the spider community, however, do not have a terrific record of faithfulness.   29

I'm not saying guys are scum. I'm saying that many guys who consider themselves to be committed to their marriages will stray if they are confronted with overwhelming temptation, defined as "virtually any temptation."   30

Okay, so maybe I *am* saying guys are scum. But they're not *mean-spirited* scum. And few of them—even when they are out of town on business trips, far from their wives, and have a clear-cut opportunity—will poop on the floor.   31

[4] I also have a female dog, Earnest, who *never* breaks the rules.
[5] I am taking some liberties here with Zippy's vocabulary. More likely, in his mind, he uses the term *mitigating*.

XXXXXXXXXXXXXXXXXXX **FOR DISCUSSION** XXXXXXXXXXXXXXXXXXX

1. Dave Barry starts to DEFINE what he means by "guys" and then says, "I don't know. I haven't thought that much about it" (5). He's being funny, right? Does his extended DEFINITION of guys lead you to believe that he has thought intelligently about what guys are? How so?

2. Males, says Barry, can be DIVIDED into two basic categories. What are the distinguishing CHARACTERISTICS of each?

3. To write his humor column, Barry doesn't ever need to buy a new, more powerful computer. But he says in paragraph 13 that he will do it anyway. What principle of guy behavior is he illustrating here?

4. In paragraph 16, Barry develops his definition of guys as neat-stuff-buying animals by CONTRASTING them with women. How does he define women in this paragraph? Do you think his definition is accurate? If not, how would you revise what he says?

5. Do you agree or disagree with Barry that "virtually all" sports fall into the "pointless challenge" category (25)? What about U.S. foreign policy?

6. Guys, says Barry, "are similar" to his dog Zippy (26). This is a definition by ANALOGY. What specific characteristics, according to Barry, do guys and Zippy have in common? Do you think the COMPARISON is just? In what one way, at least, does even Barry admit that unleashed guys are generally superior to dogs?

XXXXXXXXXXXXX **STRATEGIES AND STRUCTURES** XXXXXXXXXXXXX

1. Beginning in paragraph 6, Barry DEFINES guys by citing three of their distinguishing "guy CHARACTERISTICS." What are they? How does Barry use these characteristics to organize his entire essay in definition?

2. The basic logic behind defining something is to put it into a set of ever-narrower categories. In Barry's definition, guys belong to the category of males who like challenges. But this is still a very broad category; so Barry narrows it down further by adding the qualifier "pointless." Following this logic, why can't the high-school poet in paragraph 19 be defined as a guy? Please point out other EXAMPLES of this logic of elimination in Barry's essay, such as his definition of guys as "scum" in paragraph 31.

3. Why do you think Barry is so careful to specify the gender of God in paragraph 17?

4. From reading Barry's title, you might expect "Guys vs. Men" to be an essay that is primarily COMPARISON and CONTRAST. Where *and why* does Barry switch from drawing a comparison between the two kinds of males to defining one kind to the exclusion of the other?

5. Barry's humor often comes from his use of specific examples, as in "violent crime, war, spitting, and ice hockey" (3). Please point out where his scrupulous examples help define specific terms. Where would this essay be *without* all the examples? Why is Barry being (or pretending to be) so rigorous?

XXXXXXXXXXXX **WORDS AND FIGURES OF SPEECH** XXXXXXXXXXXX

1. How does Barry DEFINE "male" (2)? How about "manly" (2)? So, according to Barry's definitions, is "manly male" an OXYMORON? (Barry would probably make a joke here, one that would not be complimentary either to males or oxen.)

2. How would you define *loons* (3)? How do they differ from *goobers* (3)?

3. Why does Barry capitalize "Big Trouble" in paragraph 26?

4. Translate the following Barry phrase into standard English: "one humongous and spectacularly gizmo-intensive item of hardware" (15).

XXXXXXXXXXXXXXXXXXXXX **FOR WRITING** XXXXXXXXXXXXXXXXXXXXX

1. Rightly or wrongly, Barry has been called a humorist. How would *you* DEFINE one? Make a list of the distinguishing CHARACTERISTICS that make a good humorist in your view, and give EXAMPLES of humorists who you think represent these characteristics (you might want to use Barry as an example, or not).

2. How would you define "guys"? What characteristics does Barry leave out? Can a guy be female (as in "When we go shopping, my grandmother is just one of the guys")? Write an essay setting forth your definition of the term "guys," or one of the following gender terms: *man, woman, girl, girlfriend, lady.*

PICO IYER

IN PRAISE OF THE HUMBLE COMMA

Pico Iyer (b. 1957) is a novelist and travel writer who defines himself as "a global village on two legs." Iyer was born in England to Indian parents, moved to California as a boy, returned to England for schooling, and now lives in Japan. His latest book is *The Global Soul: Jet Lag, Shopping Malls, and the Search for Home* (2000). In this 1988 essay from *Time* magazine, Iyer visits a tiny corner of the world of print and writing, the "humble" comma, which he defines in strikingly human terms. Once you have seen the qualities and characteristics that Iyer sees in these old friends (or enemies), you will better understand the vital supporting roles they play in your own writing.

XXXXXXXXXXXXXXXXXXXXXXXXXXXXXXXXXXXXXXXXXXXXXXXXXXXXXXXXXXXXXXXXXXX

The gods, they say, give breath, and they take it away. But the same could be said—could it not?—of the humble comma. Add it to the present clause, and, of a sudden, the mind is, quite literally, given pause to think; take it out if you wish or forget it and the mind is deprived of a resting place. Yet still the comma gets no respect. It seems just a slip of a thing, a pedant's tick, a blip on the edge of our consciousness, a kind of printer's smudge almost. Small, we claim, is beautiful (especially in the age of the microchip). Yet what is so often used, and so rarely recalled, as the comma—unless it be breath itself?

Punctuation, one is taught, has a point: to keep up law and order. Punctuation marks are the road signs placed along the highway of our communications—to control speeds, provide directions and prevent head-on collisions. A period has the unblinking finality of a red light; the comma is a flashing yellow light that asks us only to slow down; and the semicolon is a stop sign that tells us to ease gradually to a halt, before gradually starting up again. By establishing the relations between words, punctuation establishes the relations between the people using words.

That may be one reason why schoolteachers exalt it and lovers defy it ("We love each other and belong to each other let's don't ever hurt each other Nicole let's don't ever hurt each other," wrote Gary Gilmore to his girlfriend).[1] A comma, he must have known, "separates inseparables," in the clinching words of H. W. Fowler, King of English Usage.

Punctuation, then, is a civic prop, a pillar that holds society upright. (A run-on sentence, its phrases piling up without division, is as unsightly as a sink piled high with dirty dishes.) Small wonder, then, that punctuation was one of the first proprieties of the Victorian age, the age of the corset, that the modernists threw off: the sexual revolution might be said to have begun when Joyce's Molly Bloom spilled out all her private thoughts in 36 pages of unbridled, almost unperioded and officially censored prose; and another rebellion was surely marked when E. E. Cummings first felt free to commit "God" to the lower case.[2]   3

Punctuation thus becomes the signature of cultures. The hot-blooded Spaniard seems to be revealed in the passion and urgency of his doubled exclamation points and question marks *("¡Caramba! ¿Quién sabe?")*, while the impassive Chinese traditionally added to his so-called inscrutability by omitting directions from his ideograms. The anarchy and commotion of the '60s were given voice in the exploding exclamation marks, riotous capital letters and Day-Glo italics of Tom Wolfe's spray-paint prose;[3] and in Communist societies, where the State is absolute, the dignity—and divinity—of capital letters is reserved for Ministries, Sub-Committees and Secretariats.   4

Yet punctuation is something more than a culture's birthmark; it scores the music in our minds, gets our thoughts moving to the rhythm of our hearts. Punctuation is the notation in the sheet music of our words, telling us where to rest, or when to raise our voices; it acknowledges that the meaning of our discourse, as of any symphonic composition, lies not   5

---

[1]Gary Gilmore, multiple murderer, executed by firing squad in January 1977.

[2]Molly Bloom appears in *Ulysses* (1922), by Irish writer James Joyce (1882–1941); the American poet E. E. Cummings (1894–1962) was known for his use of lowercase letters for capitals.

[3]In *The Electric Kool-Aid Acid Test* (1968), novelist and journalist Tom Wolfe (b. 1931) tells the story of a cross-country journey by "hippies" in a spray-painted bus.

in the units but in the pauses, the pacing and the phrasing. Punctuation is the way one bats one's eyes, lowers one's voice or blushes demurely. Punctuation adjusts the tone and color and volume till the feeling comes into perfect focus, not disgust exactly, but distaste; not lust, or like, but love.

Punctuation, in short, gives us the human voice, and all the meanings that lie between the words. "You aren't young, are you?" loses its innocence when it loses the question mark. Every child knows the menace of a dropped apostrophe (the parent's "Don't do that" shifting into the more slowly enunciated "Do not do that"), and every believer, the ignominy of having his faith reduced to "faith." Add an exclamation point to "To be or not to be . . ." and the gloomy Dane has all the resolve he needs; add a comma, and the noble sobriety of "God save the Queen" becomes a cry of desperation bordering on double sacrilege.

Sometimes, of course, our markings may be simply a matter of aesthetics. Popping in a comma can be like slipping on the necklace that gives an outfit quiet elegance, or like catching the sound of running water that complements, as it completes, the silence of a Japanese landscape. When V. S. Naipaul,[4] in his latest novel, writes, "He was a middle-aged man, with glasses," the first comma can seem a little precious. Yet it gives the description a spin, as well as a subtlety, that it otherwise lacks, and it shows that the glasses are not part of the middle-agedness, but something else.

Thus all these tiny scratches give us breadth and heft and depth. A world that has only periods is a world without inflections. It is a world without shade. It has a music without sharps and flats. It is a martial music. It has a jackboot rhythm. Words cannot bend and curve. A comma, by comparison, catches the gentle drift of the mind in thought, turning in on itself and back on itself, reversing, redoubling and returning along the course of its own sweet river music; while the semicolon brings clauses and thoughts together with all the silent discretion of a hostess arranging guests around her dinner table.

[4]V. S. Naipaul (b. 1932), Trinidadian-born British writer who won the Nobel Prize in Literature in 2001.

Punctuation, then, is a matter of care. Care for words, yes, but also, and more important, for what the words imply. Only a lover notices the small things: the way the afternoon light catches the nape of a neck, or how a strand of hair slips out from behind an ear, or the way a finger curls around a cup. And no one scans a letter so closely as a lover, searching for its small print, straining to hear its nuances, its gasps, its sighs and hesitations, poring over the secret messages that lie in every cadence. The difference between "Jane (whom I adore)" and "Jane, whom I adore," and the difference between them both and "Jane—whom I adore—" marks all the distance between ecstasy and heartache. "No iron can pierce the heart with such force as a period put at just the right place," in Isaac Babel's[5] lovely words: a comma can let us hear a voice break, or a heart. Punctuation, in fact, is a labor of love. Which brings us back, in a way, to gods.

9

ᗢᗢᗢᗢᗢᗢᗢᗢᗢᗢᗢᗢᗢ **FOR DISCUSSION** ᗢᗢᗢᗢᗢᗢᗢᗢᗢᗢᗢᗢᗢ

1. Why does Pico Iyer praise the humble comma? What does he say is so special about it?

2. Along with the comma, Iyer DEFINES several other punctuation marks. What CHARACTERISTICS does he ascribe to each?

3. How (and where) does Iyer define punctuation in general?

4. Is Iyer justly praising the comma and other punctuation marks, in your opinion? Why or why not?

ᗢᗢᗢᗢᗢᗢᗢᗢᗢᗢᗢ **STRATEGIES AND STRUCTURES** ᗢᗢᗢᗢᗢᗢᗢᗢᗢᗢᗢ

1. Iyer begins his essay with a series of (false) DEFINITIONS of the comma: "It seems just a slip of a thing, a pedant's tick, a blip on the edge of our consciousness, a kind of printer's smudge almost" (1). This is defining in its most basic form: X is Y. Give EXAMPLES of other places in his essay where Iyer uses this fundamental form of definition.

---

[5]Isaac Babel (1894–1940), internationally influential Soviet Jewish prose writer, most famous for his short stories.

2. Beginning with paragraph 1, Iyer illustrates what he is saying about punctuation by the way he punctuates his own writing. Where else does he use this device, and to what effect?

3. "By establishing the relations between words," says Iyer, "punctuation establishes the relations between the people using words" (2). How (and how well) does his example of murderer Gary Gilmore's letter to his girlfriend, Nicole, demonstrate this proposition? Where else in his essay does Iyer show relations between people by using punctuation? Give examples from the text.

4. Besides at least two murders, Gary Gilmore committed one long *run-on sentence* in his letter to his girlfriend. What are run-on sentences and why do teachers of writing regard them as errors?

5. Many of Iyer's definitions are definitions by ANALOGY, as when he explains what commas are by saying, "Popping in a comma can be like slipping on the necklace that gives an outfit quiet elegance" (7). Point out other instances throughout his essay where Iyer defines something by COMPARING it to other things with similar CHARACTERISTICS? Do you think his definitions by analogy are effective? Why or why not?

XXXXXXXXXXXXXX **WORDS AND FIGURES OF SPEECH** XXXXXXXXXXXX

1. *Personification* is the attributing of human CHARACTERISTICS to inanimate objects, as Iyer does to the comma. Point out several other instances in his essay of Iyer's use of this FIGURE OF SPEECH.

2. "Punctuation," says Iyer, "is the notation in the sheet music of our words" (5). What are the two things Iyer COMPARES in this METAPHOR? Do you think the comparison works? Why or why not?

3. A noun of direct address names the person or thing to whom a statement or request is directed. So where would you put a comma in "God save the Queen" to turn it into "a cry of desperation" (6)? Why do you think Iyer DESCRIBES the edited version the way he does?

4. Iyer says that punctuation is a "labor of love" (9). To what kind of tasks is this phrase normally applied? How does Iyer justify using it to DEFINE something so mundane as punctuation?

XXXXXXXXXXXXXXXXXXXXXX **FOR WRITING** XXXXXXXXXXXXXXXXXXXXXX

1. Write an extended DEFINITION of some grammatical or other term that interests you: the emoticon, the non sequitur, MLA style.

2. Henry Watson Fowler (1858–1933), to whom Iyer refers in paragraph 2, is the author of *The King's English* (1906), referred to in later printings as Fowler's *Modern English Usage*. A standard reference work for writers available in the reference section of your library, Fowler's book came out in a third edition in 1998. Examine a copy, either of the older edition or the new, and write an essay—based on Fowler's introduction and some of his EXAMPLES—in which you define what is meant by "usage" in writing and speaking. Keep in mind Fowler's advice that "anyone who wishes to become a good writer should . . . be direct, simple, brief, vigorous, and lucid."

How Come the Quantum?

John Archibald Wheeler (b. 1911) is a nuclear physicist credited with inventing the term *black hole*. A colleague of Albert Einstein and Niels Bohr, Wheeler helped formulate the standard theory of nuclear fission. In 2000, he wrote the following essay for the *New York Times* in honor of the one hundredth anniversary of Max Planck's discovery of the "quantum" principle. The quantum principle can be defined, Wheeler has said elsewhere, as the idea "that things in nature change in jumps or pulses, not smoothly." He does more than simply define the quantum in this essay, however. His "vision of the world" is that everything has a reason for being but that the reason behind "the magnificent edifice of quantum mechanics" remains unknown. "I may not live to see that reason unearthed," says Wheeler, "but I try, in my small way, to encourage the young to pursue that vision and find the reason."

XXXXXXXXXXXXXXXXXXXXXXXXXXXXXXXXXXXXXXXXXXXXXXXXXXXXXXXXXXXXXX

What is the greatest mystery in physics today? Different physicists have different answers. My candidate for greatest mystery is a question now a century old, "How come the quantum?" What is this thing, the "quantum"? It's a bundle of energy, an indivisible unit that can be sliced no more. Max Planck showed us a hundred years ago that light is emitted not in a smooth, steady flow, but in quanta. Then physicists found quantum jumps of energy, the quantum of electric charge and more. In the small-scale world, everything is lumpy.

And more than just lumpy. When events are examined closely enough, uncertainty prevails; cause and effect become disconnected. Change occurs in little explosions in which matter is created and destroyed, in which chance guides what happens, in which waves are particles and particles are waves.

Despite all this uncertainty, quantum physics is both a practical tool and the basis of our understanding of much of the physical world. It has explained the structure of atoms and molecules, the thermonuclear burning that lights the stars, the behavior of semiconductors and superconductors, the radioactivity that heats the earth, and the comings and goings of particles from neutrinos to quarks.

Successful, yes, but mysterious, too. Balancing the glory of quantum achievements, we have the shame of not knowing "how come." Why does the quantum exist?   4

My mentor, the Danish physicist Niels Bohr, made his peace with the quantum. His "Copenhagen interpretation" promulgated in 1927 bridged the gap between the strangeness of the quantum world and the ordinariness of the world around us. It is the act of measurement, said Bohr, that transforms the indefiniteness of quantum events into the definiteness of everyday experience. And what one can measure, he said, is necessarily limited. According to his principle of complementarity, you can look at something in one way or in another way, but not in both ways at once. It may be, as one French physicist put it, "the fog from the north," but the Copenhagen interpretation remains the best interpretation of the quantum that we have.   5

Albert Einstein, for one, could never accept this world view. In on-again, off-again debates over more than a dozen years, Bohr and Einstein argued the issues—always in a spirit of great mutual admiration and respect. I made my own effort to convince Einstein, but without success. Once, around 1942, I went around to his house in Princeton to tell him of a new way of looking at the quantum world developed by my student Richard Feynman.   6

Feynman pictured an electron getting from point A to point B not by one or another possible path, but by taking all possible paths at once. Einstein, after listening patiently, said, as he had on other occasions, "I still cannot believe God plays dice." Then he added, "But maybe I have earned the right to make my mistakes."   7

Feynman's superposed paths are eerie enough. In the 1970s, I got interested in another way to reveal the strangeness of the quantum world. I called it "delayed choice." You send a quantum of light (a photon) into an apparatus that offers the photon two paths. If you measure the photon that leaves the apparatus in one way, you can tell which path it took.   8

If you measure the departing photon in a different way (a complementary way), you can tell if it took both paths at once. You can't make both kinds of measurements on the same photon, but you can decide, after the photon has entered the apparatus, which kind of measurement you want to make.

Is the photon already wending its way through the apparatus along the first path? Too bad. You decide to look to see if it took both paths at once, and you find that it did. Or is it progressing along both paths at once? Too bad. You decide to find out if it took just one path, and it did.

At the University of Maryland, Carroll Alley, with Oleg Jakubowicz and William Wickes, took up the challenge I offered them and confirmed that the outcome could be affected by delaying the choice of measurement technique—the choice of question asked—until the photon was well on its way. I like to think that we may one day conduct a delayed-choice experiment not just in a laboratory, but in the cosmos.

One hundred years is, after all, not so long a time for the underpinning of a wonderfully successful theory to remain murky. Consider gravity. Isaac Newton, when he published his monumental work on gravitation in the 17th century, knew he could not answer the question, "How come gravity?" He was wise enough not to try. "I frame no hypotheses," he said.

It was 228 years later when Einstein, in his theory of general relativity, attributed gravity to the curvature of spacetime. The essence of Einstein's lesson can be summed up with the aphorism, "Mass tells spacetime how to curve, and spacetime tells mass how to move." Even that may not be the final answer. After all, gravity and the quantum have yet to be joined harmoniously.

On the windowsill of my home on an island in Maine I keep a rock from the garden of Academe, a rock that heard the words of Plato and Aristotle as they walked and talked. Will there someday arise an equivalent to that garden where a few thoughtful colleagues will see how to put it all together and save us from the shame of not knowing "how come the quantum"? Of course, in this century, that garden will be as large as the earth itself, a "virtual" garden where the members of my imagined academy will stroll and converse electronically.

Here, a hundred years after Planck, is quantum physics, the intellectual foundation for all of chemistry, for biology, for computer technology, for astronomy and cosmology. Yet, proud foundation for so much, it does not yet know the foundation for its own teachings. One can believe, and I do believe, that the answer to the question, "How come the quantum?" will prove to be also the answer to another question, "How come existence?"   15

XXXXXXXXXXXXXXXXXXXXX **FOR DISCUSSION** XXXXXXXXXXXXXXXXXXXXX

1. John Archibald Wheeler gives a simple (in form, at least) DEFINITION of the quantum in paragraph 2. How does he define it?

2. What is the "Copenhagen interpretation" of the quantum (5)?

3. Explain the problem of measurement that Wheeler is defining in paragraphs 8 through 11.

4. Isaac Newton identified and defined gravity in the seventeenth century. What explanation did Einstein give, 228 years later, for why gravity exists?

5. Wheeler is not just defining the quantum in his essay. He is defining a "mystery" (1). What is the nature of that mystery?

XXXXXXXXXXXXXX **STRATEGIES AND STRUCTURES** XXXXXXXXXXXXXX

1. In paragraphs 8 through 11, Wheeler recalls attempts to measure the quantum. How is this section related to the rest of his essay, especially his basic DEFINITION of the quantum?

2. Wheeler refers to a "virtual" garden in paragraph 14. What is he defining here, and how does he define it?

3. Wheeler begins his essay by introducing a great "mystery" of modern physics. How does he end it? How effective do you find his ending—and why?

4. Why does Wheeler tell the ANECDOTE about visiting Einstein in Princeton in 1942 (6)? How does this NARRATIVE help develop his definition of the quantum "mystery"?

XXXXXXXXXXXXX **WORDS AND FIGURES OF SPEECH** XXXXXXXXXXXX

1. Wheeler uses "lumpy" and "murky" (2, 12) to DEFINE quantum theory and the state of modern physics. Where else in the essay does he use informal language instead of the technical vocabulary of science? Why do you think he does so?

2. In paragraph 12, Wheeler COMPARES the quantum theory of modern physics to Newton's theory of gravity. Why does he draw this ANALOGY, and how does he develop it?

3. What modern word do we derive from "Academe," the name of the garden or grove outside Athens where Plato and his colleagues discussed philosophy (14)?

4. Wheeler uses the word "mystery" throughout his essay. How would you define this word as he uses it?

5. What do you think Einstein meant by the "plays dice" METAPHOR in paragraph 7?

XXXXXXXXXXXXXXXXXXXXX **FOR WRITING** XXXXXXXXXXXXXXXXXXXXX

1. Write a brief DEFINITION of quantum physics, spacetime, chaos theory, evolution, black hole, nebula, dwarf star, electron, ohm, or some other concept that interests you.

2. Write an extended definition of the term you chose in the preceding question.

BOP

Langston Hughes (1902–1967) was born in Joplin, Missouri, spent much of his childhood in Lawrence, Kansas, and graduated from high school in Cleveland. By the 1930s, however, he was known as "the bard of Harlem," producing more than a dozen books of poetry that celebrate the language and rhythms of everyday African American speech. In 1943, Hughes invented Jesse B. Semple ("Simple"), a streetwise Harlemite who appeared in Hughes's newspaper columns and books until 1965. "Bop," first published in the *Chicago Defender* in 1949 and revised and collected in *Simple Takes a Wife* (1953), defines a popular form of "cool" jazz by tracing the origin of its name and other distinguishing features.

XXXXXXXXXXXXXXXXXXXXXXXXXXXXXXXXXXXXXXXXXXXXXXXXXXXXXXXXXXXXXXXXXXX

Somebody upstairs in Simple's house had the combination turned up loud with an old Dizzy Gillespie record spinning like mad filling the Sabbath with Bop as I passed.   1

"Set down here on the stoop with me and listen to the music," said Simple.   2

"I've heard your landlady doesn't like tenants sitting on her stoop," I said.   3

"Pay it no mind," said Simple. "Ool-ya-koo," he sang. "Hey Ba-Ba-Re-Bop! Be-Bop! Mop!"   4

"All that nonsense singing reminds me of Cab Calloway back in the old *scat* days," I said, "around 1930 when he was chanting, 'Hi-de-*hie*-de-ho! Hee-de-*hee*-de-hee!' "   5

"Not at all," said Simple, "absolutely not at all."   6

"Re-Bop certainly sounds like scat to me," I insisted.   7

"No," said Simple, "Daddy-o, you are wrong. Besides, it was not *Re*-Bop. It is *Be*-Bop."   8

"What's the difference," I asked, "between *Re* and *Be*?"   9

"A lot," said Simple. "Re-Bop was an imitation like most of   10
the white boys play. Be-Bop is the real thing like the colored boys
play."

"You bring race into everything," I said, "even music."   11

"It is in everything," said Simple.   12

"Anyway, Be-Bop is passé, gone, finished."   13

"It may be gone, but its riffs remain behind," said Simple. "Be-Bop   14
music was certainly colored folks' music—which is why white folks found
it so hard to imitate. But there are some few white boys that latched onto
it right well. And no wonder, because they sat and listened to Dizzy,
Thelonius, Tad Dameron, Charlie Parker, also Mary Lou, all night long
every time they got a chance, and bought their records by the dozens
to copy their riffs. The ones that sing tried to make up new Be-Bop
words, but them white folks don't know what they are singing about,
even yet."

"It all sounds like pure nonsense syllables to me."   15

"Nonsense, nothing!" cried Simple. "Bop makes plenty of sense."   16

"What kind of sense?"   17

"You must not know where Bop comes from," said Simple, aston-   18
ished at my ignorance.

"I do not know," I said. "Where?"   19

"From the police," said Simple.   20

"What do you mean, from the police?"   21

"From the police beating Negroes' heads," said Simple. "Every time   22
a cop hits a Negro with his billy club, that old club says, 'BOP! BOP!....
BE-BOP! ... MOP! ... BOP!'

"That Negro hollers, 'Ooool-ya-koo! Ou-o-o!'   23

"Old Cop just keeps on, 'MOP! MOP! ... BE-BOP! ... MOP!' That's   24
where Be-Bop came from, beaten right out of some Negro's head into
them horns and saxophones and piano keys that plays it. Do you call
that nonsense?"

"If it's true, I do not," I said.   25

"That's why so many white folks don't dig Bop," said Simple.   26
"White folks do not get their heads beat *just for being white*. But me—a
cop is liable to grab me almost any time and beat my head—*just* for
being colored.

"In some parts of this American country as soon as the polices see   27
me, they say, 'Boy, what are you doing in this neighborhood?'

"I say, 'Coming from work, sir.'   28

"They say, 'Where do you work?'   29

"Then I have to go into my whole pedigree because I am a black   30
man in a white neighborhood. And if my answers do not satisfy them,
BOP! MOP! . . . BE-BOP! . . . MOP! If they do not hit me, they have already
hurt my soul. *A dark man shall see dark days.* Bop comes out of them
dark days. That's why real Bop is mad, wild, frantic, crazy—and not to
be dug unless you've seen dark days, too. Folks who ain't suffered much
cannot play Bop, neither appreciate it. They think Bop is nonsense—like
you. They think it's just *crazy* crazy. They do not know Bop is also MAD
CRAZY, SAD CRAZY, FRANTIC WILD CRAZY—beat out of somebody's head!
That's what Bop is. Them young colored kids who started it, they know
what Bop is."

"Your explanation depresses me," I said.   31

"Your nonsense depresses me," said Simple.   32

XXXXXXXXXXXXXXXXXXX **FOR DISCUSSION** XXXXXXXXXXXXXXXXXXX

1. The "I" who converses with Simple in Langston Hughes's newspaper columns
is Hughes himself. How does he first DEFINE Be-Bop after listening to it for a
while?

2. How does Simple define Be-Bop? Where does he say it gets its name? How
is Simple's definition different from Hughes's?

3. As they part at the end of the essay, how does Hughes react to Simple's
"explanation" of what Bop is and where it comes from (31)? How does Simple
define what Hughes has said about the music?

4. Do you find Simple's definition of Bop and its origins accurate? Why or why
not?

5. How "simple" is Simple? Please explain your answer.

XXXXXXXXXXXXX **STRATEGIES AND STRUCTURES** XXXXXXXXXXXXX

1. Hughes's entire essay is rendered in DIALOGUE, except for the first paragraph.
What is the function of that paragraph?

2. Simple's speech CONTRASTS sharply with that of Hughes. How would you DESCRIBE the differences? Why do you think Hughes, writing in 1949, chose to portray two African American men with such different speech patterns?

3. "You bring race into everything, . . . even music," Hughes says to Simple (11). How does Simple respond? How does his explanation of the origin of Bop support his position?

4. Who is the straight man in this essay, Hughes or Simple? What is the straight man's role in the conversation?

5. An important part of Simple's definition of Bop takes the form of an ANECDOTE about his own dealings with the police. Where does he tell that story, and what is his point in doing so?

XXXXXXXXXXXXX **WORDS AND FIGURES OF SPEECH** XXXXXXXXXXXXX

1. *Bop*, as Simple explains it, is an ONOMATOPOEIA. How does its sound suggest its meaning?

2. If *Bop* is onomatopoeic, what other sounds might it derive from besides the ones Simple mentions?

3. Simple seems to be using the word "crazy" in two different senses in paragraph 30. What are they?

4. What's the PUN, or play on words, in Simple's reference to "dark days" (30)?

XXXXXXXXXXXXXXXXXXXXX **FOR WRITING** XXXXXXXXXXXXXXXXXXXXX

1. Write your own DEFINITION of Bop, taking into account other players and origins that Simple leaves out.

2. Write an essay defining a genre of music you listen to. Be sure to consider (and include in your definition) its influences and origins.

GEETA KOTHARI

IF YOU ARE WHAT YOU EAT, THEN WHAT AM I?

Geeta Kothari teaches writing at the University of Pittsburgh. She is the editor of *Did My Mama Like to Dance? and Other Stories about Mothers and Daughters* (1994). Her stories and essays have appeared in various newspapers and journals, including the *Toronto South Asian Review* and the *Kenyon Review,* from which these complete selections of a longer article are taken. Kothari's essay (1999) presents a problem in personal definition. The Indian food she eats, says Kothari, is not really Indian like her mother's; nor is the American food she eats American like her husband's. So, Kothari wonders, if we are defined by what we eat—and the culture it represents—how are she and her culture to be defined?

XXXXXXXXXXXXXXXXXXXXXXXXXXXXXXXXXXXXXXXXXXXXXXXXXXXXXXXXXXX

> To belong is to understand the tacit codes of the people you live with.
>
> —MICHAEL IGNATIEFF, *BLOOD AND BELONGING*

The first time my mother and I open a can of tuna, I am nine years old. We stand in the doorway of the kitchen, in semidarkness, the can tilted toward daylight. I want to eat what the kids at school eat: bologna, hot dogs, salami—foods my parents find repugnant because they contain pork and meat byproducts, crushed bone and hair glued together by chemicals and fat. Although she has never been able to tolerate the smell of fish, my mother buys the tuna, hoping to satisfy my longing for American food.   1

Indians, of course, do not eat such things.   2

The tuna smells fishy, which surprises me because I can't remember anyone's tuna sandwich actually smelling like fish. And the tuna in those sandwiches doesn't look like this, pink and shiny, like an internal organ.   3

In fact, this looks similar to the bad foods my mother doesn't want me to eat. She is silent, holding her face away from the can while peering into it like a half-blind bird.

"What's wrong with it?" I ask.   4

She has no idea. My mother does not know that the tuna everyone   5
else's mothers made for them was tuna *salad*.

"Do you think it's botulism?"   6

I have never seen botulism, but I have read about it, just as I have   7
read about but never eaten steak and kidney pie.

There is so much my parents don't know. They are not like other   8
parents, and they disappoint me and my sister. They are supposed to
help us negotiate the world outside, teach us the signs, the clues to proper
behavior: what to eat and how to eat it.

We have expectations, and my parents fail to meet them, especially   9
my mother, who works full-time. I don't understand what it means, to
have a mother who works outside and inside the home; I notice only the
ways in which she disappoints me. She doesn't show up for school plays.
She doesn't make chocolate-frosted cupcakes for my class. At night, if I
want her attention, I have to sit in the kitchen and talk to her while she
cooks the evening meal, attentive to every third or fourth word I say.

We throw the tuna away. This time my mother is disappointed. I   10
go to school with tuna eaters. I see their sandwiches, yet cannot explain
the discrepancy between them and the stinking, oily fish in my mother's
hand. We do not understand so many things, my mother and I.

When we visit our relatives in India, food prepared outside the house is   11
carefully monitored. In the hot, sticky monsoon months in New Delhi and
Bombay, we cannot eat ice cream, salad, cold food, or any fruit that can't
be peeled. Definitely no meat. People die from amoebic dysentery, unex-
plained fevers, strange boils on their bodies. We drink boiled water only,
no ice. No sweets except for jalebi, thin fried twists of dough in dripping
hot sugar syrup. If we're caught outside with nothing to drink, Fanta,
Limca, Thums Up (after Coca-Cola is thrown out by Mrs. Gandhi) will
do. Hot tea sweetened with sugar, served with thick creamy buffalo milk,
is preferable. It should be boiled, to kill the germs on the cup.

My mother talks about "back home" as a safe place, a silk cocoon   12
frozen in time where we are sheltered by family and friends. Back home,
my sister and I do not argue about food with my parents. Home is where
they know all the rules. We trust them to guide us safely through the
maze of city streets for which they have no map, and we trust them to
feed and take care of us, the way parents should.

Finally, though, one of us will get sick, hungry for the food we see   13
our cousins and friends eating, too thirsty to ask for a straw, too polite
to insist on properly boiled water.

At my uncle's diner in New Delhi, someone hands me a plate of   14
aloo tikki, fried potato patties filled with mashed channa dal and served
with a sweet and a sour chutney. The channa, mixed with hot chilies and
spices, burns my tongue and throat. I reach for my Fanta, discard the
paper straw, and gulp the sweet orange soda down, huge drafts that sting
rather than soothe.

When I throw up later that day (or is it the next morning, when a   15
stomachache wakes me from deep sleep?), I cry over the frustration of
being singled out, not from the pain my mother assumes I'm feeling as
she holds my hair back from my face. The taste of orange lingers in my
mouth, and I remember my lips touching the cold glass of the Fanta
bottle.

At that moment, more than anything, I want to be like my cousins.   16

In New York, at the first Indian restaurant in our neighborhood, my   17
father orders with confidence, and my sister and I play with the silverware until the steaming plates of lamb biryani arrive.

What is Indian food? my friends ask, their noses crinkling up.   18

Later, this restaurant is run out of business by the new Indo-Pak-   19
Bangladeshi combinations up and down the street, which serve similar
food. They use plastic cutlery and Styrofoam cups. They do not distinguish between North and South Indian cooking, or between Indian, Pakistani, and Bangladeshi cooking, and their customers do not care. The
food is fast, cheap, and tasty. Dosa, a rice flour crepe stuffed with masala
potato, appears on the same trays as chicken makhani.

Now my friends want to know, Do you eat curry at home?   20

One time my mother makes lamb vindaloo for guests. Like dosa, this is a South Indian dish, one that my Punjabi mother has to learn from a cookbook. For us, she cooks everyday food—yellow dal, rice, chapati, bhaji. Lentils, rice, bread, and vegetables. She has never referred to anything on our table as "curry" or "curried," but I know she has made chicken curry for guests. Vindaloo, she explains, is a curry too. I understand then that curry is a dish created for guests, outsiders, a food for people who eat in restaurants. 21

I look around my boyfriend's freezer one day and find meat: pork chops, ground beef, chicken pieces, Italian sausage. Ham in the refrigerator, next to the homemade bolognese sauce. Tupperware filled with chili made from ground beef and pork. 22

He smells different from me. Foreign. Strange. 23

I marry him anyway. 24

He has inherited blue eyes that turn gray in bad weather, light brown hair, a sharp pointy nose, and excellent teeth. He learns to make chili with ground turkey and tofu, tomato sauce with red wine and portobello mushrooms, roast chicken with rosemary and slivers of garlic under the skin. 25

He eats steak when we are in separate cities, roast beef at his mother's house, hamburgers at work. Sometimes I smell them on his skin. I hope he doesn't notice me turning my face, a cheek instead of my lips, my nose wrinkled at the unfamiliar, musky smell. 26

I have inherited brown eyes, black hair, a long nose with a crooked bridge, and soft teeth with thin enamel. I am in my twenties, moving to a city far from my parents, before it occurs to me that jeera, the spice my sister avoids, must have an English name. I have to learn that haldi = turmeric, methi = fenugreek. What to make with fenugreek, I do not know. My grandmother used to make methi roti for our breakfast, cornbread with fresh fenugreek leaves served with a lump of homemade butter. No one makes it now that she's gone, though once in a while my mother will get a craving for it and produce a facsimile ("The cornmeal here is wrong") that only highlights what she's really missing: the smells and tastes of her mother's house. 27

I will never make my grandmother's methi roti or even my mother's 28
unsatisfactory imitation of it. I attempt chapati; it takes six hours, three
phone calls home, and leaves me with an aching back. I have to write
translations down: jeera = cumin. My memory is unreliable. But I have
always known garam = hot.

If I really want to make myself sick, I worry that my husband will one 29
day leave me for a meat-eater, for someone familiar who doesn't sniff
him suspiciously for signs of alimentary infidelity.

Indians eat lentils. I understand this as absolute, a decree from an uni- 30
dentifiable authority that watches and judges me.

So what does it mean that I cannot replicate my mother's dal? She 31
and my father show me repeatedly, in their kitchen, in my kitchen. They
coach me over the phone, buy me the best cookbooks, and finally write
down their secrets. Things I'm supposed to know but don't. Recipes that
should be, by now, engraved on my heart.

Living far from the comfort of people who require no explanation 32
for what I do and who I am, I crave the foods we have shared. My mother
convinces me that moong is the easiest dal to prepare, and yet it fails me
every time: bland, watery, a sickly greenish yellow mush. These imperfect
imitations remind me only of what I'm missing.

But I have never been fond of moong dal. At my mother's table it 33
is the last thing I reach for. Now I worry that this antipathy toward dal
signals something deeper, that somehow I am not my parents' daughter,
not Indian, and because I cannot bear the touch and smell of raw meat,
though I can eat it cooked (charred, dry, and overdone), I am not American either.

I worry about a lifetime purgatory in Indian restaurants where I will 34
complain that all the food looks and tastes the same because they've used
the same masala.

XXXXXXXXXXXXXXXXXXXX **FOR DISCUSSION** XXXXXXXXXXXXXXXXXXXX

1. How does Geeta Kothari DEFINE "meat byproducts" (1)? Why is she so concerned with different kinds of food in this essay? Who or what is she trying to define here?

2. How do Kothari and her mother define "back home" in paragraph 12?

3. Why is Kothari angry with herself in paragraphs 15 and 16? What "rule" has she momentarily forgotten?

4. Kothari's friends ask for a definition of Indian food in paragraph 18. How does she answer them (and us)?

5. What's wrong, from Kothari's POINT OF VIEW, with the "Indo-Pak-Bangladeshi" restaurants that spring up in her neighborhood (19)?

XXXXXXXXXXXXXX **STRATEGIES AND STRUCTURES** XXXXXXXXXXXXX

1. How does Kothari go about answering the DEFINITION question that she raises in her title? Give specific EXAMPLES of her strategy.

2. Why does Kothari recall the tuna incident in paragraphs 1 through 10? What does this ANECDOTE illustrate about her relationship with her mother? About her "Americanness?"

3. Why does Kothari introduce the matter of heredity in paragraphs 25 and 27? How do these paragraphs anticipate the reference to "something deeper" in paragraph 33?

4. According to Kothari, is culture something we inherit or something we learn? How do paragraphs 31 and 32 contribute to her definition of culture?

5. Marriage is an important event in anyone's biography, but why is it especially central in Kothari's case?

6. Kothari's essay is largely made up of specific examples, particularly culinary ones. How do they relate to the matters of personal and cultural identity she is defining? Should she have made these connections more explicit? Why or why not?

XXXXXXXXXXXXX **WORDS AND FIGURES OF SPEECH** XXXXXXXXXXXX

1. What is usually meant by the saying "You are what you eat"? How is Kothari interpreting this adage?

2. What does Kothari mean by "alimentary infidelity" (29)? What ANALOGY is she drawing here?

3. What is "purgatory" (34)? Why does Kothari end her essay with a reference to it?

4. *Synecdoche* is the FIGURE OF SPEECH that substitutes a part for the whole. What part does Kothari substitute for what whole when she uses the phrase "meat-eater" (29). Can we say her entire essay works by means of synecdoche? Why?

XXXXXXXXXXXXXXXXXXXXX **FOR WRITING** XXXXXXXXXXXXXXXXXXXXX

1. Write an extended DEFINITION about your favorite type of food. Be sure to relate how your food and food customs help to define who you are.

2. Food and food customs are often regional, as Kothari points out. Write an essay in which you define one of the following: New England, Southern, or Midwestern cooking; California cuisine; Tex-Mex, French, or Chinese food; fast food; or some other distinctive cuisine.

3. Write an essay about the culture of food and eating in your neighborhood. Food and food customs are often regional and, as Kothari shows in her essay, can be tied to family and personal identity. Be sure to include EXAMPLES of these elements in your definitions.

CHAPTER EIGHT

CAUSE AND EFFECT

XXXXXXXXXXXXXXXXXXXXXXXXXXXXXXXXXXXXXXXXXXXXXXXXXXXXXXXXXXXXXXX

If you were at home on vacation and read in the morning paper that the physics building at your school had burned down, the first question you would probably ask would be "How? What caused the fire?" If the newspaper went on to say that the cause was arson and that the fire was set by your old roommate, Larry, the next question you would likely ask would be "Why? Why did Larry do it?"

Essays in CAUSE AND EFFECT* answer these two fundamental questions—how and why—about the effects or end results of a chain of events, in this case a burned-out building. The first of these two related questions addresses the *immediate* cause, the one nearest in time to the effect. The second question addresses the *ultimate* cause, the one that set the chain of events going in the first place. In our EXAMPLE, the immediate cause would be the arsonist's match, and the ultimate cause might be Larry's failure on a physics test, the event that turned him into an angry pyromaniac.

The sum of all the causes that culminate in a particular effect is called the "complex" cause. Like those in this chapter, most of the essays in cause and effect that you write should address as fully as possible the complex cause of the effect or effects in question. There are two reasons for this. One is to avoid oversimplification. Interesting questions are usually complex, and complex questions probably have complex answers. (Was Larry depressed before he took the physics test? What were his feelings toward his father, the physics professor?)

*Words printed in SMALL CAPITALS are defined in the Glossary.

The second reason for addressing the complex cause rather than the ultimate cause alone, or the immediate cause, or some other, single "contributing" cause is to anticipate objections that the reader might raise against your ANALYSIS. A clever writer will often run through a whole chain of possible causes to show that he or she has considered all the possibilities before settling on one or two. When, for example, a clergyman asked journalist Lincoln Steffens to name the ultimate cause of corruption in city government, Steffens replied with the following analysis:

> Most people, you know, say it was Adam. But Adam, you remember, he said that it was Eve, the woman; she did it. And Eve said no, no, it wasn't she; it was the serpent. And that's where you clergy have stuck ever since. You blame the serpent, Satan. Now I come and I am trying to show you that it was, it is, the apple.
>
> LINCOLN STEFFENS, *AUTOBIOGRAPHY*

Steffens was giving an original answer to the old question of original sin. Our fallen state, he said, is due not to innate depravity, but to economic conditions. Is his causal analysis accurate?

Two basic conditions have to be met to prove causation. The cause has to be both *sufficient* and *necessary* to produce the effect in question. That is, it must be shown that (1) the alleged cause (and only the alleged cause) has the power to produce the effect; and (2) that the alleged cause *always* accompanies that effect. Steffens's analysis of the causes for the fall of humankind is perhaps too difficult a case to test easily by this standard. Also, it happened only once. So let's take a simpler example.

The following passage is from a book on statistics. The authors are recalling the days before the Salk vaccine defeated polio:

> Before the introduction of this vaccine investigators looked at the relationship between the incidence of polio and the number of soft drinks sold. For each week of the year, they tabulated the number of soft drinks sold that week, and the number of new cases of polio reported. These data points showed strong positive

correlation. During weeks when more soft drinks were sold, there were more new cases of polio; when fewer soft drinks were sold, there were fewer such cases.

The correlation between the sale of soft drinks and the incidence of polio fooled no one, however. Though polio and soft drinks *always* seemed to go together, this correlation satisfied only half of the twofold test that every cause must meet. Even if soft drinks appeared to meet the first criterion (necessity), nobody expected them to meet the second (sufficiency). Some other cause must be operating, researchers theorized; perhaps there was a third factor driving both variables—season.

Hot weather was the clear cause of the aggravated thirst that went with an increased incidence of both polio and the drinking of soft drinks; but was the heat necessary *and* sufficient to produce the paralyzing disease? It might appear necessary (always accompanying the effect), but hot weather alone hardly seemed to be sufficient to do so much harm. So Jonas Salk and his colleagues searched for a factor that always increased with hot weather but that was medically more harmful than sunlight in normal doses. Eventually, of course, they isolated the poliomyelitis virus. This tiny killer met both tests for true causality: it appeared in every case, and it was the only factor capable of producing the dire effect ascribed to it. It was both sufficient and necessary.

As Dr. Salk knew from the beginning, mere sequence in time—cases of polio increase as, or immediately after, the consumption of soft drinks increases—is not sufficient to prove causation. The hero of *Adventures of Huckleberry Finn* is not so astute. Here is Huck alone in the woods one night when he sees an evil omen:

> Pretty soon a spider went crawling up my shoulder, and I flipped it off and it lit in the candle; and before I could budge it was all shriveled up. I didn't need anybody to tell me that that was an awful bad sign and would fetch me some bad luck, so I was scared and most shook the clothes off of me. I got up and turned around in my tracks three times and crossed my breast every time; and then I tied up a little lock of my hair to keep witches away. But I hadn't no confidence.

MARK TWAIN, *ADVENTURES OF HUCKLEBERRY FINN*

Huck is right to be scared; all sorts of misadventures are going to befall him. But he wrongly thinks that because the misadventures followed the burning of the spider, they were actually caused by it: he confuses mere sequence with causation. This mistake in causal analysis is commonly known as the *post hoc, ergo propter hoc* fallacy, Latin for "after this, therefore because of this." Huck is pretty smart, but he makes this mistake because he doesn't know about the two conditions that must be met before causation may be accurately inferred.

Those two conditions can be expressed as a formula:

B cannot have happened without A;
Whenever A happens, B must happen.

The chemist who observes again and again that a flammable substance burns (B) only when combined with oxygen (A) and that it always burns when so combined, may accurately conclude that oxidation causes combustion. Such an analysis can only take us so far, however.

It might, for example, help to explain *how* Larry burned down the physics building, but it would not explain *why* he did it. Especially when we are dealing with psychological and social rather than purely physical factors, the *complex* cause—all the hows and whys—may defy simple analysis. Suppose we looked for answers to the following question: Why does Mary smoke? This looks like a simple question, but it is a difficult one to answer simply because there are so many complicated reasons for the increase in the incidence of smoking by young women like Mary. The best way for a writer to approach this kind of causal analysis might be simply to enumerate as many of the contributing causes as his or her analysis can turn up:

MARY:	"I smoke because I need something to do with my hands."
MARY'S BOYFRIEND:	"Mary smokes because she thinks it looks sophisticated."
MEDICAL DOCTOR:	"Because Mary has developed a physical addiction to tobacco."
PSYCHOLOGIST:	"Because of peer pressure."

SOCIOLOGIST: "Because 30 percent of all female Americans under twenty years of age now smoke. Mary is part of a trend."

ADVERTISER: "Because she's come a long way, baby."

When you enumerate particular causes like this, be as specific as you can without oversimplifying. When you enumerate *effects*, be even more specific. Don't just say "Smoking is bad for your health" or "Smoking causes some people to recoil in disgust." Be disgustingly particular, as in this analysis of the effects of smoking, written by England's King James I (of the King James Bible), who in 1604 found smoking to be

> a custom lothsome to the eye, hatefull to the Nose, harmefull to the braine, dangerous to the Lungs, and in the blacke stinking fume thereof, neerest resembling the horrible Stigian smoke of the pit that is bottomelesse.
>
> JAMES I, *COUNTER-BLASTE TO TOBACCO*

The cigar-smoking Mark Twain would not have agreed. His Huck Finn has a more laid-back attitude toward tobacco and a few other commodities. On the raft, says Huck, "it was kind of lazy and jolly laying off comfortable all day, smoking and fishing, and no books nor study."

In a more recent essay on the evils of tobacco, Erik Eckholm strikes a grimmer note. "The most potentially tragic victims of cigarettes," he writes, "are the infants of mothers who smoke. They are more likely than the babies of nonsmoking mothers to be born underweight and thus to encounter death or disease at birth or during the initial months of life."

In singling out the effects of smoking upon unwitting infants, Eckholm has chosen an example that might be just powerful enough to convince some smokers to quit. Your examples need not be so grim, but they must be specific to be powerful. And they must be selected with the interests of your audience in mind. Eckholm is addressing the young women who are smoking more today than ever before. When writing for a middle-aged audience, he points out that smoking causes cancer and heart disease at a rate 70 percent higher among one-pack-a-day men and women than among nonsmokers.

Your audience needs to be taken into account because when you analyze causes and effects, you are also making an ARGUMENT about the causes or effects of an event or trend. It is a form of reasoning that must carry the reader step by step through some kind of proof. Your analysis may be instructive, amusing, or startling; but it must be persuasive.

Chip Brown's old tent smells bad; that much he knows. But what's the cause of the awful smell? To find out, he consults "The Wild File," a question-and-answer column in *Outside* magazine. This response to Chip's inquiry points to the culprit, butyric acid. In this case, butyric acid is only the *immediate* cause of the effect (barf smell) in question. The release of the foul-smelling acid is a side effect of the breakdown of cellulose acetate butyrate (CAB) in the tent's waterproof coating—an abnormal condition, according to the manufacturer. What caused the normally stable chemical coating of Chip's tent to deteriorate in the first place? Apparently, the tent was improperly stored. Chip himself is the *ultimate* cause of the bad smell. There's no way to get rid of the smell other than by throwing out the old tent and buying a new tent. Now that he knows what caused the problem, however, he'll be able to prevent it from happening again—which is why we engage in this sort of problem solving in the first place.

CONSIDER FURTHER . . .

1. Explanations of cause and effect may give equal weight to each, but they often emphasize one or the other, depending on which is known. In explaining why some old tents smell bad, does the *Outside* columnist spend more time enumerating causes or effects? Why? Which is known, and which is to be discovered?

2. Here are a few other questions that readers have thrown at the editor of "The Wild File": Why does the skin on our fingers turn pruney in water? What causes knuckles to crack? What makes snow squeak when you walk on it? What makes stars twinkle? Why do fireflies light up? Each of these questions specifies an effect for which the questioner seeks a cause or causes. What questions would you like to ask *Outside*'s wild experts? Formulate several as clear inquiries into particular effects.

Q Why do old tents smell like barf?

—*Chip Brown, New York, New York*

A People will tell you it's mildew, but they're wrong. Tents do suffer from mildew, of course, but that's another problem and another smell. The real culprit here is cellulose acetate butyrate (CAB), which is commonly added to the polyurethane coatings used on tents. When CAB breaks down over time, one of its many by-products is butyric acid, which gives off a distinctly puky odor. (*Butyric* comes from the Latin word for butter; butyric acid is the substance that gives rancid butter its endearing fragrance.) According to Kris Krishnan, technical director of Raffi & Swanson, a manufacturer of polyurethane coatings, the odor is "not normal—it's an abused condition." You can avoid CAB breakdown by taking a few simple precautions: Keep your tent out of excessive sunlight. Don't store it wet. And don't leave it cooking in your car trunk for weeks at a time.

MARISSA NUÑEZ

CLIMBING THE GOLDEN ARCHES

Marissa Nuñez (b. 1974) was nineteen when she wrote this essay about working for McDonald's. Nuñez started at the bottom (the "fried products" station) and worked her way up to management training—and still higher ambitions. "Climbing the Golden Arches" not only tells the story of this ascent, it also analyzes the effects, personal and professional, of learning to do a job, dealing with the public, and being part of a team. An essay about making choices and becoming oneself, "Climbing the Golden Arches" originally appeared in *New Youth Connections*, a magazine that publishes work by student authors.

XXXXXXXXXXXXXXXXXXXXXXXXXXXXXXXXXXXXXXXXXXXXXXXXXXXXXXXXXXXXX

1   Two years ago, while my cousin Susie and I were doing our Christmas shopping on Fourteenth Street, we decided to have lunch at McDonald's.

2   "Yo, check it out," Susie said. "They're hiring. Let's give it a try." I looked at her and said, "Are you serious?" She gave me this look that made it clear that she was.

3   After we ate our food, I went over to the counter and asked the manager for two applications. I took them back to our table and we filled them out. When we finished, we handed them in to the manager and he told us he'd be calling.

4   When Susie and I got home from school one day about a month later, my mother told us that McDonald's had called. They wanted to interview us both. We walked straight over there. They asked us why we wanted to work at McDonald's and how we felt about specific tasks, like cleaning the bathrooms. Then they told us to wait for a while. Finally the manager came out and said we had the job.

5   When we got outside, I looked over at Susie and laughed because

I hadn't thought it would work. But I was happy to have a job. I would be able to buy my own stuff and I wouldn't have to ask my mother for money anymore.

A week and a half later we went to pick up our uniforms (a blue and white striped shirt with blue pants or a blue skirt) and to find out what days we'd be working. We were also told the rules and regulations of the work place. "No stealing" was at the top of the list. A couple of the others were: "Leave all your problems at home" and "Respect everyone you work with."

Before you can officially start working, you have to get trained on every station. I started on "fried products," which are the chicken nuggets, chicken sandwiches, and Filet-o-Fish. Then I learned to work the grill, which is where we cook the burgers. Next was the assembly table where we put all the condiments (pickles, onions, lettuce, etc.) on the sandwiches. After all that, you have to learn the french fry station. Then finally you can learn to work the register. It was a month before I could be left alone at any station.

The most difficult thing was learning how to work the grill area. We use a grill called a clamshell which has a cover. It cooks the whole burger in forty-four seconds without having to flip it over. At first I didn't like doing this. Either I wouldn't lay the meat down right on the grill and it wouldn't cook all the way through or I would get burned. It took a few weeks of practicing before I got the hang of it. Now, after a lot more practice, I can do it with no problem.

My first real day at work was a lot of fun. The store had been closed for remodeling and it was the grand opening. A lot of people were outside waiting for the store to open. I walked around just to get the feel of things before we let the customers come in. I was working a register all by myself. My cousin was at the station next to me and we raced to see who could get the most customers and who could fill the orders in fifty-nine seconds. I really enjoyed myself.

Susie worked for only three months after our grand opening, but I stayed on. I liked having a job because I was learning how to be a responsible person. I was meeting all kinds of people and learning a lot about them. I started making friends with my co-workers and getting to know many of the customers on a first-name basis. And I was in charge of my own money for the first time. I didn't have to go asking Mom for money when I wanted something anymore. I could just go and buy it.

Working at McDonald's does have its down side. The worst thing about the job is that the customers can be real jerks sometimes. They just don't seem to understand the pressure we're under. At times they will try to jerk you or make you look stupid. Or they will blame you for a mistake they made. If you don't watch and listen carefully, some of them will try to short-change you for some money. 11

The most obnoxious customer I ever had came in one day when it was really busy. She started saying that one of my co-workers had over-charged her. I knew that wasn't the case, so I asked her what the problem was. She told me to mind my own business, so I told her that she was my business. She started calling me a "Spanish b-tch" and kept on calling me names until I walked away to get the manager. If I had said anything back to her, I would have gotten in trouble. 12

Another time, a woman wanted to pay for a $2.99 Value Meal with a $100 bill. No problem, we changed it. She walked away from the counter with her food and then came back a few minutes later saying we had given her a counterfeit $20 bill in her change. We knew it was a lie. She wouldn't back down and even started yelling at the manager. He decided that we should call the cops and get them to settle it. That got her so mad that she threw her tray over the counter at us. Then she left. Of course, not all our customers are like this. Some are very nice and even take the time to tell the manager good things about me. 13

Sometimes we make up special events to make the job more fun for everyone. For example, we'll have what we call a "battle of the sexes." On those days, the women will work the grill area and the french fry station and all the other kitchen jobs and the men will work the registers. For some reason, the guys usually like to hide in the grill area. The only time they'll come up front and pretend they are working there is to see some female customer they are interested in. Still, they always act like working the grill is so much harder than working the register. I say the grill is no problem compared to working face-to-face with customers all day. After a battle of the sexes, the guys start to give the girls more respect because they see how much pressure we're under. 14

Every six months, our job performance is reviewed. If you get a good review, you get a raise and sometimes a promotion. After my first six months on the job I got a raise and was made a crew trainer. I became the one who would show new employees how to work the register, fry station, and yes, even the grill area. 15

When I made a year and a half, I was asked if I would like to become a manager-trainee. To move to that level, your performance has to be one hundred percent on all stations of the store. That means doing every job by the book with no shortcuts. The managers have to trust you, and you have to set a good example for your co-workers. I was so happy. Of course I said yes. 16

Now that I've been there two years, the managers trust me to run a shift by myself. I am working to get certified as a manager myself. To do that I have to attend a class and take an exam, and my manager and supervisor have to observe the way I work with everyone else and grade my performance. I have been in the program for nine months now and expect to get certified this month. I'm thinking about staying on full-time after I graduate from high school. 17

Working at McDonald's has taught me a lot. The most important thing I've learned is that you have to start at the bottom and work your way up. I've learned to take this seriously—if you're going to run a business, you need to know how to do all the other jobs. I also have more patience than ever and have learned how to control my emotions. I've learned to get along with all different kinds of people. I'd like to have my own business someday, and working at McDonald's is what showed me I could do that. 18

XXXXXXXXXXXXXXXXXXXXX **FOR DISCUSSION** XXXXXXXXXXXXXXXXXXXXX

1. Marissa Nuñez had been working for McDonald's for two years when she wrote this essay. What EFFECTS did the experience have on her? What were some of the main CAUSES of those effects?

2. What particular work experiences did Nuñez find most instructive? How did they help bring about the personal changes she mentions?

3. What does Nuñez hope to become by working at McDonald's? How does she expect to accomplish that goal?

4. What do you think of Nuñez's response to the customer who calls her a name?

5. "Climbing the Golden Arches" was originally published in a magazine for teenagers. What attitudes and values does the essay promote? How well do you think it succeeds?

XXXXXXXXXXXXXX **STRATEGIES AND STRUCTURES** XXXXXXXXXXXXXX

1. In paragraph 10, Nuñez sums up what she is learning in her new job. Where does she sum up what she *has* learned? If Nuñez had left out these two paragraphs, how would the focus and direction of her essay be changed?

2. How does the following sentence, which comes approximately halfway through her essay, help Nuñez to present different aspects of her work experience: "Working at McDonald's does have its down side" (11)? What sort of CAUSES is she ANALYZING now? What EFFECT do they have on her?

3. In addition to analyzing causes and effects, "Climbing the Golden Arches" tells a story. What is the role of the "most obnoxious customer" and of the woman who throws her tray (12–13)? What roles do these people play in her analysis of causes and effects?

4. Nuñez's essay covers a two-year work period that might be broken down into application, apprenticeship, "officially working," management training, future plans. Where does each stage begin and end? How effective do you find such a scheme for organizing an account of someone's work life?

5. The phases of Nuñez's NARRATIVE resemble the steps or stages of much PROCESS ANALYSIS, or how-to writing (Chapter 5). Why is this? Besides examining the effects on her life of working at McDonald's, what process or processes does she analyze by telling her story?

XXXXXXXXXXXXX **WORDS AND FIGURES OF SPEECH** XXXXXXXXXXXXX

1. Why does Nuñez put "battle of the sexes" in quotation marks (14)?

2. What does the word "station" mean in connection with restaurant work (7)?

3. Explain the METAPHOR in Nuñez's title. What figurative meaning does the word "arches" take on in an account of someone's career goals? How about "golden" arches?

4. How does Nuñez DEFINE the word "fun" in this essay (9)? What specific

EXAMPLES does she give? What does her distinctive use of the word tell you about her as a person?

XXXXXXXXXXXXXXXXXXXXX **FOR WRITING** XXXXXXXXXXXXXXXXXXXXX

1. Write a letter of application for your ideal job. Explain your qualifications, your career goals, and how you expect to achieve them.

2. Write a personal NARRATIVE of your work experience or some other experience that taught you a lot. Break it into phases, if appropriate, and explain how specific aspects and events of the experience caused you to become who you are. In other words, tell what happened to you, but also ANALYZE the specific EFFECTS the experience had on you and your life.

JOHN EDWARDS

PRISON MAN CONSIDERS TURKEY

John Edwards is a former inmate and prison-reform activist. He is the author of *Coming Clean: Grim Truths about Sex* (2000) and *Prison Man Learns Things*, a book about the criminal justice system that will include "Prison Man Considers Turkey," a winning essay in a National Public Radio writing competition. Locked up for growing marijuana, Edwards is separated from his wife and son. But on his second Thanksgiving behind bars, prison life is starting to have strange effects upon him. During a visit from his wife, marital tension runs high, and Edwards discovers that he is beginning to prefer his new "family" of psychos and felons to the one outside that he has failed so miserably.

XXXXXXXXXXXXXXXXXXXXXXXXXXXXXXXXXXXXXXXXXXXXXXXXXXXXXXXXXXXXXXX

A first Thanksgiving in prison may be laden with maudlin sentimentality, and a last with hard-boiled familiarity, but in the middle are moments when clearly defined feelings fray and you can't be sure exactly who you are. During my first Thanksgiving season in prison, I was sitting alone in The Hole, and my last was mere weeks before I walked out of there, as they say, a free man. The second Thanksgiving the shock of being locked up was gone, as was the truculent refusal to enjoy anything pleasant a prison experience might offer. But gone also was the novelty, especially for my family, tired of long drives and disrupted holidays. This second Thanksgiving in federal prison was celebrated by someone called *Me*, but I didn't know quite who he was, and neither did anyone back home. He tutored crack dealers for their GED exams, taught Shakespeare on Thursday nights, but prison can absorb you, and he was becoming the kind of guy who would rather teach classes in prison than have visits from his family. Because family meant guilt and failed responsibility. By comparison, prison was freedom.

Chief Running Mouth, believing Thanksgiving to be a celebration of Native American genocide, had tried to get the black guys to join his boycott. Nobody was going to do *that*. Psycho, missing the point completely, had said, "What'd them Pilgrims ever do for me?" Snakebite added, "When the white man wants to feed me some good food for a change, you want me to do *what*?" Even Toilet Paper Man, ever fearful of cosmic rays emanating from the mess hall, was there along with Bed-Sore, Bird, Stoney, and all the rest of us, standing in line, hoping the best turkey wouldn't be gone by the time we got there.

I'd finally found a seat with my little tray of turkey when a guard   3
came up and said, "Edwards, you got a visit." I eyed my food, then looked at the other guys at the table. "Here," I said, "any you guys want this?" I got up, leaving my decent federal Thanksgiving dinner to the vultures. Up in the visiting room, families were arriving. Some inmates would let their families wait while they ate, but for most of us, family came first, even if that meant missing a special meal. Still, it was hard not to be torn between family and your buddies, the ones with whom you ate and worked and watched movies and read books and wrote to lawyers, and counted the days. The ones who were cooking contraband right now.

I had been down long enough to know that while we waited for our   4
official meal, an unofficial one was being prepared back in the cellblock living units. Former car thieves, now with contacts in the kitchen, would be sneaking trays of turkey and pumpkin pie out the back door. And the Italian guys could prepare a meal worth a prison sentence to eat. The marijuana growers were the next best. These were men in their forties like me—exactly like me, middle-class ex-hippies busted with little gardens in our cellars. We like good food.

My four-year-old son ran up to me and gave me a big hug. I looked   5
at Mary. "Hi," I said tentatively, and got a dark look in response. "What? What'd I do?" I asked. "What's the matter with you?" she demanded. I thought about that one a while. "Is something wrong?" I asked. "Just never mind," she spat. Now, of course something was wrong. I was in prison for growing marijuana and she was stuck alone with our child. As guys were wolfing down my Thanksgiving dinner, I ate a microwave mini-pizza from the vending machine and tried to hear Mary, over the din of the visiting room, recite her stream of complaints, which I could do nothing about. Prison visiting rooms are never comfortable, and on

holidays they are always crowded and hot and loud. This was our second Thanksgiving here, and eighteen months of this was getting to her. "You never give me what I need," she said. "I can't. I'm in prison," I tried lamely. "We were waiting here for almost an hour," she said. "Well, things were a little chaotic down in the chow hall . . ." "Sometimes I think you'd rather be with your friends than with us," she said. She wasn't far from wrong.

Each of us was torn, I between this hellish racket of the visiting room and the camaraderie of the prison, and she between this same hellish racket and the camaraderie that would await her when she left me for the day: prison wives sitting around a Formica table in the motel restaurant, probably ordering turkey dinner, bad-mouthing us and exchanging nightmarish tales of handling the house and kids back home alone with community and family disapproval looming over their tired shoulders. We'd dragged them into this and now, hundreds of miles from home, missing home-cooked dinners at their own parents' houses, they were prison wives whose children played together while we snuck food and cookery behind the backs of the guards who themselves would rather have been home on Thanksgiving. It was our fault for putting everybody through this, and the guilt we felt was in part because, under these conditions, we knew we were beginning to prefer each other's company to that of our real families.

Visiting hours were over and I went back to my cell. A plate of turkey with all the clearly contraband goodies was waiting for me. Somebody, knowing I'd missed dinner, had cooked it up and made sure I got it. I have no idea who that might have been. Maybe Chief Running Mouth. Maybe Psycho.

✗✗✗✗✗✗✗✗✗✗✗✗✗✗✗✗✗✗✗✗ **For Discussion** ✗✗✗✗✗✗✗✗✗✗✗✗✗✗✗✗✗✗✗✗

1. How is John Edwards's second Thanksgiving in federal prison different from his first one?

2. One of the main EFFECTS that prison had on him and some of his fellow inmates, says Edwards, was an overpowering sense of "guilt and failed responsibility" (1). Why does being in prison CAUSE him to feel this way?

3. What effect does the visit from his family have on Edwards's feelings, particularly his sense of guilt and remorse? How does he compensate for being made to feel so uncomfortable?

4. What difference, if any, would it make in our attitude toward him and his story if Edwards had been locked up for rape or murder?

5. Why do you suppose Edwards chose to write this piece? What might his reasons be, besides telling a good story?

XXXXXXXXXXXXXX **STRATEGIES AND STRUCTURES** XXXXXXXXXXXXX

1. "Prison Man Considers Turkey" might be the caption for a newspaper photograph of a "typical" inmate celebrating an official holiday. Like prison itself, such words and pictures can turn people into objects of public disdain. How does Edwards indicate that being incarcerated had a dehumanizing EFFECT on him? Explain by citing specific passages from his essay.

2. Edwards is writing about the effects of prison on his identity as well as his feelings. That second Thanksgiving, he says, was "celebrated by someone called *Me*, but I didn't know quite who he was, and neither did anyone back home" (1). How does he explain what he means by this statement?

3. By becoming Prison Man and speaking from inside the bars, Edwards shifts the normal perspective from which we usually view people convicted of crimes. What does Prison Man do and say to make himself and his buddies look like ordinary human beings? Cite specific EXAMPLES.

4. From whose perspective is paragraph 5 told? Paragraph 6? Why do you think Edwards employs DIALOGUE in one but not in the other?

5. How does the ending (7) resolve the tension in this scene of marital strife? Without this paragraph, how would Edwards's essay be different?

XXXXXXXXXXXXX **WORDS AND FIGURES OF SPEECH** XXXXXXXXXXXXX

1. How does Edwards's use of nicknames in his essay confirm the dehumanizing EFFECTS of prison life? How do the nicknames counter those effects?

2. The root meaning of "truculent" is "savage" or "fierce" (1). How well do these CONNOTATIONS DEFINE the feelings that Edwards is DESCRIBING?

3. To what "contraband" is Edwards referring (3)? Why is this use of official language funny, and how does it influence the reader's judgment of Prison Man's and the others' actions?

4. What kind of lingo is "been down" (4)? What are the implications of the author's pairing "decent" and "federal" (3)?

5. Edwards's wife doesn't literally "spit" in paragraph 5. What does she actually do? Why the HYPERBOLE?

XXXXXXXXXXXXXXXXXXXXX **FOR WRITING** XXXXXXXXXXXXXXXXXXXXX

1. The amino acids (tryptophans) in turkey induce a natural "high," or sense of well-being, in some people and cats. What is your favorite comfort food? Write a paragraph explaining how it makes you feel.

2. Write a personal NARRATIVE recalling your adaptation to a difficult period in your life, perhaps one that challenged or even changed your idea of who you are. Mention specific CAUSES of the difficulty and ways it affected you.

JARED DIAMOND

WHO KILLED EASTER ISLAND?

Jared Diamond (b. 1937) is a professor of physiology in the School of Medicine at the University of California, Los Angeles. His technical research focuses on biological membranes, ecology, and evolutionary biology, especially of bird faunas of New Guinea and other southwest Pacific Islands. Diamond is the author of hundreds of articles and numerous books, including *Gun, Germs, and Steel: The Fates of Human Societies* (1997), which won a Pulitzer Prize. "Who Killed Easter Island?" (editor's title) first appeared in *Discover* magazine. It analyzes the possible causes of the fall and decline of a mysterious, isolated civilization in the South Pacific—and elsewhere.

XXXXXXXXXXXXXXXXXXXXXXXXXXXXXXXXXXXXXXXXXXXXXXXXXXXXXXXXXXX

A mong vanished civilizations, the former Polynesian society on Easter Island remains unsurpassed in mystery and isolation.   1

The mystery stems especially from the island's gigantic stone statues and its impoverished landscape.   2

David Steadman, a paleontologist, has been working with a number of other researchers who are carrying out the first systematic excavations on Easter intended to identify the animals and plants that once lived there.   3

Their work is contributing to a new interpretation of the island's history that makes it a tale not only of wonder but of warning as well.   4

Easter Island, with an area of only sixty-four square miles, is the world's most isolated scrap of habitable land.   5

It lies in the Pacific Ocean more than 2,000 miles west of the nearest continent (South America), 1,400 miles from even the nearest habitable island (Pitcairn).   6

Its subtropical location helps give it a rather mild climate, while its volcanic origins make its soil fertile. In theory, this combination of blessings should have made Easter a miniature paradise.   7

The island derives its name from its "discovery" by the Dutch   8
explorer Jacob Roggeveen, on Easter (April 5) in 1722.

Roggeveen's first impression was not of a paradise but of a waste-   9
land: "We originally, from a further distance, have considered the said
Easter Island as sandy. The reason for that is this, that we counted as
sand the withered grass, hay or other scorched and burnt vegetation,
because its wasted appearance could give no other impression than of a
singular poverty and barrenness."

Roggeveen wrote that the Easter Islanders who greeted his ships did   10
so by swimming or paddling leaky canoes that were "bad and frail."

The canoes, only ten feet long, held at most two people, and only   11
three or four canoes were observed on the entire island.

With such flimsy craft, these people could never have colonized   12
Easter from even the nearest island, nor could they have traveled far
offshore to fish. The islanders Roggeveen met were totally isolated,
unaware that other people existed.

Easter Island's most famous feature is its huge stone statues, more   13
than 200 of which once stood on massive stone platforms lining the coast.

At least 700 more, in all stages of completion, were abandoned in   14
quarries or on ancient roads between the quarries and the coast.

Most of the erected statues were carved in a single quarry and then   15
somehow transported as far as six miles—despite heights as great as
thirty-three feet and weights up to eighty-two tons. The abandoned statues, meanwhile, were as much as sixty-five feet tall and weighed up to
270 tons.

The stone platforms were equally gigantic: up to 500 feet long and   16
ten feet tall, with facing slabs weighing up to ten tons.

How did these people transport the giant statues for miles, even   17
before erecting them?

To deepen the mystery, the statues were still standing in 1770, but   18
by 1864 all had been pulled down by the islanders themselves.

Why then did they carve them in the first place? And why did they   19
stop?

Most importantly, what happened to those settlers?   20

The fanciful theories of the past must give way to evidence gathered   21 by hardworking practitioners in three fields: archaeology, pollen analysis and paleontology.

The earliest radiocarbon dates associated with human activities on Easter Island are around 400 to 700, in reasonable agreement with the approximate settlement date of 400 estimated by linguists.   22

The period of statue construction peaked around 1200 to 1500, with few if any statues erected thereafter.   23

Densities of archaeological sites suggest a large population—an estimate of 7,000 people is widely quoted by archaeologists, but other estimates range up to 20,000.   24

Archaeologists also have enlisted surviving islanders in experiments aimed at figuring out how the statues might have been carved and erected.   25

Twenty people, using only stone chisels, could have carved even the largest completed statue within a year.   26

Given enough timber and fiber for making ropes, teams of at most a few hundred people could have loaded the statues onto wooden sleds, dragged them over lubricated wooden tracks or rollers and used logs as levers to maneuver them into a standing position.   27

Rope could have been made from the fiber of a small native tree, related to the linden, called the hauhau.   28

However, that tree is now extremely scarce on Easter, and hauling one statue would have required hundreds of yards of rope. Did Easter's now barren landscape once support the necessary trees?   29

That question can be answered by the technique of pollen analysis, which involves boring out a column of sediment from a swamp or pond. The absolute age of each layer of sediment can be dated by radiocarbon methods.   30

Then begins the hard work: examining tens of thousands of pollen grains under a microscope, counting them and identifying the plant species that produced each one.   31

Scientists John Flenley, now at Massey University in New Zealand, and Sarah King of the University of Hull in England performed the analysis and were rewarded by the striking new picture that emerged of Easter's prehistoric landscape.   32

For at least 30,000 years before human arrival and during the early years of Polynesian settlement, Easter was a subtropical forest. Woody bushes towered over shrubs, herbs, ferns and grasses.

What did the first settlers of Easter Island eat when they were not glutting themselves on the local equivalent of maple syrup?

Recent excavations by David Steadman, of the New York State Museum at Albany, have yielded a picture of Easter's original animal world.

Less than a quarter of the bones in Easter Island's early garbage heaps (from the period 900 to 1300) belonged to fish; instead, nearly one-third of all bones came from porpoises.

On Easter, porpoises would have been the largest animal available. The porpoise species identified at Easter—the common dolphin—weighs up to 165 pounds. It generally lives out at sea, so it could not have been hunted by line fishing or spear fishing from shore.

Instead, it must have been harpooned far offshore, in big seaworthy canoes built from the extinct palm tree.

In addition to porpoise meat, Steadman found the early Polynesian settlers were feasting on sea birds and land birds.

Bird stew would have been seasoned with meat from large numbers of rats, which the Polynesian colonists inadvertently brought with them.

Porpoises, seabirds, land birds and rats did not complete the list of meat sources formerly available on Easter. A few bones hint at the possibility of breeding seal colonies as well.

All these delicacies were cooked in ovens fired by wood from the island's forests.

Such evidence lets us imagine the island onto which Easter's first Polynesian colonists stepped ashore some 1,600 years ago, after a long canoe voyage from eastern Polynesia. They found themselves in a pristine paradise.

What then happened to it?

The pollen grains and the bones yield a grim answer. Pollen records show that destruction of Easter's forests was well under way by the year 800, just a few centuries after the start of human settlement.

Then charcoal from wood fires came to fill the sediment cores, while 46
pollen of palms and other trees and woody shrubs decreased or disappeared, and pollen of the grasses that replaced the forest became more
abundant.

The fifteenth century marked the end not only for Easter's palm 47
but for the forest itself. Its doom had been approaching as people cleared
land to plant gardens; as they felled trees to build canoes, to transport
and erect statues, and to burn; as rats devoured seeds; and probably as
the native birds died out that had pollinated the trees' flowers and dis-
persed their fruit.

The overall picture is among the most extreme examples of forest 48
destruction anywhere in the world.

The destruction of the island's animals was as extreme as that of 49
the forest: Without exception, every species of native land bird became
extinct.

Even shellfish were over-exploited. Porpoise bones disappeared 50
abruptly from garbage heaps around 1500. No one could harpoon porpoises anymore, since the trees used for constructing the big seagoing
canoes no longer existed.

The colonies of more than half of the seabird species breeding on 51
Easter or on its offshore islets were wiped out.

In place of these meat supplies, the Easter Islanders intensified their 52
production of chickens.

They also turned to the largest remaining meat source available: 53
humans, whose bones became common in late Easter Island garbage
heaps. Oral traditions of the islanders are rife with cannibalism.

Intensified chicken production and cannibalism replaced only part 54
of all those lost foods. Preserved statuettes with sunken cheeks and visible
ribs suggest that people were starving.

By around 1700, the population began to crash toward between one- 55
quarter and one-tenth of its former number. People took to living in caves
for protection against their enemies.

By 1864 the last statue had been thrown down and desecrated. 56

By now the meaning of Easter Island for us should be chillingly 57
obvious. Easter Island is Earth writ small.

Today, again, a rising population confronts shrinking resources. We   58
too have no emigration valve, because all human societies are linked by
international transport, and we can no more escape into space than the
Easter Islanders could flee into the ocean.

If we continue to follow our present course, we shall have exhausted   59
the world's major fisheries, tropical rain forests, fossil fuels and much of
our soil by the time my sons reach my current age.

Every day newspapers report details of famished countries where   60
soldiers have appropriated the wealth or where central government is
yielding to local gangs of thugs.

With the risk of nuclear war receding, the threat of our ending with   61
a bang no longer has a chance of galvanizing us to halt our course. Our
risk now is of winding down, slowly, in a whimper.

The Easter Islanders had no books and no histories of other doomed   62
societies. Unlike the Easter Islanders, we have histories of the past—
information that can save us.

My main hope for my sons' generation is that we may now choose   63
to learn from the fates of societies such as Easter's.

XXXXXXXXXXXXXXXXXXXX **For Discussion** XXXXXXXXXXXXXXXXXXXX

1. In this chilling account of the decline of an island paradise, Jared Diamond
attempts to solve an ancient "mystery" (2). What is it, and what solution does
he propose?

2. Diamond issues a "warning" in paragraph 4 that he then states explicitly
much later in the essay when he says that "Easter Island is Earth writ small"
(57). What does he mean by this statement?

3. We have something the Easter Islanders did not have: a written history. How,
according to Diamond, might this advantage help us to avoid their fate?

4. How plausible do you find Diamond's explanation of who or what killed
Easter Island? How does he establish (or fail to establish) his credibility as a
scientific detective? Why is being credible so important to his purpose in the
rest of his essay?

5. Diamond presents an ANALOGY, or unexpected COMPARISON, near the end
of his essay. What is he comparing to what? List his specific points of comparison.

XXXXXXXXXXXXXX **STRATEGIES AND STRUCTURES** XXXXXXXXXXXXX

1. "Who Killed Easter Island" begins by examining EFFECTS (the evidence of decline on Easter Island) and later switches to speculating about CAUSES (the reasons for that decline). With what specific RHETORICAL QUESTION does the author signal this shift in emphasis?

2. Why the sequence of effects first and then causes rather than the other way around? Remember that Diamond is writing a sort of scientific detective story.

3. According to Diamond, the destruction of the forest (43–47) and the depletion of its animals and fish (49–51) were the primary causes of the decline of civilization on Easter Island. What does he say were some of the secondary causes? What makes them secondary?

4. Diamond never speculates about why the Easter Islanders carved their mammoth stone statues, why the carving ceased, or why existing statues were pulled down. Why not? Can Diamond maintain his authority as a scientific detective without answering these questions? Why or why not?

5. By comparing earth to a desert island, Diamond is advancing an ARGUMENT by ANALOGY. What is the gist of his argument?

6. Arguments by analogy are only as strong as the analogy is close. How effective, in your opinion, is this analogy?

XXXXXXXXXXXX **WORDS AND FIGURES OF SPEECH** XXXXXXXXXXX

1. Many of the verbs in this essay are in the subjunctive mood: "might have been carved" (25), "could have been made" (28). Why do you think Diamond uses the subjunctive instead of the indicative (were carved, was made)?

2. Easter Island's mysterious stone statues, says Diamond, were all "desecrated" by 1864 (56). Why do you think Diamond uses this word rather than *destroyed* or *demolished*?

3. *Archaeology* deals with the "human remains," including such physical structures as stone statues, of past cultures; *paleontology* deals with the remains of plants and animals (21). Look up the root meanings of these terms in a dictionary. Why are they essentially the same?

4. "Easter Island," says Diamond, "is Earth writ small" (57). Why the archaic, almost biblical language here?

5. Why do you think Diamond refers to his revisionist history of Easter Island as a "tale" (4)? What NARRATIVE elements does he incorporate into his scientific ANALYSIS of CAUSE AND EFFECT?

XXXXXXXXXXXXXXXXXXXXXXX **FOR WRITING** XXXXXXXXXXXXXXXXXXXXXXXX

1. Drawing either on historical events or events from your own experience, write an essay in which you show how some CAUSE in the past has had a significant EFFECT on the present.

2. Write a cause and effect essay about a closet or room in an old house (or an attic or a barn or warehouse or other storage place) with its relics of the past. Tell what the place looks and smells like and how it makes you feel. Examine a number of the objects in the place, and explain who and where you think they came from and how they got there. Do the relics seem to give evidence of progress or decline, or simply of time passing?

HENRY LOUIS GATES JR.

A GIANT STEP

Henry Louis Gates Jr. (b. 1950) is Chair of the African American Studies Department at Harvard. He is the author or editor of many works on black literature and history and of literary criticism, including *The Signifying Monkey: A Theory of Afro-American Literary Criticism* (1988) and *The Norton Anthology of African American Literature* (1997). Gates grew up in Piedmont, West Virginia, the small town depicted in this personal narrative from the *New York Times Magazine*. He later incorporated this essay into *Colored People: A Memoir* (1994), a book that tells of events and people in the author's past from the standpoint of the present. But "A Giant Step" is also an essay in cause and effect, playfully examining the social attitudes that caused young Gates to be misdiagnosed as an "overachiever" and showing how he sidestepped the potentially crippling effects of both physical disability and racial prejudice on his way to becoming a distinguished scholar.

XXXXXXXXXXXXXXXXXXXXXXXXXXXXXXXXXXXXXXXXXXXXXXXXXXXXXXXXXXXX

"What's this?" the hospital janitor said to me as he stumbled over my right shoe.   1

"My shoes," I said.   2

"That's not a shoe, brother," he replied, holding it to the light. "That's a brick."   3

It *did* look like a brick, sort of.   4

"Well, we can throw these in the trash now," he said.   5

"I guess so."   6

We had been together since 1975, those shoes and I. They were orthopedic shoes built around molds of my feet, and they had a 2¼-inch lift. I had mixed feelings about them. On the one hand, they had given me a more or less even gait for the first time in 10 years. On the other hand, they had marked me as a "handicapped person," complete with   7 cane and special license plates. I went through a pair a year, but it was always the same shoe, black, wide, weighing about four pounds.

It all started 26 years ago in Piedmont, W. Va., a backwoods town of 2,000 people. While playing a game of touch football at a Methodist summer camp, I incurred a hairline fracture. Thing is, I didn't know it yet. I was 14 and had finally lost the chubbiness of my youth. I was just learning tennis and beginning to date, and who knew where that might lead?

Not too far. A few weeks later, I was returning to school from lunch when, out of the blue, the ball-and-socket joint of my hip sheared apart. It was instant agony, and from that time on nothing in my life would be quite the same.

I propped myself against the brick wall of the schoolhouse, where the school delinquent found me. He was black as slate, twice my size, mean as the day was long and beat up kids just because he could. But the look on my face told him something was seriously wrong, and—bless him—he stayed by my side for the two hours it took to get me into a taxi.

"It's a torn ligament in your knee," the surgeon said. (One of the signs of what I had—a "slipped epithysis"—is intense knee pain, I later learned.) So he scheduled me for a walking cast.

I was wheeled into surgery and placed on the operating table. As the doctor wrapped my leg with wet plaster strips, he asked about my schoolwork.

"Boy," he said, "I understand you want to be a doctor."

I said, "Yessir." Where I came from, you always said "sir" to white people, unless you were trying to make a statement.

Had I taken a lot of science courses?

"Yessir. I enjoy science."

"Are you good at it?"

"Yessir, I believe so."

"Tell me, who was the father of sterilization?"

"Oh, that's easy, Joseph Lister."

Then he asked who discovered penicillin.

Alexander Fleming.

And what about DNA?

Watson and Crick.

The interview went on like this, and I thought my answers might get me a pat on the head. Actually, they just confirmed the diagnosis he'd come to.

He stood me on my feet and insisted that I walked. When I tried, the joint ripped apart and I fell on the floor. It hurt like nothing I'd ever known.

The doctor shook his head. "Pauline," he said to my mother, his voice kindly but amused, "there's not a thing wrong with that child. The problem's psychosomatic. Your son's an overachiever."

Back then, the term didn't mean what it usually means today. In Appalachia, in 1964, "overachiever" designated a sort of pathology: the overstraining of your natural capacity. A colored kid who thought he could be a doctor—just for instance—was headed for a breakdown.

What made the pain abate was my mother's reaction. I'd never, ever heard her talk back to a white person before. And doctors, well, their words were scripture.

Not this time. Pauline Gates stared at him for a moment. "Get his clothes, pack his bags—we're going to the University Medical Center," which was 60 miles away.

Not great news: the one thing I knew was that they only moved you to the University Medical Center when you were going to die. I had three operations that year. I gave my tennis racket to the delinquent, which he probably used to club little kids with. So I wasn't going to make it to Wimbledon. But at least I wasn't going to die, though sometimes I wanted to. Following the last operation, which fitted me for a metal ball, I was confined to bed, flat on my back, immobilized by a complex system of weights and pulleys. It was six weeks of bondage—and bedpans. I spent my time reading James Baldwin, learning to play chess and quarreling daily with my mother, who had rented a small room—which we could ill afford—in a motel just down the hill from the hospital.

I think we both came to realize that our quarreling was a sort of ritual. We'd argue about everything—what time of day it was—but the arguments kept me from thinking about that traction system.

I limped through the next decade—through Yale and Cambridge . . . as far away from Piedmont as I could get. But I couldn't escape the pain, which increased as the joint calcified and began to fuse over the next 15 years. My leg grew shorter, as the muscles atrophied and the ball of the ball-and-socket joint migrated into my pelvis. Aspirin, then Motrin, heating pads and massages, became my traveling companions.

Most frustrating was passing store windows full of fine shoes. I used to dream about walking into one of those stores and buying a pair of shoes. "Give me two pairs, one black, one cordovan," I'd say. "Wrap 'em up." No six-week wait as with the orthotics in which I was confined. These would be real shoes. Not bricks.

In the meantime, hip-joint technology progressed dramatically. But no surgeon wanted to operate on me until I was significantly older, or until the pain was so great that surgery was unavoidable. After all, a new hip would last only for 15 years, and I'd already lost too much bone. It wasn't a procedure they were sure they'd be able to repeat.

This year, my 40th, the doctors decided the time had come.

I increased my life insurance and made the plunge.

The nights before my operations are the longest nights of my life— but never long enough. Jerking awake, grabbing for my watch, I experience a delicious sense of relief as I discover that only a minute or two have passed. You never want 6 A.M. to come.

And then the door swings open. "Good morning, Mr. Gates," the nurse says. "It's time."

The last thing I remember, just vaguely, was wondering where amnesiac minutes go in one's consciousness, wondering if I experienced the pain and sounds, then forgot them, or if these were somehow blocked out, dividing the self on the operating table from the conscious self in the recovery room. I didn't like that idea very much. I was about to protest when I blinked.

"It's over, Mr. Gates," says a voice. But how could it be over? I had merely *blinked*. "You talked to us several times," the surgeon had told me, and that was the scariest part of all.

Twenty-four hours later, they get me out of bed and help me into a "walker." As they stand me on my feet, my wife bursts into tears. "Your foot is touching the ground!" I am afraid to look, but it is true: the surgeon has lengthened my leg with that gleaming titanium and chrome-cobalt alloy ball-and-socket-joint.

"You'll need new shoes," the surgeon says. "Get a pair of Dock-Sides; they have a secure grip. You'll need a ¾-inch lift in the heel, which can be as discreet as you want." 43

I can't help thinking about those window displays of shoes, those elegant shoes that, suddenly, I will be able to wear. Dock-Sides and sneakers, boots and loafers, sandals and brogues. I feel, at last, a furtive sympathy for Imelda Marcos, the queen of soles. 44

The next day, I walk over to the trash can, and take a long look at the brick. I don't want to seem ungracious or unappreciative. We have walked long miles together. I feel disloyal, as if I am abandoning an old friend. I take a second look. 45

Maybe I'll have them bronzed. 46

XXXXXXXXXXXXXXXXXXXXX **For Discussion** XXXXXXXXXXXXXXXXXXXX

1. The doctor misdiagnoses Gates's injury in paragraph 11. What does he misdiagnose in paragraph 27? What CAUSES the doctor to make the first mistake? The second?

2. What EFFECTS did each misdiagnosis have on Gates? On his mother, Pauline?

3. "Where I came from," says Gates, "you always said 'sir' to white people, unless you were trying to make a statement" (14). What "statement" is Gates making about race and "natural capacity" in this essay (28)?

4. Why does Gates think of having his old shoes "bronzed" (46)?

XXXXXXXXXXXXX **Strategies and Structures** XXXXXXXXXXXXXX

1. Gates begins the story of his physical injury with "It all started 26 years ago in Piedmont, W. Va." (8). What clues does he give us that this is going to be a story about overcoming adversity rather than giving in to it?

2. Besides the EFFECTS of physical pain, young Gates also had to deal with the effects of racism. How does the incident involving his mother and the doctor who "interviews" him show both what he is up against and what strengths he has that will enable him to succeed (13–30)?

3. How does the bedridden boy in paragraphs 13 through 32 foreshadow the chaired professor who is writing about him?

4. Gates takes a giant step when he gets a new hip. Up until then, however, his life story has been shaped around an earlier turning point. What is it? How do the two "steps" differ? How does each influence his life?

5. How much time elapses between when the "bricks" first go in the trash can and when Gates thinks of having them bronzed (5, 46)? How many distinct time periods does Gates identify? What do these elements of NARRATIVE contribute to Gates's essay?

XXXXXXXXXXXXX **WORDS AND FIGURES OF SPEECH** XXXXXXXXXXXX

1. How, according to Gates, has the meaning of "overachiever" changed since 1964 (28)?

2. A "slipped epithysis" is a medical pathology (11). What kind of pathology is Gates referring to in paragraph 28?

3. What are the multiple meanings of each of the following words as Gates uses them here: "breakdown," "bondage," "limped" (28, 31, 33).

4. Why does Gates profess to feel "disloyal" in paragraph 45? What does it mean to say to someone, "You've been a brick"?

XXXXXXXXXXXXXXXXXXXXX **FOR WRITING** XXXXXXXXXXXXXXXXXXXXX

1. Write a paragraph about an object you might like to have bronzed. Be sure to ANALYZE why it's so important to you.

2. Write an essay that examines the EFFECTS of dealing with some kind of adversity.

RUTH RUSSELL

THE WOUNDS THAT CAN'T BE STITCHED UP

Ruth Russell was a student at a community college in Greenfield, Massachusetts, when she wrote an essay entitled "Full Circle," about a chance encounter with the drunk driver who had almost killed her mother and sister. With a few changes and a new title, "The Wounds That Can't Be Stitched Up" was published as a "My Turn" column in *Newsweek* in 1999. In it, the author warily confronts not only the source of her trauma, but also its lingering psychological and emotional effects.

XXXXXXXXXXXXXXXXXXXXXXXXXXXXXXXXXXXXXXXXXXXXXXXXXXXXXXXXXXXXXXXXXXXX

It was a mild December night. Christmas was only two weeks away. The evening sky was overcast, but the roads were dry. All was quiet in our small town as I drove to my grandmother's house.   1

I heard the sirens first. Red lights and blue lights strobed in tandem. Ambulances with their interiors lit like television screens in a dark room flew by, escorted by police cruisers on the way to the hospital.   2

When I arrived at my gram's, she was on the porch steps struggling to put on her coat. "Come on," she said breathlessly, "your mother has been in an accident." I was 17 then, and it would take a long time before sirens lost their power to reduce me to tears.   3

Twenty-three years have passed, but only recently have I realized how deeply affected I was by events caused by a drunk driver so long ago.   4

When the accident occurred, my youngest brother was 8. He was sitting in the back seat of our family's large, sturdy sedan. The force of the crash sent him flying headlong into the back of the front seat, leaving him with a grossly swollen black eye. He was admitted to the hospital for observation. He didn't talk much when I visited him that night. He just sat in bed, a lonely little figure in a darkened hospital room.   5

My sister, who was 12, was sitting in the front seat. She confided   6
to me later how much she missed the beautiful blue coat she'd been
wearing at the time. It was an early Christmas present, and it was
destroyed beyond repair by the medical personnel who cut it off her body
as they worked to save her life. She had a severely fractured skull that
required immediate surgery. The resulting facial scar became for our family a permanent reminder of how close she came to dying that night.

My mother was admitted to the intensive-care unit to be stabilized   7
before her multiple facial cuts could be stitched up. Dad tried to prepare
me before we went in to see her by telling me that she looked and
sounded worse than she was. One eye was temporarily held in place by
a bandage wrapped around her head. Her lower lip hideously gaped,
exposing a mouthful of broken teeth. Delirious, she cried out for her
children and apologized for an accident she neither caused nor could have
avoided. An accident that happened when her car was hit head-on by a
drunk driver speeding down the wrong side of the road in a half-ton
truck with no headlights.

My dad, my brothers, my sister and I spent Christmas at the hos-   8
pital visiting my mother. Sometimes she was so out of it from medication
that she barely recognized us. We celebrated two of my brothers' birth-
days—one only days after Christmas and the other in early January—
there too.

I remember watching the police escort the drunk driver out of the   9
hospital the night of the accident. He looked about 35 years old, but his
face was so distorted by rage and alcohol that I could only guess. A
bandaged wrist was his only visible injury. He kept repeating that he'd
done nothing wrong as several officers tried to get him into the cruiser
waiting outside the emergency-room exit.

The man was jailed over the weekend and lost his license for 30   10
days for driving while intoxicated. I don't know if that was his first
alcohol-related traffic violation, but I know it wasn't the last. Now and
then I'd see his name in the court log of our local paper for another
DWI, and wonder how he could still be behind the wheel.

Sometimes when I tell this story, I'd be asked in an accusatory tone   11
if my mom and siblings were wearing seat belts. I think that's a lot like

asking a rape victim how she was dressed. The answer is no. This all happened before seat-belt-awareness campaigns began. In fact, if they had been in a smaller car, seat belts or not, I believe my mother and sister would have died.

Many local people who know the driver are surprised when they hear about the accident, and they are quick to defend him. They tell me he was a war hero. His parents aren't well. He's an alcoholic. Or my favorite: "He's a good guy when he doesn't drink." 12

Two years ago I discovered this man had moved into my apartment building. I felt vaguely apprehensive, but I believed the accident was ancient history. Nothing could have prepared me for what happened next. 13

It was a mild afternoon, just a few days before Christmas. I had started down the back staircase of the building, on my way to visit my son, when I recognized my neighbor's new pickup truck as it roared down the street. The driver missed the entrance to our shared parking lot. He reversed crookedly in the road, slammed the transmission into forward, then quickly pulled into his parking space. Gravel and sand flew as he stomped on the brakes to halt his truck just inches from where I stood frozen on the staircase. As he staggered from his vehicle, he looked at me and asked drunkenly, "Did I scare you?" 14

XXXXXXXXXXXXXXXXXXXX **For Discussion** XXXXXXXXXXXXXXXXXXXX

1. What are the "wounds that can't be stitched up," and who has them? What is the CAUSE of the wounds, and what lasting EFFECTS do they have?

2. What "permanent reminder" of her and her family's trauma does Ruth Russell mention? What are some other yearly reminders?

3. "Now and then I'd see his name in the court log of our local paper for another DWI, and wonder how he could still be behind the wheel" (10). What ARGUMENT is Russell advancing here?

4. Russell DESCRIBES the drunk driver as being solely guilty for the accident (7). Where and why does she also give EXAMPLES of blaming the victim?

5. Like Henry Louis Gates Jr.'s "Giant Steps" (see the preceding selection), Russell's essay is about both literal and figurative wounds. How does Russell's account differ from Gates's?

312 ♠ *Cause and Effect*

XXXXXXXXXXXXXXX **STRATEGIES AND STRUCTURES** XXXXXXXXXXXXXX

1. "Nothing could have prepared me for what happened next," says Russell in paragraph 13. How is she preparing us as readers for what happens in the last paragraph of her essay?

2. The first sentence of Russell's last paragraph echoes the first sentence of her first paragraph. How does this repetition in her essay support what she has to say about drunk drivers and the psychological traumas they cause?

3. The last paragraph of Russell's essay is a complete NARRATIVE. What constitutes the beginning? the middle? the end?

4. How did the scrap of DIALOGUE in Russell's last paragraph affect you as a reader? Where else does she use dialogue effectively?

5. What clue does Russell give us that she has told this story over and over to different audiences? Again, what does the repetition tell us?

6. What ARGUMENT does Russell's essay imply about drunk drivers and the laws that let them stay on the road?

XXXXXXXXXXXX **WORDS AND FIGURES OF SPEECH** XXXXXXXXXXXX

1. Why do you think Russell DESCRIBES the man's face in paragraph 9 as "distorted" rather than "changed" or "influenced"?

2. Explain the IRONY in Russell's use of the phrase "my favorite" (12).

3. Both SIMILES and METAPHORS draw COMPARISONS; but in one case the comparison is stated, and in the other it is implied. Which is the case here: "I stood frozen on the staircase" (14)? Or here: "Ambulances with their interiors lit like television screens in a dark room flew by" (2)?

4. Not only do Russell's wounds not heal, they can't even be "stitched up." What are the implications of this metaphor?

XXXXXXXXXXXXXXXXXXXX **FOR WRITING** XXXXXXXXXXXXXXXXXXXX

1. Try to recall a brief encounter with someone who scared or startled you. Write a paragraph in which you recapture the entire scene. Tell where you were standing when you first saw the other person, what he or she said and did, and how the episode ended. Be sure to DESCRIBE what things about that person caused your fear and to explain any other emotional EFFECTS the experience had for you.

2. The auto accident described in Russell's essay took place twenty-three years ago, but "only recently" has she realized "how deeply affected" she was by that event (4). Have you ever had a delayed reaction to stress or a traumatic event? Write a personal essay in which you examine both the CAUSES of that stress or trauma and the effects that it had on you later, even much later.

CHAPTER NINE

ARGUMENT

XXXXXXXXXXXXXXXXXXXXXXXXXXXXXXXXXXXXXXXXXXXXXXXXXXXXXXXXXXXXXXXXXX

ARGUMENT* is the strategic use of language to move an audience to agree with you on an issue or act in a way that you think is right. People can be moved in three ways: (1) by appealing to reason, (2) by appealing to their emotions, and (3) by appealing to their sense of ethics (their standards of what constitutes proper behavior). The essays in this chapter illustrate all three appeals.

The writer who wants to appeal to a reader's sense of reason cannot do so simply by affirming that a position or belief is rational and reasonable. The writer must supply proofs. There are basically two kinds of logical reasoning on which such proofs can be built: DEDUCTION and INDUCTION. When we deduce something, we reason from general premises to particular conclusions. When we reason by induction, we proceed the other way—from particulars to generalities.

Here is a piece of inductive reasoning about an unusual bird:

> Flamingos feed with their heads upside down. They stand in shallow water and swing their heads down to the level of their feet, subtly adjusting the head's position by lengthening or shortening the s-curve of the neck. This motion naturally turns the head upside down, and the bills therefore reverse their conventional roles in feeding. . . . Has this unusual behavior led to any changes of form and, if so, what and how?
>
> STEPHEN JAY GOULD, *THE FLAMINGO'S SMILE*

Here biologist Stephen Jay Gould observes several particulars of flamingo feeding habits: (1) they always feed with their heads upside down;

---

*Words printed in SMALL CAPITALS are defined in the Glossary.

(2) the birds' heads are held so low in feeding that they approximate the level of their feet; (3) the normal functions of the jaws are reversed: the upper beak serves as a lower jaw, and the lower jaw serves as an upper beak. On the basis of these particulars, Gould, reasoning inductively, poses a generalization: perhaps a structural change has occurred, over time, in the flamingo's beak to fit the bird's peculiar eating habits. And so it has. The flamingo, as Gould notes, has "developed a highly mobile ball and socket joint between upper and lower jaws."

Inductive reasoning like this depends upon EXAMPLES—the more, the better. If you are trying to convince someone that UFOs exist, you will be more persuasive if you can cite fifty eyewitnesses rather than one or two. In a short essay, however, you probably will not have enough room to cite all the examples you would like, so you will have to choose your best, most representative ones.

Otherwise, you may sound like the Duchess in *Alice in Wonderland*:

> "Very true," said the Duchess: "flamingos and mustard both bite. And the moral of that is—'Birds of a feather flock together.' "
>
> "Only mustard isn't a bird," Alice remarked.
>
> "Right as usual," said the Duchess: "what a clear way you have of putting things."
>
> LEWIS CARROLL, *ALICE IN WONDERLAND*

Carroll's Duchess is guilty of a serious lapse in inductive reasoning. Two examples are few enough, but her two examples are not even remotely related. Flamingos and mustard may bite, but not in the same sense. They are definitely not birds of a feather, as your examples must be if you are to construct solid arguments.

In a moment we will look an effective argument built on a few, well-chosen examples, but first let's examine the other kind of logical argumentation—deduction. Whereas inductive arguments move from the particular to the general, deductive arguments move from the general to the less general. The general proposition that a deductive argument purports to prove is called the *conclusion*, and the general claims on which that conclusion is based are called the *premises*.

Here is perhaps the most famous of all deductive arguments:

Major premise: All men are mortal.

Minor premise: Socrates is a man.

Conclusion: Therefore, Socrates is mortal.

Since Socrates was long dead when Aristotle posed this argument, the younger philosopher was reasonably confident that it would not be seriously challenged. He also had logic on his side. If we grant the major premise that all men must die and the minor premise that Socrates is a man, the conclusion follows inevitably that Socrates must die.

When a conclusion follows logically from the premises or (in inductive reasoning, from the examples), we say that the argument is valid. An argument can be valid without being true, however. Consider this exercise in wishful thinking:

Major premise: All human beings are immortal.

Minor premise: Socrates is a man.

Conclusion: Therefore, Socrates is immortal.

This argument is properly drawn, but it is untrue because its major premise is false. Most debates arise in real life because people disagree over the truth of one or more of their primary assumptions. And these are the sorts of argument that tend to be worth writing about. If differences of opinion make horse races, as Mark Twain once said, they also make essays far more interesting than they would be if everyone agreed on the point at issue.

Take, for example, the idea that the world's leaders "should start an international campaign to promote imports from sweatshops." Nicholas D. Kristof argues in favor of this controversial proposition in an article in the *New York Times* entitled "Let's Hear It for Third-World Sweatshops." Kristof's essay is an instructive example of how all the techniques of argumentation can work together.

Kristof knows that arguing in favor of sweatshops is likely to be an uphill battle. Like any writer with a point to make, especially a controversial one, he needs to win the reader's trust. One way to do this is to anticipate objections the reader might be expected to raise. So before anyone can accuse him of being totally out of his head for promoting sweatshops, Kristof writes: "The Gentle Reader will think I've been smoking Pakistani opium. But sweatshops are the only hope of kids like Ahmed Zia, 14, here in Attock, a gritty center for carpet weaving."

Right away, Kristof is hoping to convince his audience that they are hearing the words of an ethical person who deserves to be heeded. Next, he tugs at the readers' heart strings:

> Ahmed earns $2 a day hunched over the loom, laboring over a rug that will adorn some American's living room. It is a pittance, but the American campaign against sweatshops could make his life much more wretched by inadvertently encouraging mechanization that could cost him his job.
>
> "Carpet-making is much better than farm work," Ahmed said. "This makes much more money and is more comfortable."

Kristof's logical claim in citing Ahmed's case is that his plight is *representative* of that of most factory workers in poor countries. "Indeed," writes Kristof, "talk to Third World factory workers and the whole idea of 'sweatshops' seems a misnomer. It is farmers and brick-makers who really sweat under the broiling sun, while sweatshop workers merely glow."

The same claim—that other cases are like this one—also lies behind Kristof's second example: "But before you spurn a shirt made by someone like Kamis Saboor, 8, an Afghan refugee whose father is dead and who is the sole breadwinner in the family, answer this question: How does shunning sweatshop products help Kamis? All the alternatives for him are worse." Kristof is appealing to the reader's emotions and sense of ethics, and he is using logical reasoning. If we grant Kristof's major premise that in really poor countries "all the alternatives" to sweatshop labor are worse, we must logically concede his main point that, for these workers, "a sweatshop job is the first step on life's escalator" and, therefore, that sweatshops are to be supported.

Kristof has not finished marshaling his reasons yet, however. Unlike flamingos and mustard, Kristof's first two examples *do* belong to the same general category—underage workers in poor countries. But to strengthen his argument, Kristof introduces another, broader example, one that Americans are more likely to be familiar with:

> Nike has 35 contract factories in Taiwan, 49 in South Korea, only three in Pakistan and none at all in Afghanistan—if it did, critics would immediately fulminate about low wages, glue vapors, the mistreatment of women.
>
> But the losers are the Afghans, and especially Afghan women. The country is full of starving widows who can find no jobs. If Nike hired them at 10 cents an hour to fill all-female sweatshops, they and their country would be hugely better off.
>
> Nike used to have two contract factories in impoverished Cambodia, among the neediest countries in the world. Then there was an outcry after BBC reported that three girls in one factory were under 15 years old. So Nike fled controversy by ceasing production in Cambodia.
>
> The result was that some of the 2,000 Cambodians (90 percent of them young women) who worked in three factories faced layoffs. Some who lost their jobs probably were ensnared in Cambodia's huge sex slave industry—which leaves many girls dead of AIDS by the end of their teenage years.

Again, we can dispute Kristof's premises. Can the widows of Afghanistan find no decent jobs whatsoever? Will they actually starve if they don't? Will the young women of Cambodia inevitably die of AIDS because Nike has pulled out of their impoverished country? (Notice that Kristof qualifies this assertion with "probably.") We can even dispute Kristof's reasoning based on statistics. In statistics, when it is not possible to poll every individual in the set being ANALYZED, sound practice requires at least a representative sampling. Has Kristof given us a truly representative sampling of *all* the workers in Third World sweatshops?

We can pick away at Kristof's logic, but with the exception of a court of law, a good argument does not have to prove its point beyond a shadow of a doubt. It only has to convince the reader. Whether or not you're convinced by Kristof's argument, you can learn from his tactics. Here are a few "rules" that Kristof and other good arguers follow for winning even skeptical readers over to their side in an argument—and a few blunders (fallacies) to avoid:

- Do not condescend. Address all members of your potential audience with respect even when you disagree with them.
- Do not attribute questionable motives to others unless you're willing to lose them to your cause. If you do, be prepared to defend your own motives against sharp criticism.
- Avoid name-calling. Having referred to "heartless conservatives," Kristoff tries to be evenhanded in his criticism by mentioning "muddle-headed liberals." But such name-calling does not help his (or your) cause. You'll end up preaching to the choir because everyone else has left.
- Stay away from ad hominem attacks that go after an opponent's character rather than his or her ideas: "How would this old guy know what he is talking about? He's too ancient to understand anybody under thirty."
- Avoid tautologies. A *tautology* is a circular argument: "If we had some ham, we could have some ham and eggs—if we had the eggs."
- Don't beg the question. This form of circular reasoning gets around an issue by assuming what it purports to prove: "The quarterback could not have flunked the midterm because he is an 'A' student."
- Look out for red herrings. These are lines of argument that will throw the reader off the track of the real argument: "I know my paper is full of spelling errors, but English is not a very phonetic language. Now if we were writing in Spanish. . . ."
- *Post hoc, ergo propter hoc*. This is faulty reasoning that says: After this, therefore because of this. For example: "Most people believe it is bad for athletes in training to drink beer. From my experience with distance running, I have found not only that this is not true, but that drinking beer is a good thing to do before a race. One Friday night I was out with my friends and couldn't resist drinking a few beers even though I had a meet the next day. I was a little worried at first, but during the race I felt great and ended up running one of my best races ever."
- The *"tu quoque"* argument. Like the red herring, the "you're one, too" argument goes off on a tangent—for example, saying to a teacher: "So what if my paper does not make sense. Neither do your lectures."
- The fallacy of the undistributed middle. This has nothing to do with diet. It is the blunder in deduction of giving an argument the following shape: All A are B; all C are B; therefore, all A are C. Not likely to be tripped up by such clearly spurious reasoning? Consider the following near-universal adaptation of this faulty form: *Major premise:* Discriminating people buy Fisquick. *Minor premise:* You buy Fisquick, and *Conclusion:* You'll be a discriminating person.

Like the rest of America, Don Jones of Delhi, New York, owner of the frame house pictured here, was angered and saddened by the attacks on the World Trade Center. "Three weeks after Sept. 11," says Jones, "I bought a 4-by-6 American flag and wrote those words on the house." Jones's message is plain. It is the underlying message inscribed on much loftier monuments: never forget. His message, like any argument, is an imperative of sorts: do this, do that, or, at the very least, agree with me. Argumentative writing is audience-centered. Even more than other kinds, it delivers a message directly *to* someone with whom the writer converses. "I still have people stopping by to take pictures of it," says Jones of the house he has turned into a billboard. A message presumes not only a recipient, but also a messenger. Jones sees his house as relaying a message from the nation's highest authorities: "I don't know," he says, "if it was Colin Powell or that Department of Defense guy what's-his-name [Secretary of Defense Donald Rumsfeld] or maybe it was John McCain that made the comment 'God forgives but we don't.' But it stuck with me." The message not only stuck in the messenger's mind; by writing it on the side of his house for all to see, he appropriated it as his own: "I stole that guy's words," Jones admits, "but I took it one step further."

CONSIDER FURTHER . . .

1. Never to forgive is never to forget. Besides a message about never forgetting those who died in the World Trade Center attacks, "God forgives, but we don't" also carries a warning. What is the nature of that warning, and to whom is it addressed?

2. How does the presence of the American flag on the side of Don Jones's house contribute to the argument he is making? What kind of appeal does it make?

3. "I like to think I'm a freethinker," Jones says. "My mom always said it would get me into trouble. I don't follow a Republican or Democratic Party line." How does Jones's message capture this spirit of freethinking individualism?

THOMAS JEFFERSON

THE DECLARATION OF INDEPENDENCE

Thomas Jefferson (1743–1826) was the third president of the United States. He was as much philosopher as politician, however, and the Declaration of Independence (1776), which announced the colonies' break with England, was as much an argument for human rights as a political document. Drafted by Jefferson and revised by Benjamin Franklin, John Adams, and the Continental Congress at large, the Declaration is a well-reasoned, logical argument for independence that skillfully combines inductive and deductive reasoning. The version reprinted here is that published on the Web site of the United States National Archives, www.archives.gov.

XXXXXXXXXXXXXXXXXXXXXXXXXXXXXXXXXXXXXXXXXXXXXXXXXXXXXXXXXXXXXXXX

When in the Course of human events, it becomes necessary for one people to dissolve the political bands which have connected them with another, and to assume among the powers of the earth, the separate and equal station to which the Laws of Nature and of Nature's God entitle them, a decent respect to the opinions of mankind requires that they should declare the causes which impel them to the separation.

We hold these truths to be self-evident, that all men are created equal, that they are endowed by their Creator with certain unalienable Rights, that among these are Life, Liberty and the pursuit of Happiness. That to secure these rights, Governments are instituted among Men, deriving their just powers from the consent of the governed. That whenever any Form of Government becomes destructive of these ends, it is the Right of the People to alter or to abolish it, and to institute new Government, laying its foundation on such principles and organizing its powers in such form, as to them shall seem most likely to effect their Safety and Happiness. Prudence, indeed, will dictate that Governments long established should not be changed for light and transient causes;

and accordingly all experience hath shewn, that mankind are more disposed to suffer, while evils are sufferable, than to right themselves by abolishing the forms to which they are accustomed. But when a long train of abuses and usurpations pursuing invariably the same Object evinces a design to reduce them under absolute Despotism, it is their right, it is their duty, to throw off such Government, and to provide new Guards for their future security. Such has been the patient sufferance of these Colonies; and such is now the necessity which constrains them to alter their former Systems of Government. The history of the present King of Great Britain[1] is a history of repeated injuries and usurpations, all having in direct object the establishment of absolute Tyranny over these States. To prove this, let Facts be submitted to a candid world.

He has refused his Assent to Laws, the most wholesome and necessary for the public good. 3

He has forbidden his Governors to pass Laws of immediate and pressing importance, unless suspended in their operation till his Assent should be obtained; and when so suspended, he has utterly neglected to attend to them. 4

He has refused to pass other Laws for the accommodation of large districts of people, unless those people would relinquish the right of Representation in the Legislature, a right inestimable to them and formidable to tyrants only. 5

He has called together legislative bodies at places unusual, uncomfortable, and distant from the depository of their public Records, for the sole purpose of fatiguing them into compliance with his measures. 6

He has dissolved Representative Houses repeatedly, for opposing with manly firmness his invasions on the rights of the people. 7

He has refused for a long time, after such dissolutions, to cause others to be elected; whereby the Legislative powers, incapable of Annihilation, have returned to the People at large for their exercise; the State remaining in the mean time exposed to all the dangers of invasion from without, and convulsions within. 8

He has endeavoured to prevent the population of these States; for that purpose obstructing the Laws of Naturalization of Foreigners; refus- 9

[1]George III (ruled 1760–1820).

ing to pass others to encourage their migration hither, and raising the conditions of new Appropriations of Lands.

He has obstructed the Administration of Justice, by refusing his Assent to Laws for establishing Judiciary powers.

He has made Judges dependent on his Will alone, for the tenure of their offices, and the amount and payment of their salaries.

He has erected a multitude of New Offices, and sent hither swarms of Officers to harass our people, and eat out their substance.

He has kept among us, in time of peace, Standing Armies without the Consent of our legislatures.

He has affected to render the Military independent of and superior to the Civil power.

He has combined with others to subject us to a jurisdiction foreign to our constitution, and unacknowledged by our laws; giving his Assent to their acts of pretended Legislation:

For Quartering large bodies of armed troops among us:

For protecting them, by a mock Trial, from punishment for any Murders which they should commit on the Inhabitants of these States:

For cutting off our Trade with all parts of the world:

For imposing Taxes on us without our Consent:

For depriving us in many cases, of the benefits of Trial by Jury:

For transporting us beyond the Seas to be tried for pretended offenses:

For abolishing the free System of English Laws in a neighbouring Province, establishing therein an Arbitrary government, and enlarging its Boundaries so as to render it at once an example and fit instrument for introducing the same absolute rule into these Colonies:

For taking away our Charters, abolishing our most valuable Laws, and altering fundamentally the Forms of our Governments:

For suspending our own Legislatures, and declaring themselves invested with power to legislate for us in all cases whatsoever.

He has abdicated Government here, by declaring us out of his Protection and waging War against us.

He has plundered our seas, ravaged our Coasts, burnt our towns and destroyed the lives of our people.

He is at this time transporting large Armies of foreign Mercenaries   27
to compleat the works of death, desolation and tyranny, already begun
with circumstances of Cruelty & perfidy scarcely paralleled in the most
barbarous ages, and totally unworthy the Head of a civilized nation.

He has constrained our fellow Citizens taken Captive on the high   28
Seas to bear Arms against their Country, to become the executioners of
their friends and Brethren, or to fall themselves by their Hands.

He has excited domestic insurrections amongst us, and has endea-   29
voured to bring on the inhabitants of our frontiers, the merciless Indian
Savages, whose known rule of warfare, is an undistinguished destruction
of all ages, sexes and conditions.

In every stage of these Oppressions We have Petitioned for Redress   30
in the most humble terms: Our repeated Petitions have been answered
only by repeated injury. A Prince, whose character is thus marked by
every act which may define a Tyrant, is unfit to be the ruler of a free
people.

Nor have We been wanting in attentions to our Brittish brethren.   31
We have warned them from time to time of attempts by their legislature
to extend an unwarrantable jurisdiction over us. We have reminded them
of the circumstances of our emigration and settlement here. We have
appealed to their native justice and magnanimity, and we have conjured
them by the ties of our common kindred to disavow these usurpations,
which would inevitably interrupt our connections and correspondence.
They too have been deaf to the voice of justice and of consanguinity. We
must, therefore acquiesce in the necessity, which denounces our Separation, and hold them, as we hold the rest of mankind, Enemies in War,
in Peace Friends.

We, therefore, the Representatives of the United States of America,   32
in General Congress, Assembled, appealing to the Supreme Judge of the
world for the rectitude of our intentions, do, in the Name, and by
Authority of the good People of these Colonies, solemnly publish and
declare, That these United Colonies are, and of Right ought to be Free
and Independent States; that they are Absolved from all Allegiance to
the British Crown, and that all political connection between them and
the State of Great Britain, is and ought to be totally dissolved; and that

as Free and Independent States, they have full Power to levy War, conclude Peace, contract Alliances, establish Commerce, and to do all other Acts and Things which Independent States may of right do. And for the support of this Declaration, with a firm reliance on the protection of divine Providence, we mutually pledge to each other our Lives, our Fortunes and our sacred Honor.

XXXXXXXXXXXXXXXXXXXX **For Discussion** XXXXXXXXXXXXXXXXXXXX

1. What is the purpose of government, according to Thomas Jefferson?

2. On what basis does Jefferson ARGUE that a new government is justified in America?

3. "We hold these truths to be self-evident . . ." (2). A self-evident "truth" stated at the beginning of an argument is called a *premise*. What are the premises on which Jefferson's entire argument is built?

4. Which of Jefferson's premises is most crucial to the rest of his logical argument?

5. Which of the many "injuries and usurpations" that Jefferson attributes to the British king seem most intolerable to you (2)? Why?

XXXXXXXXXXXXXX **Strategies and Structures** XXXXXXXXXXXXXX

1. A HYPOTHESIS is a theory or supposition to be tested by further proof in a logical ARGUMENT. What is the hypothesis, introduced in paragraph 2, that Jefferson's long list of "facts" is meant to test?

2. Where does Jefferson indirectly restate his hypothesis as an established conclusion? What is it? Does he arrive at this conclusion by INDUCTION (from EXAMPLES to generalizations) or DEDUCTION (from premises to particular conclusions)?

3. Is the underlying logical argument of the Declaration basically inductive or deductive? Please explain your answer.

4. The signers of the Declaration of Independence wanted to appear as men of good reason, and they approved the logical form that Jefferson gave that document. Many of the specific issues their reason addressed, however, were highly emotional. What words does Jefferson use in bringing charges against the king that show his strong feelings? Give specific examples.

5. Why do you think Jefferson includes paragraph 31, which seems to be a digression from his main line of argument?

XXXXXXXXXXXXX **WORDS AND FIGURES OF SPEECH** XXXXXXXXXXXX

1. Look up "unalienable" (or *inalienable*) in your dictionary (2). What does it mean? What does it CONNOTE?

2. What single word does Jefferson use to indicate each time he introduces a new proposition into his ARGUMENT?

3. What is "consanguinity" (31)? How can it be said to have a "voice"?

4. *Metonymy* is the use of one word or name in place of another one closely associated with it. What EXAMPLE of this FIGURE OF SPEECH can you find in paragraph 32?

5. DEFINE five of the following words: "transient" (2), "usurpations" (2), "evinces" (2), "Despotism" (2), "constrains" (2), "candid" (2), "abdicated" (25), "perfidy" (27), "Redress" (30), "magnanimity" (31), "conjured" (31), "acquiesce" (31), "rectitude" (32).

XXXXXXXXXXXXXXXXXXXXXX **FOR WRITING** XXXXXXXXXXXXXXXXXXXXXX

1. Imagine you are King George. Compose a reply to Jefferson's charges, defending your actions and policies toward the colonies.

2. Jefferson lists "the pursuit of Happiness" as one of our basic rights (2). Construct an ARGUMENT disagreeing with this assertion, perhaps saying that this promise was unwise, that happiness cannot be guaranteed, and that the unbridled pursuit of anything can lead to chaos in the life of the individual. Or, alternatively, defend Jefferson's position on the pursuit of happiness.

JOHNSON C. MONTGOMERY

THE ISLAND OF PLENTY

Johnson C. Montgomery was a California attorney and an early member
of the organization Zero Population Growth. Montgomery's "The Island
of Plenty," which first appeared as a "My Turn" column in *Newsweek* in
1974, is an "elitist" argument in favor of American social isolationism.
Until we have enough food to feed all Americans plentifully, Montgomery reasons, Americans should not share their material resources with
other countries of the world.

✗✗✗

The United States should remain an island of plenty in a sea of hun-   1
ger. The future of mankind is at stake. We are not responsible for
the rest of humanity. We should not accept responsibility for all humanity. We owe more to the hundreds of billions of *Homo futurans* than we
do to the hungry millions—soon to be billions—of our own generations.

Ample food and resources exist to nourish man and all other crea-   2
tures indefinitely into the future. This planet is indeed an Eden—to date
our only Eden. Admittedly our Eden is plagued by pollution. Some of
us have polluted the planet by reproducing too many of us. Too many
people have made excessive demands on the long-range carrying capacity
of our garden; and during the last 200 years there has been dramatic,
ever-increasing destruction of the web of life on earth. If we try to save
the starving millions today, we will simply destroy what's left of Eden.

The problem is not that there is too little food. The problem is   3
there are too many people—many too many. It is not that the children
should never have been born. It is simply that we have mindlessly tried
to cram too many of us into too short a time span. Four billion humans
are fine—but they should have been spread over several hundred years.

But the billions are already here. What should we do about them?   4
Should we send food, knowing that each child saved in Southeast Asia,

India or Africa will probably live to reproduce and thereby bring more people into the world to live even more miserably? Should we eat the last tuna fish, the last ear of corn and utterly destroy the garden? That is what we have been doing for a long time and all the misguided efforts have merely increased the number who go to bed hungry each night. There have never been more miserable, deprived people in the world than there are right now.

It was obvious even in the late 1950s that the famine the world now 5 faces was coming unless people immediately began exercising responsibility for reducing population levels. It was also obvious that too many people contributed to the risk of nuclear war, global pestilence, illiteracy and even to many problems that are usually classified as purely economic. For example, unemployment is having too many people for the available jobs. Inflation is in part the result of too much demand from too many people. But in the 1950s, population control was taboo and those who warned of impending disasters received a cool reception.

By the time Zero Population Growth, Inc., was formed, those of us 6 who wanted to do something useful decided to concentrate our initial efforts on our own families and friends and then on the white American middle and upper classes. Our belief was that by setting an example, we could later insist that others pay attention to our proposals.

I think I was the first in the original ZPG group to have had a 7 vasectomy. Nancy and I had two children—each doing superbly well and each getting all the advantages of the best nutrition, education, attention, love and other resources available. I think Paul Ehrlich[1] (one child) was the next. Now don't ask me to cut my children back to the same number of calories that children from large families eat. In fact, don't ask me to cut my children back on anything. I won't do it without a fight; and in today's world, power is in knowledge, not numbers. Nancy and I made a conscious decision to limit the number of our children so each child could have a larger share of whatever we could make available. We intend to keep the best for them.

The future of mankind is indeed with the children. But it is with 8 the nourished, educated and loved children. It is not with the starving,

[1]Biology professor at Stanford, founder and past-president of Zero Population Growth.

uneducated and ignored. This is of course a highly elitist point of view. But that doesn't make the view incorrect. As a matter of fact, the lowest reproductive rate in the nation is that of one of the most elite groups in the world—black, female Ph.D.'s. They had to be smart and effective to make it. Having made it, they are smart enough not to wreck it with too many kids.

We in the United States have made great progress in lowering our   9
birth rates. But now, because we have been responsible, it seems to some that we have a great surplus. There is, indeed, waste that should be eliminated, but there is not as much fat in our system as most people think. Yet we are being asked to share our resources with the hungry peoples of the world. But why should we share? The nations having the greatest needs are those that have been the least responsible in cutting down on births. Famine is one of nature's ways of telling profligate peoples that they have been irresponsible in their breeding habits.

Naturally, we would like to help; and if we could, perhaps we   10
should. But we can't be of any use in the long run—particularly if we weaken ourselves.

Until we have at least a couple of years' supply of food and other   11
resources on hand to take care of our own people and until those asking for handouts are doing at least as well as we are at reducing existing excessive population-growth rates, we should not give away our resources—not so much as one bushel of wheat. Certainly we should not participate in any programs that will increase the burden that mankind is already placing on the earth. We should not deplete our own soils to save those who will only die equally miserably a decade or so down the line—and in many cases only after reproducing more children who are inevitably doomed to live and die in misery.

We know the world is finite. There is only so much pie. We may   12
be able to expand the pie, but at any point in time, the pie *is* finite. How big a piece each person gets depends in part on how many people there are. At least for the foreseeable future, the fewer of us there are, the more there will be for each. That is true on a family, community, state, national and global basis.

At the moment, the future of mankind seems to depend on our   13
maintaining the island of plenty in a sea of deprivation. If everyone

shared equally, we would all be suffering from protein-deficiency brain damage—and that would probably be true even if we ate every last animal on earth.

As compassionate human beings, we grieve for the condition of mankind. But our grief must not interfere with our perception of reality and our planning for a better future for those who will come after us. Someone must protect the material and intellectual seed grain for the future. It seems to me that that someone is the U.S. We owe it to our children—and to their children's children's children's children. 14

These conclusions will be attacked, as they have been within Zero Population Growth, as simplistic and inhumane. But truth is often very simple and reality often inhumane. 15

XXXXXXXXXXXXXXXXXXXX **FOR DISCUSSION** XXXXXXXXXXXXXXXXXXXX

1. What is Johnson C. Montgomery's main claim?

2. Which of Montgomery's reasons for his position do you find most persuasive? Why? What counterarguments would you make?

3. In paragraph 4, what is the last sentence intended to prove? Why do you think Montgomery includes it?

4. Montgomery warns us not to ask him "to cut my children back on anything" (7). How is this position consistent with what he says about there not being enough food to go around?

XXXXXXXXXXXXX **STRATEGIES AND STRUCTURES** XXXXXXXXXXXXX

1. The logic of Montgomery's basic ARGUMENT can be represented by a SYLLOGISM:

> *Major premise:* To provide undamaged human stock for the future, some people must remain healthy.
>
> *Minor premise:* All will suffer if all share equally in the world's limited bounty.
>
> *Conclusion:* Therefore, some must not share what they have.

How sound is this logic? Do you think Montgomery's premises are true? Why or why not? Do they affect the validity of his argument?

2. Montgomery's hard-headed realism not only intends to show us the "truth" of the human condition, but also to move us to action (15). What would Montgomery have us do?

3. Logic is only part of Montgomery's persuasive arsenal. Where in his essay does he appeal more to emotion and ethics than to logic? Give specific examples from the text.

4. Montgomery seems to be speaking from a position of authority. Where does he get his authority, and how much weight does it carry in your opinion?

5. Montgomery admits that his position is elitist (8). How does he head off the charge that it is racist?

6. Are you persuaded by Montgomery's essay? Why or why not?

7. Montgomery's argument is based on a COMPARISON. What is he comparing to what? Which specific points of his comparison do you find most convincing? Why?

XXXXXXXXXXXXX **WORDS AND FIGURES OF SPEECH** XXXXXXXXXXXX

1. How does Montgomery use the METAPHOR of the island to contribute to his ARGUMENT?

2. For the sake of the future, says Montgomery, we must save some "material and intellectual seed grain" (14). Explain this metaphor. What does he COMPARE to what?

3. *Homo futurans*, meaning "man of the future," is modeled after such scientific terms as *Homo erectus* ("upright man") and *Homo sapiens* ("thinking man"). Why do you think Montgomery uses the language of science at the beginning of his argument?

4. How does Montgomery's use of the word "mindlessly" epitomize his entire argument (3)?

5. What is the meaning of "profligate" (9)? Why does Montgomery use this term?

XXXXXXXXXXXXXXXXXXX **FOR WRITING** XXXXXXXXXXXXXXXXXXXX

1. Write an essay agreeing or disagreeing with Montgomery's position, particularly his assumption that "the future of mankind seems to depend on our maintaining the island of plenty in a sea of deprivation" (13).

2. Read Jonathan Swift's "A Modest Proposal" in the next chapter, and write a "modest proposal" of your own in which you ARGUE for a way to solve one of the world's great problems—such as feeding the masses, sharing the world's wealth, regulating human breeding habits, reversing the greenhouse effect, or eliminating terrorism.

KORI QUINTANA

THE PRICE OF POWER:
LIVING IN THE NUCLEAR AGE

Kori Quintana was a student at the University of New Mexico when she wrote "The Price of Power" (1990), an essay arguing that "an unsuspecting public" remains at risk to exposure to dangerous levels of radiation. Quintana's term paper, complete with citations, is more than a logical argument, however. She grew up in Utah, where she contracted Lupus at age seventeen. Most of the female members of her immediate family have suffered from similar afflictions. Bad genes? Quintana wonders. Or was her family a victim of the nuclear testing in nearby Nevada in the 1950s? Quintana's deductive reasoning may not be conclusive, but by reasoning inductively about her particular case, she makes a strong appeal to the reader's emotions and sense of fair play.

XXXXXXXXXXXXXXXXXXXXXXXXXXXXXXXXXXXXXXXXXXXXXXXXXXXXXXXXXXXXXX

I became interested in the topic of genetic mutation last May after coming across an article in *Time* magazine entitled "Legacy of a Disaster." The article included photos and descriptions of animal deformities caused by the nuclear meltdown at Chernobyl. Having always been fascinated by biology and genetics, I was intrigued with the subject of environmentally induced changes in genetic structure. What I did not know when I began researching the connection between radioactivity and genetic damage was that I would find the probable cause of my own family's battle with cancer and other health problems.

Hailing from Utah, the state known for its Mormon population's healthy lifestyle, my family has been plagued with a number of seemingly unrelated health problems. My grandmother was recently diagnosed as having bone cancer. My mother has suffered from allergies and thyroid problems most of her life. When I was diagnosed at the age of 17 as having Lupus, an auto-immune disease with an unknown cause, I accepted it as being determined by fate. Assuming that our family was just genetically predisposed to such ailments, I never considered any external causes, until now.

During my research on the effects of radiation on human genes, I noticed that there were several references to studies of Mormons in Utah. My curiosity piqued, I studied on. Apparently, the atmospheric bomb tests of the 1950s over Nevada were performed only when winds were blowing away from Las Vegas toward Utah. Subsequent studies of residents of towns with high nuclear fallout showed that various illnesses, especially leukemia, had stricken people who had no family history of them. Of course, it is possible that the emergence of my family's illnesses following the bomb tests is purely coincidental; however, as the evidence against radiation unfolded before me, I became convinced that some sort of connection did exist. I also wondered if the cell damage sustained by people exposed to radiation could be passed on to future generations.

Once met by the public with wild enthusiasm for their potential benefits to humanity, X-rays, radium, nuclear energy, and nuclear arms now generate fear and foreboding as their unforeseen side effects become known. While it is true that radiation occurs naturally from the sun and cosmic rays, these levels are minuscule when compared to the levels that humans are exposed to from fallout, nuclear accidents, medical treatments, consumer products and nuclear waste. Considering that nuclear power has only been available for the past 25 years, we have just begun to see the effects of widespread exposure to radiation.

According to Catherine Caufield, author of *Multiple Exposures: Chronicles of the Radiation Age*, radiation sets off a "chain of physical, chemical, and biological changes that can result in serious illness, genetic defects, or death" (Caufield 10). It is possible for radiation damage to be inherited by offspring because the beta and gamma rays affect the most basic elements of the human body, the genes. Radiation alters the electrical charge of the atoms and molecules that make up our cells. Within the cell lies the DNA, containing the genetic code that controls the function and reproduction of the cell. Genetic mutations, which are basically changes in the composition of the DNA, occur whenever a gene is chemically or structurally changed. When a radioactive particle collides with a cell, the cell usually dies. But when the damaged cell lives, it may function normally for a while until one day, maybe years later, it "goes berserk and manufactures billions of identically damaged cells" (Caldicott, 40). Cancerous tumors are formed this way.

Although mutations do occur naturally in organisms over the course of many generations, research has shown that environmental factors—radiation and chemicals—increase the rates and types of mutations. A prime example of this is the enormous increase in animal deformations in areas surrounding the Chernobyl nuclear plant. Since the accident, 197 deformed calves (some with up to eight legs) and about 200 abnormal piglets have been born. The severity of these deformities is frightening, including animals with no eyes, deformed skulls, and distorted mouths (Toufexis 70). There have also been indications that human babies have been born in the area with gross deformities, but due to the Soviets' strict control over such information, no evidence has been made public. The disaster was followed immediately by an overwhelming rise in human mortality, spanning several countries and continents. Residents of the area continue to experience dramatic rises in cases of thyroid disease, anemia, and cancer as well as a drop in immunity levels.

In *Secret Fallout*, Ernest Sternglass, a well known authority on radiation and health, claims that a human, "especially during the stage of early embryonic life, is hundreds or thousands of times more sensitive to radiation than anyone had ever suspected" (Sternglass 17). Fetuses formed from a mutated egg or sperm cell usually spontaneously abort. This explains the unusually high miscarriage rate for areas surrounding nuclear plants. If the fetus survives pregnancy, Sternglass says that it may turn out to be a "sickly, deformed individual with a shortened life span" (Sternglass 41). Down's Syndrome is caused by a chromosomal abnormality sometimes linked to radiation damage. According to genetic principles, if an affected person reproduces, one half of his or her children will inherit the deformities or illnesses.

In addition to contributing to a higher infant mortality rate and birth defects, the damage sustained by radiation manifests itself as a myriad of diseases including: leukemia; lymphoid, brain, liver and lung cancers; Hodgkin's disease, and central nervous system diseases (Gould 184).

Among Japan's bomb survivors, instances of stomach, ovary, breast, bowel, lung, bone and thyroid cancers doubled. In addition, some researchers have theorized that radiation may have created many new organisms that take advantage of weakened immune systems. In their new book, *Deadly Deceit*, Jay Gould and Benjamin Goldman give an example of this hypothesis. In 1975, after huge releases of radiation from the nearby Millstone nuclear reactor, the town of Old Lyme experienced an outbreak of the previously rare disease now bearing its name, Lyme disease. The disease, which is carried by ticks, had been virtually unknown to humans for several generations. The authors suggest that radiation caused a sudden lethal change in the ticks, so that its bite became lethal to the victim. Gould and Goldman also link the recent emergence of AIDS to radiation by applying this hypothesis to the muta-tion of viruses.

Scientists and government officials have known for several years that radiation causes the mutations I have described, which lead to illness, genetic damage, and death; yet, they continue to allow the unsuspecting public to be exposed to dangerous levels of radiation, and to have their food, water, and air contaminated by it. Ernest Sternglass made the com-ment that because of man's fascination with nuclear power, "it appears that we have unwittingly carried out an experiment with ourselves as guinea pigs on a worldwide scale" (Sternglass 189). Millions of innocent people have paid the price of nuclear power through their suffering and untimely deaths. By inheriting genetic damage caused by radiation, the future generations of mankind may bear the burden as well. A multi-million dollar settlement was awarded to Utah residents who proved that their cancers were caused by radioactive fallout. Whether or not radiation is indeed responsible for my own illness may never be proven. Never-theless, the image I once had of my grandparents' farm in Utah as an unspoiled, safe haven, untouched by the tainted hands of modern evils, has been forever changed in my mind. I must live with the knowledge that, because of atmospheric bomb tests performed before I was born, I am a prime candidate for developing some form of cancer in my lifetime, and if that happens, it won't be because of fate or the will of God, but because of man's unleashing a power he cannot control.

9

Works Consulted

Caldicott, Dr. Helen. "Radiation: Unsafe at Any Level." *Medical Hazards of Radiation Packet*. Boston: Autumn, 1978.
Caufield, Catherine. *Multiple Exposures: Chronicles of the Radiation Age*. New York: Perennial, 1989.
Congress of the United States. *Technologies for Detecting Heritable Mutagens in Human Beings*. Washington: GPO, 1986.
Gould, Jay M., and Benjamin Goldman. *Deadly Deceit: Low-Level Radiation, High-Level Cover-Up*. New York: Four Walls Eight Windows, 1990.
Kotulak, Ronald, and Peter Gorner. "The Gene Is Out of the Bottle." *Chicago Tribune* 8 Apr. 1990: A1.
Science Policy Research Division, Congressional Research Service, Library of Congress. *Genetic Engineering, Human Genetics and Cell Biology: Evolution of Technological Issues*. Supplemental Report III. Washington: GPO, 1980.
Sternglass, Ernest. *Secret Fallout*. New York: McGraw, 1981.
Toufexis, Anastasia. "Legacy of a Disaster." *Time* 9 Apr. 1990: 68–70.
World Health Organization. *Health Aspects of Human Rights*. Geneva: WHO, 1976.

XXXXXXXXXXXXXXXXXXXX **FOR DISCUSSION** XXXXXXXXXXXXXXXXXXXX

1. What is the main point of Kori Quintana's ARGUMENT? How well do you think she makes it? How convinced are you?

2. Is Quintana arguing that nuclear fallout from the fifties directly CAUSED her and her family's diseases? Please explain.

3. In paragraph 3, Quintana asks if cell damage due to radiation can be inherited. What does she conclude?

4. Energy from nuclear power plants emits far less radiation than do nuclear accidents or unprotected nuclear waste. Yet Quintana lumps all of these together in paragraph 4. Is she implying guilt by association? Is it fair or foul, in your opinion, to group these causes together?

XXXXXXXXXXXXXX **STRATEGIES AND STRUCTURES** XXXXXXXXXXXXX

1. INDUCTIVE reasoning examines specific EXAMPLES and particular cases. What's *inductive* about Quintana's reasoning in "The Price of Power"? Does her inductive reasoning appeal more to reason or to the reader's emotions and sense of ethics? Give examples that explain why you think so.

2. Where does Quintana use DEDUCTIVE reasoning in her essay? What conclusions does she draw from this line of ARGUMENT?

3. "X-rays, radium, nuclear energy, and nuclear arms," says Quintana, "now generate fear and foreboding as their unforeseen side effects become known" (4). Is this an appeal to reason, to emotion, or to both? Please explain.

4. Why does Quintana cite all those other writers? How does that affect the persuasive power of her argument?

5. Why does Quintana, in paragraph 9, refer to her grandparents' farm? How does this conclusion recall the opening paragraphs of her essay?

6. Quintana's argument is also, in part, a study in CAUSE AND EFFECT (Chapter 8). According to Quintana, what are the probable causes of her mother's and her grandmother's illnesses? Of her own?

XXXXXXXXXXXXX **WORDS AND FIGURES OF SPEECH** XXXXXXXXXXXXX

1. Quintana uses the word *power* in at least two senses here. What are they, and where does she use them?

2. What is Lupus? What is the connection between the Latin origin of the disease's name and some of the disease's symptoms, including discoloration and disfiguring lesions of the skin?

3. Her grandparents' farm, says Quintana, once seemed to her "untouched by the tainted hands of modern evils" (9). How does this language differ from the prevailing language of her essay—that of paragraph 6, for example? Why might she be using a different type of language here?

XXXXXXXXXXXXXXXXXXXXX **FOR WRITING** XXXXXXXXXXXXXXXXXXXXX

1. Imagine you are entering a debate about nuclear energy. Choose two among the possible audiences you might need to persuade about this issue—a teacher, a grandparent, a senator, a voter, or some other listener. What evidence would you give to appeal to each? Come up with specific EXAMPLES, and explain how you would best approach an ARGUMENT for each type of audience.

2. Coal-burning power plants release far more radiation (in the form of radon) than properly functioning nuclear power plants. Write a persuasive essay *defending* the use of nuclear energy as a safe and economical means of generating power.

ROGER VERHULST

BEING PREPARED IN SUBURBIA

Roger Verhulst is a professional advertising writer. His essays have appeared in various newspapers and magazines, including *Newsweek*, from which this essay on gun control is reprinted. Verhulst was a believer in the effectiveness of gun-control legislation until he acquired a Crossman 760 for a Cub Scout den's target practice. He developed an irrational attachment to his weapon that, he says, is stronger than any rational arguments against owning deadly firearms. "Being Prepared in Suburbia" (1976) is his analysis of what happens to rational debate when emotion triumphs over reason.

XXXXXXXXXXXXXXXXXXXXXXXXXXXXXXXXXXXXXXXXXXXXXXXXXXXXXXXXXXXXX

Gun legislation is dead for another year. As a result, if statistics are any guide, there's every likelihood that a lot of people now living will also be dead before the year is over.   1

There's no point in citing those statistics again; they may prove something, but they're not likely to prompt any concrete action. There is nothing very moving about statistics.   2

What is needed to produce results is passion—and that's where the antigun-control lobby has it all over the rest of us. Those who favor stronger gun legislation—a solid majority of Americans—can't hold a candle to the lovers of guns when it comes to zeal.   3

I had a taste of that passion recently, and I begin to understand something of what it is that fosters in gun libbers such dedicated resolve. Thanks to a bunch of Cub Scouts and an absurd little creature that went bump in the night, I've begun to realize why cold, unemotional tabulations of gun deaths will never lead to effective gun control. It's because of what can happen to people—even sane, rational, firearm-hating people like me—when they get their hands on a genuine, authentic, real-life gun.   4

Until last fall, I had never owned any weapon more lethal than a   5 water pistol. I opposed guns as esthetically repugnant, noisy, essentially churlish devices whose only practical purpose was to blast holes of various sizes in entities that would thereby be rendered less functional than they would otherwise have been. I didn't object merely to guns that killed people; I also objected to guns that killed animals, or shattered windows, or plinked away at discarded beer bottles. Whenever a gun was put to effective use, I insisted, something broke; and it seemed absurd to go through life breaking things.

With arguments such as these, bolstered by assorted threats, I tried to instill holy terror also in my sons. Initially, I imposed an absolute ban on even toy guns. When that didn't work—their determination to possess such toys exceeding by scores of decibels my determination to ban them—I tried substituting lectures on the merits of nonviolence and universal love. Nice try. 6

Then, last fall, I became co-leader of a Cub Scout den here in Grand Rapids, Mich., consisting of half a dozen 9-, 10- and 11-year-old boys. Sharing the leadership responsibilities with me was a kind and gentle man named Mickey Shea, who happens to be extremely fond of outdoor activities—including, of course, hunting. 7

It was in Mickey's basement, in full view of an imposing gun rack, that I yielded to the pressure of pleading Cubbers and agreed to add target shooting to our scheduled activities. (Though I should make it clear that it wasn't Mickey who forced, or even strongly urged, that agreement; it was rather a wish to be accepted by the boys—to be regarded as appropriately adult and masculine—that prompted my decision. I've no one to blame but myself.) 8

So, for the sake of my kids and under the auspices of the Boy Scouts of America, I bought a gun—a Crossman Power Master 760 BB Repeater pump gun, with bolt action, adjustable sight and a satisfying heft. It was capable of putting holes in all sorts of things. 9

A few nights later we got the Cubs together and spent an hour or two aiming and firing at targets taped to paper-filled cardboard cartons. After which I unloaded the gun and locked it in my study, intending to leave it there until future target shoots came along to justify bringing it out again. But a roving opossum that took up residence in our garage for a few cold nights in January undermined my good intentions. 10

We were entertained, at first. We called the kids down to see our   11
visitor perched on the edge of the trash barrel; we recorded the event on
film. We regarded the presence of authentic wild animals in our corner
of suburbia as delightfully diverting.

Almost at once, however, the rat-faced prowler began to make him-   12
self obnoxious. There was the midnight clatter of falling objects, and the
morning-after disarray of strewn garbage. The possum, we decided,
would have to go.

But he proved to be not only an unwelcome but also a recalcitrant   13
guest. It was cold outside, and rather than waddling willingly back
through the open garage door he took refuge behind a pile of scrap lumber; my vigorous thrusts with a broomstick were parried by obstinacy,
and an occasional grunt.

I was cold, too, by now; and tired; and becoming frustrated. Drastic   14
action was indicated; I poured a handful of BB's into the Crossman 760,
pumped it up, pointed the barrel blindly into the woodpile and pulled
the trigger.

Nothing happened. The opossum did not move. Shivering, I went   15
back inside the house, still holding my weapon. I sat down with a drink
and a cigarette to warm up.

With little else to do, I put the gun to my shoulder and aimed it   16
idly at the clock above the fireplace; I aimed it at a light fixture across
the room, pressing gently against the trigger; I aimed it at a row of glasses
behind the bar, imagining the snap and shatter of breaking glass; I aimed
it at my own reflection in the TV set, thinking how absurdly easy it
would be to eliminate television from my life.

The more imaginary targets I selected, the stronger became the urge   17
to shoot—something, anything. The gun extended my potential range of
influence to everyone within sight; I could alter the world around me
without even moving from the couch, simply by pulling the trigger. Gun
in hand, I was bravely prepared to defend myself against any intruder,
man or beast. I felt omnipotent as Zeus,[1] with lightning bolts at my
fingertips.

No wonder, I thought, that people become hooked on guns. This   18
is the feeling that explains their passion, their religious fervor, their

---

[1]Ruler of the Greek gods; lightning was his special weapon.

refusal to yield. It's rooted in the gut, not in the head. And in the recurrent struggle over gun legislation it is no wonder that their stamina exceeds mine.

I can understand that passion because I've felt it in my own gut. 19 I've felt the gun in my hand punch psychic holes in my intellectual convictions. And having felt all that, I do not have much hope that private ownership of deadly weapons will be at all regulated or controlled in the foreseeable future.

XXXXXXXXXXXXXXXXXXXXXX **FOR DISCUSSION** XXXXXXXXXXXXXXXXXXXX

1. According to Roger Verhulst, what is the special appeal of guns to those who own them? In which paragraph does he explain that appeal most explicitly?

2. Verhulst thinks that gun-control legislation is doomed. Why? What is his main reason?

3. Why do you think Verhulst explicitly points out that he came into contact with guns through the Cub Scouts?

4. In paragraph 19, Verhulst says that his gun opened "psychic holes" in his resolve. What does he mean by this? How does this statement confirm his original theory about the appeal of guns?

5. Why is Verhulst's subject especially suited to an appeal to emotion?

XXXXXXXXXXXXXX **STRATEGIES AND STRUCTURES** XXXXXXXXXXXXX

1. Verhulst writes as a "convert," a gun-control supporter who has come reluctantly to understand the appeal of firearms. Does this stance strengthen his ARGUMENT or weaken it, in your opinion? Why?

2. Verhulst dismisses the effectiveness of statistical evidence in paragraphs 1 and 2. On what grounds does he do so? How effective do you think this strategy is?

3. Why do you suppose Verhulst makes himself look foolish, even mean, in the encounter with the possum (10–15)?

4. Far from assuming that a writer stirs emotion in the reader by being emotional, Verhulst comes across as reasonably coolheaded. How does he create this impression? Give specific examples from the text.

5. Who do you think is Verhulst's audience? In which paragraph does he, in effect, DEFINE it? Why is his approach a good one for this particular readership?

6. By telling the story of his conversion, Verhulst uses NARRATIVE to help achieve

his persuasive aim. Where does the narrative begin and end? How appealing and convincing do you find Verhulst's story? Why?

7. As a general rule, do you think ANECDOTES and other narratives appeal more to emotion or to reason? Please explain.

XXXXXXXXXXXX **WORDS AND FIGURES OF SPEECH** XXXXXXXXXXX

1. What are the CONNOTATIONS of "hooked" in paragraph 18?

2. "Holey terror" and "delightfully diverting" represent two different levels of DICTION (6, 11). How would you DEFINE the two levels? Point out other EXAMPLES of each. Why do you think Verhulst mixes them?

3. "Psychic" (19) has two basic meanings. What are they? Which one does Verhulst intend here?

4. Look up five of the following words in your dictionary: "esthetically" (5), "churlish" (5), "decibels" (6), "auspices" (9), "recalcitrant" (13), "obstinacy" (13), "omnipotent" (17), and "fervor" (18).

XXXXXXXXXXXXXXXXXXXXX **FOR WRITING** XXXXXXXXXXXXXXXXXXXXXXX

1. Find an essay online that presents a stance on gun control, and summarize it. How is it the same as or different from Verhulst's?

2. Write a persuasive essay in favor of gun-control legislation on the basis that guns are "esthetically repugnant, noisy, essentially churlish devices" (5).

MEGHAN DAUM

SAFE-SEX LIES

Meghan Daum (b. 1970) is the author of *My Misspent Youth* (2002), a collection of her essays from the *New Yorker*, the *New York Times Book Review, GQ,* and *Vogue,* among others. The subjects that Daum chooses to write about, she says, are "ideas or events that have not only affected me personally but seem to resonate with the culture at large." The subject of "Safe-Sex Lies" (1996) is the AIDS epidemic and its effects upon Daum's own intimate relationships and those of her contemporaries. Although it argues that AIDS awareness has bred a generation of "liars," Daum's essay is more an argument for honesty than an analysis of CAUSE AND EFFECT. As you read, notice how Daum appeals to the reader's emotions and trust. This essay first appeared in the *New York Times Magazine.*

XXXXXXXXXXXXXXXXXXXXXXXXXXXXXXXXXXXXXXXXXXXXXXXXXXXXXXXXXXXXXX

I have been tested for HIV three times. I've gone to clinics and stuck   1
my arm out for those disposable needles, each time forgetting the fear
and nausea that descend upon me before the results come back, those
minutes spent in a publicly financed waiting room staring at a video loop
about "living with" this thing that kills you. These tests have taken place
over five years, and the results have always been negative—not surprisingly in retrospect, since I am not a member of a "high-risk group,"
don't sleep around and don't take pity on heroin-addicted bass players
by going to bed with them in the hopes of being thanked in the liner
notes of their first major independent release. Still, getting tested always
seemed like the thing to do. Despite my demographic profile, despite the
fact that I grew up middle class, attended an elite college and do not
personally know any women or straight men within that demographic
profile who have the AIDS virus, I am terrified of this disease. I went to
a college where condoms and dental dams lay in baskets in dormitory
lobbies, where it seemed incumbent on health service counselors to give

us the straight talk, to tell us never, ever to have sex without condoms unless we wanted to die; that's right, *die*, shrivel overnight, vomit up our futures, pose a threat to others. (And they'd seen it happen, oh, yes, they had.) They gave us pamphlets, didn't quite explain how to use dental dams, told us where we could get tested, threw us more fistfuls of condoms (even some glow-in-the-dark brands, just for variety). This can actually be fun, they said, if only we'd adopt a better attitude.

We're told we can get this disease and we believe it and vow to protect ourselves, and intend (really, truly) to stick by this rule, until we don't because we just can't, because it's just not fair, because our sense of entitlement exceeds our sense of vulnerability. So we blow off precaution again and again, and then we get scared and get tested, and when it comes out O.K., we run out of the clinic, pamphlets in hand, eyes cast upward, promising ourselves we'll never be stupid again. But of course we are stupid, again and again. And the testing is always for the same reasons and with the same results, and soon it becomes more like fibbing about SAT scores ten years after the fact than lying about whether we practice unsafe sex, a lie that sounds like such a breach of contract with ourselves that we might as well be talking about putting a loaded gun under our pillow every night.

Still, I've gone into more than a few relationships with the safest of intentions and discarded them after the fourth or fifth encounter. Perhaps this is a shocking admission, but my hunch is that I'm not the only one doing it. My suspicion is, in fact, that very few of us—"us" being the demographic profile frequently charged with thinking we're immortal, the population accused of being cynical and lazy and weak—have really responded to the AIDS crisis the way the Federal Government and educators would like us to believe. My guess is that we're all but ignoring it and that almost anyone who claims otherwise is lying.

It seems there is a lot of lying going around. One of the main tenets of the safe-sex message is that ageless mantra "you don't know where he's been," meaning that everyone is a potential threat, that we're all either scoundrels or ignoramuses. "He didn't tell me he was shooting drugs," says an HIV-positive woman on a public-service advertisement. Safe-sex "documentaries" on MTV and call-in radio shows on pop stations give us woman after woman whose boyfriend "claimed he loved me but was sleeping around." The message we receive is that trusting anyone is itself an irresponsible act, that having faith in an intimate partner, particularly women in relation to men, is a symptom of such profound naïveté that we're obviously not mature enough to be having sex anyway.

I find this reasoning almost more troubling than the disease itself. 5 It flies in the face of the social order from which I, as someone born in 1970, was supposed to benefit. That this reasoning runs counter to almost any feminist ideology—the ideology that proclaimed, at least back in the seventies, that women should feel free to ask men on dates and wear jeans and have orgasms—is an admission that no AIDS-concerned citizen is willing to make. Two decades after *The Joy of Sex* made sexual pleasure permissible for both sexes and three decades after the pill put a government-approved stamp on premarital sex, we're still told not to trust each other. We've entered a period where mistrust equals responsibility, where fear signifies health.

Since I spent all of the seventies under the age of ten, I've never 6 known a significantly different sexual and social climate. Supposedly this makes it easier to live with the AIDS crisis. Health educators and AIDS activists like to think that people of my generation can be made to unlearn what we never knew, to break the reckless habits we didn't actually form. But what we have learned thoroughly is how not to enjoy ourselves. Just like our mothers, whose adolescences were haunted by the abstract taboo against being "bad" girls, my contemporaries and I are discouraged from doing what feels good. As it did with our mothers, the onus falls largely on the women. We know that it's much easier for women to contract HIV from a man than the other way around. We know that an "unsafe" man generally means someone who has shot drugs or slept with other men, or possibly slept with prostitutes. We find ourselves wondering about these things over dinner dates. We look for any hints of homosexual tendencies, any references to a hypodermic moment. We try to catch him in the lie we've been told he'll tell.

What could be sadder? We're not allowed to believe anyone any- 7 more. And the reason we're not isn't so much because of AIDS but because of the anxiety that ripples around the disease. The information about AIDS that is supposed to produce "awareness" has been subsumed into the aura of style. AIDS awareness has become so much a part of the pop culture that not only is it barely noticeable, it is largely ineffectual. MTV runs programs about safe sex that are barely distinguishable from documentaries about Madonna. A print advertisement for Benetton features a collage of hundreds of tiny photographs of young people, some of whom are shaded with the word AIDS written across their faces. Many are white and blond and have the tousled, moneyed look common to more traditional fashion spreads or even yearbooks from colleges like the one I attended. There is no text other than the company's slogan. There is no explanation of how these faces were chosen, no public statement of whether these people actually have the disease or not. I called Benetton for clarification and was told that the photographs were supposed to represent people from all over the world and that no one was known to be HIV-positive—just as I suspected. The advertisement was a work of art, which meant I could interpret the image any way I liked. This is how the deliverers of the safe-sex message shoot themselves in the foot. Confronted with arty effects instead of actual information, people like me are going to believe what we want to believe, which, of course, is whatever isn't too scary. So we turn the page.

Since I am pretty sure I do not sleep with bisexual men or IV drug users, my main personal concern about AIDS is that men can get the virus from women and subsequently pass it on to other women. According to the Centers for Disease Control's National AIDS Clearinghouse surveillance report, less than three-quarters of 1 percent of white non-Hispanic men with HIV infection contracted the virus through heterosexual sex with a non-IV drug-using woman. (Interestingly, the CDC labels this category as "risk not specified.") But this statistic seems too dry for MTV and campus health brochures, whose eye-catching "sex kills" rhetoric tells us nothing other than to ignore what we don't feel like thinking about. Obviously, there are still too many cases of HIV; there is a deadly risk in certain kinds of sexual behavior and therefore reason to take precautions. But until more people appear on television, look into the camera and tell me that they contracted HIV through heterosexual sex with someone who had no risk factors, I will continue to disregard the message.

Besides, the very sophistication that allows people like me to filter out much of the hype behind music videos, fashion magazines and television talk shows is what we use to block out the safe-sex message. We are not a population that makes personal decisions based on the public service work of a rock star. We're not going to sacrifice the thing we believe we deserve, the experiences we waited for, because Levi Strauss is a major sponsor of MTV's coverage of World AIDS Day.

So the inconsistent behavior continues, as do the confessions among   10
friends and the lies to health care providers during routine exams, because we just can't bear the terrifying lectures that ensue when we confess to not always protecting ourselves. Life in your twenties is fraught not only with financial and professional uncertainty, but also with a specter of death that floats above the pursuit of a sex life. And there is no solution, only the conclusion that invariably finishes the hushed conversations: the whole thing simply "sucks." It's a bummer on a grand scale.

Heterosexuals are receiving vague signals. We're told that if we are   11
sufficiently vigilant, we will probably be all right. We're being told to assume the worst and to not invite disaster by hoping for the best. We're being encouraged to keep our fantasies on a tight rein, otherwise we'll lose control of the whole buggy, and no one can say we weren't warned. So for us AIDS remains a private hell, smoldering beneath intimate conversations among friends and surfacing on those occasional sleepless nights when it occurs to us to wonder about it, upon which that dark hysteria sets in, and those catalogues of whom we've done it with and whom they might have done it with and oh-my-God-I'll-surely-die seem to project themselves onto the ceiling, the way fanged monsters did when we were children. But we fall asleep and then we wake up. And nothing has changed except our willingness to forget about it, which has become the ultimate survival mechanism. What my peers and I are left with is a generalized anxiety, a low-grade fear and anger that resides at the core of everything we do. Our attitudes have been affected by the disease by leaving us scared, but our behavior has stayed largely the same. One result is a corrosion of the soul, a chronic dishonesty and fear that will most likely damage us more than the disease itself. In this world, peace of mind is a utopian concept.

XXXXXXXXXXXXXXXXXXXXX **FOR DISCUSSION** XXXXXXXXXXXXXXXXXXXXX

1. What is Meghan Daum's "demographic profile" (1)? Given that profile, how likely is she (and others with similar profiles) to contract the AIDS virus?

2. According to Daum, most AIDS-awareness programs have become not only "barely noticeable," but "largely ineffectual" (7). Why does she think so? Do you agree or disagree, and why?

3. Why is Daum critical of the Benetton safe-sex campaign (7)? Are you persuaded by her ARGUMENT?

4. To what kind of "sophistication" is Daum referring in paragraph 9? How, according to her, does that sophistication clash with government and / or school safe-sex awareness programs?

5. Why, according to Daum, do she and others of her generation "vow to protect ourselves" and then fail to do so (2)?

6. Daum charges that the "lies" and misinformation her generation has been given about AIDS prevention may do more "damage" than the disease itself (11). What does she mean by "damage"? How persuaded are you by this argument?

XXXXXXXXXXXXXX **STRATEGIES AND STRUCTURES** XXXXXXXXXXXXXX

1. Why do you think Daum begins her complaint against traditional safe-sex awareness programs with her "demographic profile" (1)? Based on this inclusion, who would you say is the primary audience for her ARGUMENTS?

2. What "shocking admission" does Daum make in paragraph 3? Why do you think she makes it?

3. "I find this reasoning almost more troubling than the disease itself," says Daum in paragraph 5. What line of reasoning is she talking about? How does Daum counter: with a logical argument, an appeal to feeling and emotion, or both? Please explain.

4. How does Daum, in paragraph 6, establish her credibility (or lack of it) as an authority on the effect of AIDS awareness upon social and personal relationships?

5. "What could be sadder? We're not allowed to believe anyone anymore" (7). Daum's RHETORICAL QUESTION is an obvious appeal to the reader's emotions. Is the conclusion she draws about not being able to trust anyone based more on emotion or logical reasoning? Please explain.

6. Daum's claim to the reader's sympathy is not so much that she is virtuous, but that she is honest. How does she go about establishing that claim?

7. Daum's argument relies on some CAUSAL ANALYSES. By her reasoning, what are the principal causes of the "corrosion of the soul" (11)?

XXXXXXXXXXXXX **WORDS AND FIGURES OF SPEECH** XXXXXXXXXXXX

1. Demography is the study of the characteristics of human populations. In what ways is Daum's essay a demographic study?

2. What are the CONNOTATIONS of "scoundrels and ignoramuses" in paragraph 4?

3. AIDS is an acronym for Acquired Immune Deficiency Syndrome. What is an *acronym*? What is a *syndrome*?

4. What does Daum COMPARE to a "buggy" in paragraph 11? Why do you think she uses this METAPHOR? Is it effective, in your opinion? Why or why not?

5. What is the effect of Daum's UNDERSTATEMENT in paragraph 1, where she says she doesn't "take pity on heroin-addicted bass players by going to bed with them"?

XXXXXXXXXXXXXXXXXXXX **FOR WRITING** XXXXXXXXXXXXXXXXXXXXXX

1. "Safe-Sex Lies" was first published in the *New York Times Magazine*. Write a letter to the *Times* responding to Daum's argument.

2. Daum raises the question of whether or not "trusting anyone," especially in an intimate relationship, is an act of "profound naïveté" (4). Write a persuasive essay in which you take a clear stand on this issue, and carefully defend your position.

REPLY TO THE U.S. GOVERNMENT

Chief Seattle (1786–1866) was the leader of the Dwamish, Suquamish, and allied Native American tribes living in the region of the city that now bears his name. The Reply printed here purports to be his response to the U.S. government's offer to buy 2 million acres of Indian land in 1854. It is said to have been "translated" by Henry A. Smith, but Smith's earliest published version (on which this one is based) did not appear until 1887. Smith's version bears little resemblance to Chief Seattle's two short speeches, preserved among the documents accompanying the Port Elliott Treaty, which Chief Seattle signed with the government in 1855. Perhaps Smith based his version upon extensive notes from his diary of the event. At any rate, it is a model of the kind of persuasion that wins over an audience because it convinces them that they are listening to the words of an ethical person who is telling the truth.

XXXXXXXXXXXXXXXXXXXXXXXXXXXXXXXXXXXXXXXXXXXXXXXXXXXXXXXXXXXXXXX

Yonder sky that has wept tears of compassion upon my people for centuries untold, and which to us appears changeless and eternal, may change. Today is fair. Tomorrow may be overcast with clouds. My words are like the stars that never change. Whatever Seattle says the great chief at Washington can rely upon with as much certainty as he can upon the return of the sun or the seasons. The White Chief says that Big Chief at Washington sends us greetings of friendship and goodwill. That is kind of him for we know he has little need of our friendship in return. His people are many. They are like the grass that covers vast prairies. My people are few. They resemble the scattering trees of a storm-swept plain. The great, and—I presume—good, White Chief sends us word that he wishes to buy our lands but is willing to allow us enough to live comfortably. This indeed appears just, even generous, for the Red Man no longer has rights that he need respect, and the offer may be wise also, as we are no longer in need of an extensive country. . . . I will not dwell on, nor mourn over, our untimely decay, nor reproach our paleface brothers with hastening it, as we too may have been somewhat to blame.

Youth is impulsive. When our young men grow angry at some real   2
or imaginary wrong, and disfigure their faces with black paint, it denotes that their hearts are black, and then they are often cruel and relentless, and our old men and old women are unable to restrain them. Thus it has ever been. Thus it was when the white men first began to push our forefathers further westward. But let us hope that the hostilities between us may never return. We would have everything to lose and nothing to gain. Revenge by young men is considered gain, even at the cost of their own lives, but old men who stay at home in times of war, and mothers who have sons to lose, know better.

Our good father at Washington—for I presume he is now our father   3
as well as yours, since King George[1] has moved his boundaries further north—our great good father, I say, sends us word that if we do as he desires he will protect us. His brave warriors will be to us a bristling wall of strength, and his wonderful ships of war will fill our harbors so that our ancient enemies far to the northward—the Hydas and Tsimpsians—will cease to frighten our women, children, and old men. Then in reality will he be our father and we his children. But can that ever be? Your God is not our God! Your God loves your people and hates mine. He folds his strong and protecting arms lovingly about the paleface and leads him by the hand as a father leads his infant son—but He has forsaken His red children—if they really are his. Our God, the Great Spirit, seems also to have forsaken us. Your God makes your people wax strong every day. Soon they will fill the land. Our people are ebbing away like a rapidly receding tide that will never return. The white man's God cannot love our people or He would protect them. They seem to be orphans who can look nowhere for help. How then can we be brothers? How can your God become our God and renew our prosperity and awaken in us dreams of returning greatness? If we have a common heavenly father He must be partial—for He came to his paleface children. We never saw Him. He gave you laws but He had no word for His red children whose teeming

[1]George IV, king of England from 1820 to 1830.

multitudes once filled this vast continent as stars fill the firmament. No; we are two distinct races with separate origins and separate destinies. There is little in common between us.

To us the ashes of our ancestors are sacred and their resting place is hallowed ground. You wander far from the graves of your ancestors and seemingly without regret. Your religion was written upon tables of stone by the iron finger of your God so that you could not forget. The Red Man could never comprehend nor remember it. Our religion is the traditions of our ancestors—the dreams of our old men, given them in solemn hours of night by the Great Spirit; and the visions of our sachems; and it is written in the hearts of our people.

Your dead cease to love you and the land of their nativity as soon as they pass the portals of the tomb and wander way beyond the stars. They are soon forgotten and never return. Our dead never forget the beautiful world that gave them being.

Day and night cannot dwell together. The Red man has ever fled the approach of the White Man, as the morning mist flees before the morning sun. However, your proposition seems fair and I think that my people will accept it and will retire to the reservation you offer them. Then we will dwell apart in peace, for the words of the Great White Chief seem to be the words of nature speaking to my people out of dense darkness.

It matters little where we pass the remnant of our days. They will not be many. A few more moons; a few more winters—and not one of the descendants of the mighty hosts that once moved over this broad land or lived in happy homes, protected by the Great Spirit, will remain to mourn over the graves of a people once more powerful and hopeful than yours. But why should I mourn at the untimely fate of my people? Tribe follows tribe, and nation follows nation, like the waves of the sea. It is the order of nature, and regret is useless. Your time of decay may be distant, but it will surely come, for even the White Man whose God walked and talked with him as friend with friend, cannot be exempt from the common destiny. We may be brothers after all. We will see.

We will ponder your proposition, and when we decide we will let you know. But should we accept it, I here and now make this condition that we will not be denied the privilege without molestation of visiting at any time the tombs of our ancestors, friends and children. Every part of this soil is sacred in the estimation of my people. Every hillside, every valley, every plain and grove, has been hallowed by some sad or happy event in days long vanished. . . . The very dust upon which you now stand responds more lovingly to their footsteps than to yours, because it is rich with the blood of our ancestors and our bare feet are conscious of the sympathetic touch. . . . Even the little children who lived here and rejoiced here for a brief season will love these somber solitudes and at eventide they greet shadowy returning spirits. And when the last Red Man shall have perished, and the memory of my tribe shall have become a myth among the White Men, these shores will swarm with the invisible dead of my tribe, and when your children's children think themselves alone in the field, the store, the shop, upon the highway, or in the silence of the pathless woods, they will not be alone. . . . At night when the streets of your cities and villages are silent and you think them deserted, they will throng with the returning hosts that once filled and still love this beautiful land. The White Man will never be alone.

Let him be just and deal kindly with my people, for the dead are not powerless. Dead, did I say? There is no death, only a change of worlds.

9

XXXXXXXXXXXXXXXXXXXX **For Discussion** XXXXXXXXXXXXXXXXXXX

1. Does Chief Seattle appear trustworthy to you in this speech? Why or why not?

2. Why, according to Chief Seattle, did the young men of his tribe paint their faces and go to war (2)? What was their motive, and what was the meaning of their war paint?

3. Why and for what is Chief Seattle appealing to the White Man? What slightly veiled threat does he make in paragraphs 8 and 9 of his speech?

4. Why does the Dwamish chief doubt that the White Man and the Red Man will ever be brothers? In what sense may they prove "brothers after all" (7)?

5. The last paragraph of Chief Seattle's speech sounds similar at first to a Christian denial of death and affirmation of heavenly life. But what does he mean by "a change of worlds" (9)? What other differences does Chief Seattle mention between his religion and the Christianity of the White Man?

6. Chief Seattle refuses to mourn the "untimely fate" of his people or to grant the eternal supremacy of his conquerors (7). Why?

XXXXXXXXXXXXX **STRATEGIES AND STRUCTURES** XXXXXXXXXXXXX

1. How does Chief Seattle establish his authority and trustworthiness in paragraph 1? Give specific EXAMPLES.

2. What personal qualities do you attribute to Chief Seattle after reading his speech? Point out specific statements and phrases that help to characterize him.

3. How does paragraph 2 show Chief Seattle's wisdom?

4. What distinction is Chief Seattle making when he refers to the "great, and—I presume—good, White Chief" (1)? How does making this distinction help to qualify Chief Seattle as a person worthy of appealing to his audience's sense of ethical behavior?

5. The Dwamish chief pays his respects to the Big Chief at Washington. How does Chief Seattle also show that he is not afraid of the Big Chief? Give specific examples from the text.

6. Chief Seattle's appeal also appeals to both ethics and emotion. How and where do the two work together? What particular emotions does his oration speak to?

XXXXXXXXXXXXX **WORDS AND FIGURES OF SPEECH** XXXXXXXXXXXXX

1. The White Man, we are told, is like "the grass that covers vast prairies," and the Native American is like "scattering trees" or like a "receding tide," though he once was like the "stars" (1,3). How do these nature METAPHORS fit in with Chief Seattle's mentions of decay and the cycle of the seasons?

2. What does this metaphor mean: "Day and night cannot dwell together" (6)?

3. In what sense is the translator using the word "sympathetic" when he reports Seattle as saying that "our bare feet are conscious of the sympathetic touch" (8)?

4. What extended ANALOGY does Chief Seattle draw when he DESCRIBES the role of the ideal leader or chief in paragraph 3?

XXXXXXXXXXXXX **FOR WRITING** XXXXXXXXXXXXX

1. A class you want to take is overenrolled, and you have been closed out of it. You go to the instructor for permission to enter the full class, and the instructor asks you to give the reasons why you should be admitted. You figure you have to make the case for yourself as a valuable addition to the class. What ARGU-MENT would you advance?

2. Speaking on behalf of the Big Chief in Washington, compose an appropriate reply to Chief Seattle's speech that might convince him and his tribespeople that they are hearing the words of an ethical person.

CHAPTER TEN

CLASSIC ESSAYS

XXXXXXXXXXXXXXXXXXXXXXXXXXXXXXXXXXXXXXXXXXXXXXXXXXXXXXXXXXXXXXXX

The essays in this chapter are "classics"—timeless EXAMPLES* of good writing from three centuries. What makes them timeless? Jonathan Swift's "A Modest Proposal," for instance, is nearly 275 years old. The speaker is a "projector," a word that in Swift's day meant a person who was full of projects, in this case for ridding Ireland of hunger and poverty. But the issue that Swift addresses is as timely now as it was in the eighteenth century: his well-to-do countrymen, Swift charges—not to mention English landlords and "a very knowing American of my acquaintance"—will do anything for money (9).

E. B. White's nostalgic "Once More to the Lake" is explicitly about time—or, rather, timelessness. When White takes his young son fishing at the quiet lake where he himself had spent so many summers as a boy, a dragonfly lands on the tip of White's rod, and time seems to stand still: "It was the arrival of this fly that convinced me beyond any doubt that everything was as it always had been, that the years were a mirage and that there had been no years" (5). The suspension of time is an illusion, of course, and White's essay ends with the shock we all feel when waking up from a dream that is better than life.

Whether it is White skimming the lake for signs of eternal youth, or the cub pilot, Mark Twain, reading the faces of nature in the Mississippi, or George Orwell looking beneath the surfaces of language itself, these writers distill universal meanings for us, and they invoke people who seem familiar even when they are as exotic as those Joan Didion describes as she takes notes beside the pool at the Beverly Hills Hotel.

What's so good about these essays on timeless themes? The writer

---

*Words printed in SMALL CAPITALS are defined in the Glossary.

of each one has a brilliant command of language and of the fundamental forms and patterns of written discourse. By taking these great essays apart, however, you will find that they are constructed around the same basic strategies and techniques of writing you have been studying in *The Norton Sampler*. All the MODES OF WRITING are here—NARRATION, DESCRIPTION, EXPOSITION, and ARGUMENT—but interwoven as seamlessly as the layers of time in White's essay.

Let's look more closely at Virginia Woolf's influential "The Death of the Moth" as an example of how a great writer combines the basic patterns of writing into a unified whole. These patterns are all the more tightly woven together because Woolf's essay not only makes connections, it is *about* the connectedness of all living things.

As in Annie Dillard's essay on the same subject at the beginning of this book, the eponymous moth gives Woolf's essay a visual and thematic focal point. (*Eponymous*, meaning "name-giving," is not a word you get to use every day.) Thus much of her essay is devoted to a detailed DESCRIPTION of "the present specimen, with his narrow hay-coloured wings, fringed with a tassel" (1). The moth's little world is so limited that we wonder, at first, why Woolf is bothering to show it to us: "He flew vigorously to one corner" of the surrounding window pane and, "after waiting there a second, flew across to the other. What remained for him," Woolf wonders, "but to fly to a third corner and then to a fourth?" (2).

This question is soon answered, and we discover that the physical setting Woolf describes here is the framework of a NARRATIVE. All that remains for the moth is to die. Just when the narrator, deeply absorbed in her book, has forgotten the moth, it catches her attention again: "He was trying to resume his dancing, but seemed either so stiff or so awkward that he could only flutter to the bottom of the window-pane; and when he tried to fly across it he failed" (4).

At first, Woolf's narrator does not realize the significance of what she sees. "Being intent on other matters," she says, "I watched these futile attempts for a time without thinking, unconsciously waiting for him to resume his flight, as one waits for a machine, that has stopped momentarily, to start again without considering the reason for its failure" (4).

Here is the basic plot of Woolf's narrative—not the death of a moth but the narrator's *observation* of the little creature's death. The drama here is a mental one, and Woolf develops it through an EXPOSITION of what the narrator is thinking. Specifically, she uses the techniques of COMPARISON and DEFINITION.

The narrator's window looks out onto the nearby fields and downs, the rolling grassy hills near where men and horses are to be seen plowing under the remains of the harvest to make way for winter. It is mid-September. Above the downs the "rooks" (1), or blackbirds, are rising and falling in the air. What could all this "vigour" possibly have to do with the frail moth (1)? The idea of a connection rises in the narrator's mind, and she makes a direct comparison between the moth and the out-side world: "The same energy which inspired the rooks, the ploughmen, the horses, and even, it seemed, the lean bare-backed downs, sent the moth fluttering from side to side of his square of the window-pane" (2).

That energy is "pure life" (3). But what is life, essentially? Woolf's narrator can now answer this momentous question because she has made the connection between the moth and the scene outside her window: "It was as if someone had taken a tiny bead of pure life and decking it as lightly as possible with down and feathers, had set it dancing and zig-zagging to show us the true nature of life" (3).

Life is to be DEFINED, at bottom, as motion, animation, and when that motion ceases, that is death: "One could only watch the extraordi-nary efforts made by those tiny legs against an oncoming doom which could, had it chosen, have submerged an entire city, not merely a city, but masses of human beings; nothing, I knew, had any chance against death" (5). (This essay was written shortly before Woolf's suicide by drowning.)

Woolf's essay, then, is a DESCRIPTION of the moth and the downs, a NARRATIVE about the woman watching them, and an EXPOSITION on the nature of life and death. It is also an ARGUMENT. Having defined life, Woolf subtly makes the case for how it should be lived. If a mere moth, a "tiny bead of pure life," expends its little energy "dancing and zigzag-ging" to the fullest extent that its meager compass will allow (3), then the woman musing aloud to herself on this "pleasant morning, mid-September, mild, benignant, yet with a keener breath than that of the summer months" (1), should perhaps convince herself (and us) to do likewise.

To reduce Woolf's subtle essay to another moth-to-the-flame message about being inspired by life or making hay while the sun shines, however, would kill it. The meaning of a complex piece of writing is not to be extracted like pulling a thread from a tapestry. We can dissect a great essay into its constituent parts, but its meaning derives from the essay as a whole—from all the MODES OF WRITING working together. Keep this lesson in mind as you study the other fine specimens in this chapter.

JONATHAN SWIFT

A MODEST PROPOSAL

Jonathan Swift (1667–1745) was born in Ireland and educated at Trinity College, Dublin, where he was censured for breaking the rules of discipline, graduating only by "special grace." He was ordained as a clergyman in the Anglican Church in 1694 and became dean of St. Patrick's, Dublin, in 1713. Swift's SATIRES in prose and verse, including *Gulliver's Travels* (1726), addressed three main issues: political relations between England and Ireland; Irish social questions; and matters of church doctrine. Swift's best-known essay was published in 1729 under the full title "A Modest Proposal For Preventing the Children of poor People in Ireland, from being a Burden to their Parents or Country; and for making them beneficial to the Publick." Using IRONY as his weapon, Swift pours into the essay his deep contempt for materialism and for logic without compassion.

XXXXXXXXXXXXXXXXXXXXXXXXXXXXXXXXXXXXXXXXXXXXXXXXXXXXXXXXXXXXX

It is a melancholy object to those who walk through this great town[1] or travel in the country, when they see the streets, the roads, and cabin doors, crowded with beggars of the female sex, followed by three, four, or six children, all in rags and importuning every passenger for an alms. These mothers, instead of being able to work for their honest livelihood, are forced to employ all their time in strolling to beg sustenance for their helpless infants, who, as they grow up, either turn thieves for want of work, or leave their dear native country to fight for the Pretender in Spain, or sell themselves to the Barbadoes.[2]

1

[1]Dublin, capital city of Ireland.

[2]The pretender to the throne of England was James Francis Edward Stuart (1688–1766), son of the deposed James II. Barbados is an island in the West Indies.

I think it is agreed by all parties that this prodigious number of   2
children in the arms, or on the backs, or at the heels of their mothers,
and frequently of their fathers, is in the present deplorable state of the
kingdom a very great additional grievance; and therefore whoever could
find out a fair, cheap, and easy method of making these children sound,
useful members of the commonwealth would deserve so well of the public
as to have his statue set up for a preserver of the nation.

But my intention is very far from being confined to provide only   3
for the children of professed beggars; it is of a much greater extent, and
shall take in the whole number of infants at a certain age who are born
of parents in effect as little able to support them as those who demand
our charity in the streets.

As to my own part, having turned my thoughts for many years   4
upon this important subject and maturely weighed the several schemes
of other projectors,[3] I have always found them grossly mistaken in their
computation. It is true, a child just dropped from its dam may be supported by her milk for a solar year, with little other nourishment; at most
not above the value of two shillings,[4] which the mother may certainly
get, or the value in scraps, by her lawful occupation of begging; and it
is exactly at one year old that I propose to provide for them in such a
manner as instead of being a charge upon their parents or the parish, or
wanting food and raiment for the rest of their lives, they shall on the
contrary contribute to the feeding, and partly to the clothing, of many
thousands.

There is likewise another great advantage in my scheme, that it will   5
prevent those voluntary abortions, and that horrid practice of women
murdering their bastard children, alas, too frequent among us, sacrificing
the poor innocent babes, I doubt, more to avoid the expense than the
shame, which would move tears and pity in the most savage and inhuman
breast.

The number of souls in this kingdom being usually reckoned one   6
million and a half, of these I calculate there may be about two hundred

---

[3]Men whose heads were full of foolish schemes or projects.

[4]The British pound sterling was made up of twenty shillings; five shillings made a crown.

thousand couple whose wives are breeders; from which number I subtract thirty thousand couples who are able to maintain their own children, although I apprehend there cannot be so many under the present distress of the kingdom; but this being granted, there will remain an hundred and seventy thousand breeders. I again subtract fifty thousand for those women who miscarry, or whose children die by accident or disease within the year. There only remain an hundred and twenty thousand children of poor parents annually born. The question therefore is, how this number shall be reared and provided for, which, as I have already said, under the present situation of affairs, is utterly impossible by all the methods hitherto proposed. For we can neither employ them in handicraft or agriculture; we neither build houses (I mean in the country) nor cultivate land. They can very seldom pick up a livelihood by stealing till they arrive at six years old, except where they are of towardly parts,[5] although I confess they learn the rudiments much earlier, during which time they can however be looked upon only as probationers, as I have been informed by a principal gentleman in the county of Cavan, who protested to me that he never knew above one or two instances under the age of six, even in a part of the kingdom so renowned for the quickest proficiency in that art.

I am assured by our merchants that a boy or a girl before twelve years old is no salable commodity; and even when they come to this age they will not yield above three pounds, or three pounds and half a crown at most on the Exchange; which cannot turn to account either to the parents or the kingdom, the charge of nutriment and rags having been at least four times that value.

I shall now therefore humbly propose my own thoughts, which I hope will not be liable to the least objection.

I have been assured by a very knowing American of my acquaintance in London, that a young healthy child well nursed is at a year old a most delicious, nourishing, and wholesome food, whether stewed, roasted, baked, or boiled; and I make no doubt that it will equally serve in a fricassee or a ragout.

[5]Having natural ability.

I do therefore humbly offer it to public consideration that of the   10
hundred and twenty thousand children, already computed, twenty thousand may be reserved for breed, whereof only one fourth part to be males,
which is more than we allow to sheep, black cattle, or swine; and my
reason is that these children are seldom the fruits of marriage, a circum-
stance not much regarded by our savages, therefore one male will be
sufficient to serve four females. That the remaining hundred thousand
may at a year old be offered in sale to the persons of quality and fortune
through the kingdom, always advising the mother to let them suck plentifully in the last month, so as to render them plump and fat for a good
table. A child will make two dishes at an entertainment for friends; and
when the family dines alone, the fore or hind quarter will make a reasonable dish, and seasoned with a little pepper or salt will be very good
boiled on the fourth day, especially in winter.

I have reckoned upon a medium that a child just born will weigh   11
twelve pounds, and in a solar year if tolerably nursed increaseth to
twenty-eight pounds.

I grant this food will be somewhat dear, and therefore very proper   12
for landlords, who, as they have already devoured most of the parents,
seem to have the best title to the children.

Infant's flesh will be in season throughout the year, but more plen-   13
tiful in March, and a little before and after. For we are told by a grave
author, an eminent French physician,[6] that fish being a prolific diet, there
are more children born in Roman Catholic countries about nine months
after Lent than at any other season; therefore, reckoning a year after Lent,
the markets will be more glutted than usual, because the number of
popish infants is at least three to one in this kingdom; and therefore it
will have one other collateral advantage, by lessening the number of
Papists among us.

I have already computed the charge of nursing a beggar's child (in   14
which list I reckon all cottagers, laborers, and four fifths of the farmers)
to be about two shillings per annum, rags included; and I believe no
gentleman would repine to give ten shillings for the carcass of a good fat

[6]François Rabelais (1494?–1553), French satirist.

child, which, as I have said, will make four dishes of excellent nutritive meat, when he hath only some particular friend or his own family to dine with him. Thus the squire will learn to be a good landlord, and grow popular among the tenants; the mother will have eight shillings net profit, and be fit for work till she produces another child.

Those who are more thrifty (as I must confess the times require) may flay the carcass; the skin of which artificially[7] dressed will make admirable gloves for ladies, and summer boots for fine gentlemen. 15

As to our city of Dublin, shambles[8] may be appointed for this purpose in the most convenient parts of it, and butchers we may be assured will not be wanting; although I rather recommend buying the children alive, and dressing them hot from the knife as we do roasting pigs. 16

A very worthy person, a true lover of his country, and whose virtues I highly esteem, was lately pleased in discoursing on this matter to offer a refinement upon my scheme. He said that many gentlemen of this kingdom, having of late destroyed their deer, he conceived that the want of venison might be well supplied by the bodies of young lads and maidens, not exceeding fourteen years of age nor under twelve, so great a number of both sexes in every country being now ready to starve for want of work and service; and these to be disposed of by their parents, if alive, or otherwise by their nearest relations. But with due deference to so excellent a friend and so deserving a patriot, I cannot be altogether in his sentiments; for as to the males, my American acquaintance assured me from frequent experience that their flesh was generally tough and lean, like that of our schoolboys, by continual exercise, and their taste disagreeable; and to fatten them would not answer the charge. Then as to the females, it would, I think with humble submission, be a loss to the public, because they soon would become breeders themselves: and besides, it is not improbable that some scrupulous people might be apt to censure such a practice (although indeed very unjustly) as a little bordering upon cruelty; which, I confess, hath always been with me the strongest objection against any project, how well 'soever intended. 17

[7]Skillfully, artfully.

[8]Slaughterhouses.

But in order to justify my friend, he confessed that this expedient   18
was put into his head by the famous Psalmanazar,[9] a native of the island
Formosa, who came from thence to London above twenty years ago, and
in conversation told my friend that in his country when any young person
happened to be put to death, the executioner sold the carcass to persons
of quality as a prime dainty; and that in his time the body of a plump
girl of fifteen, who was crucified for an attempt to poison the emperor,
was sold to his Imperial Majesty's prime minister of state, and other great
mandarins of the court, in joints from the gibbet, at four hundred crowns.
Neither indeed can I deny that if the same use were made of several
plump young girls in this town, who without one single groat to their
fortunes cannot stir abroad without a chair, and appear at the playhouse
and assemblies in foreign fineries which they never will pay for, the kingdom would not be the worse.

Some persons of a desponding spirit are in great concern about that   19
vast number of poor people who are aged, diseased, or maimed, and I
have been desired to employ my thoughts what course may be taken to
ease the nation of so grievous an encumbrance. But I am not in the least
pain upon that matter, because it is very well known that they are every
day dying and rotting by cold and famine, and filth and vermin, as fast
as can be reasonably expected. And as to the younger laborers, they are
now in almost as hopeful a condition. They cannot get work, and consequently pine away for want of nourishment to a degree that if at any
time they are accidentally hired to common labor, they have not strength
to perform it; and thus the country and themselves are happily delivered
from the evils to come.

I have too long digressed, and therefore shall return to my subject.   20
I think the advantages by the proposal which I have made are obvious
and many, as well as of the highest importance.

For first, as I have already observed, it would greatly lessen the   21
number of Papists, with whom we are yearly overrun, being the principal
breeders of the nation as well as our most dangerous enemies; and who

---

[9]George Psalmanazar (1679?–1763), a Frenchman, fooled English society for several years
by masquerading as a pagan Formosan.

stay at home on purpose to deliver the kingdom to the Pretender, hoping to take their advantage by the absence of so many good Protestants, who have chosen rather to leave their country than stay at home and pay tithes against their conscience to an Episcopal curate.[10]

Secondly, the poorer tenants will have something valuable of their own, which by law may be made liable to distress, and help to pay their landlord's rent, their corn and cattle being already seized and money a thing unknown.

22

Thirdly, whereas the maintenance of an hundred thousand children, from two years old and upward, cannot be computed at less than ten shillings a piece per annum, the nation's stock will be thereby increased fifty thousand pounds per annum, besides the profit of a new dish introduced to the tables of all gentlemen of fortune in the kingdom who have any refinement in taste. And the money will circulate among ourselves, the goods being entirely of our own growth and manufacture.

23

Fourthly, the constant breeders, besides the gain of eight shillings sterling per annum by the sale of their children, will be rid of the charge of maintaining them after the first year.

24

Fifthly, this food would likewise bring great custom to taverns, where the vintners will certainly be so prudent as to procure the best receipts for dressing it to perfection, and consequently have their houses frequented by all the fine gentlemen, who justly value themselves upon their knowledge in good eating; and a skillful cook, who understands how to oblige his guests, will contrive to make it as expensive as they please.

25

Sixthly, this would be a great inducement to marriage, which all wise nations have either encouraged by rewards or enforced by laws and penalties. It would increase the care and tenderness of mothers toward their children, when they were sure of a settlement for life to the poor babes, provided in some sort by the public, to their annual profit instead of expense. We should see an honest emulation among the married women, which of them could bring the fattest child to the market. Men would become as fond of their wifes during the time of their pregnancy

26

---

[10]Swift blamed much of Ireland's poverty upon large landowners who avoided church tithes by living (and spending their money) abroad.

as they are now of their mares in foal, their cows in calf, or sows when they are ready to farrow; nor offer to beat or kick them (as is too frequent a practice) for fear of a miscarriage.

Many other advantages might be enumerated. For instance, the addition of some thousand carcasses in our exportation of barreled beef, the propagation of swine's flesh, and improvement in the art of making good bacon, so much wanted among us by the great destruction of pigs, too frequent at our tables, which are no way comparable in taste or magnificence to a well-grown, fat, yearling child, which roasted whole will make a considerable figure at a lord mayor's feast or any other public entertainment. But this and many others I omit, being studious of brevity.

Supposing that one thousand families in this city would be constant customers for infants' flesh, besides others who might have it at merry meetings, particularly weddings and christenings, I compute that Dublin would take off annually about twenty thousand carcasses, and the rest of the kingdom (where probably they will be sold somewhat cheaper) the remaining eighty thousand.

I can think of no one objection that will possibly be raised against this proposal, unless it should be urged that the number of people will be thereby much lessened in the kingdom. This I freely own, and it was indeed one principal design in offering it to the world. I desire the reader will observe, that I calculate my remedy for this one individual kingdom of Ireland and for no other that ever was, is, or I think ever can be upon earth. Therefore let no man talk to me of other expedients:[11] of taxing our absentees at five shillings a pound: of using neither clothes nor household furniture except what is of our own growth and manufacture: of utterly rejecting the materials and instruments that promote foreign luxury: of curing the expensiveness of pride, vanity, idleness, and gaming in our women: of introducing a vein of parsimony, prudence, and temperance: of learning to love our country, in the want of which we differ even from Laplanders and the inhabitants of Topinamboo:[12] of quitting our animosities and factions, nor acting any longer like the Jews, who

27

28

29

[11]The following are all measures that Swift himself proposed in various pamphlets.
[12]In Brazil.

were murdering one another at the very moment their city[13] was taken: of being a little cautious not to sell our country and conscience for nothing: of teaching landlords to have at least one degree of mercy toward their tenants: lastly, of putting a spirit of honesty, industry, and skill into our shopkeepers; who, if a resolution could now be taken to buy only our native goods, would immediately unite to cheat and exact upon us in the price, the measure, and the goodness, nor could ever yet be brought to make one fair proposal of just dealing, though often and earnestly invited to it.

Therefore I repeat, let no man talk to me of these and the like 30 expedients, till he hath at least some glimpse of hope that there will ever be some hearty and sincere attempt to put them in practice.

But as to myself, having been wearied out for many years with 31 offering vain, idle, visionary thoughts, and at length utterly despairing of success, I fortunately fell upon this proposal, which, as it is wholly new, so it hath something solid and real, of no expense and little trouble, full in our own power, and whereby we can incur no danger in disobliging England. For this kind of commodity will not bear exportation, the flesh being of too tender a consistence to admit a long continuance in salt, although perhaps I could name a country[14] which would be glad to eat up our whole nation without it.

After all, I am not so violently bent upon my own opinion as to 32 reject any offer proposed by wise men, which shall be found equally innocent, cheap, easy, and effectual. But before something of that kind shall be advanced in contradiction to my scheme, and offering a better, I desire the author or authors will be pleased maturely to consider two points. First, as things now stand, how they will be able to find food and raiment for an hundred thousand useless mouths and backs. And secondly, there being a round million of creatures in human figure throughout this kingdom, whose sole subsistence put into a common stock would leave them in debt two millions of pounds sterling, adding those who are beggars by profession to the bulk of farmers, cottagers, and laborers, with

[13]Jerusalem, sacked by the Romans in A.D. 70.
[14]England.

their wives and children who are beggars in effect; I desire those politicians who dislike my overture, and may perhaps be so bold to attempt an answer, that they will first ask the parents of these mortals whether they would not at this day think it a great happiness to have been sold for food at a year old in the manner I prescribe, and thereby have avoided such a perpetual scene of misfortunes as they have since gone through by the oppression of landlords, the impossibility of paying rent without money or trade, the want of common sustenance, with neither house nor clothes to cover them from the inclemencies of the weather, and the most inevitable prospect of entailing the like or greater miseries upon their breed forever.

I profess, in the sincerity of my heart, that I have not the least   33
personal interest in endeavoring to promote this necessary work, having no other motive than the public good of my country, by advancing our trade, providing for infants, relieving the poor, and giving some pleasure to the rich. I have no children by which I can propose to get a single penny; the youngest being nine years old, and my wife past childbearing.

ⵝⵝⵝⵝⵝⵝⵝⵝⵝⵝⵝⵝ UNDERSTANDING THE WHOLE ESSAY ⵝⵝⵝⵝⵝⵝⵝⵝⵝⵝⵝⵝ

1. Swift's essay is celebrated for its IRONY, which is sometimes misdefined as saying the opposite of what is meant. But Swift is not really arguing that the people of Ireland should *not* eat children. What *is* he arguing? (Clue: see paragraph 29.) How would you define IRONY based on this example?

2. SATIRE is writing that exposes vice and wrongdoing to ridicule for the purpose of correcting them. Who are the wrongdoers addressed in Swift's great satire?

3. Swift's projector offers what he considers a serious solution to a serious problem. How would you DESCRIBE his personality and TONE of voice? How does his presence contribute to Swift's irony throughout the essay? Give specific examples from the text.

4. "A Modest Proposal" uses both PROCESS ANALYSIS (how to solve Ireland's economic woes) and CAUSE AND EFFECT (the causes of Ireland's poverty and moral condition; the effects of the proposed "improvements"). How do these two MODES OF WRITING work together to support the projector's logical argument?

5. Swift's persona is the soul of reason, yet what he proposes is so horrible and bizarre that any reader, except perhaps Hannibal Lecter, would reject it. Why do you think Swift resorts to the METAPHOR of cannibalism? How does it help him to critique arguments that depend on pure reason, even when the situations they address are truly desperate?

GEORGE ORWELL

POLITICS AND THE ENGLISH LANGUAGE

George Orwell is the pen name of Eric Arthur Blair (1903–1950), a British novelist and essayist born in Bengal, India. After attending school in England, Blair served with the Indian Imperial Police in Burma from 1922 to 1927. He also served briefly in the Spanish Civil War, was wounded, and afterward settled in Hertfordshire, England. A brilliant political satirist, Orwell is best known for *Animal Farm* (1945) and *Nineteen Eighty-Four* (1949), both attacks on totalitarianism. "Politics and the English Language" (1946) is a logical appeal—based on the premise that language is "an instrument which we shape for our own purposes" (1)—for the responsible use of language, especially in political writing and speech making.

xxxxxxxxxxxxxxxxxxxxxxxxxxxxxxxxxxxxxxxxxxxxxxxxxxxxxxxxxxxxxxxxxxxx

Most people who bother with the matter at all would admit that the English language is in a bad way, but it is generally assumed that we cannot by conscious action do anything about it. Our civilization is decadent and our language—so the argument runs—must inevitably share in the general collapse. It follows that any struggle against the abuse of language is a sentimental archaism, like preferring candles to electric light or hansom cabs to aeroplanes. Underneath this lies the half-conscious belief that language is a natural growth and not an instrument which we shape for our own purposes.

Now, it is clear that the decline of a language must ultimately have political and economic causes: it is not due simply to the bad influence of this or that individual writer. But an effect can become a cause, reinforcing the original cause and producing the same effect in an intensified form, and so on indefinitely. A man may take to drink because he feels himself to be a failure, and then fail all the more completely because he drinks. It is rather the same thing that is happening to the English language. It becomes ugly and inaccurate because our thoughts are foolish, but the slovenliness of our language makes it easier for us to have foolish thoughts. The point is that the process is reversible. Modern English, especially written English, is full of bad habits which spread by imitation and which can be avoided if one is willing to take the necessary trouble. If one gets rid of these habits one can think more clearly, and to think clearly is a necessary first step towards political regeneration: so that the fight against bad English is not frivolous and is not the exclusive concern of professional writers. I will come back to this presently, and I hope that by that time the meaning of what I have said here will have become clearer. Meanwhile, here are five specimens of the English language as it is now habitually written.

These five passages have not been picked out because they are especially bad—I could have quoted far worse if I had chosen—but because they illustrate various of the mental vices from which we now suffer. They are a little below the average, but are fairly representative samples. I number them so that I can refer back to them when necessary: 3

1. I am not, indeed, sure whether it is not true to say that the Milton who once seemed not unlike a seventeenth-century Shelley had not become, out of an experience ever more bitter in each year, more alien [sic] to the founder of that Jesuit sect which nothing could induce him to tolerate.

Professor Harold Laski (Essay in *Freedom of Expression*)

2. Above all, we cannot play ducks and drakes with a native battery of idioms which prescribes such egregious collocations of vocables as the Basic *put up with* for *tolerate* or *put at a loss* for *bewilder*.

Professor Lancelot Hogben (*Interglossa*)

3. On the one side we have the free personality: by definition it is not neurotic, for it has neither conflict nor dream. Its desires, such as they are, are transparent, for they are just what institutional approval keeps in the forefront of consciousness; another institutional pattern would alter their number and intensity; there is little in them that is natural, irreducible, or culturally

dangerous. But *on the other side*, the social bond itself is nothing but the mutual reflection of these self-secure integrities. Recall the definition of love. Is not this the very picture of a small academic? Where is there a place in this hall of mirrors for either personality or fraternity?

Essay on psychology in *Politics* (New York)

4. All the 'best people' from the gentlemen's clubs, and all the frantic fascist captains, united in common hatred of Socialism and bestial horror of the rising tide of the mass revolutionary movement, have turned to acts of provocation, to foul incendiarism, to medieval legends of poisoned wells, to legalize their own destruction of proletarian organizations, and rouse the agitated petty-bourgeoisie to chauvinistic fervour on behalf of the fight against the revolutionary way out of the crisis.

Communist pamphlet

5. If a new spirit is to be infused into this old country, there is one thorny and contentious reform which must be tackled, and that is the humanization and galvinization of the B.B.C. Timidity here will bespeak cancer and atrophy of the soul. The heart of Britain may be sound and of strong beat, for instance, but the British lion's roar at present is like that of Bottom in Shakespeare's *Midsummer Night's Dream*—as gentle as any sucking dove. A virile new Britain cannot continue indefinitely to be traduced in the eyes, or rather ears, of the world by the effete languors of Langham Place, brazenly masquerading as 'standard English'. When the Voice of Britain is heard at nine o'clock, better far and infinitely less ludicrous to hear aitches honestly dropped than the present priggish, inflated, inhibited, schoolma'amish arch braying of blameless bashful mewing maidens!

Letter in *Tribune*

Each of these passages has faults of its own, but, quite apart from avoidable ugliness, two qualities are common to all of them. The first is staleness of imagery: the other is lack of precision. The writer either has a meaning and cannot express it, or he inadvertently says something else, or he is almost indifferent as to whether his words mean anything or not. This mixture of vagueness and sheer incompetence is the most marked characteristic of modern English prose, and especially of any kind of political writing. As soon as certain topics are raised, the concrete melts into the abstract and no one seems able to think of turns of speech that are not hackneyed: prose consists less and less of *words* chosen for the sake of their meaning, and more and more of *phrases* tacked together like the sections of a prefabricated hen-house. I list below, with notes and examples, various of the tricks by means of which the work of prose-construction is habitually dodged:

Dying Metaphors

A newly invented metaphor assists thought by evoking a visual image, while on the other hand a metaphor which is technically "dead" (e.g. *iron resolution*) has in effect reverted to being an ordinary word and can generally be used without loss of vividness. But in between these two classes there is a huge dump of worn-out metaphors which have lost all evocative power and are merely used because they save people the trouble of inventing phrases for themselves. Examples are *Ring the changes on, take up the cudgels for, toe the line, ride roughshod over, stand shoulder to shoulder with, play into the hands of, no axe to grind, grist to the mill, fishing in troubled waters, on the order of the day, Achilles' heel, swan song, hotbed.* Many of these are used without knowledge of their meaning (what is a "rift", for instance?), and incompatible metaphors are frequently mixed, a sure sign that the writer is not interested in what he is saying. Some metaphors now current have been twisted out of their original meaning without those who use them even being aware of the fact. For example, *toe the line* is sometimes written *tow the line*. Another example is *the hammer and the anvil*, now always used with the implication that the anvil gets the worst of it. In real life it is always the anvil that breaks the hammer, never the other way about: a writer who stopped to think what he was saying would be aware of this, and would avoid perverting the original phrase.

Operators or Verbal False Limbs

These save the trouble of picking out appropriate verbs and nouns, and at the same time pad each sentence with extra syllables which give it an appearance of symmetry. Characteristic phrases are: *render inoperative, militate against, make contact with, be subjected to, give rise to, give grounds for, have the effect of, play a leading part (role) in, make itself felt, take effect, exhibit a tendency to, serve the purpose of, etc., etc.* The keynote is the elimination of simple verbs. Instead of being a single word, such as *break, stop, spoil, mend, kill,* a verb becomes a *phrase,* made up of a noun or adjective tacked on to some general-purposes verb such as *prove, serve, form, play, render.* In addition, the passive voice is wherever possible used in preference to the active, and noun constructions are used instead of gerunds (*by examination of* instead of *by examining*). The range of verbs is further cut down by means of the *-ize* and *de-* formation, and the banal statements are given an appearance of profundity by means of the *not un-* formation. Simple conjunctions and prepositions are replaced by such phrases as *with respect to, having regard to, the fact that, by dint of, in view of, in the interests of, on the hypothesis that;* and the ends of sentences are saved from anticlimax by such resounding commonplaces as *greatly to be desired, cannot be left out of account, a development to be expected in the near future, deserving of serious consideration, brought to a satisfactory conclusion,* and so on and so forth.

Pretentious Diction

Words like *phenomenon, element, individual* (as noun), *objective, categorical, effective, virtual, basic, primary, promote, constitute, exhibit, exploit, utilize, eliminate, liquidate,* are used to dress up simple statements and give an air of scientific impartiality to biased judgments. Adjectives like *epoch-making, epic, historic, unforgettable, triumphant, age-old, inevitable, inexorable, veritable,* are used to dignify the sordid processes of international politics, while writing that aims at glorifying war usually takes on an archaic colour, its characteristic words being: *realm, throne, chariot, mailed fist, trident, sword shield, buckler, banner, jackboot, clarion.* Foreign words and expressions such as *cul de sac, ancien régime, deus ex machina, mutatis mutandis, status quo, gleichschaltung, weltanschauung* are used to give an air of culture and elegance. Except for the useful abbreviations *i.e., e.g.,* and *etc.,* there is no real need for any of the hundreds of foreign phrases now current in English. Bad writers, and especially scientific, political and sociological writers, are nearly always haunted by the notion that Latin or Greek words are grander than Saxon ones, and unnecessary words like *expedite, ameliorate, predict, extraneous, deracinated, clandestine, subaqueous* and hundreds of others constantly gain ground from their Anglo-Saxon opposite numbers.[1] The jargon peculiar to Marxist writing (*hyena, hangman, cannibal, petty bourgeois, these gentry, lacquey, flunkey, mad dog, White Guard,* etc.) consists largely of words and phrases translated from Russian, German or French; but the normal way of coining a new word is to use a Latin or Greek root with the appropriate affix and, where necessary, the- *ize* formation. It is often easier to make up words of this kind (*deregionalize, impermissible, extramarital, nonfragmentatory* and so forth) than to think up the English words that will cover one's meaning. The result, in general, is an increase in slovenliness and vagueness.

Meaningless Words

In certain kinds of writing, particularly in art criticism and literary criticism, it is normal to come across long passages which are almost completely lacking in meaning.[2] Words like *romantic, plastic, values, human, dead, sentimental, natural, vitality,* as used in art criticism, are strictly meaningless in the sense that they not only do not point to any discoverable object, but are hardly ever expected to do so by the reader. When one critic writes, "The outstanding feature of Mr. X's work is its living quality", while another writes, "The immediately striking thing about

[1] An interesting illustration of this is the way in which the English flower names which were in use till very recently are being ousted by Greek ones, *snapdragon* becoming *antirrhinum, forget-me-not* becoming *myosotis,* etc. It is hard to see any practical reason for this change of fashion: it is probably due to an instinctive turning-away from the more homely word and a vague feeling that the Greek word is scientific [Orwell's note].

[2] Example: "Comfort's catholicity of perception and image, strangely Whitmanesque in range, almost the exact opposite in aesthetic compulsion, continues to evoke that trembling atmospheric accumulative hinting at a cruel, an inexorably serene timelessness . . . Wrey Gardiner scores by aiming at simple bull's-eyes with precision. Only they are not so simple, and through this contented sadness runs more than the surface bittersweet of resignation" (*Poetry Quarterly*) [Orwell's note].

Mr. X's work is its peculiar deadness", the reader accepts this as a simple difference of opinion. If words like *black* and *white* were involved, instead of the jargon words *dead* and *living*, he would see at once that language was being used in an improper way. Many political words are similarly abused. The word *Fascism* has now no meaning except in so far as it signifies "something not desirable". The words *democracy, socialism, freedom, patriotic, realistic, justice,* have each of them several different meanings which cannot be reconciled with one another. In the case of a word like *democracy*, not only is there no agreed definition, but the attempt to make one is resisted from all sides. It is almost universally felt that when we call a country democratic we are praising it: consequently the defenders of every kind of régime claim that it is a democracy, and fear that they might have to stop using the word if it were tied down to any one meaning. Words of this kind are often used in a consciously dishonest way. That is, the person who uses them has his own private definition, but allows his hearer to think he means something quite different. Statements like *Marshal Pétain was a true patriot, The Soviet Press is the freest in the world, The Catholic Church is opposed to persecution,* are almost always made with intent to deceive. Other words used in variable meanings, in most cases more or less dishonestly, are: *class, totalitarian, science, progressive, reactionary, bourgeois, equality.*

Now that I have made this catalogue of swindles and perversions, let me give another example of the kind of writing that they lead to. This time it must of its nature be an imaginary one. I am going to translate a passage of good English into modern English of the worst sort. Here is a well-known verse from *Ecclesiastes*:

9

> I returned and saw under the sun, that the race is not to the swift, nor the battle to the strong, neither yet bread to the wise, nor yet riches to men of understanding, nor yet favour to men of skill; but time and chance happeneth to them all.

Here it is in modern English:

10

> Objective consideration of contemporary phenomena compels the conclusion that success or failure in competitive activities exhibits no tendency to be commensurate with innate capacity,

but that a considerable element of the unpredictable must invariably be taken into account.

This is a parody, but not a very gross one. Exhibit (3), above, for instance, contains several patches of the same kind of English. It will be seen that I have not made a full translation. The beginning and ending of the sentence follow the original meaning fairly closely, but in the middle the concrete illustrations—race, battle, bread—dissolve into the vague phrase "success or failure in competitive activities". This had to be so, because no modern writer of the kind I am discussing—no one capable of using phrases like "objective consideration of contemporary phenomena"—would ever tabulate his thoughts in that precise and detailed way. The whole tendency of modern prose is away from concreteness. Now analyse these two sentences a little more closely. The first contains forty-nine words but only sixty syllables, and all its words are those of everyday life. The second contains thirty-eight words of ninety syllables: eighteen of its words are from Latin roots, and one from Greek. The first sentence contains six vivid images, and only one phrase ("time and chance") that could be called vague. The second contains not a single fresh, arresting phrase, and in spite of its ninety syllables it gives only a shortened version of the meaning contained in the first. Yet without a doubt it is the second kind of sentence that is gaining ground in modern English. I do not want to exaggerate. This kind of writing is not yet universal, and outcrops of simplicity will occur here and there in the worst-written page. Still, if you or I were told to write a few lines on the uncertainty of human fortunes, we should probably come much nearer to my imaginary sentence than to the one from *Ecclesiastes*.

As I have tried to show, modern writing at its worst does not consist in picking out words for the sake of their meaning and inventing images in order to make the meaning clearer. It consists in gumming together long strips of words which have already been set in order by someone else, and making the results presentable by sheer humbug. The attraction of this way of writing is that it is easy. It is easier—even quicker, once you have the habit—to say *In my opinion it is a not unjustifiable assumption that* than to say *I think*. If you use ready-made phrases, you not only don't have to hunt about for words; you also don't have to bother with the rhythms of your sentences, since these phrases are generally so arranged as to be more or less euphonious. When you are composing in a hurry—when you are dictating to a stenographer, for instance, or making a public speech—it is natural to fall into a pretentious, Latinized style. Tags like *a consideration which we should do well to bear in mind* or *a conclusion to which all of us would readily assent* will save many a sentence from coming down with a bump. By using stale metaphors, similes and idioms, you save much mental effort, at the cost of leaving your meaning vague, not only for your reader but for yourself. This is the significance of mixed metaphors. The sole aim of a metaphor is to call up a visual image. When these images clash—as in *The Fascist octopus has sung its swan song, the jack-boot is thrown into the melting pot*—it can be taken as certain that the writer is not seeing a mental image of the objects he is naming; in other words he is not really thinking. Look again at the examples I gave at the beginning of this essay. Professor Laski (1) uses five negatives in fifty-three words. One of these is superfluous, making nonsense of the whole passage, and in addition there is the slip *alien* for akin, making further nonsense, and several avoidable pieces of clumsiness which increase the general vagueness. Professor Hogben (2) plays ducks and drakes with a battery which is able to write prescriptions, and, while disapproving of the everyday phrase *put up with*, is unwilling to look *egregious* up in the dictionary and see what it means. (3), if one takes an uncharitable attitude towards it, is simply meaningless: probably one could work out its intended meaning by reading the whole of the article in which it occurs. In (4), the writer knows more or less what he wants to say, but an accumulation of stale phrases chokes him like tea leaves blocking a sink. In (5), words and meaning have almost parted company. People who write in this manner usually have a general emotional meaning—they dislike one thing and want to express solidarity with another—but they are not interested in the detail of what they are saying. A scrupulous writer, in every sentence that he writes, will ask himself at least four questions, thus: What am I trying to say? What words will express it? What image or idiom will make it clearer? Is this image fresh enough to have an effect? And he will probably ask himself two more: Could I put it more shortly? Have I said anything that is avoidably ugly? But you are not obliged to go to all this trouble. You can shirk it by simply throwing your mind open and letting the ready-made phrases come crowding in. They will construct your sentences for you—even think your thoughts for you, to a certain extent—and at need they will perform the important service of partially concealing your meaning even from yourself. It is at this point that the special connection between politics and the debasement of language becomes clear.

In our time it is broadly true that political writing is bad writing. Where it is not true, it will generally be found that the writer is some kind of rebel, expressing his private opinions and not a "party line". Orthodoxy, of whatever colour, seems to demand a lifeless, imitative style. The political dialects to be found in pamphlets, leading articles, manifestos, White Papers and the speeches of under-secretaries do, of course, vary from party to party, but they are all alike in that one almost never finds in them a fresh, vivid, home-made turn of speech. When one watches some tired hack on the platform mechanically repeating the familiar phrases—*bestial atrocities, iron heel, bloodstained tyranny, free peoples of the world, stand shoulder to shoulder*—one often has a curious feeling that one is not watching a live human being but some kind of dummy: a feeling which suddenly becomes stronger at moments when the light catches the speaker's spectacles and turns them into blank discs which seem to have no eyes behind them. And this is not altogether fanciful. A speaker who uses that kind of phraseology has gone some distance towards turning himself into a machine. The appropriate noises are coming out of his larynx, but his brain is not involved as it would be if he were choosing his words for himself. If the speech he is making is one that he is accustomed to make over and over again, he may be almost unconscious of what he is saying, as one is when one utters the responses in church. And this reduced state of consciousness, if not indispensable, is at any rate favourable to political conformity. 13

In our time, political speech and writing are largely the defence of the indefensible. Things like the continuance of British rule in India, the Russian purges and deportations, the dropping of the atom bombs on Japan, can indeed be defended, but only by arguments which are too brutal for most people to face, and which do not square with the professed aims of political parties. Thus political language has to consist largely of euphemism, question-begging and sheer cloudy vagueness. 14

Defenceless villages are bombarded from the air, the inhabitants driven out into the countryside, the cattle machine-gunned, the huts set on fire with incendiary bullets: this is called *pacification*. Millions of peasants are robbed of their farms and sent trudging along the roads with no more than they can carry: this is called *transfer of population* or *rectification of frontiers*. People are imprisoned for years without trial, or shot in the back of the neck or sent to die of scurvy in Arctic lumber camps: this is called *elimination of unreliable elements*. Such phraseology is needed if one wants to name things without calling up mental pictures of them. Consider for instance some comfortable English professor defending Russian totalitarianism. He cannot say outright, "I believe in killing off your opponents when you can get good results by doing so". Probably, therefore, he will say something like this:

"While freely conceding that the Soviet régime exhibits certain features which the humanitarian may be inclined to deplore, we must, I think, agree that a certain curtailment of the right to political opposition is an unavoidable concomitant of transitional periods, and that the rigours which the Russian people have been called upon to undergo have been amply justified in the sphere of concrete achievement."   15

The inflated style is itself a kind of euphemism. A mass of Latin   16 words falls upon the facts like soft snow, blurring the outlines and covering up all the details. The great enemy of clear language is insincerity. When there is a gap between one's real and one's declared aims, one turns as it were instinctively to long words and exhausted idioms, like a cuttlefish squirting out ink. In our age there is no such thing as "keeping out of politics". All issues are political issues, and politics itself is a mass of lies, evasions, folly, hatred and schizophrenia. When the general atmosphere is bad, language must suffer. I should expect to find—this is a guess which I have not sufficient knowledge to verify—that the German, Russian and Italian languages have all deteriorated in the last ten or fifteen years, as a result of dictatorship.

But if thought corrupts language, language can also corrupt thought.   17 A bad usage can spread by tradition and imitation, even among people who should and do know better. The debased language that I have been discussing is in some ways very convenient. Phrases like *a not unjustifiable assumption, leaves much to be desired, would serve no good purpose, a con-*

sideration which we should do well to bear in mind, are a continuous temptation, a packet of aspirins always at one's elbow. Look back through this essay, and for certain you will find that I have again and again committed the very faults I am protesting against. By this morning's post I have received a pamphlet dealing with conditions in Germany. The author tells me that he "felt impelled" to write it. I open it at random, and here is almost the first sentence that I see: "(The Allies) have an opportunity not only of achieving a radical transformation of Germany's social and political structure in such a way as to avoid a nationalistic reaction in Germany itself, but at the same time of laying the foundations of a cooperative and unified Europe." You see, he "feels impelled" to write—feels, presumably, that he has something new to say—and yet his words, like cavalry horses answering the bugle, group themselves automatically into the familiar dreary pattern. This invasion of one's mind by ready-made phrases (*lay the foundations, achieve a radical transformation*) can only be prevented if one is constantly on guard against them, and every such phrase anaesthetizes a portion of one's brain.

I said earlier that the decadence of our language is probably curable. Those who deny this would argue, if they produced an argument at all, that language merely reflects existing social conditions, and that we cannot influence its development by any direct tinkering with words and constructions. So far as the general tone or spirit of a language goes, this may be true, but it is not true in detail. Silly words and expressions have often disappeared, not through any evolutionary process but owing to the conscious action of a minority. Two recent examples were *explore every avenue* and *leave no stone unturned*, which were killed by the jeers of a few journalists. There is a long list of flyblown metaphors which could similarly be got rid of if enough people would interest themselves in the job; and it should also be possible to laugh the *not un-* formation out of existence,[3] to reduce the amount of Latin and Greek in the average sentence, to drive out foreign phrases and strayed scientific words, and, in general, to make pretentiousness unfashionable. But all these are minor

18

---

[3]One can cure oneself of the *not un-* formation by memorizing this sentence: *A not unblack dog was chasing a not unsmall rabbit across a not ungreen field* [Orwell's note].

points. The defence of the English language implies more than this, and perhaps it is best to start by saying what it does not imply.

To begin with it has nothing to do with archaism, with the salvaging   19
of obsolete words and turns of speech, or with the setting up of a "standard English" which must never be departed from. On the contrary, it is especially concerned with the scrapping of every word or idiom which has outworn its usefulness. It has nothing to do with correct grammar and syntax, which are of no importance so long as one makes one's meaning clear, or with the avoidance of Americanisms, or with having what is called a "good prose style". On the other hand it is not concerned with fake simplicity and the attempt to make written English colloquial. Nor does it even imply in every case preferring the Saxon word to the Latin one, though it does imply using the fewest and shortest words that will cover one's meaning. What is above all needed is to let the meaning choose the word, and not the other way about. In prose, the worst thing one can do with words is to surrender to them. When you think of a concrete object, you think wordlessly, and then, if you want to describe the thing you have been visualizing you probably hunt about till you find the exact words that seem to fit. When you think of something abstract you are more inclined to use words from the start, and unless you make a conscious effort to prevent it, the existing dialect will come rushing in and do the job for you, at the expense of blurring or even changing your meaning. Probably it is better to put off using words as long as possible and get one's meaning as clear as one can through pictures or sensations. Afterwards one can choose—not simply accept—the phrases that will best cover the meaning, and then switch round and decide what impression one's words are likely to make on another person. This last effort of the mind cuts out all stale or mixed images, all prefabricated phrases, needless repetitions, and humbug and vagueness generally. But one can often be in doubt about the effect of a word or a phrase, and one needs rules that one can rely on when instinct fails. I think the following rules will cover most cases:

(i) Never use a metaphor, simile or other figure of speech which you are used to seeing in print.

(ii) Never use a long word where a short one will do.

(iii) If it is possible to cut a word out, always cut it out.

(iv) Never use the passive where you can use the active.

(v) Never use a foreign phrase, a scientific word or a jargon word if you can think of an everyday English equivalent.

(vi) Break any of these rules sooner than say anything outright barbarous.

These rules sound elementary, and so they are, but they demand a deep change of attitude in anyone who has grown used to writing in the style now fashionable. One could keep all of them and still write bad English, but one could not write the kind of stuff that I quoted in those five specimens at the beginning of this article.

I have not here been considering the literary use of language, but merely language as an instrument for expressing and not for concealing or preventing thought. Stuart Chase and others have come near to claiming that all abstract words are meaningless, and have used this as a pretext for advocating a kind of political quietism. Since you don't know what Fascism is, how can you struggle against Fascism? One need not swallow such absurdities as this, but one ought to recognize that the present political chaos is connected with the decay of language, and that one can probably bring about some improvement by starting at the verbal end. If you simplify your English, you are freed from the worst follies of orthodoxy. You cannot speak any of the necessary dialects, and when you make a stupid remark its stupidity will be obvious, even to yourself. Political language—and with variations this is true of all political parties, from Conservatives to Anarchists—is designed to make lies sound truthful and murder respectable, and to give an appearance of solidity to pure wind. One cannot change this all in a moment, but one can at least change one's own habits, and from time to time one can even, if one jeers loudly enough, send some worn-out and useless phrase—some *jackboot*, *Achilles' heel*, *hotbed*, *melting pot*, *acid test*, *veritable inferno* or other lump of verbal refuse—into the dustbin where it belongs.

XXXXXXXXXX **UNDERSTANDING THE WHOLE ESSAY** XXXXXXXXXX

1. George Orwell's essay is virtually a catalogue of EXAMPLES (9). Examples of what? What does he exemplify?

2. Exemplification is a means to a larger end for Orwell. What larger purpose does Orwell have for giving so many examples? What conclusion(s) about the (then) present state of English does Orwell draw from them?

3. Orwell uses the conclusion of his INDUCTIVE ARGUMENT—the one based upon examples—as a premise in a DEDUCTIVE ARGUMENT about politics. What is he arguing here?

4. Besides exemplification and argument, Orwell's arsenal also includes the ANALYSIS of CAUSE AND EFFECT: "But an effect can become a cause," he says in paragraph 2, "reinforcing the original cause and producing the same effect in an intensified form, and so on indefinitely." What causes and effects is he referring to? How does the following sentence fit into his analysis: "But if thought corrupts language, language can also corrupt thought" (17)?

5. In paragraph 3, Orwell cites five passages (which he numbers and refers to later) as examples of the state of "modern English prose" (4). This is an inductive argument. If you were trying to refute it, on what grounds would you argue? How would you attempt to prove the contrary?

6. "Politics and the English Language" was written in 1946, after World War II had ended and the Cold War was beginning. How might this help to account for Orwell's use of language like "drive out foreign phrases"; "the defence of the English language"; "the worst thing one can do with words is to surrender to them"; "one needs rules that one can rely on" (18, 19).

7. The following words are central to Orwell's discourse: "decadent" (1), "vices" (3), "foreign" (7), "slovenliness" (7), "improper" (8), "dishonest" (8), "perversions" (9), "humbug" (12, 19), "easy" (12), "shirk" (12), "insincerity" (16). What do the meanings of these words have in common? Given his goal, why might Orwell use such a vocabulary?

MARK TWAIN

LEARNING THE RIVER

Mark Twain is the pen name of Samuel Langhorne Clemens (1835–1910), author of *The Adventures of Tom Sawyer* (1876), *Adventures of Huckleberry Finn* (1884), and *A Connecticut Yankee in King Arthur's Court* (1889). Clemens was born and raised on the banks of the Mississippi River, and as a young man he apprenticed himself to a steamboat captain as a cub pilot. "Learning the River" is a chapter from *Life on the Mississippi* (1883), Clemens's personal narrative of those early days before he became Mark Twain. A narrative of education, it includes many fine descriptive passages of the great river, but it is also a COMPARISON AND CONTRAST of two fundamentally different ways of seeing the natural world.

XXXXXXXXXXXXXXXXXXXXXXXXXXXXXXXXXXXXXXXXXXXXXXXXXXXXXXXXXXXXXXXXX

There was no use in arguing with a person like this [Horace Bixby, the steamboat captain who has vowed to teach young Clemens the river]. I promptly put such a strain on my memory that by and by even the shoal water and the countless crossing-marks began to stay with me. But the result was just the same. I never could more than get one knotty thing learned before another presented itself. Now I had often seen pilots gazing at the water and pretending to read it as if it were a book; but it was a book that told me nothing. A time came at last, however, when Mr. Bixby seemed to think me far enough advanced to bear a lesson on water-reading. So he began:—

"Do you see that long slanting line on the face of the water? Now, that 's a reef. Moreover, it 's a bluff reef. There is a solid sand-bar under it that is nearly as straight up and down as the side of a house. There is plenty of water close up to it, but mighty little on top of it. If you were

"THAT'S A REEF."

to hit it you would knock the boat's brains out. Do you see where the
line fringes out at the upper end and begins to fade away?"

"Yes, sir."

"Well, that is a low place; that is the head of the reef. You can climb
over there, and not hurt anything. Cross over, now, and follow along
close under the reef—easy water there—not much current."

3

4

I followed the reef along till I approached the fringed end. Then
Mr. Bixby said,—

"Now get ready. Wait till I give the word. She won't want to mount
the reef; a boat hates shoal water. Stand by—wait—*wait*—keep her well
in hand. *Now* cramp her down! Snatch her! snatch her!"

He seized the other side of the wheel and helped to spin it around
until it was hard down, and then we held it so. The boat resisted, and
refused to answer for a while, and next she came surging to starboard,
mounted the reef, and sent a long, angry ridge of water foaming away
from her bows.

"Now watch her; watch her like a cat, or she 'll get away from you.
When she fights strong and the tiller slips a little, in a jerky, greasy sort
of way, let up on her a trifle; it is the way she tells you at night that the
water is too shoal; but keep edging her up, little by little, toward the
point. You are well up on the bar, now; there is a bar under every point,
because the water that comes down around it forms an eddy and allows
the sediment to sink. Do you see those fine lines on the face of the water
that branch out like the ribs of a fan? Well, those are little reefs; you
want to just miss the ends of them, but run them pretty close. Now look
out—look out! Don't you crowd that slick, greasy-looking place. There
ain't nine feet there; she won't stand it. She begins to smell it; look sharp,
I tell you! Oh blazes, there you go! Stop the larboard wheel! Quick! Ship
up to back! Set her back!"

The engine bells jingled and the engines answered promptly, shooting white columns of steam far aloft out of the 'scape pipes, but it was
too late. The boat had "smelt" the bar in good earnest; the foamy ridges
that radiated from her bows suddenly disappeared, a great dead swell
came rolling forward and swept ahead of her, she careened far over to
larboard, and went tearing away toward the other shore as if she were
about scared to death. We were a good mile from where we ought to
have been, when we finally got the upper hand of her again.

During the afternoon watch the next day, Mr. Bixby asked me if I
knew how to run the next few miles. I said:—

"Go inside the first snag above the point, outside the next one, start
out from the lower end of Higgins's wood-yard, make a square crossing
and"—

"That's all right. I 'll be back before you close up on the next point." 12

But he was n't. He was still below when I rounded it and entered 13
upon a piece of river which I had some misgivings about. I did not know
that he was hiding behind a chimney to see how I would perform. I went
gayly along, getting prouder and prouder, for he had never left the boat
in my sole charge such a length of time before. I even got to "setting"
her and letting the wheel go, entirely, while I vaingloriously turned my
back and inspected the stern marks and hummed a tune, a sort of easy
indifference which I had prodigiously admired in Bixby and other great
pilots. Once I inspected rather long, and when I faced to the front again:
my heart flew into my mouth so suddenly that if I hadn't clapped my
teeth together I should have lost it. One of those frightful bluff reefs was
stretching its deadly length right across our bows! My head was gone in
a moment; I did not know which end I stood on; I gasped and could not
get my breath; I spun the wheel down with such rapidity that it wove
itself together like a spider's web; the boat answered and turned square
away from the reef, but the reef followed her! I fled, and still it followed
still it kept—right across my bows! I never looked to see where I was
going, I only fled. The awful crash was imminent—why didn't that vil-
lain come! If I committed the crime of ringing a bell, I might get thrown
overboard. But better that than kill the boat. So in blind desperation I
started such a rattling "shivaree" down below as never had astounded an
engineer in this world before, I fancy. Amidst the frenzy of the bells the
engines began to back and fill in a furious way, and my reason forsook
its throne—we were about to crash into the woods on the other side of
the river. Just then Mr. Bixby stepped calmly into view on the hurricane
deck. My soul went out to him in gratitude. My distress vanished;
I would have felt safe on the brink of Niagara, with Mr. Bixby on
the hurricane deck. He blandly and sweetly took his tooth-pick out of
his mouth between his fingers, as if it were a cigar—we were just in the
act of climbing an overhanging big tree, and the passengers were scudding astern like rats—and lifted up these commands to me ever so
gently—

"Stop the starboard. Stop the larboard. Set her back on both." 14

The boat hesitated, halted, pressed her nose among the boughs a 15
critical instant, then reluctantly began to back away.

"Stop the larboard. Come ahead on it. Stop the starboard. Come ahead on it. Point her for the bar." 16

I sailed away as serenely as a summer's morning. Mr. Bixby came in and said, with mock simplicity,— 17

"When you have a hail, my boy, you ought to tap the big bell three times before you land, so that the engineers can get ready." 18

I blushed under the sarcasm, and said I had n't had any hail. 19

"Ah! Then it was for wood, I suppose. The officer of the watch will tell you when he wants to wood up." 20

I went on consuming, and said I was n't after wood. 21

"Indeed? Why, what could you want over here in the bend, then? Did you ever know of a boat following a bend up-stream at this stage of the river?" 22

"No, sir, and *I* was n't trying to follow it. I was getting away from a bluff reef." 23

"No, it was n't a bluff reef; there isn't one within three miles of where you were." 24

"But I saw it. It was as bluff as that one yonder." 25

"Just about. Run over it!" 26

"Do you give it as an order?" 27

"Yes. Run over it." 28

"If I don't, I wish I may die." 29

"All right; I am taking the responsibility." 30

I was just as anxious to kill the boat, now, as I had been to save her before. I impressed my orders upon my memory, to be used at the inquest, and made a straight break for the reef. As it disappeared under our bows I held my breath; but we slid over it like oil. 31

"Now don't you see the difference? It was n't anything but a *wind* reef. The wind does that." 32

"So I see. But it is exactly like a bluff reef. How am I ever going to tell them apart?" 33

"I can't tell you. It is an instinct. By and by you will just naturally *know* one from the other, but you never will be able to explain why or how you know them apart." 34

It turned out to be true. The face of the water, in time, became a wonderful book—a book that was a dead language to the uneducated 35 passenger, but which told its mind to me without reserve, delivering its most cherished secrets as clearly as if it uttered them with a voice. And it was not a book to be read once and thrown aside, for it had a new story to tell every day. Throughout the long twelve hundred miles there was never a page that was void of interest, never one that you could leave unread without loss, never one that you would want to skip, thinking you could find higher enjoyment in some other thing. There never was so wonderful a book written by man; never one whose interest was so absorbing, so unflagging, so sparklingly renewed with every re-perusal. The passenger who could not read it was charmed with a peculiar sort of faint dimple on its surface (on the rare occasions when he did not overlook it altogether); but to the pilot that was an *italicized* passage; indeed, it was more than that, it was a legend of the largest capitals, with a string of shouting exclamation points at the end of it; for it meant that a wreck or a rock was buried there that could tear the life out of the strongest vessel that ever floated. It is the faintest and simplest expression the water ever makes, and the most hideous to a pilot's eye. In truth, the passenger who could not read this book saw nothing but all manner of pretty pictures in it, painted by the sun and shaded by the clouds, whereas to the trained eye these were not pictures at all, but the grimmest and most dead-earnest of reading-matter.

Now when I had mastered the language of this water and had come to know every trifling feature that bordered the great river as familiarly as I knew the letters of the alphabet, I had made a valuable acquisition. But I had lost something, too. I had lost something which could never be restored to me while I lived. All the grace, the beauty, the poetry had gone out of the majestic river! I still keep in mind a certain wonderful sunset which I witnessed when steamboating was new to me. A broad expanse of the river was turned to blood; in the middle distance the red hue brightened into gold, through which a solitary log came floating, black and conspicuous; in one place a long, slanting mark lay sparkling upon the water; in another the surface was broken by boiling, tumbling rings, that were as many-tinted as an opal; where the ruddy flush was faintest, was a smooth spot that was covered with graceful circles and radiating lines, ever so delicately traced; the shore on our left was densely wooded, and the sombre shadow that fell from this forest was broken in one place by a long, ruffled trail that shone like silver; and high above the forest wall a clean-stemmed dead tree waved a single leafy bough that glowed like a flame in the unobstructed splendor that was flowing from the sun. There were graceful curves, reflected images, woody heights, soft distances; and over the whole scene, far and near, the dissolving lights drifted steadily, enriching it, every passing moment, with new marvels of coloring.

I stood like one bewitched. I drank it in, in a speechless rapture. The world was new to me, and I had never seen anything like this at home. But as I have said, a day came when I began to cease from noting the glories and the charms which the moon and the sun and the twilight wrought upon the river's face; another day came when I ceased altogether to note them. Then, if that sunset scene had been repeated, I should have looked upon it without rapture, and should have commented upon it, inwardly, in this fashion: This sun means that we are going to have wind to-morrow; that floating log means that the river is rising, small thanks to it; that slanting mark on the water refers to a bluff reef which is going to kill somebody's steamboat one of these nights, if it keeps on stretching out like that; those tumbling "boils" show a dissolving bar and a changing channel there; the lines and circles in the slick water over yonder are a warning that that troublesome place is shoaling up dangerously; that silver streak in the shadow of the forest is the "break" from a new snag, and he has located himself in the very best place he could have found to fish for steamboats; that tall dead tree, with a single living branch, is not going to last long, and then how is a body ever going to get through this blind place at night without the friendly old landmark?

No, the romance and the beauty were all gone from the river. All the value any feature of it had for me now was the amount of usefulness it could furnish toward compassing the safe piloting of a steamboat. Since those days, I have pitied doctors from my heart. What does the lovely flush in a beauty's cheek mean to a doctor but a "break" that ripples above some deadly disease? Are not all her visible charms sown thick with what are to him the signs and symbols of hidden decay? Does he ever see her beauty at all, or does n't he simply view her professionally, and comment upon her unwholesome condition all to himself? And does n't he sometimes wonder whether he has gained most or lost most by learning his trade?

XXXXXXXXXXX **UNDERSTANDING THE WHOLE ESSAY** XXXXXXXXXXX

1. This essay is a personal NARRATIVE of young Samuel Clemens's apprenticeship as a steamboat pilot on the great river. It is also an essay in COMPARISON and CONTRAST. How do these two MODES OF WRITING work together here?

2. Besides comparing the river as it appeared to his "uneducated" eye with the river as he came to see it with a "trained eye," Twain also compares the river to a book (1, 35). How does *this* comparison help to unify his essay?

3. To what else does Twain compare the natural markings on the "face" of the river (8)? How has this comparison been prepared for earlier?

4. In the first half of the nineteenth century and before, the "book" of nature was presumed to be the work of a divine author who revealed His will through it. What happens to this conception of nature in Twain's late nineteenth-century view? Who or what gives meaning to the book he is trying to read here?

5. What is the role of the "great pilot," Mr. Bixby, in Twain's narrative (13)?

6. Twain has been called both a literary realist and a sentimentalist. How and where are these two ways of "reading" the world—one utilitarian, the other inspired by beauty and emotion—EXEMPLIFIED in this essay? How does Twain reconcile the two views?

VIRGINIA WOOLF

The Death of the Moth

Virginia Woolf (1882–1941) was a distinguished novelist and essayist, the center of the "Bloomsbury Group" of writers and artists that flourished in London from about 1907 to 1930. Suffering from recurrent mental depression, she drowned herself in the river Ouse near her home at Rodmell, England. *The Voyage Out* (1915), *Mrs. Dalloway* (1925), *To the Lighthouse* (1927), *Orlando* (1928), and *The Waves* (1931) are among her works that helped to alter the course of the novel in English. Today she is recognized as a psychological novelist especially gifted at exploring the minds of her female characters. "The Death of the Moth" is the title essay of a collection published in 1942, soon after her suicide. It is a personal narrative in which she depicts herself at her desk, being distracted by a moth that expires on her windowsill. This "tiny bead of pure life" causes her to reflect on the life force infusing the natural world beyond her study (3).

XXXXXXXXXXXXXXXXXXXXXXXXXXXXXXXXXXXXXXXXXXXXXXXXXXXXXXXXXXXXXXXXX

Moths that fly by day are not properly to be called moths; they do not excite that pleasant sense of dark autumn nights and ivy-blossom which the commonest yellow underwing asleep in the shadow of the curtain never fails to rouse in us. They are hybrid creatures, neither gay like butterflies nor sombre like their own species. Nevertheless the present specimen, with his narrow hay-coloured wings, fringed with a tassel of the same colour, seemed to be content with life. It was a pleasant morning, mid-September, mild, benignant, yet with a keener breath than that of the summer months. The plough was already scoring the field opposite the window, and where the share had been, the earth was pressed flat and gleamed with moisture. Such vigour came rolling in from the fields and the down beyond that it was difficult to keep the eyes strictly turned upon the book. The rooks too were keeping one of their annual festivities; soaring round the tree-tops until it looked as if a vast net with thousands of black knots in it has been cast up into the air; which, after a few moments sank slowly down upon the trees until every twig seemed to have a knot at the end of it. Then, suddenly, the net would be thrown into the air again in a wider circle this time, with the utmost clamour and vociferation, as though to be thrown into the air and settle slowly down upon the tree-tops were a tremendously exciting experience.

The same energy which inspired the rooks, the ploughmen, the horses, and even, it seemed, the lean bare-backed downs, sent the moth fluttering from side to side of his square of the window-pane. One could not help watching him. One was, indeed, conscious of a queer feeling of pity for him. The possibilities of pleasure seemed that morning so enormous and so various that to have only a moth's part in life, and a day moth's at that, appeared a hard fate, and his zest in enjoying his meagre opportunities to the full, pathetic. He flew vigorously to one corner of his compartment, and, after waiting there a second, flew across to the other. What remained for him but to fly to a third corner and then to a fourth? That was all he could do, in spite of the size of the downs, the width of the sky, the far-off smoke of houses, and the romantic voice, now and then, of a steamer out at sea. What he could do he did. Watching him, it seemed as if a fiber, very thin but pure, of the enormous energy of the world had been thrust into his frail and diminutive body. As often as he crossed the pane, I could fancy that a thread of vital light became visible. He was little or nothing but life. 2

Yet, because he was so small, and so simple a form of the energy that was rolling in at the open window and driving its way through so many narrow and intricate corridors in my own brain and in those of other human beings, there was something marvelous as well as pathetic about him. It was as if someone had taken a tiny bead of pure life and decking it as lightly as possible with down and feathers, had set it dancing and zigzagging to show us the true nature of life. Thus displayed one could not get over the strangeness of it. One is apt to forget all about life, seeing it humped and bossed and garnished and cumbered so that it has to move with the greatest circumspection and dignity. Again, the thought of all that life might have been had he been born in any other shape caused one to view his simple activities with a kind of pity. 3

After a time, tired by his dancing apparently, he settled on the 4
window ledge in the sun, and the queer spectacle being at an end, I forgot
about him. Then, looking up, my eye was caught by him. He was trying
to resume his dancing, but seemed either so stiff or so awkward that he
could only flutter to the bottom of the window-pane; and when he tried
to fly across it he failed. Being intent on other matters I watched these
futile attempts for a time without thinking, unconsciously waiting for
him to resume his flight, as one waits for a machine, that has stopped
momentarily, to start again without considering the reason for its failure.
After perhaps a seventh attempt he slipped from the wooden ledge and
fell, fluttering his wings, on to his back on the window-sill. The help-
lessness of his attitude roused me. It flashed upon me that he was in
difficulties; he could no longer raise himself; his legs struggled vainly.
But, as I stretched out a pencil, meaning to help him to right himself, it
came over me that the failure and awkwardness were the approach of
death. I laid the pencil down again.

The legs agitated themselves once more. I looked as if for the enemy 5
against which he struggled. I looked out of doors. What had happened
there? Presumably it was midday, and work in the fields had stopped.
Stillness and quiet had replaced the previous animation. The birds had
taken themselves off to feed in the brooks. The horses stood still. Yet the
power was there all the same, massed outside indifferent, impersonal, not
attending to anything in particular. Somehow it was opposed to the little
hay-coloured moth. It was useless to try to do anything. One could only
watch the extraordinary efforts made by those tiny legs against an oncoming doom which could, had it chosen, have submerged an entire city, not
merely a city, but masses of human beings; nothing, I knew, had any
chance against death. Nevertheless after a pause of exhaustion the legs
fluttered again. It was superb this last protest, and so frantic that he
succeeded at last in righting himself. One's sympathies, of course, were
all on the side of life. Also, when there was nobody to care or to know,
this gigantic effort on the part of an insignificant little moth, against a
power of such magnitude, to retain what no one else valued or desired
to keep, moved one strangely. Again, somehow, one saw life, a pure bead.
I lifted the pencil again, useless though I knew it to be. But even as I
did so, the unmistakable tokens of death showed themselves. The body

relaxed, and instantly grew stiff. The struggle was over. The insignificant little creature now knew death. As I looked at the dead moth, this minute wayside triumph of so great a force over so mean an antagonist filled me with wonder. Just as life had been strange a few minutes before, so death was now as strange. The moth having righted himself now lay most decently and uncomplainingly composed. O yes, he seemed to say, death is stronger than I am.

XXXXXXXXXX **UNDERSTANDING THE WHOLE ESSAY** XXXXXXXXXX

1. In this personal NARRATIVE, Virginia Woolf presents herself with pencil in hand, perhaps sitting alone in her study or workroom reading and writing. Why are there no other people in the room? What is the significance of Woolf's keeping a window open to the world outside?

2. Woolf DESCRIBES the moth in considerable detail. Why do you think she tells us so little about what she herself and her room look like? What does this CONTRAST achieve in the essay?

3. Woolf seems to have trouble concentrating on her work. Why? How does she show us that this is the case?

4. How would you describe Woolf's general state of mind in the essay? How does it COMPARE with the "vigour" of the scene outside (1)? What is the significance of her finding both life and death to be "strange" (5)?

5. Published posthumously in 1942, "The Death of the Moth" was written shortly before Woolf experienced a mental breakdown and committed suicide. Are these facts relevant to a reading of the essay? Why or why not?

E. B. WHITE

ONCE MORE TO THE LAKE

Elwyn Brooks White (1899–1985) was considered by many to be the leading American essayist of his day. For more than fifty years, White contributed regularly to the *New Yorker, Harper's,* and other magazines. He also wrote books for children, among them *Charlotte's Web* (1952). "Once More to the Lake" originally appeared in *Harper's* in 1941; it is a personal narrative about time and the generations. When asked about the process of composing this American classic, White responded: "The 'process' is probably every bit as mysterious to me as it is to some of your students—if that will make them feel any better. As for the revising I did, it was probably quite a lot. I always revise the hell out of everything. It's the only way I know how to write."

xxxxxxxxxxxxxxxxxxxxxxxxxxxxxxxxxxxxxxxxxxxxxxxxxxxxxxxxxxxxxxxxxxxxxx

One summer, along about 1904, my father rented a camp on a lake in Maine and took us all there for the month of August. We all got ringworm from some kittens and had to rub Pond's Extract on our arms and legs night and morning, and my father rolled over in a canoe with all his clothes on; but outside of that the vacation was a success and from then on none of us ever thought there was any place in the world like that lake in Maine. We returned summer after summer—always on August 1 for one month. I have since become a salt-water man, but sometimes in summer there are days when the restlessness of the tides and the fearful cold of the sea water and the incessant wind that blows across the afternoon and into the evening make me wish for the placidity of a lake in the woods. A few weeks ago this feeling got so strong I bought myself a couple of bass hooks and a spinner and returned to the lake where we used to go, for a week's fishing and to revisit old haunts. 1

I took along my son, who had never had any fresh water up his nose and who had seen lily pads only from train windows. On the journey 2 over to the lake I began to wonder what it would be like. I wondered how the time would have marred this unique, this holy spot—the coves and streams, the hills that the sun set behind, the camps and the paths behind the camps. I was sure that the tarred road would have found it out, and I wondered in what other ways it would be desolated. It is strange how much you can remember about places like that once you allow your mind to return into the grooves that lead back. You remember one thing, and that suddenly reminds you of another thing. I guess I remembered clearest of all the early mornings, when the lake was cool and motionless, remembered how the bedroom smelled of the lumber it was made of and of the wet woods whose scent entered through the screen. The partitions in the camp were thin and did not extend clear to the top of the rooms, and as I was always the first up I would dress softly so as not to wake the others, and sneak out into the sweet outdoors and start out in the canoe, keeping close along the shore in the long shadows of the pines. I remembered being very careful never to rub my paddle against the gunwale for fear of disturbing the stillness of the cathedral.

The lake had never been what you would call a wild lake. There were cottages sprinkled around the shores, and it was in farming country although the shores of the lake were quite heavily wooded. Some of the cottages were owned by nearby farmers, and you would live at the shore and eat your meals at the farmhouse. That's what our family did. But although it wasn't wild, it was a fairly large and undisturbed lake and there were places in it that, to a child at least, seemed infinitely remote and primeval. 3

I was right about the tar: it led to within half a mile of the shore. But when I got back there, with my boy, and we settled into a camp near a farmhouse and into the kind of summertime I had known, I could tell that it was going to be pretty much the same as it had been before—I knew it, lying in bed the first morning, smelling the bedroom and hearing the boy sneak quietly out and go off along the shore in a boat. I began to sustain the illusion that he was I, and therefore, by simple transposition, that I was my father. This sensation persisted, kept cropping up all the time we were there. It was not an entirely new feeling, but in this setting, it grew much stronger. I seemed to be living a dual existence. I would be in the middle of some simple act, I would be picking up a bait 4 box or laying down a table fork, or I would be saying something, and suddenly it would be not I but my father who was saying the words or making the gesture. It gave me a creepy sensation.

We went fishing the first morning. I felt the same damp moss covering the worms in the bait can, and saw the dragonfly alight on the tip of my rod as it hovered a few inches from the surface of the water. It was the arrival of this fly that convinced me beyond any doubt that everything was as it always had been, that the years were a mirage and that there had been no years. The small waves were the same, chucking the rowboat under the chin as we fished at anchor, and the boat was the same boat, the same color green and the ribs broken in the same places, and under the floorboards the same freshwater leavings and débris—the dead helgramite, the wisps of moss, the rusty discarded fishhook, the dried blood from yesterday's catch. We stared silently at the tips of our rods, at the dragonflies that came and went. I lowered the tip of mine into the water, tentatively, pensively dislodging the fly, which darted two feet away, poised, darted two feet back, and came to rest again a little farther up the rod. There had been no years between the ducking of this dragonfly and the other one—the one that was part of memory. I looked at the boy, who was silently watching his fly, and it was my hands that held his rod, my eyes watching. I felt dizzy and didn't know which rod I was at the end of.

We caught two bass, hauling them in briskly as though they were mackerel, pulling them over the side of the boat in a businesslike manner without any landing net, and stunning them with a blow on the back of the head. When we got back for a swim before lunch, the lake was exactly where we had left it, the same number of inches from the dock, and there was only the merest suggestion of a breeze. This seemed an utterly enchanted sea, this lake you could leave to its own devices for a few hours and come back to, and find that it had not stirred, this constant and trustworthy body of water. In the shallows, the dark, water-soaked sticks and twigs, smooth and old, were undulating in clusters on the bottom against the clean ribbed sand, and the track of the mussel was plain. A school of minnows swam by, each minnow with its small individual shadow, doubling the attendance, so clear and sharp in the sunlight. Some of the other campers were in swimming, along the shore, one of them with a cake of soap, and the water felt thin and clear and unsubstantial. Over the years there had been this person with the cake of soap, this cultist, and here he was. There had been no years.

Up to the farmhouse to dinner through the teeming, dusty field, the road under our sneakers was only a two-track road. The middle track was missing, the one with the marks of the hooves and the splotches of dried, flaky manure. There had always been three tracks to choose from in choosing which track to walk in; now the choice was narrowed down to two. For a moment I missed terribly the middle alternative. But the way led past the tennis court, and something about the way it lay there in the sun reassured me; the tape had loosened along the backline, the alleys were green with plantains and other weeds, and the net (installed in June and removed in September) sagged in the dry noon, and the whole place steamed with midday heat and hunger and emptiness. There was a choice of pie for dessert, and one was blueberry and one was apple, and the waitresses were the same country girls, there having been no passage of time, only the illusion of it as in a dropped curtain—the waitresses were still fifteen; their hair had been washed, that was the only difference—they had been to the movies and seen the pretty girls with the clean hair. 7

Summertime, oh, summertime, pattern of life indelible, the fade-proof lake, the woods unshatterable, the pasture with the sweetfern and the juniper forever and ever, summer without end; this was the background, and the life along the shore was the design, the cottages with their innocent and tranquil design, their tiny docks with the flagpole and the American flag floating against the white clouds in the blue sky, the little paths over the roots of the trees leading from camp to camp and the paths leading back to the outhouses and the can of lime for sprinkling, and at the souvenir counters at the store the miniature birch-bark canoes and the postcards that showed things looking a little better than they looked. This was the American family at play, escaping the city heat, wondering whether the newcomers in the camp at the head of the cove were "common" or "nice," wondering whether it was true that the people who drove up for Sunday dinner at the farmhouse were turned away because there wasn't enough chicken. 8

It seemed to me, as I kept remembering all this, that those times and those summers had been infinitely precious and worth saving. There had been jollity and peace and goodness. The arriving (at the beginning 9 of August) had been so big a business in itself, at the railway station the farm wagon drawn up, the first smell of the pine-laden air, the first glimpse of the smiling farmer, and the great importance of the trunks and your father's enormous authority in such matters, and the feel of the wagon under you for the long ten-mile haul, and at the top of the last long hill catching the first view of the lake after eleven months of not seeing this cherished body of water. The shouts and cries of the other campers when they saw you, and the trunks to be unpacked, to give up their rich burden. (Arriving was less exciting nowadays, when you sneaked up in your car and parked it under a tree near the camp and took out the bags and in five minutes it was all over, no fuss, no loud wonderful fuss about trunks.)

Peace and goodness and jollity. The only thing that was wrong now,   10
really, was the sound of the place, an unfamiliar nervous sound of the outboard motors. This was the note that jarred, the one thing that would sometimes break the illusion and set the years moving. In those other summertimes all motors were inboard; and when they were at a little distance, the noise they made was a sedative, an ingredient of summer sleep. They were one-cylinder and two-cylinder engines, and some were make-and-break and some were jump-spark, but they all made a sleepy sound across the lake. The one-lungers throbbed and fluttered, and the twin-cylinder ones purred and purred, and that was a quiet sound, too. But now the campers all had outboards. In the daytime, in the hot mornings, these motors made a petulant, irritable sound; at night, in the still evening when the afterglow lit the water, they whined about one's ears like mosquitoes. My boy loved our rented outboard, and his great desire was to achieve single-handed mastery over it, and authority, and he soon learned the trick of choking it a little (but not too much), and the adjustment of the needle valve. Watching him I would remember the things you could do with the old one-cylinder engine with the heavy flywheel, how you could have it eating out of your hand if you got really close to it spiritually. Motorboats in those days didn't have clutches, and you would make a landing by shutting off the motor at the proper time and coasting in with a dead rudder. But there was a way of reversing them, if you learned the trick, by cutting the switch and putting it on again exactly on the final dying revolution of the flywheel, so that it would kick

back against compression and begin reversing. Approaching a dock in a strong following breeze, it was difficult to slow up sufficiently by the ordinary coasting method, and if a boy felt he had complete mastery over his motor, he was tempted to keep it running beyond its time and then reverse it a few feet from the dock. It took a cool nerve, because if you threw the switch a twentieth of a second too soon you would catch the flywheel when it still had speed enough to go up past center, and the boat would leap ahead, charging bull-fashion at the dock.

We had a good week at the camp. The bass were biting well and the sun shone endlessly, day after day. We would be tired at night and lie down in the accumulated heat of the little bedrooms after the long hot day and the breeze would stir almost imperceptibly outside and the smell of the swamp drift in through the rusty screens. Sleep would come easily and in the morning the red squirrel would be on the roof, tapping out his gay routine. I kept remembering everything, lying in bed in the mornings—the small steamboat that had a long rounded stern like the lip of a Ubangi, and how quietly she ran on the moonlight sails, when the older boys played their mandolins and the girls sang and we ate doughnuts dipped in sugar, and how sweet the music was on the water in the shining night, and what it had felt like to think about girls then. After breakfast, we would go up to the store and the things were in the same place—the minnows in a bottle, the plugs and spinners disarranged and pawed over by the youngsters from the boys' camp, the Fig Newtons and the Beeman's gum. Outside, the road was tarred and cars stood in front of the store. Inside, all was just as it had always been, except there was more Coca-Cola and not so much Moxie[1] and root beer and birch beer and sarsaparilla. We would walk out with the bottle of pop apiece and sometimes the pop would backfire up our noses and hurt. We explored the streams, quietly, where the turtles slid off logs and dug their way into the soft bottom; and we lay on the town wharf and fed worms to the tame bass. Everywhere we went I had trouble making out which was I, the one walking at my side, the one walking in my pants.

One afternoon while we were there at that lake a thunderstorm came up. It was like the revival of an old melodrama that I had seen long ago

11

12

[1]Brand name of an old-fashioned soft drink.

with childish awe. The second-act climax of the drama of the electrical disturbance over a lake in America has not changed in any important respect. This was the big scene, still the big scene. The whole thing was so familiar, the first feeling of oppression and heat and a general air around camp of not wanting to go very far away. In midafternoon (it was all the same) a curious darkening of the sky, and a lull in everything that had made life tick; and then the way the boats suddenly swung the other way at their moorings with the coming of a breeze out of the new quarter, and the premonitory rumble. Then the kettle drum, then the snare, then the bass drum and cymbals, then crackling light against the dark, and the gods grinning and licking their chops in the hills. Afterward the calm, the rain steadily rustling in the calm lake, the return of light and hope and spirits, and the campers running out in joy and relief to go swimming in the rain, their bright cries perpetuating the deathless joke about how they were getting simply drenched, and the children screaming with delight at the new sensation of bathing in the rain, and the joke about getting drenched linking the generations in a strong indestructible chain. And the comedian who waded in carrying an umbrella.

When the others went swimming, my son said he was going in, too. He pulled his dripping trunks from the line where they had hung all through the shower and wrung them out. Languidly, and with no thought of going in, I watched him, his hard little body, skinny and bare, saw him wince slightly as he pulled up around his vitals the small, soggy, icy garment. As he buckled the swollen belt, suddenly my groin felt the chill of death. 13

XXXXXXXXXXX **UNDERSTANDING THE WHOLE ESSAY** XXXXXXXXXXX

1. "Once More to the Lake" combines many MODES OF WRITING: it is a personal NARRATIVE; it DESCRIBES the lake and its environs in detail; and it gives EXAMPLES of what the narrator and his son find there. If the basic PLOT of E. B. White's narrative is the return to youth, how do the description and exemplification contribute to that plot?

2. White's narrative is told from the POINT OF VIEW of the father; and even though he at times "becomes" the boy, he always speaks from the older man's perspective. What does he know that his young son cannot? How does White reveal this?

3. His son, White says, "loved our rented outboard, and his great desire was to achieve single-handed mastery over it, and authority" (10). How does he relate this statement to the earlier one about "the great importance of the trunks and your father's enormous authority in such matters" (9)?

4. When he and his son first journey to the lake, White speaks of returning "into the grooves that lead back" (2). And later, when they go to eat at the farmhouse, he is disturbed because the middle "track" in the old road is missing (7). How are the two events (or musings) related? Where are these "grooves" and "tracks" located? How does this detail relate to the time themes White explores?

5. White's lake is said to be "utterly enchanted," and much of his essay has the air of a reverie or dream (6). How does White's treatment of time throughout contribute to this dreamlike quality?

6. White often speaks of the natural peace and placidity of the lake, broken only by the whine of the outboard motors. How does White's "theatrical" presentation of the noisy thunderstorm in paragraph 12 keep it from posing any real threat to the peace or safety of the campers? How is that tranquillity broken permanently by the last line of the essay?

7. "This was the American family at play," says White (8). What, according to White, are the typical attributes of this (mythical?) institution? In your opinion, has the passage of time altered its portrait since 1941? If so, how?

JOAN DIDION

On Keeping a Notebook

Joan Didion (b. 1934) is a novelist and one of America's leading essayists. She is the author of *A Book of Common Prayer* (1977), *The White Album* (1979), and *The Last Thing He Wanted* (1996), among others. "On Keeping a Notebook" is from the collection *Slouching towards Bethlehem* (1968). An account of one of Didion's life-long writing habits, it shows how keeping a notebook helps the writer to remember not only how the past felt to her, but also who she once was. A personal NARRATIVE, this essay also ANALYZES the PROCESS of making coherent narratives out of the fragments of memory. A few of these "bits of the mind's string," Didion admits, are pure "embroidery, worked into the day's pattern to lend verisimilitude" to her sampler of memories (11, 7).

xxxxxxxxxxxxxxxxxxxxxxxxxxxxxxxxxxxxxxxxxxxxxxxxxxxxxxxxxxxxxx

" 'That woman Estelle,' " the note reads, " 'is partly the reason why George Sharp and I are separated today.' *Dirty crepe-de-Chine wrapper, hotel bar, Wilmington RR, 9:45 a.m. August Monday morning.*"

Since the note is in my notebook, it presumably has some meaning to me. I study it for a long while. At first I have only the most general notion of what I was doing on an August Monday morning in the bar of the hotel across from the Pennsylvania Railroad station in Wilmington, Delaware (waiting for a train? missing one? 1960? 1961? why Wilmington?), but I do remember being there. The woman in the dirty crepe-de-Chine wrapper had come down from her room for a beer, and the bartender had heard before the reason why George Sharp and she were separated today. "Sure," he said, and went on mopping the floor. "You told me." At the other end of the bar is a girl. She is talking, pointedly, not to the man beside her but to a cat lying in the triangle of sunlight cast through the open door. She is wearing a plaid silk dress from Peck & Peck, and the hem is coming down.

Here is what it is: the girl has been on the Eastern Shore, and now she is going back to the city, leaving the man beside her, and all she can see ahead are the viscous summer sidewalks and the 3 a.m. long-distance calls that will make her lie awake and then sleep drugged through all the steaming mornings left in August (1960? 1961?). Because she must go directly from the train to lunch in New York, she wishes that she had a safety pin for the hem of the plaid silk dress, and she also wishes that she could forget about the hem and the lunch and stay in the cool bar that smells of disinfectant and malt and make friends with the woman in the crepe-de-Chine wrapper. She is afflicted by a little self-pity, and she wants to compare Estelles. That is what that was all about.

Why did I write it down? In order to remember, of course, but exactly what was it I wanted to remember? How much of it actually happened? Did any of it? Why do I keep a notebook at all? It is easy to deceive oneself on all those scores. The impulse to write things down is a peculiarly compulsive one, inexplicable to those who do not share it, useful only accidentally, only secondarily, in the way that any compulsion tries to justify itself. I suppose that it begins or does not begin in the cradle. Although I have felt compelled to write things down since I was five years old, I doubt that my daughter ever will, for she is a singularly blessed and accepting child, delighted with life exactly as life presents itself to her, unafraid to go to sleep and unafraid to wake up. Keepers of private notebooks are a different breed altogether, lonely and resistant rearrangers of things, anxious malcontents, children afflicted apparently at birth with some presentiment of loss.

My first notebook was a Big Five tablet, given to me by my mother with the sensible suggestion that I stop whining and learn to amuse myself by writing down my thoughts. She returned the tablet to me a few years ago; the first entry is an account of a woman who believed herself to be freezing to death in the Arctic night, only to find, when day broke, that she had stumbled onto the Sahara Desert, where she would die of the heat before lunch. I have no idea what turn of a five-year-old's mind could have prompted so insistently "ironic" and exotic a story, but it does reveal a certain predilection for the extreme which has dogged me into adult life; perhaps if I were analytically inclined I would find it a truer story than any I might have told about

Donald Johnson's birthday party or the day my cousin Brenda put Kitty Litter in the aquarium.

So the point of my keeping a notebook has never been, nor is it now, to have an accurate factual record of what I have been doing or thinking. That would be a different impulse entirely, an instinct for reality which I sometimes envy but do not possess. At no point have I ever been able successfully to keep a diary; my approach to daily life ranges from the grossly negligent to the merely absent, and on those few occasions when I have tried dutifully to record a day's events, boredom has so overcome me that the results are mysterious at best. What is this business about "shopping, typing piece, dinner with E, depressed"? Shopping for what? Typing what piece? Who is E? Was this "E" depressed, or was I depressed? Who cares?

In fact I have abandoned altogether that kind of pointless entry; instead I tell what some would call lies. "That's simply not true," the members of my family frequently tell me when they come up against my memory of a shared event. "The party was not for you, the spider was *not* a black widow, *it wasn't that way at all.*" Very likely they are right, for not only have I always had trouble distinguishing between what happened and what merely might have happened, but I remain unconvinced that the distinction, for my purposes, matters. The cracked crab that I recall having for lunch the day my father came home from Detroit in 1945 must certainly be embroidery, worked into the day's pattern to lend verisimilitude; I was ten years old and would not now remember the cracked crab. The day's events did not turn on cracked crab. And yet it is precisely that fictitious crab that makes me see the afternoon all over again, a home movie run all too often, the father bearing gifts, the child weeping, an exercise in family love and guilt. Or that is what it was to me. Similarly, perhaps it never did snow that August in Vermont; perhaps there never were flurries in the night wind, and maybe no one else felt the ground hardening and summer already dead even as we pretended to bask in it, but that was how it felt to me, and it might as well have snowed, could have snowed, did snow.

How it felt to me: that is getting closer to the truth about a notebook. I sometimes delude myself about why I keep a notebook, imagine that some thrifty virtue derives from preserving everything observed. See enough and write it down, I tell myself, and then some morning when the world seems drained of wonder, some day when I am only going through the motions of doing what I am supposed to do, which is write— on that bankrupt morning I will simply open my notebook and there it will all be, a forgotten account with accumulated interest, paid passage back to the world out there: dialogue overheard in hotels and elevators and at the hat-check counter in Pavillon (one middle-aged man shows his hat check to another and says, "That's my old football number"); impressions of Bettina Aptheker and Benjamin Sonnenberg and Teddy ("Mr. Acapulco") Stauffer; careful *aperçus* about tennis bums and failed fashion models and Greek shipping heiresses, one of whom taught me a significant lesson (a lesson I could have learned from F. Scott Fitzgerald, but perhaps we all must meet the very rich for ourselves) by asking, when I arrived to interview her in her orchid-filled sitting room on the second day of a paralyzing New York blizzard, whether it was snowing outside.

I imagine, in other words, that the notebook is about other people. But of course it is not. I have no real business with what one stranger said to another at the hat-check counter in Pavillon; in fact I suspect that the line "That's my old football number" touched not my own imagination at all, but merely some memory of something once read, probably "The Eighty-Yard Run." Nor is my concern with a woman in a dirty crepe-de-Chine wrapper in a Wilmington bar. My stake is always, of course, in the unmentioned girl in the plaid silk dress. *Remember what it was to be me:* that is always the point.

It is a difficult point to admit. We are brought up in the ethic that others, any others, all others, are by definition more interesting than ourselves; taught to be diffident, just this side of self-effacing. ("You're the least important person in the room and don't forget it," Jessica Mitford's governess would hiss in her ear on the advent of any social occasion; I copied that into my notebook because it is only recently that I have been able to enter a room without hearing some such phrase in my inner ear.) Only the very young and the very old may recount their dreams at breakfast, dwell upon self, interrupt with memories of beach picnics and favorite Liberty lawn dresses and the rainbow trout in a creek near Colorado

Springs. The rest of us are expected, rightly, to affect absorption in other people's favorite dresses, other people's trout.

And so we do. But our notebooks give us away, for however duti- 11 fully we record what we see around us, the common denominator of all we see is always, transparently, shamelessly, the implacable "I." We are not talking here about the kind of notebook that is patently for public consumption, a structural conceit for binding together a series of graceful *pensées*,[1] we are talking about something private, about bits of the mind's string too short to use, an indiscriminate and erratic assemblage with meaning only for its maker.

And sometimes even the maker has difficulty with the meaning. 12 There does not seem to be, for example, any point in my knowing for the rest of my life that, during 1964, 720 tons of soot fell on every square mile of New York City, yet there it is in my notebook, labeled "FACT." Nor do I really need to remember that Ambrose Bierce liked to spell Leland Stanford's[2] name "£eland $tanford" or that "smart women almost always wear black in Cuba," a fashion hint without much potential for practical application. And does not the relevance of these notes seem marginal at best?:

> In the basement museum of the Inyo County Courthouse in Independence, California, sign pinned to a mandarin coat: "This MANDARIN COAT was often worn by Mrs. Minnie S. Brooks when giving lectures on her TEAPOT COLLECTION."

> Redhead getting out of car in front of Beverly Wilshire Hotel, chinchilla stole, Vuitton bags with tags reading:

> MRS LOU FOX
> HOTEL SAHARA
> VEGAS

Well, perhaps not entirely marginal. As a matter of fact, Mrs. Min- 13 nie S. Brooks and her MANDARIN COAT pull me back into my own child-hood, for although I never knew Mrs. Brooks and did not visit Inyo

[1]Thoughts, reflections.

[2]A nineteenth-century American millionaire.

County until I was thirty, I grew up in just such a world, in houses cluttered with Indian relics and bits of gold ore and ambergris and the souvenirs my Aunt Mercy Farnsworth brought back from the Orient. It is a long way from that world to Mrs. Lou Fox's world, where we all live now, and is it not just as well to remember that? Might not Mrs. Minnie S. Brooks help me to remember what I am? Might not Mrs. Lou Fox help me to remember what I am not?

But sometimes the point is harder to discern. What exactly did I have in mind when I noted down that it cost the father of someone I know $650 a month to light the place on the Hudson in which he lived before the Crash?[3] What use was I planning to make of this line by Jimmy Hoffa: "I may have my faults, but being wrong ain't one of them"? And although I think it interesting to know where the girls who travel with the Syndicate have their hair done when they find themselves on the West Coast, will I ever make suitable use of it? Might I not be better off just passing it on to John O'Hara? What is a recipe for sauerkraut doing in my notebook? What kind of magpie keeps this notebook? *"He was born the night the Titanic went down."* That seems a nice enough line, and I even recall who said it, but is it not really a better line in life than it could ever be in fiction? 14

But of course that is exactly it: not that I should ever use the line, but that I should remember the woman who said it and the afternoon I heard it. We were on her terrace by the sea, and we were finishing the wine left from lunch, trying to get what sun there was, a California winter sun. The woman whose husband was born the night the *Titanic* went down wanted to rent her house, wanted to go back to her children in Paris. I remember wishing that I could afford the house, which cost $1,000 a month. "Someday you will," she said lazily. "Someday it all comes." There in the sun on her terrace it seemed easy to believe in someday, but later I had a low-grade afternoon hangover and ran over a black snake on the way to the supermarket and was flooded with inexplicable fear when I heard the checkout clerk explaining to the man ahead of me why she was finally divorcing her husband. "He left me no choice," she said over and over as she punched the register. "He has a little seven- 15

[3]The stock market crash of 1929.

month-old baby by her, he left me no choice." I would like to believe that my dread then was for the human condition, but of course it was for me, because I wanted a baby and did not then have one and because I wanted to own the house that cost $1,000 a month to rent and because I had a hangover.

It all comes back. Perhaps it is difficult to see the value in having one's self back in that kind of mood, but I do see it; I think we are well advised to keep on nodding terms with the people we used to be whether we find them attractive company or not. Otherwise they turn up unannounced and surprise us, come hammering on the mind's door at 4 a.m. of a bad night and demand to know who deserted them, who betrayed them, who is going to make amends. We forget all too soon the things we thought we could never forget. We forget the loves and the betrayals alike, forget what we whispered and what we screamed, forget who we were. I have already lost touch with a couple of people I used to be; one of them, a seventeen-year-old, presents little threat, although it would be of some interest to me to know again what it feels like to sit on a river levee drinking vodka-and-orange-juice and listening to Les Paul and Mary Ford and their echoes sing "How High the Moon" on the car radio. (You see I still have the scenes, but I no longer perceive myself among those present, no longer could even improvise the dialogue.) The other one, a twenty-three-year-old, bothers me more. She was always a good deal of trouble, and I suspect she will reappear when I least want to see her, skirts too long, shy to the point of aggravation, always the injured party, full of recriminations and little hurts and stories I do not want to hear again, at once saddening me and angering me with her vulnerability and ignorance, an apparition all the more insistent for being so long banished. 16

It is a good idea, then, to keep in touch, and I suppose that keeping in touch is what notebooks are all about. And we are all on our own when it comes to keeping those lines open to ourselves: your notebook will never help me, nor mine you. *"So what's new in the whiskey business?"* What could that possibly mean to you? To me it means a blonde in a Pucci bathing suit sitting with a couple of fat men by the pool at the Beverly Hills Hotel. Another man approaches, and they all regard one another in silence for a while. "So what's new in the whiskey business?" 17

one of the fat men finally says by way of welcome, and the blonde stands up, arches one foot and dips it in the pool, looking all the while at the cabaña where Baby Pignatari is talking on the telephone. That is all there is to that, except that several years later I saw the blonde coming out of Saks Fifth Avenue in New York with her California complexion and a voluminous mink coat. In the harsh wind that day she looked old and irrevocably tired to me, and even the skins in the mink coat were not worked the way they were doing them that year, not the way she would have wanted them done, and there is the point of the story. For a while after that I did not like to look in the mirror, and my eyes would skim the newspapers and pick out only the deaths, the cancer victims, the premature coronaries, the suicides, and I stopped riding the Lexington Avenue IRT[4] because I noticed for the first time that all the strangers I had seen for years—the man with the seeing-eye dog, the spinster who read the classified pages every day, the fat girl who always got off with me at Grand Central—looked older than they once had.

It all comes back. Even that recipe for sauerkraut: even that brings   18
it back. I was on Fire Island when I first made that sauerkraut, and it was raining, and we drank a lot of bourbon and ate the sauerkraut and went to bed at ten, and I listened to the rain and the Atlantic and felt safe. I made the sauerkraut again last night and it did not make me feel any safer, but that is, as they say, another story.

XXXXXXXXXXXX **UNDERSTANDING THE WHOLE ESSAY** XXXXXXXXXXXX

1. In a sense, the first three paragraphs of Joan Didion's essay form a miniversion of the whole. How so? How does the NARRATOR's perspective shift from one paragraph to the next? How is it that Didion knows so much about what the girl in the plaid dress is thinking?

2. Where else in her essay does Didion replicate the whole essay in a constituent part or EXAMPLE? Give examples, and explain.

3. In paragraphs 12 and 13, Didion COMPARES AND CONTRASTS Mrs. Minnie S. Brooks of Independence, California, with Mrs. Lou Fox of "Vegas." What point does she make with this comparison?

---

[4]A New York City subway line; one of its stops is the Grand Central railway terminal.

4. The reason for her keeping a notebook, says Didion, "has never been . . . to have an accurate factual record of what I have been doing or thinking" (6). How does she illustrate this throughout her essay? Give specific examples.

5. So why *does* Didion keep a notebook? Just what (or who) is she trying to remember? How does the incident of the blonde in paragraph 17 exemplify her real reasons for the notebook? What is "the point of the story"—and of the others she tells (17)?

6. "Your notebook will never help me, nor mine you" (17). So Didion says, but she is referring to the content of her notebook, not to her methods and her reasons for keeping one. How might these methods and reasons indeed "help" you as a writer?

GLOSSARY

XXXXXXXXXXXXXXXXXXXXXXXXXXXXXXXXXXXXXXXXXXXXXXXXXXXXXXXXXXX

ABSTRACT   General, having to do with essences and ideas: Liberty, truth, and beauty are abstract concepts. Most writers depend upon abstractions to some degree; however, abstractions that are not fleshed out with vivid particulars are not likely to hold a reader's interest. See CONCRETE.

ALLUSION   A passing reference, especially to a work of literature. When feminist Lindsy Van Gelder put forth the "modest proposal" that words of feminine gender be used whenever English traditionally uses masculine words, she had in mind Jonathan Swift's essay by that title (reprinted here in Chapter 10). This single brief reference carries the weight of Swift's entire essay behind it, humorously implying that the idea being advanced is about as modest as Swift's tongue-in-cheek proposal that Ireland eat its children as a ready food supply for a poor country. Allusions, therefore, are an efficient means of enlarging the scope and implications of a statement. They work best, of course, when they refer to works most readers are likely to know.

ANALOGY   A comparison that explains aspects of something unfamiliar by likening it to something that is more familiar. In expository writing, analogies are used as aids to explanation and as organizing devices. In a persuasive essay, a writer may argue that what is true in one case is also true in the similar case that he or she is advancing. An argument "by analogy" is only as strong as the terms of the analogy.

ANALYSIS   The separation of an idea or topic into its constituent parts. An analysis of bread making, for example, would break the process into several steps, such as sifting, mixing, baking, cooling, serving. (As a mode of writing, process analysis is discussed in Chapter 5.)

ANECDOTE   A brief narrative or humorous story, often told for the purpose of exemplifying or explaining a larger point. Anecdotal evidence is proof based on such stories rather than on rigorous statistical or scientific inquiry.

ARGUMENT   An argument makes a case or proves a point. It seeks to convince someone to act in a certain way or to believe in the truth or validity of a statement. According to traditional definitions of argumentation and persuasion, a writer can convince a reader in one of three ways: by appealing to reason, by appealing to the reader's emotions, or by appealing to the reader's sense of ethics.

CAUSE AND EFFECT   A strategy of exposition. Cause and effect essays analyze why an event occurred and/or trace its consequences. See the introduction to Chapter 8 for further discussion of this strategy.

CLASSIFICATION   A strategy of exposition that places an object (or person) within a group of similar objects and then focuses on the characteristics distinguishing it from others in the group. Classification is a mode of organizing an essay as well as a means of obtaining knowledge. The introduction to Chapter 4 defines this strategy in detail.

CLICHÉ   A tired expression that has lost its original power to surprise because of overuse: *We came in on a wing and a prayer. The quarterback turned the tables and saved the day.*

CLIMAX   An aspect of plot in narrative writing. The climax is the moment when the action of a narrative is most intense—the culmination, after which the dramatic tension is released.

COMPARISON AND CONTRAST   A strategy of expository writing that explores the similarities and differences between two persons, places, things, or ideas. See Chapter 6 for a more detailed explanation.

CONCRETE   Definite, particular, capable of being perceived directly. Opposed to *abstract. Rose, Mississippi, pinch* are more concrete words than *flower, river, touch.* Five-miles-per-hour is a more concrete idea than slowness. It is a good practice to make your essays as concrete as possible, even when you are writing on a general topic. If you are defining an ideal wife or husband, cite specific wives or husbands you have known or heard about.

CONNOTATIONS   The implied meanings of a word; its overtones and associations over and above its literal meaning. The strict meaning of *home*, for example, is "the place where one lives"; but the word connotes comfort, security, and love.

DEDUCTION   A form of logical reasoning or explaining that proceeds from general premises to specific conclusions. For example, from the general premises that all men are mortal and that Socrates is a man, we can deduce that Socrates is mortal. See the introduction to Chapter 9 for more examples.

DEDUCTIVE   See DEDUCTION.

DEFINITION   A basic strategy of expository writing. Definitions give the essential meaning of something. Extended definitions enlarge upon that basic meaning by analyzing the qualities, recalling the history, explaining the purpose, or giving synonyms of whatever is being defined. See the introduction to Chapter 7 for a full treatment of definition.

DESCRIPTION   One of the four modes of writing. Description appeals to the senses: it tells how something looks, feels, sounds, smells, or tastes. "Scientific" description reports these qualities; "evocative" description re-creates them. See the introduction to Chapter 1 for an extended definition of the descriptive mode.

DIALOGUE   Direct speech, especially between two or more speakers, quoted word for word.

DICTION   Word choice. Mark Twain was talking about diction when he said that the difference between the almost right word and the right word is the difference "between the lightning bug and the lightning." "Standard" diction is defined by dictionaries and other authorities as the language taught in schools and used in the national media. "Nonstandard" diction includes words like *ain't* that are generally not used in formal writing.

Slang includes the figurative language of a group (*moll*, *gat*, *heist*) or fashionable, coined words (*boondoggle*, *weirdo*) and extended meanings (*dead soldier* for an empty bottle; *garbage* for nonsense). Slang words often pass quickly into the standard language or just as quickly fade away.

Informal (or colloquial) language is less informal than slang, and longer lasting. "I am crazy about you, Virginia," is informal rather than nonstandard. *Regional* language is that spoken in certain geographic areas—for example, *remuda*, a word for a herd of riding horses, is used in the Southwest. *Obsolete* language includes terms like *pantaloons* and *palfrey* (saddle horse) that were once standard but are no longer used.

DIVISION   An aspect of classification. Strictly speaking, classification assigns individuals to categories (*This coin is an Indian-Head penny*), and division separates individuals in a group according to a given trait or traits (*Put the pennies in this box, the nickels in this one, and give me the quarters and half dollars*).

DOMINANT IMPRESSION   In descriptive writing, the main impression that a writer gives about something he or she describes.

ETYMOLOGY   A word history or the practice of tracing such histories. The modern English word *march*, for example, is derived from the French *marcher* ("to walk"), which in turn is derived from the Latin word *marcus* ("a hammer"). The etymological definition of *march* is thus "to walk with a measured tread, like the rhythmic pounding of a hammer." In most dictionaries, the derivation, or etymology, of a word is explained in parentheses or brackets before the first definition is given.

EXAMPLE   A concrete illustration of a general idea. Among "things that have given males a bad name," for example, humorist Dave Barry cites "violent crime, war, spitting, and ice hockey."

EXPOSITION   One of the four modes of writing. Expository writing is informative writing. It explains or gives directions. All the items in this glossary are written in the expository mode; and most of the practical prose that you write in the coming years will be—e.g., papers and examinations, job applications, business reports, insurance claims, your last will and testament. See the Introduction for a discussion of how exposition is related to the other modes of writing.

FIGURES OF SPEECH   Colorful words and phrases used in a nonliteral sense. Some common figures of speech: *Simile:* A stated comparison, usually with *like* or *as: He stood like a rock. Metaphor:* A comparison that equates two objects without the use of a stated connecting word: *Throughout the battle, Sergeant Phillips was a rock. Metonymy:* The use of one word or name in place of another commonly associated with it: *The White House* [for the president] *awarded the sergeant a medal. Personification:* The assignment of human traits to nonhuman objects: *The very walls have ears. Hyperbole:* Conscious exaggeration: *The mountain reached to the sky. Understatement:* The opposite of hyperbole, a conscious playing down: *After forty days of climbing the mountain, we felt that we had made a start. Rhetorical Question:* A question to which the author expects no answer or that he answers himself: *Why climb the mountain? Because it is there.*

HYPERBOLE   Exaggeration. See FIGURES OF SPEECH.

HYPOTHESIS   A tentative explanation; a theory to be tested. One hypothesis for explaining the extinction of the dinosaurs, for example, is that they were killed off by a cataclysmic event, such as a meteor striking the earth. The statement of such a theory in writing—"Dinosaurs, most scientists now believe, did not die out gradually but perished over a short period of time as the result of some cataclysmic event"—is a hypothesis.

INDUCTION   A form of logical reasoning or explanation that proceeds from specific examples to general principles. As a rule, an inductive argument is only as valid as its examples are representative. See the introduction to Chapter 9.

IRONY   A statement that implies something other than what the words generally mean. For example, when Russell Baker writes that New Yorkers find

Toronto "hopelessly bogged down in civilization," what he implies is that New Yorkers define "civilization" in an uncivilized way. Irony of situation, as opposed to *verbal* irony, occurs when events in real life or in a narrative turn out differently than the characters or people had expected. It was ironic that Hitler, with his dream of world domination, committed suicide in the end.

METAPHOR   A direct comparison that identifies one thing with another. See FIGURES OF SPEECH.

MODES OF WRITING   Basic patterns of writing, including description, narration, exposition, and argumentation. Description is explained in detail in Chapter 1 of *The Norton Sampler;* narration, in Chapter 2; exposition, in Chapters 3–8; and argumentation, in Chapter 9.

NARRATION   One of the four modes of writing. An account of actions and events that have befallen someone or something. Because narration is essentially story-telling, it is the mode most often used in fiction; however, it is also an important element in almost all writing and speaking. The opening of Lincoln's *Gettysburg Address,* for example, is in the narrative mode: "Fourscore and seven years ago our fathers brought forth on this continent a new nation. . . ."

ONOMATOPOEIA   The use of words that sound like what they refer to, as in "What's the buzz?" or "The cat purred, the dog barked, and the clock ticked."

OXYMORON   An apparent contradiction or bringing together of opposites for rhetorical or humorous effect, as in *eloquent silence, mournful optimist,* or (some would say) *military intelligence, civic organization.*

PERSUASION   The art of moving an audience to action or belief. According to traditional definitions, a writer can persuade a reader in one of three ways: by appealing to the reader's reason, emotions, or sense of ethics. For a full explanation of persuasion and argumentation, see the introduction to Chapter 9.

PLOT   An aspect of narrative. Plot is the sequence of events in a story. It therefore has more to do with actions than with ideas.

POINT OF VIEW   The vantage from which a story is told or an account given. Point of view is often described according to the grammatical person of a narrative. An "I" narrative, for example, is told from the "first-person" point of view. A narrative that refers to "he" or "she" is told from the "third-person" point of view. If the speaker of a third-person narrative seems to know everything about his or her subject, including their thoughts, the point of view is "omniscient"; if the speaker's knowledge is incomplete, the point of view is third-person "limited."

PROCESS ANALYSIS   A form of expository writing that breaks a process into its component operations or that gives directions. Most "how to" essays are essays in process analysis: how to write an essay; how to operate a fork lift; how to avoid a shark bite. Process analyses are usually divided into stages or steps arranged in chronological order. They differ from narratives in that they tell how something functions rather than what happens to something or someone. See the introduction to Chapter 5 for further discussion of this expository technique.

PUN   A play on words, usually involving different words that sound alike, or different meanings of the same word (*The undertaker was a grave man*).

QUALIFIERS   A verbal or grammatical element that limits or modifies the meaning of another word, phrase, or statement. In the sentence *I have been true to you after my fashion*, "after my fashion" is a qualifier both in the sense that it is a prepositional phrase modifying "have been" and in the sense that it restricts the meaning of the statement.

RHETORIC   The art of using language effectively in speech and in writing. The term originally belonged to oratory, and it implies the presence of both a speaker (or writer) and a listener (or reader). This book is a collection of the rhetorical techniques and strategies that some successful writers have found helpful for communicating effectively with an audience.

RHETORICAL QUESTION   A question that is really a statement. See FIGURES OF SPEECH.

SATIRE   A form of writing that attacks a person or practice in hopes of improving either. For example, in "A Modest Proposal" (Classic Essays), Jonathan Swift satirizes the materialism that had reduced his native Ireland to extreme poverty. His intent was to point out the greed of many of his countrymen and thereby shame them all into looking out for the public welfare. This desire to correct vices and follies distinguishes *satire* from *sarcasm*, which is intended primarily to wound. See also IRONY.

SATIRIZE   See SATIRE.

SETTING   The physical place or scene in which an action or event takes place, especially in narrative and descriptive writing.

SIMILE   A comparison that likens one thing to another, usually with *like* or *as*. See FIGURES OF SPEECH.

SYLLOGISM   A common way of organizing a logical argument, in which a conclusion is drawn from a major (or wider) premise or assumption and a minor (or narrower) premise. For example: *Major premise:* All borogroves are mimsy. *Minor premise:* Grog is a borogrove. *Conclusion:* Grog is mimsy.

SYNONYMS Words or phrases that have essentially the same meaning, such as *cope, carry on, get by, make do, manage, survive.*

THESIS The main point that a paragraph or an essay is intended to make or prove. A *thesis statement* is a direct statement of that point.

TONE An author's attitude toward his or her subject or audience: sympathy, longing, amusement, shock, sarcasm—the range is endless. When analyzing the tone of a passage, consider what quality of voice you would use in reading it aloud.

UNDERSTATEMENT A verbal playing down or softening for humorous or ironic effect. See FIGURES OF SPEECH.

PERMISSIONS
ACKNOWLEDGMENTS

XXXXXXXXXXXXXXXXXXXXXXXXXXXXXXXXXXXXXXXXXXXXXXXXXXXXXXXXXXXX

Isaac Asimov: "What Do You Call a Platypus?" From the March/April 1971 issue of *National Wildlife*. Reprinted with permission of the Estate of Isaac Asimov, c/o Ralph M. Vicinanza Ltd.

Dave Barry: "Guys vs. Men." From *Dave Barry's Complete Guide to Guys: A Fairly Short Book*. Copyright © 1995 by Dave Barry. Used with the permission of Random House, Inc.

Baseball stats: images of Dave Winfield and Kirby Puckett reprinted courtesy of Corbis. Text from "Winfield and Puckett Elected to Hall of Fame" reprinted courtesy of *The New York Times* from the article by Jack Curry, originally run on January 17, 2001.

Thomas Beller: "The Ashen Guy: Lower Broadway, September 11, 2001." Reprinted from *Before and After: Stories from New York* (Mr. Beller's Neighborhood Books, 2002), edited by Thomas Beller.

Malcolm Browne: "The Invisible Flying Cat." From *Princeton Anthology of Writing*. Copyright © 1981 The New York Times. Reprinted with the permission of *The New York Times*.

Bruce Catton: "Grant and Lee: A Study in Contrasts." From *The American Story*, edited by Earl Schenck Miers. Copyright U.S. Capital Historical Society, all rights reserved.

Chico's Silver Ox Cuff Watch image courtesy of Chico's Inc.

dailycandy.com page reprinted courtesy of Daily Candy, Inc.

Deborah Dalfonso: "Grammy Rewards." Originally appeared in *Parenting Magazine* as "Summer Fun 1992" by Deborah Dalfonso. Reprinted with permission of *Parenting Magazine*.

Debi Davis: "Body Imperfect." First appeared in *The Norton Textra Extra*, February 1992, Vol. 1, No. 2. Used by permission of W. W. Norton & Company, Inc.

Meghan Daum: "Safe-Sex Lies." Copyright © 1996 by Meghan Daum. First appeared in the *New York Times*. Reprinted by the permission of International Creative Management, Inc.

430 Permissions Acknowledgments

Every effort has been made to contact the copyright holders of each of the selections. Rights holders of any selections not credited should contact W. W. Norton & Company, Inc., 500 Fifth Avenue, New York, NY 10110 for a correction to be made in the next reprinting of our work.

INDEX

XXXXXXXXXXXXXXXXXXXXXXXXXXXXXXXXXXXXXXXXXXXXXXXXXXXXXXXXXX